THE ARAB MIND

RAPHAEL PATAI

THE
ARAB
MIND

CHARLES SCRIBNER'S SONS, NEW YORK

CONTENTS

CONTENTS

CONTENTS

PREFACE: ON A PERSONAL NOTE

WHEN IT COMES TO THE ARABS, I MUST ADMIT TO AN INCURABLE romanticism; nay, more than that: to having had a life-long attachment to Araby. When exactly and how it all started I can no longer remember. But some events and experiences which, to put it more prosaically this time, first awakened and then deepened my interest in the Arabs, have etched themselves indelibly into my memory.

I was not yet ten years old when, one day, my father took me along on a visit to Ignaz Goldziher. On our way back home, my father said to me: "Remember you shook hands with the greatest Orientalist alive."

At the age of eleven or twelve I began reading, first in Hungarian translation, then in the German original, the adventure stories of Karl May, and I was especially impressed by those of his imaginary exploits which took place in the Arabian Desert. One day, thumbing through a Hungarian literary journal, I came across a Hungarian translation of Walter de la Mare's hauntingly beautiful poem on Arabia. Although years later I read the poem in the original English, I still remember lines of it in Hungarian. Furthermore, I still have in my possession a self-portrait in pen and India ink which I drew when I was fourteen and which shows my frowning face enveloped in an Arab kefiyya (lit. *kūfiyya*) and agal (lit. *'iqāl*), headcloth and rope crown.

1

It must have been about the same time, if not earlier, that I first visited the most famous monument that remained in Budapest from the days of Turkish rule: the tomb of Gül Baba. While I was by that time well aware of the distinction between Arabs and Turks, the fact that both peoples were Muslims led me to connect in my mind the fascinating, domed Turkish structure with its turbaned tombstone and the Arabs about whom I had by then read several books.

In the first year of my university studies in Budapest, I attended classes in Arabic, Syriac, Persian, readings in the Koran, the history of Arabic literature, the history of the ancient Near East, the economic history of ancient Egypt, and some others as well. Although I received an "Excellent" in Arabic, I could not have learned too much of the language, because in the next year, during which I studied at the University of Breslau in Germany, I again took a course in Arabic for beginners, under the great Semitic linguist Carl Brockelmann. It so happened that there was only one other student in that course who, however, did not continue into the second term. Thus, I had the rare privilege of getting what amounted to private tutoring from Brockelmann. We met twice a week for an hour in a small classroom of the university (except for once or twice when the university, which was a Catholic institution, was closed because of a Catholic holiday, and Professor Brockelmann, who was a Protestant and did not want to miss a single session, asked me to come to his office for the lesson). Brockelmann was a demanding teacher, and I still remember that I had to put in three or four hours of work in advance of each session in order to be reasonably well prepared. With Brockelmann I also took Hebrew syntax, biblical Aramaic, Syriac, Persian, Fiqh texts, and South Arabian inscriptions, as well as attending his lecture course on Semitic peoples and languages and Arabic historiography.

After two semesters in Breslau, during which I also attended the Jewish Theological Seminary of that city, I returned to Budapest and continued to study both the Arabic language and the masterpieces of its literature, such as the pre-Islamic *mu'allaqāt,* and, of course, the Koran. One of the courses at the Rabbinical Seminary of Budapest, where I was also enrolled as a student, was a seminar devoted to readings in medieval Jewish philosophy. Much of this course centered on the *Guide of the Perplexed* of Maimonides, which was read by the class in its medieval Hebrew translation. I, however, got permission from the instructor, Professor Bernhard Heller—not only an outstanding biblical scholar and folklorist, but also a fine Arabist—to read the *Guide* in the Arabic original whenever my turn came to present a section, translate, and explain it.

In the spring of 1933, after I passed my Dr. Phil. orals at the University of Budapest, I left for Palestine. There, to my dismay, I soon discovered that I could neither speak Arabic nor understand Arabs speaking their language. Although I already was the proud possessor of a doctorate in philosophy, which at Central European universities a student could earn after four years of study, I enrolled at the Hebrew University of Jerusalem (which had been founded only eight years earlier) at the age of twenty-two as a "research student," the term used for a graduate student at the time. I concentrated on two subjects: Palestinology, which comprised the history, historical geography, and topography of the country; and Arabic. In the latter, I was again fortunate to have an excellent teacher, Professor Joseph J. Rivlin, who later helped me found the Palestine Institute of Folklore and Ethnology, co-edited with me the Institute's journal *Edoth (Communities), A Quarterly for Folklore and Ethnology,* and remained a good friend of mine until he passed away in 1971 at the age of eighty-one.

Also, soon after my arrival in Jerusalem, I got acquainted with an Arab teacher and scholar, a shaykh of the famous al-Azhar of Cairo and a scion of one of the great Arab families of Jerusalem, Aḥmad Fakhr al-Dīn al-Kin-ānī al-Khaṭīb. Although Aḥmad was several years my senior, we became good friends, and throughout the fifteen years I spent in Jerusalem we met at least once a week on the average, with the avowed purpose of enabling him to practice and perfect his Hebrew, and me my Arabic. It was through Aḥmad that I gained first an insight into, and gradually a familiarity with, Arab Jerusalem. He introduced me to many of his friends, and taught me the delicate arts of bargaining in the bazaar, slurping Turkish coffee, and "drinking" the narghila. When the tension between the Arabs and the Jews of Palestine mounted, Aḥmad and I promised each other that, should one of us be in danger of his life, the other would take in him and his family to shelter and protect them.

In 1934–35, I taught Arabic at a high school in Talpiyot, a suburb of Jerusalem. In 1936, I got my second doctorate from the Hebrew University of Jerusalem, which, incidentally, happened to be the first Ph.D. to be awarded by that institution. Thereafter, for several years, my scholarly work focused more and more on the cultural anthropology of the Middle Eastern Jewish communities in Palestine, but my interest in, and sympathy for, the Arabs never flagged. I made many more Arab friends, undertook in their company trips to all parts of Arab Palestine, and visited the neighboring Arab countries. But my favorite haunt remained the Old City of Jerusalem. I used to visit the Khālidī Library and chat with its venerable keeper, Shaykh Amīn al-Anṣārī, than whom I have never seen a more beautiful and gracious man. With Aḥmad I went several times to see the Ḥaram and the inside of the fabulous Dome of the Rock with the primeval stone in the middle of its pavement. I sat around in the cafés of the Old City on Ramaḍān nights, listened to the traditional storytellers, and watched the rapt faces around me. While my means were very limited, I was unable to resist buying samples of Arab folk art, some of which I still have: lamps, amulets, "hands of Fāṭima," inkwells, robes, caps, baskets, chairs, rugs, and the like.

In 1947 I received a Viking Fund Fellowship, and in the fall of that year I came to New York. Here, at the Fund's weekly supper conferences, I met many fellow anthropologists who knew of my work as the author of the first and (to this day) only Hebrew textbook of anthropology and the editor of *Edoth,* and read my study *On Culture Contact and Its Working in Modern Palestine,* which was published just then in the American Anthropological Association Memoir Series. Professor William Duncan Strong invited me to teach a course on the Peoples and Cultures of the Middle East as Honorary Visiting Lecturer in Anthropology at Columbia University in the spring term of 1948. In the academic year 1948–49, I taught the same course as Visiting Professor in Anthropology at the University of Pennsylvania in Philadelphia, at the invitation of Professor Loren Eiseley; and from the fall of 1948 to 1957 I was Professor of Anthropology at the Dropsie College in Philadelphia. Throughout my term of service there, one of the courses I taught was "Peoples and Cultures of the Middle East"; another was "Society and Culture of Israel." Concurrently, but for shorter periods, I also taught the same subjects at the New School for Social Research, New York University, Columbia University, and Ohio State University. In 1951, I was asked by the Department of Social Affairs of the United Nations Secretariat to prepare a report on the social conditions in the Middle East, which was subsequently published (in 1952) anonymously, as required by the rules of the Secretariat. From 1952 to 1954, at the invitation of Professor Philip K. Hitti, I taught a course on the Peoples and Cultures of the Middle East in the Department of Oriental Studies of Princeton University. In 1955, I was asked by the Human Relations Area Files, Inc., of New Haven, Connecticut, to direct a research project which resulted in three country handbooks, one on Lebanon, one on Syria, and one on Jordan, and an annotated bibliography on those three countries. I myself wrote several of the chapters in each of these country handbooks, while others were contributed by Arab, Israeli, and American Middle East specialists.

Next, I collected some of the papers I had written in the course of twenty years, and arranged them, with the addition of several new studies, into a volume entitled *Golden River to Golden Road: Society, Culture and Change in the Middle East,* which was published by the University of Pennsylvania Press in 1962. To date, this book has been published in three editions, each of which was augmented by new chapters, and as a paperback reprint.

As this brief résumé indicates, much of my attention throughout these years was devoted to the study of the Middle East, with the Arabs, their society and culture, as the focal point.

After settling in New York, I was a frequent visitor to Palestine—now independent Israel. On these visits I missed the Old City and my Arab friends who lived on the other side of the border. Instead, whenever I could, I visited other Arab or Muslim countries. Finally, a few weeks after the Six Day War of June, 1967, when I was again back in Jerusalem, I picked up the telephone directory of East Jerusalem, and at random called a number whose owner was listed as living in the Shaykh Jarrāḥ quarter. A woman answered. "Do you know the ustāẓ Aḥmad al-Khaṭīb? How is he?" I asked her. "I know him. He is well, and so is his family," she answered. I asked her to send over somebody to tell Aḥmad that his old friend Rafa'īl Baṭā'ī would come to see him next morning. She promised to do so, and next morning I stood in front of Aḥmad's house. I knocked. Aḥmad's wife opened the door, and bade me welcome. I sat down in the living room, and a moment later Aḥmad entered. I had not seen him for twenty years. He was now well over seventy. As we embraced and cried, I was reminded of Jacob and Esau who, too, met after a separation of twenty years and fell on each other's necks and wept.

The present book, as must be clear from the foregoing remarks, is the result of my life-long interest in the Arabs and their world. It presents some of the things I have learned from talking to Arabs over many years, informally in most cases, but not infrequently in formal interviews as well, and from observing them and absorbing innumerable little details of their behavior, attitudes and expressions, movements and gestures, and words both uttered and left unsaid. Sometimes I even became guilty of some unplanned eavesdropping, as when during a recent sojourn in the Old City of Jerusalem my window overlooked the courtyard of a small mosque and I found myself the involuntary witness of the prayer meetings of a small group of Arabs, most of whom stayed on after the ṣalāt to drink coffee and converse in the loud, animated voices so characteristic of them.

It goes without saying that a book like this cannot be written on the basis of personal observations alone. Reading what others wrote about the Arabs has been one of my constant occupations throughout the years I spent in Jerusalem as well as thereafter; in the last three years, this work has been intensified to such an extent that it became a major preoccupation. The written sources I perused consisted not only of printed books, pamphlets, and articles, but also of mimeographed reports, records, and minutes of meetings. From all of them I learned; many proved invaluable, and some are found referred to in the footnotes. Of special importance in connection with the present book were the writings of Arab authors, because these supplemented in a written form the type of information I obtained orally from my Arab friends and acquaintances; they enabled me, that is, to learn more about what Arabs think about Arabs, how they judge them, and what they consider the positive and what the negative sides of the Arab personality. Whether they gave me of the fruit of their knowledge orally or in writing, I consider all of them my teachers and masters and say to them, *"Allāh yukaththir khayrakum,"* "May Allah increase your wellbeing."

Of the many Arab friends and casual acquaintances who helped me in writing this book I wish to thank, in particular, my friend Aḥmad (Shaykh Aḥmad Fakhr al-Dīn al-Kinānī al-Khaṭīb), Dr. Sami Farah Geraisy (Jeraysi), ‘Abdu ’l-‘Azīz Zu‘bī, and the late Shaykh Amīn al-Anṣārī and Ribḥī Nashāshībī. I am also indebted to Professor Halil Inalcik of the University of Ankara, with whom I repeatedly discussed, both in New York and in Turkey, historical problems of Islam; to Dean Edwin Terry Prothro of the American University of Beirut; Professor Charles Issawi of Columbia University; Professor Ehsan Yar Shater of Columbia University; Professor M. M. Bravmann of Columbia University; Professor Majid Khadduri of Johns Hopkins University; Professor Victor Sanua of the University of the City of New York; Professor Y. Harkabi of the Hebrew University of Jerusalem; Professor Jacob Landau of the Hebrew University of Jerusalem. My thanks are also due to the directors and staffs of those libraries who made accessible to me many of the books I needed to consult, and, in particular, to Mr. Francis Paar of the New York Public Library; Miss

Sylvia Landress of the Zionist Archives and Library; Miss Annette Bruhwiler of the library of Fairleigh Dickinson University, Rutherford, N.J.; and Miss Madeleine Neige of the Bibliothèque Nationale of Paris. And, last but not least, I wish to thank my wife Frances, whose voracious reading habits made her something of an extension of my own two eyes in tracking down, or else fortuitously alighting on and calling my attention to, data pertaining to the subject of this book, in addition to helping me in its writing in many other ways.

Forest Hills, N.Y.   RAPHAEL PATAI
November, 1972

A NOTE ON TRANSLITERATION

I HAVE FOLLOWED THE SYSTEM OF TRANSLITERATION OF arabic words and names in general use in the scholarly literature, except in the case of names which are familiar to the English reader in a simplified Anglicized form from the daily press or from other non-scholarly sources. Thus, for example, I have used Koran instead of *Qur'ān;* King Hussein (Ḥusayn); President Nasser (Nāṣir); King Ibn Saud; and so on. Occasionally, the transliteration had to show some inconsistency, because authors often use a simple Anglicized transliteration of Arabic names in their books; also, Arab authors' names in the English editions of their books appear in a variety of simplified transliterations (e.g. Ḥāmid 'Ammār as Hamed Ammar; Aḥmad Abu-Zayd as Ahmed Abou-Zeid; Husayn as Husain, Hussein; 'Abdu 'l-Raḥmān as 'Abdarrahmān, etc.). When referring to such authors, or in quotations from such books I had, of course, to retain their transliteration.

I

THE ARABS AND THE WORLD

1. ISLAM, MIDDLE EAST, ARABS

IN HIS LITTLE BOOK *Egypt's Liberation: The Philosophy of the Revolution,* Gamal Abdul Nasser outlined the position of his country in relation to the world in terms of three concentric circles. The innermost of the three was the "Arab circle," which surrounds Egypt and which "is a part of us, and we are a part of it, our history being inextricably part of its history." The second circle is that of the continent of Africa, to which Egypt is bound by geography, by the Nile, by the responsibilities of leadership, and by an "enlightened African consciousness." The third circle "which circumscribes continents and oceans is the domain of our brothers in faith," that is, the circle of Islam.[1] It is, of course, clear that this construct is based primarily on the political goals Nasser set for Egypt in the early days after King Faruk was overthrown: he saw Egypt as destined to occupy the central, and hence leading, position in the three groupings of nations constituting the worlds of the Arabs, of Africa, and of Islam.[2] From the cultural point of view, only two of Nasser's concentric circles have validity; the third one is meaningless. Culturally, Egypt—as indeed every other Arab country—belongs to the Arab world, as well as to the world of Islam which is many times larger. But as far as the cultural factor is concerned, neither Egypt,

9

nor any of the other Arab countries which line the African coast of the Mediterranean, is part of Africa. As to the Sudan—an Arab country by its own definition—the situation is less clear-cut, although as an overall gener-alization it can be stated that only its southern one-third belongs to Africa, while its northern two-thirds form culturally, as well as ethnically and linguistically, a part of the Arab world.

While from the cultural point of view the Arab countries have nothing —or at the most very little—in common with Black Africa, there is a third circle to which all Arab countries do belong and which in size lies between the smaller Arab world and the larger world of Islam. This third, intermedi-ary circle is that of the Middle East, a culturally clearly definable area which lies geographically between Europe, Black Africa, and Central and South-ern Asia.

The circle of Islam is based on the great monotheistic world religion founded by the Arabian Prophet Muḥammad (570–632). The victorious sweep of Islam within a few decades after Muḥammad's death across a major part of the Old World constitutes a unique phenomenon in human history. Islam continued dominant until the fifteenth century, when it was forced to retreat in Spain before Christianity. In Hungary a Muslim power, Turkey, managed to keep its hold until the eighteenth century. Elsewhere, and especially in Central Africa, Islam has continued to expand. Today, from one-seventh to one-sixth of all mankind are Muslims, or, in absolute figures, between 400 and 500 million. In a huge area, extending roughly from the Atlantic coast of Africa to West Pakistan and from Central Asia to the Sahara, Islam is the religion of some 90 per cent of the population, as it is in East Pakistan and Indonesia. On the peripheries of this solidly Muslim bloc, there are large contiguous areas in which more than half of the population is Muslim. These, in turn, are surrounded by yet another ring of territories with sizable Muslim minorities.[3]

Within the Muslim world lies the second circle, the Middle East. Except where it abuts on the sea, the Middle East is everywhere surrounded by areas which are part of the "House of Islam." While the Muslim world derives its identity from the religion of Islam alone, the Middle East is not a religious but a cultural concept. It is, as I have termed it elsewhere, a "culture continent," characterized by a distinct cultural configuration.[4] One of the most important features in this configuration is Islam (though Islam alone is not enough to place a people into the Middle Eastern context).

On the basis of certain cultural criteria, the Middle East can be said to comprise the area bounded in the west by the Atlantic Ocean; in the north by the Mediterranean, the Black Sea, the Caucasus, the Caspian Sea, and the Turkmen, Kazakh, and Tadzhik Soviet Republics; in the east by the Indus River; in the southeast by the Arabian Sea; and in the south by the Sudan belt. In several Middle Eastern countries there are numerous and sizable Christian minority groups, as well as a few remaining Jewish minorities, especially in Turkey and Morocco. About half of the population of Lebanon is Christian, and Israel is populated primarily by Jews.

Without losing sight of the existence and importance of the non-Muslim minorities, one can state that the Middle East is, on the whole, as Muslim as Europe and America are Christian; and, with all the due caution called for in dealing with figures in a statistically largely unsurveyed area, one can estimate that some 90 per cent of the Middle Eastern population is Muslim.

Coming now finally to the Arab world, we can begin by stating that just as the Middle East is surrounded by the world of Islam, so the Arab world is surrounded by the Middle East. In other words, the Arab world constitutes the core area within the Middle East. The great bodies of water—the Mediterranean, the Black Sea, the Arabian Sea—bound the world of Islam and the Middle East as well as the Arab world. But to the north and east, the Arab world borders on the non-Arab Muslim Middle Eastern countries of Turkey, Iran, Afghanistan, and Pakistan; while to the south, in Africa, the Arab world gradually gives way to the non-Arab Muslim Middle Eastern areas of the Saharan and Sudanic countries.[5]

The Arab world itself is divided geographically into two major parts: one of them lies in Southwest Asia, the other in North Africa. The Southwest Asian part, as well as Egypt, is characterized by the almost total predominance of Arabic as the mother tongue of the inhabitants. To the west of Egypt, along the southern coast of the Mediterranean, lie the Arab countries of North Africa in which sizable minorities have to this day retained Berber as their mother tongue, and in which, to a much greater extent than in Egypt and the Asian Arab countries, European languages, primarily French, have been accepted as the medium of the educated classes.

Five of the Arab countries line the southern shore of the Mediterranean: Morocco, Algeria, Tunisia, Libya, and Egypt; south of Egypt lies the largest Arab country, Sudan; to the northeast are the countries of the Fertile Crescent: Jordan, Lebanon, Syria, and Iraq; while due east lies the Arabian Peninsula, which comprises Saudi Arabia, Yemen, Southern Yemen, and the Persian Gulf principalities. The total extent of this area is 4,658,063 square miles; in 1970 it was inhabited by a population of about 121 million (see Appendix I, page 314).

2. WHO IS AN ARAB?

Of the three successively larger concentric circles—Arabs, Middle East, Islam—only the first and the third figure prominently in Arab consciousness. The Arabs are, of course, well acquainted with the middle one as well; in fact, in modern Arab political writings one encounters frequently the expression *al-sharq al-awsaṭ,* "the Middle East." But this term has been adopted and translated from the European languages, primarily English and French, in which it had come into vogue only during the World War II years. Having had no indigenous term for it, one suspects that the concept of the area as the locale of a specific cultural configuration did not exist in the Arab mind.

The term "Arab" referred in pre-Islamic times to the people who inhabited the Arabian Peninsula and the Syrian Desert. It appears in Assyrian records: in 854 B.C. Gindibu the Arab with one thousand camel troops from Aribi territory joined Bir-'idri of Damascus (who is none other than the biblical Benhadad II) against Shalmanassar III in the Battle of Qarqar. In this first historical appearance of the Arabs they are associated with camels —evidently they were camel-herding desert Bedouins—and throughout the ensuing twenty-eight centuries, the association between Arabs and the desert has never ceased. "Like an Arab in the desert" is a simile used by Jeremiah (3:2) about 600 B.C. in the tone in which one refers to a well-known fact, and more than a century earlier Isaiah (13:20) refers to the Arab pitching his tent, which presupposes a nomadic, desert-dwelling existence. The conceptual association between Arab and Bedouin was and remained so close that frequently when an Arab author uses "Arab" what he actually means is "Bedouin." This is how Ibn Khaldūn, the famous fourteenth-century historian, uses the term "Arab," and this is how the Bedouins refer to themselves to this day.

The foundation of Islam by the Prophet Muḥammad (570–632) and the Islamization of Arabia during his lifetime marked the beginning of the large-scale Arab expansion outside the Arabian Peninsula and the Syrian Desert. From this time on, the term "Arab" assumed a second meaning: it came to denote all the peoples who, after having been converted to Islam, gave up their ancestral languages and adopted Arabic instead. Simultaneously, the Arab conquerors of the new lands lost their originally tribal character, settled down, and became town dwellers. The fate of the Arabic language in these new countries differed from place to place, but in general it can be stated that in several countries the initial distinction between the Arab conquerors and the local populations gradually diminished and disappeared. Within a relatively short period the "Arabs" had become the only, or the predominant, population element in a huge area in North Africa and in Southwest Asia.[6]

Numerous scholars, both Arab and Western, have struggled to answer the question, Who is an Arab? The answers usually include one or more of the following criteria: Arabs are those who speak Arabic, are brought up in Arab culture, live in an Arab country, believe in Muḥammad's teachings, cherish the memory of the Arab Empire, are members of any of the Arab nations.[7] A moment's reflection will suffice to show that of all these criteria, only the linguistic one holds good for all Arabs and for almost nobody else but Arabs. Persons whose mother tongue is Arabic may be brought up in a non-Arab culture (e.g., in French culture in North Africa), and still consider themselves Arabs and be so considered by others. They may live in a non-Arab country—witness the many Arabs who live in France, the United States, Latin America, and elsewhere—and still be Arabs. They may not believe in Muḥammad—the hundreds of thousands of Christian Arabs do not—and yet are as intensely Arab in their feelings and national orientation as any Muslim Arab. Many Arabs do not "cherish" in particular the memory of the Arab Empire because they are Communists, or for any of several other reasons. And, finally, there are numerous Arabs who emigrated to other countries, acquired citizenship there, and have become members of other nations, without thereby losing their Arab identity. In a similar manner, one could point out that there are individuals and groups who meet all or most of the conditions enumerated and yet are not Arabs, for example, the Christian Copts of Egypt, or the Jews of any Arab country.

For this reason, and for want of a better definition, we go along with the one suggested recently by Jabra I. Jabra, a Baghdadi critic, novelist, and poet, to the effect that an Arab is "anyone who speaks Arabic as his own language and consequently feels as an Arab."[8]

However, and this is significant for their self-image, the Arabs do not consider themselves as several separate nations or peoples who inhabit separate political entities. In the Arab view, fostered for at least one generation by almost all Arab leaders, the Arabs constitute one nation, the Arab nation, and the division of the one Arab fatherland into numerous separate countries is but a temporary condition that sooner or later must be, will be, overcome. In this theoretical or ideal view, all Arabs are brothers, children of one single *qawm* or nation.

As to Islam, all educated or even semi-educated Arabs know that it embraces, in addition to the Arabs, numerous non-Arab nations. The Arabs, of course, consider themselves the core of the Muslim nations, since they were the originators of Islam and those who spread it in the world. The world, in the traditional Arab view, is divided into two parts: an inner part, constituting the *Dār al-Islām*, or "House of Islam," and an outer one, constituting the *Dār al-Ḥarb*, or "House of War." In Arabic the antithesis between the two Houses is much more apparent and impressive than in the English translation of their names, because in Arabic the term "Islam" always carries the connotation of the word from which it is derived: *salām*, "peace." Therefore, for the Arabs, the meaning of the two Houses connotes the contrast between inner peace and outer war, just as the ancient Romans had their *pax Romana* imposed upon the "pacified" lands, separated by the *limes* from the lands beyond which were the domains of the lawless Barbarians.

Under the impact of Western domination and the irresistible penetration of Western influences, the concept of the "House of War" has in the twentieth century become obsolete even in the eyes of the traditional Arabs, let alone in those of their Westernized fellow countrymen. But if the "House of War" as such does not exist any longer, the distinction between Muslim and infidel remains and it is a sharp one. In fact, as the Arabist Clifford Geertz observed, as a result of the involvement with the West, "into what had been a fine medieval contempt for infidels crept a tense modern note of anxious envy and defensive pride."[9]

In fine, in the Arab view the world appears like a fruit that consists of three parts. At its core is the kernel, the most valuable part: this is the Arab world. Surrounding it is the flesh of the fruit, the Muslim world, enveloping the Arab core area like a protective covering. Outside is the skin, the non-Muslim world, whose very existence testifies to the inscrutability of the ways of Allah.

One last point. Despite the historical difference between the Arab world and the Muslim world, Arabs often tend to identify Arabism with Islam and Islam with Arabism. This tendency can be observed not only among uneducated Arabs who cannot be expected to know too much about the existence of non-Arab Muslims,[10] but also among Arab literati. The writings of one of the most outstanding contemporary Arab thinkers, Muḥammad Kurd 'Alī (1876–1953), can be mentioned as an example of such an absence of distinction. This prominent Syrian scholar, who was for many years the president of the Arab Academy of Damascus, wrote, among other works, a book entitled *Al-Islām wa 'l-Hadāra al-'Arabiyya (Islam and Arab Civilization),* published in two volumes in Cairo in 1934 and 1936. One would expect a book with this title to differentiate carefully between Arabs and Muslims, between the narrower and the wider of the two circles, between the part and the whole. This, however, is not the case. While Kurd 'Alī is at pains to distinguish between "Arab" and "Bedouin," he is guilty of an indiscriminate usage of "Arab and "Muslim" throughout the book.[11] This is a significant characteristic of the ethnocentricity of Arab students of Arab history. Islam, originally the religion of the Arabs, remains for them identified with the Arabs to the extent of making it practically impossible for them to distinguish between the two, despite the fact that they know very well, of course, that Islam underwent important extra-Arab developments.

II

THE GROUP ASPECTS OF THE MIND

HAVING TACKLED THE TERM "ARAB" WE MUST NEXT CLARIFY
what we mean by the second word in the title of this book: mind. In fact,
it might be asked in general, What is meant by the "mind" of any large
population aggregate, such as a nation? Is it at all legitimate to talk about
the "mind" of a human group?[1] Is not the "mind" a most personal part of
the individual and, as such, unique and uniquely his?

To begin with, it must be admitted that any statement about the mind
of a population is, of necessity, an abstraction. Concretely, there are only
individual minds (or psyches, or characters, or personalities). Still, by the
same token there are only individual human bodies, and yet we are all used
to talking about "the human body" and to being told about new discoveries
made of formerly unknown properties of "the human body."[2]

The abstractions that we do venture (about either body or mind) are
reached by processes of generalization. When we say that the cephalic index
(i.e., the width of the head divided by its length and multiplied by 100) of
the Arabian Bedouins ranges from 72 to 75, we are resorting to verbal
shorthand, the full explication of which would run something like this: On
the basis of measurements taken of the breadth and length of the heads of,
say, a thousand Arabian Bedouins, one seems to be justified in generalizing
and asserting that the cephalic index of the Arabian Bedouins in general

ranges from 72 to 75. On the basis of this generalization, in turn, one can make the statement that "the Arabian Bedouin" (which term itself is, of course, an abstraction) is dolichocephalic or long-headed. Likewise, when one ventures a statement about a certain mental characteristic of any given human group, one inevitably generalizes as well as abstracts.

In the writings of social psychologists and psychologically oriented anthropologists, one seldom encounters expressions such as "group mind," "national mind," "racial mind," and the like. They prefer, instead, to use the terms "personality" or "character," and in their studies they discuss the common elements discernible in the personalities (or characters) of individuals who are part of a given sociocultural milieu.

One of the earliest attempts to tackle the problem of the individual and his sociocultural background was made by the anthropologist Ralph Linton and the psychologist Abram Kardiner. The concept of "basic personality types," as developed by these two scholars, rests upon the following postulates:

1. That the individual's early experiences exert a lasting effect upon his personality, especially upon the development of his projective systems.
2. That similar experiences will tend to produce similar personality configurations in the individuals who are subjected to them.
3. That the techniques which the members of any society employ in the care and rearing of children are culturally patterned and will tend to be similar, although never identical, for various families within the society.
4. That the culturally patterned techniques for the care and rearing of children differ from one society to another.

If these postulates are correct, and they seem to be supported by a wealth of evidence, it follows:

1. That the members of any given society will have many elements of early experience in common.
2. That as a result of this they will have many elements of personality in common.
3. That since the early experience of individuals differs from one society to another, the personality norms for various societies will also differ.

The *basic personality type* for any society is that personality configuration which is shared by the bulk of the society's members as a result of the early experiences which they have in common. It does not correspond to the total personality of the individual but rather to the projective systems or, in different phraseology, the value-attitude systems which are basic to the individual's personality configuration. Thus the same basic personality type may be reflected in many different total personality configurations.[3]

Despite the circumspection with which the above statement was formulated, a few years after its publication another anthropologist-psychologist team, Kluckhohn and Murray, found it necessary to warn that "a group can no more have a 'common character' than they can have a common pair of legs."[4] What can be common to a group is a specific feature, or a set of specific features, that social psychologists and anthropologists have reference to when they talk about national character or modal personality. Incidentally, the very term "modal," borrowed as it is from statistics (where it refers to the value or number that occurs most frequently in a given series), shows that the personality thus described is only the statistically most significant one in the group studied, and not necessarily that of the majority.

The basis of modal personality or national character studies is the observation that human beings who grow up in a common environment exhibit, beyond their individual differences, a strong common factor in their personality. It is inevitable that this should be the case. Any sociocultural environment impresses the individuals who grow up within it with its own stamp: its values, its behavior patterns, its accepted and approved varieties of actions and reactions, as well as its culturally channeled needs and goals. During childhood, the young member of the society gradually internalizes the moral imperatives of his social environment, implanted in him by parents, nurses, teachers, priests, and other individuals in position of authority. At an early age, the channels through which this implantation takes place utilize the lure of rewards for "good," that is, conforming, behavior, and punishment or the threat of punishment for "bad," or nonconforming, behavior. After a number of years, the system of rewards and punishments becomes sufficiently internalized to develop the Freudian "superego," which takes over and continues the task begun by external agents. In this way, the successfully enculturated and socialized individual will become a true representative of his cultural and societal environment, a member of that numerically preponderant group which constitutes the modal personality.[5] I would, therefore, venture to define national character as *the sum total of the motives, traits, beliefs, and values shared by the plurality in a national population.* Since the personality of the plurality in a given population can also be designated as the modal personality, it appears that national character can be equated with modal personality.

At the same time, one can agree with those who insist on a distinction between national character and modal personality and propose that the former term should be used for the more general concept, while the latter should be applied to more narrowly delimited groups. In any population, and especially in contemporary large-scale industrial societies with their great diversity of constituent sectors, there may be several modal personality structures. This means that the national character consists of the sum total of the modal personality structures found in the national population.[6]

The issue, then, comes down to the question of cultural homogeneity. In a national population made up of several distinct culture groups (or ethnic groups), each of these groups can be made the object of a study with a view to ascertaining its modal personality. To take an example from the peripheries of the Arab world, one will undoubtedly find two rather different modal personalities in the Arab north and the Negro south of the Republic of Sudan. In fact, the difference between the two modal personalities will be so pronounced that the researcher would be hard put if he were to try to subsume the two under the general heading of the Sudanese national character.

On the other hand, if the national population studied is fairly homogeneous as far as its ethnic composition is concerned, one will find that the modal personalities of any two or more sample groups will be sufficiently similar to warrant extrapolation from them to the character of the national population at large. As a preliminary tentative estimate in this respect one can state that the Muslim Arabs, who form the overwhelming majority of the population in the Arab world, are definitely closer to this homogeneous type of cultural and personality configuration than to the disparate variety referred to in the preceding paragraph.

The value of the national character concept—with the limitations and qualifications indicated—as a tool of scholarly inquiry and an approach to portraying a large sociocultural aggregate is enhanced by the fact that the idea of a national character is present, albeit in a vague form, in the consciousness of national groups themselves. With the spread of nationalism into all parts of the world, people everywhere acquired the habit of thinking of themselves as members of a nation and as sharing certain national traits.[7] Even minority groups have, in recent years, evinced a growing tendency to view themselves as national groups, constituting a separate nation within the larger political entity in which they live.

As to the Arabs, the best minds as well as some of the simpler people among them have been and still are astute observers of their overall national character. If one reads the *Muqaddima (Introduction to History)* of Ibn Khaldūn (1332–1406)—who was undoubtedly the greatest historical genius of his times as well as the greatest ever produced by the Arabs—one is struck again and again by his observations on the Arab character, which add up to a veritable portrait of the Arab national character seen from the vantage point of a historian who could look back upon seven centuries of Arab history. A few brief quotes will suffice to show the Khaldūnian view of some features of the Arab national character. But first one must keep in mind that when Ibn Khaldūn used the name "Arabs" he was referring primarily to the Bedouin or nomadic Arabs: and that he was not entirely free of the universal tendency of intellectuals to fault rather than praise their countrymen.

Under the heading "Arabs can gain control only over flat territory," Ibn Khaldūn explains, "This is because, on account of their savage nature [the Arabs] are people who plunder and cause damage. . . . Eventually their civilization [i.e., of those whom the Arabs conquer] is wiped out. . . ." In the next section, which he entitled "Places that succumb to the Arabs are quickly ruined," Ibn Khaldūn explains, "The reason for this is that [the Arabs] are a savage nation, fully accustomed to savagery and the things that cause it. Savagery has become their character and nature. They enjoy it because it means freedom from authority and no subservience to leadership. Such a natural disposition is the negation and antithesis of civilization."

Perhaps even more remarkable is Ibn Khaldūn's insight into the psychology of the vanquished, which he based on his observations of the peoples conquered by the Arabs, but which holds equally good for the Arabs themselves after they succumbed to European colonial domination. The heading of the section in which he treats this subject reads: "The vanquished always want to imitate the victor in his distinctive mark(s), his dress, his occupation, and his other conditions and customs."[8] Thereafter, Ibn Khaldūn adds several more features to his portrait of the Arab national character. "The Arab," he says,

> can obtain authority only by making use of some religious coloring, such as prophecy or sainthood, or some great religious event in general. The reason for this is that, because of their savagery, the Arabs are least willing of nations to subordinate themselves to each other, as they are rude, proud, ambitious, and eager to be the leader.[9]

While Ibn Khaldūn's observations refer primarily to the Bedouin Arabs, his disciple Taqī al-Dīn Aḥmad al-Maqrīzī (1364–1442), the most eminent of Mamluk historians and himself an Egyptian, discusses in some detail the character of his countrymen. The Egyptians' character, he says, is dominated by inconstancy, indecision, indolence, cowardice, despondency, avarice, impatience, disdain of study, fearfulness, jealousy, slander, falsehood, readiness to denounce others to the king and to accuse them; in brief, the foundation of their character is composed of the vilest faults produced by the meanness of the soul. All of them are not like this, but these faults are encountered among most of them.

A few pages later, Maqrīzī returns to the subject and adds several more traits to his unflattering portrayal of the Egyptian character:

That which dominates in the character of the Egyptians is the love of pleasure, the propensity for enjoyments, the love of trifles, the belief in impossible things, the weakness in resolution and decision. They are extremely inclined to cunning and deceit; from their birth they excel in it and are very skilful in using it, because there is in their character a basis of flattery and adulation which makes them masters in it more than all the peoples who have lived before them or will live after them.

In a third passage Maqrīzī repeats some of the points he made in foregoing quotes, adds that the Egyptians are characterized by the "absence of reflection," and records that "our shaykh, the master Abū Zayd ʿAbdul-Raḥmān Ibn Khaldūn, told me: 'The Egyptians act as if they would never have to render account.' " As against this long list of negative traits, Maqrīzī finds only two positive features in the Egyptian character: they are not jealous of their wives, and those of them who live in seaside towns are of a gentle nature, which he attributes to the effect of the humidity.[10]

Medieval Arab generalizations about the personality of a people, such as those offered by Ibn Khaldūn and Maqrīzī, are based on personal observation and/or statements made by respected authorities. In any case, they represent attempts to describe group character by enumerating one feature discerned after another. As against them, Arab folk wisdom, as expressed in innumerable proverbs and sayings, usually picks out one particular feature which it considers characteristic of Arabs in general, or of one specific subdivision of the Arab people, and presents it in an emphatic statement. A very few examples of this kind of folk characterization will have to suffice.

One of the most frequently quoted proverbs, current in several variants in many Arab countries, is: "I and my brothers against my cousin; I and my cousins against the stranger" (or "against the world"). This is an acute comment on the Arab traits of family cohesion and hierarchical loyalties. A proverb current in Syria and Lebanon comments on Arab pride: "Even if I have to see the worm of hunger emerge from my mouth, I shall not debase myself" (i.e., by asking help). Another reflects the Arab dislike of authority: "Nothing humiliates a man like being subject to somebody else's authority." The importance of self-respect and of face-saving, as well as of independence, is emphasized again and again in Arabic proverbs: "Pass in front of your enemy when you are hungry, but not when you are naked." "Work on Sunday and holidays, and be not in need of your fortunate brother." "Better to die with honor than to live in humiliation." "Be content with a piece of wild celery, but don't humiliate yourself, O my soul!" "Shave with a hatchet, but don't be obliged to someone else."[11] There are thousands of proverbs current in the Arab world which either comment upon the Arab character as it is actually found to be, or hold out, in the form of advice, the character traits which the ideal Arab should strive to possess. A study of these proverbs would yield a fascinating folk view of the Arab character and would set forth the Arab value system as applied to personal conduct.

That there is such a thing as the "mind" of a national entity was discovered by at least one Arab intellectual about the same time as (or perhaps even earlier than) the concept came in vogue in the West. Ṭāhā Ḥusain (1889–), who has been called "probably the leading scholar-littérateur of the Arab world,"[12] operates with the concept in his book entitled *The Future of Culture in Egypt,*[13] published in Cairo in 1938. In this book, Ṭāhā Ḥusain asks the question, Is the Egyptian mind (he uses the Arabic term " *'aql"*) Eastern or Western in terms of its concept formation, perception, understanding, and judgment? And his answer is, It is Western because in the past it was part of the Mediterranean mind, and thus related to the European mind. All appearances notwithstanding, even in the modern age, Egypt has taken Europe for her model in all aspects of material life, and her spiritual life, too, is purely European. All the signs point to Egypt developing toward complete coalescence with Europe.

Another term Ṭāhā Ḥusain is fond of using closely corresponds to the English concept of national character. He talks about the *shakhṣiyya,* or "personality," of Egypt, which, he asserts, she was able to preserve intact despite the dominion exercised over her by numerous powerful nations. Egypt's own personality was formed by her unchangeable geographical situation, as well as by other factors which have remained constant. This being the case, Egypt does not have to fear that Westernization will endanger her personality or her national identity and individuality.[14]

One would expect a people so sensitive to national character traits to be aware of differences that exist between one Arab country and another, as well as between various population elements in one and the same country. And this, indeed, is the case. Well known is the Bedouin stereotype of the fellah, or Arab peasant, whom he considers to be a slave of the soil. The urbanite, too, has his own stereotype of the fellah: a dumb, subservient, docile beast of burden. He is lazy, cowardly, cringing, stupid, and evil; or, according to a more charitable view, quiet, gentle, satisfied with his lot, happy, grateful, and a hard and loyal worker. The fellah himself, knowing that patience is one of the character traits that makes his life bearable, extols it in many proverbs: "Patience demolishes mountains." "Nothing is lost with patience." "Patience is beautiful." "A patient man sees freedom." "God is with the patient." His opinion of the Bedouin and the townspeople is rarely expressed, because he fears the former and often is dependent on the latter (his landlord). One proverb nevertheless ridicules the Bedouin: "Everything is soap for the Bedouin."[15]

Nor is the observation of differences in national character between one Arab country and another a new development in the Arab world. In fact, astute Arab observers had remarked on these differences many centuries before the concept of national character was formulated in the West. A classical example is attributed by Maqrīzī to Ka'b al–Aḥbār, one of the companions of the Prophet Muḥammad. The observation is couched in an anecdotal form but its import is unmistakable: When Allah created all things, Ka'b is reported to have said, He gave them each a companion. "I am going to Syria," said Reason, "I will go with you," said Rebellion. Abundance said: "I am going to Egypt"; "I shall accompany you," said Resignation." "I am going to the Desert," said Poverty; "I shall go with you," said Health.

Carrying this a stage further, Maqrīzī goes on:

> When God created the world, He also created, it is said, ten character types: faith, honor, courage, rebellion, pride, hypocrisy, riches, poverty, humility, and misery. Faith said: "I shall go to Yemen"; "I shall accompany you," said Honor. Courage said, "I shall go to Syria"; "I shall go with you," said Rebellion. "I shall go to Iraq," said Pride; "I shall accompany you," said Humility. Poverty said, "I shall go into the Desert"; "I shall go with you," said Misery."[16]

As can be seen from these quotes from Maqrīzī, educated Arabs in the fourteenth and fifteenth century were well aware, not only of the existence of an Arab national character, but also of character differences between the Arab peoples inhabiting various countries. To this day this latter factor causes one of the main difficulties for anybody who attempts to portray the Arab mind. There seems to be no such thing as an Arab in the abstract. He is always, and has been at least since the days of Maqrīzī, an Iraqi Arab, a Syrian Arab, and so forth. These differences in character have, in turn, led to the creation in many parts of the Arab world of local tendencies, which frequently clash with the overall, larger ideal of all-Arab unity.

One of the main problems, then, in dealing with the Arab mind, or the Arab national character, is that the Arabs have for over a thousand years inhabited a larger geographical area than any comparable ethnic group and that this historico-geographic factor tends to express itself in two contrapuntal themes in the Arab mentality: the theme of all-Arab unity, which is a matter of aspiration; and that of the particularistic local Arab nationalism, which is a matter of realistic self-interest. As far as the modal Arab personality is concerned, one can, as a working hypothesis, posit the same interplay between general all-Arab and particular local Arab character traits as occurs in the cultural realm.[17]

III

ARAB CHILD-REARING PRACTICES

1. THE ISSUE OF SEVERITY

IS THERE SUCH A THING AS A GENERAL PATTERN OF CHILD-rearing practices in the Arab world? The question is of basic importance because, as several leading social psychologists have conclusively shown, child-rearing practices are among the most important factors contributing to the formation of the modal personality.[1] As so often with basic questions, this too is rather difficult to answer. In fact, for lack of sufficient data, no definitive answer at all can be given. A number of considerations nevertheless allow us to arrive at least at a tentative conclusion.

First of all, one finds that even two such widely separated cultures as those of Morocco and Iraq appear quite similar when compared with, say, the Greek, or Italian, or Sub-Saharan Negro culture. And this basic cultural similarity, which underlies the surface manifestations of local differences, is very likely to have a correlate in the basic similarity of child-rearing practices in all parts of the Arab world.

Secondly, in quite a large number of studies dealing with many different parts of the Arab world one can find at least a few observations on child-rearing practices which point to the same kind of basic similarity. One subject commented on in this area by many authors is that of corporal punishment. All those who have made first-hand observations of Arab family life agree that the incidence and severity of corporal punishment administered to Arab children is much greater than is the case in the Western world.[2] The sheer weight of this evidence makes it legitimate to conclude that, at least as far as this particular feature of Arab child-rearing practices is concerned, there is indeed a general conformity to an all-Arab basic pattern.

Thirdly, there exist a few specific studies—all too few, to be sure—of child-rearing practices in certain Arab communities in places as widely scattered as Lebanon, Palestine, Upper Egypt, and Algeria.[3] When one considers the striking similarities disclosed by these studies, one is again led to the conclusion that there must be a general all-Arab pattern of child rearing of which the cases studied are but the local manifestations.

Local and individual variations aside, the general situation in the Arab family is that it is the father who is severe, stern, and authoritarian, while the mother is, by contrast, loving and compassionate. This difference between the attitude of the two parents is so often referred to in Arabic literature, including proverbs, and in studies dealing with Arab communities, that one cannot doubt its widespread occurrence. It is because of this difference in their treatment of the child that the latter, while respecting and even fearing the father, develops a more affectionate attachment to the mother. In the lives of both sons and daughters the love for the mother remains important, even after marriage.

If the two parents have such disparate approaches to their children, one would expect the compassionate mother to disapprove of the disciplinarian measures of her husband. In fact, reports from various parts of the Arab world make explicit mention of the mother's attempts, either in open defiance or through discreet intervention, to prevent undue severity on the part of the father.[4] However, a study of Lebanese mothers found that they "were more likely to approve of the [disciplinary] actions of a severe father than those of the non-severe fathers."[5] The question arises whether this approval was not in itself conditioned by the cultural expectation of the women: they, after all, *knew* that the typical father must be a stern disciplinarian, and therefore they approved if their husbands lived up to the stereotype. Also, one can assume that a severe father was severe not only to his children but also to his wife, and that therefore the wives of severe husbands were less likely to dare or to care to express open disapproval of their husbands' child-rearing practices than the wives of less severe husbands.

2. DIFFERENTIAL EVALUATION OF BOYS AND GIRLS

Arab folk wisdom has amply commented upon the malleability of the infantile character and the consequent desirability of subjecting it at an early date to formative influences.[6] An Arab proverb current among the fellahin of Palestine as well as in other parts of the Arab world states: "Character impressed by the mother's milk cannot be altered by anything but death." Another cautions: "A child's heart is like a precious jewel without inscription; it is therefore ready to absorb whatever is engraved upon it." And numerous other sayings insist on either the ease with which a child's character can be formed, or the indelibility of childhood influences.[7]

What the proverbs recommend and sanction, folk custom translates into actual practice. Since the Arabs are convinced that it is primarily the early childhood influences that form character and personality, and since subordination of one's ego to the authority of the father (and/or the actual head of the family) is a cornerstone of the Arab social edifice, the children are disciplined, if necessary severely, in order to make them accept, and acquiesce in, paternal rule. As a result of Arab child-rearing practices, the children learn to subordinate their own personal interests to those of the family as represented by the father or grandfather.[8]

In discussing these practices we must, from the very outset, distinguish between the treatment of boys and girls. The Arabic language has no literal equivalent to the English word "child." Every noun in Arabic is either masculine or feminine. Therefore, while there are words for "boy," "son," "girl," "daughter," there are no words for "child," "baby," "infant," "toddler," and so on, which in English refer to human beings at various stages of their early development without specifying their sex. When asking a man (e.g., in connection with a census) how many children he has, the word used will be *"awlād"* (the plural of *walad,* meaning male child), and, accordingly, the answer will specify the number of *sons*. Then, the experienced census taker will have to ask again: And how many daughters *(banāt)*? Only thus can he arrive at the total of the man's progeny.

Since there are no "children" in the Arabic language but only "sons" and "daughters," there are no "children" in the Arab consciousness either, but only either "sons" or "daughters." And, accordingly, there are no "child"-rearing practices in the Arab world, but only "boy"-rearing practices on the one hand, and "girl"-rearing practices on the other.

The distinction between the sexes begins before the child is born; in fact, even before it is conceived. The overwhelming desire of all parents is to have sons, and on the very wedding day (or wedding week) the friends and relatives of the young couple wish them many sons. Once the wife becomes pregnant, she hopes and prays that she will be graced with a boy. If indeed a boy is born, he is greeted with exuberant joy. If a girl—the mother is ashamed and the father's face darkens with displeasure. In olden days, the father would even contemplate whether to let his newborn daughter live or kill her by burying her alive in the sand. Muḥammad reproached his fellow Arabs for this practice of female infanticide:

> If one of them receiveth tidings of the birth of a female, his face remaineth darkened and he is wroth inwardly. He hideth himself from the folk because of the evil of that whereof he hath had tidings (asking himself): Shall he keep it in contempt, or bury it beneath the dust. Verily evil is their judgment (Koran 16:58–59).

Despite this prophetic warning, the custom of female infanticide survived in some localities for many generations and, according to scattered reports, was practiced in a few remote and ultra-conservative areas as late as the beginning of the present century.

However, while female infanticide is, fortunately, a thing of the past, the idea that it is humiliating to beget daughters has managed to survive in conservative Arab circles down to the present. A man who has only girl children is derided as an *"abū banāt,"* "father of daughters." As the months and years pass, the feeling of disappointment with which the birth of a daughter was greeted gradually changes into one of apprehension lest she, by infringing the moral code, bring shame and disgrace upon her father and entire family. In some of the most conservative sectors of the Arab world, where the *patria potestas* is still in full force, quite recent cases are known to have occurred of fathers putting to death a daughter because her behavior brought dishonor upon them. To restore the honor of the family in this manner was in accordance with the *'urf,* or traditional local law.

As a concrete illustration of the differences in the attitude and reception accorded to a son and a daughter upon birth, let us quote Musa Alami, a scion of one of the leading Muslim Arab families of Jerusalem: After the midwife uttered the joyful cry of "It's a boy!" the baby was

> hastily washed and dressed, was being handed round the ranks of women, first in the bed-chamber and then outside. . . . Then, as it was a boy, proudly entered the father to receive congratulations and adulation all round . . . and to preen himself, for only the second time in his life (his marriage having been the first), in the smiles of a crowd of unveiled woman. . . . Very different would have been the scene had the child been a girl . . . while a girl was tolerated as a firstborn, the toleration diminished with each successive female birth so long as no son intervened, to the point where exasperated parents had been known to name the last of a string of girls "Taman," which may be freely translated as "that's the lot." On such an occasion there would have been no joyful cry from the midwife, no clamour from the rooms outside; only the silent dispersal of the throng in the face of the misfortune which had befallen the family, while the father comforted his wife.[9]

The different evaluation of boys and girls finds its expression, among other things, in the widespread folk custom of dressing boys like girls until they are five years of age. Since male children are highly prized in Arab society, folk belief holds that they are exposed to potential harm from the "evil eye," that ubiquitous malevolent influence that emanates from envious persons—often without conscious awareness—and that can endanger anybody or anything on which it alights, even if inadvertently. Apart from hanging an amulet around the neck of the child and letting it run about unwashed and unkempt, the "tried and proven" method of protecting a boy child from the evil eye is to give him the appearance of a girl: the evil eye will not notice so valueless a person as a little girl child.[10]

One would expect this relative valuation of son and daughter to find its expression in the treatment accorded to boys and girls. And this, indeed, is the case. The young wife's position in her husband's family (where, in conservative circles, she is treated initially more or less like an unpaid servant) improves only if she gives birth to a son. A woman who has daughters solely is not much better off than a childless wife: the ignominy of divorce is a threat and—as shown by numerous examples in all social classes, including Arab royalty—often becomes a reality. No wonder, then, that the emotional gratification experienced by a young mother who proudly presents her husband and his family with a boy child is reflected in her attitude toward her child. She will be much more lenient with him, will take better care of him, devote more attention to him, and be more affectionately inclined toward him than she would be to a daughter.

This differential treatment amounts, in fact, to a basic pedagogical principle which demands that a boy should be pampered but not a girl. As E. T. Prothro observed in his study of child rearing in several ethnic groups in the Lebanon, "in every group boys were treated more warmly than were girls."[11]

3. LACTATION

One of the most significant manifestations of this disparity in the treatment of boys and girls in early infancy, and one that unquestionably has a lasting influence on the character formation and mutual expectations of the two sexes, is the difference in the duration of breast feeding. Local variations, of which there are many, aside, in general a boy is suckled twice as long as a girl. A boy is breast fed for two to three years; a girl, for one to two.[12]

The reasons for this difference are not far to seek. Since the period of lactation is one in which, under the practice of demand feeding, a child is almost automatically pampered, and since the folk mores call for pampering a boy but not a girl, the mother, by cutting short the breast feeding of a girl child, in effect terminates the period in which the baby girl is pampered. A second reason is the widespread belief that while a mother nurses a child she will not become pregnant again. Having experienced the disappointment of bearing a daughter, the mother wishes to conceive again as soon as possible in the hope of presenting a son to her husband and his kin, and thereby compensating everybody (including herself) for the loss of prestige suffered through the birth of a daughter.

Under the time-honored system of demand feeding, whenever the child cries, the mother picks it up and gives it her breast. Wherever she goes, she takes the child with her. (An Arab mother carries her infant on her head, back, shoulder, or hip.) This is the period of the most intimate contact, almost a symbiosis between mother and child, a direct continuation of the prenatal mother-child unit, only one step removed from the marsupial young in the pouch.

The real break between mother and child comes with weaning. Although thereafter too the mother usually continues to give the child its food, this task among the Arabs, with their many children, is often relegated to an older daughter. In any case, the close symbiotic relationship is over, and the child, for the first time in its life, learns what deprivation means.

The very fact that weaning comes so much earlier in the life of a girl than of a boy signifies an incisive difference in the early socialization experience of the two sexes, which leaves its indelible mark on the personality of both adult male and female. For the girl child, the memory of the short paradisiac period of breast feeding soon recedes into the background under the impact of the weaning trauma and the subsequent rather matter-of-fact treatment she receives from her mother and other members of her immediate and extended families. Within a few months after weaning, the female infant is well on the way to internalizing the role she will play in life as a woman: a subordinate, a person of little importance, destined to remain most of her life in a servile position in relation to the menfolk who will dominate her life: her father, brothers, husband, sons. The extent to which this role of the obedient female is actually internalized by the time the girl reaches her fourth or fifth year is indicated by the fact that she provokes her parents to administering physical punishment to her much less frequently than a boy of the same age.

As for the boy, both the actual treatment accorded to him and the expectations he will develop are fundamentally different. While still being breast fed, there is the tendency on the part of the mother to pamper him more than she would a girl child. By the time the boy is weaned he has learned to walk, run, play, and control his elimination. What is more important, he has learned to talk and so can and does ask verbally for the mother's breast whenever he wants it. And, since the principles followed by the mother include both pampering the boy and demand feeding him, he actually gets the breast whenever he asks for it. Thus the verbalization of the one major childhood desire, that for the mother's breast, is followed, in most cases at least, by instant gratification. And, what is psychologically equally important, the emphatic verbal formulation of the wish carries in itself, almost automatically, the guarantee of its fulfillment without the need for any additional action on the part of the child. This experience, repeated several times a day for a number of months, cannot fail to leave a lasting impression on the psyche of the boy child. It may not be too far-fetched to seek a connection between this situation in childhood and a characteristic trait of the adult Arab personality which has frequently been observed and commented upon: the proclivity for making an emphatic verbal statement of intention and failing to follow it up with any action that could lead to its realization. It would seem that—at least in certain contexts and moods —stating an intention or wish in itself provides a psychological satisfaction

31

which actually can become a deterrent to undertaking the action that is averred. Examples of this type of behavior will be supplied in a later chapter, together with instances of Arab self-criticism on this score. Here it should only be remarked that there is a definite similarity between this trait and the certainty that develops in the Arab boy's psyche as to the unfailing effect produced by his uttered demand for his mother's breast (especially an emphatically uttered demand). In both child and adult, the verbally stated wish, intention, or demand is expected to bring about realization without any additional action. The only thing required is the word; the utterer can then relax and let the word bring about its own realization.

(It could be mentioned in passing that it was this kind of mentality which, among the ancient Hebrews, produced the myth of the God who creates by verbal fiat. In fact, Genesis 1, with its emphasis on creation by word rather than deed, may have been an early attempt to provide mythical justification and validation of a similar psychological over-reliance on verbal utterance.)

4. EARLY ROOTS OF THE MALE-FEMALE RELATIONSHIP

The prolonged period of lactation also impresses into the mind of the boy child a special image or archetype of the male-female relationship. For a period of up to three years, the mother was unfailingly at his beck and call. Her breast, his greatest source of pleasure and gratification, was his for the asking. This experience cannot fail to become a contributing factor in the general mold to which the boy will eventually expect his relationship to all women to conform. Here, in all probability, we come close to the origin of the characteristic Arab male attitude to women: that the destiny of women in general, and in particular of those within the family circle, is to serve the men and obey them.

This expectation is further reinforced by another childhood experience of which many male infants partake in the first years of their lives. In contrast to a girl, whose crying evokes little attention—since one is not supposed to pamper a girl—a male infant who cries is picked up and comforted. This comforting and soothing of the baby boy often takes the form of handling his genitals. Mother, grandmother, other female relatives and visitors, as well as his older siblings, will play with the penis of the boy, not only to soothe him, but also simply to make him smile.[13] Among the fellahin of Upper Egypt, the mother may attempt to prepare her son gradually for the circumcision operation "by caressing his organ and playfully endeavoring to separate the foreskin from the glans. While doing this, she would hum words to the effect that what she is doing will help to make him to become a man amongst men."[14] Since circumcision in Upper Egypt is usually performed any time before the boy attains maturity,[15] this motherly caressing of the boy's penis may well go on at an age from which the boy retains distinct memories throughout his adult life.

While this particular custom may be a local development, the association of the mother, and hence women in general, with erotic pleasure is something that Arab male infants in general experience and that predisposes them to accept the stereotype of the woman as primarily a sexual object and a creature who cannot resist sexual temptation. The most frequently stated purpose of female circumcision (clitoridectomy, or the more severe excision or infibulation), which is practiced in many parts of the Arab world, is to "calm down" the women, that is, to diminish their libido.[16]

In traditional Arabic literature there are numerous references to the sexual excitability of women. Inasmuch as these statements were written by men (and continue to be written to the present day), they, of course, testify more reliably to the sexual excitability of their male authors than of the women about whom they write. However that may be, intense and uncontrollable sexuality is the assumption that underlies the segregation of the sexes, that traditional cornerstone of Arab mores, and of the entire strict and rigid Arab code of sexual conduct. The sexuality of the male is seldom discussed expressly, but the tacitly assumed Arab male self-image is that of a man who will inevitably take advantage of any woman who strikes his fancy whenever circumstances enable him to do so. Consequently, he must be prevented by the same strict code of sexual conduct from ever being exposed to erotic temptation. Arab sexual mores assume that wherever and whenever a man and a woman of suitable ages happen to find themselves alone, they will be irresistably driven to having sexual union even if they had never before seen each other, and even if the consequences could be most disastrous. The only way to prevent such occurrences is to practice strict segregation, calculated to make it impossible for a man and woman ever to be alone, unless, of course, they are married or are first-degree blood relations.

5. THE BOY ENTERS THE MEN'S WORLD

Even after lactation is discontinued, the "pampering" of the boy by the mother goes on, including her fondling of his genitals (wherever that is practiced), and her hugging and kissing and praising him. By the time the boy is weaned, he is well accustomed to food other than mother's milk. Furthermore, at that late stage the milk of the mother tends to dry out and the boy find it less and less rewarding to exert himself sucking and tugging at the mother's breast with literally diminishing returns.

The warm, intimate, loving relationship of the mother to her son becomes the more important for him since about this time (the fourth year, more or less), the father begins to pay more attention to his son, and the boy's gradual easing over from the women's to the men's world begins. This paternal attention is, from the boy child's point of view, a mixed blessing. The father, much as he may love his son, is required by the folk mores to develop the boy's character, and the methods of fatherly socialization are often harsh. As long as he was under the exclusive tutelage of his mother, or a female mother-substitute such as an older sister, aunt, or grandmother, the boy could in general have his way. The basic, or certainly the main, task of all these women was to make him happy, to give him what he wanted, to care for him, to fulfill his whims and wishes. The men's world, as represented by the father, is very different. Here, the boy is suddenly confronted by standards. While his own wishes are disregarded more often than not, he has to learn to fulfill his father's wishes, to obey his commands, to serve him and even to be subservient to him.

This change in status is not an easy one to get used to, and it takes a long time, years in fact, for the new role of a young (for a while inevitably the youngest) male child in the men's world to become internalized. In the meantime clashes occur, and with them comes the bitter taste of the father's heavy hand, the rod, the strap, and, at least among the most tradition-bound Bedouin tribes, the saber and the dagger whose cut or stab is supposed, beyond punishing the disobedient son, to harden him for his future life.[17] No wonder that in the early period of this painful transition into the men's world, and until such time as he learns that it is shameful to do so, the boy runs back from the father's discipline to the mother's arms, in which he finds comfort, love, indulgence, reassurance. The harsh, disciplinarian father is thus counterbalanced by the compassionte, tender, loving mother. Accordingly, the budding personality of the boy develops a twofold aspect:

one expressive of his self-image and his position in the larger male world; and the other presented by him to the small world of the women, consisting of a few individuals only—his mother, his sisters, his grandmother, and a few other closest female relatives.

Soon after learning his place in relation to his father, the young boy child finds out that, in contrast to the women's world in which both older and younger females, irrespective of age, are supposed to do his bidding (within limits, of course), in the men's world age differences are of the utmost importance. He learns who his other superiors are, in addition to his father: all men older than he, including even a brother or a cousin who is his senior by only a year or so. On the other hand, he learns that he can treat boys younger than he as his inferiors, although not quite as inferior as the women, but still as persons of lesser importance than he. Once he has learned these lessons, and assuming that he has learned them well, the boy will have assumed the typical male Arab personality.

6. THE GIRL REMAINS IN THE WOMEN'S WORLD

The girl child, on the other hand, is spared this painful transition from the childhood environment to an alien world. But unless she is taken to wife by a cousin, that is, by a son of her father's brother, there is a different kind of transition, no less painful in many cases, that she must face and weather: the transition from the kind and compassionate tutelage of her mother to the much harsher and jealousy-tainted rule of her mother-in-law. While at home, the most difficult thing a girl child has to learn is to be satisfied with what must appear to her as the crumbs of her mother's love while her brothers get generous slices of it. Now, upon marrying, she finds that compared to the treatment she receives at the hand of her mother-in-law, her own mother's attitude to her was, and remains, the embodiment of lovingkindness. Only if the girl marries her father's brother's son, and both her own parents and her husband's parents still live in the home of the extended family of which her and her husband's common grandfather is the head, is she spared this often traumatic changeover from a soft to a tough superior. She remains living in the same house or compound, and the presence of her own mother, as well as the fact that she is the niece as well as the daughter-in-law of her husband's father, keeps her mother-in-law from riding her too hard.

If this is not the case, the young child-bride (the average age at marriage is only now slowly climbing toward the time of puberty) experiences hard times indeed. All the skills she has learned from her mother and elder sisters become severely tested. Can she properly perform the many chores that make up the duties of a wife? Can she fetch water from the village well, grind the corn, knead the dough, bake the bread? Kill a chicken, clean it, and cook it? Make butter, knead the dung into cakes fit for fuel? Spin and weave and sew? Is she strong enough to help her husband in plowing and sowing and reaping and threshing? And, above all, is her womb blessed and, when the time comes, can she bear sons? Inability to perform any of these things expected of a young wife, but especially failing to "bring" sons, means that she has proved a failure as a wife and must reckon with the possibility or even probability of divorce.

However, Allah is merciful and compassionate. Most wives do bear both sons and daughters, and in the course of years learn how to perform the household chores to the satisfaction of the mother-in-law, and all is well. As the years pass, the child-bride becomes a young matron, and, as the mother of sons, her position in her husband's family grows secure and even influential.

All in all one can say that the maturation process, and especially the transition from the world of childhood to the world of adults, is smoother for a girl than for a boy. For the boy it means a passing over from the women's world, in which he was protected, pampered, and admired, to the men's world, in which he is viewed critically and in which he must learn to compete and to fend for himself. As the oft-quoted Arabic proverb has it, a man must be able not only to stand up, with the help of his brother, against his cousins, but, if need be, also against his brother. For the girl, growing up means that she will have to pass over from her mother's home to that of her mother-in-law; but ultimately in both of these places she lives in a women's world, and the same virtues which made her accepted and appreciated in the first will stand by her in the second. Although there are numerous Arabic proverbs about women, expressing their hopes and fears, their joys and sorrows, typically, there is no proverb which would be the female counterpart of the one above and which would say: "I and my sister against my female cousins; I against my sister." Although brothers are members of the same family and same lineage, and often of the same household, as far as emotional attachment goes, sisters, even while living in separate households each with their husband, remain closer to each other.

7. CHILDHOOD REWARDS AND ADULT ACHIEVEMENT

While some anthropologists, following Freudian lines, have focused their attention on such emotional or affective aspects as strictness and permissiveness in weaning, toilet training, sex, and dependency, others have emphasized a different area, that of the need for achievement.[18] These studies found a wide range in the need for achievement, as well as some relationship between mother-child relations and the degree of the child's achievement need. On this basis it was argued that one of the practical outcomes of achievement need was the rate of economic development, and a three-phase causal relationship was postulated: child-rearing practices ↠ need for achievement ↠ economic development. A central part of the hypothesis was that

> differences in rate of economic development in different countries might be attributable not to natural resources, available investment capital, or technological skills alone, but also to the amount of achievement motive found in the inhabitants of that nation.[19]

What causes these observable differences in achievement need between one culture and another? The answer given by anthropologists and psychologists of the culture and personality school is that a significant factor is the extent to which parents (and especially the mother) reward acts of achievement performed by their children. To put it briefly, it was found that there is a positive correlation between parental rewarding in childhood and achievement in adult life. Parental reward, evidently, reinforces in the child the urge to achieve. The child who is consistently rewarded by the parents for his acts of achievement receives a reinforcement of his need to achieve to such an extent that he carries over this need into adult life.

Can any correlation of this kind between rewarding of achievement in childhood and record of achievement in adulthood be established in the Arab world? This is one of the questions that Prothro sets out to answer in his study *Child Rearing in the Lebanon*. To being with, one must be aware of the heterogeneous ethnic composition of the population of Lebanon. While Lebanon is unquestionably the most advanced of the Arab countries in its attitude toward Westernization and modernization, within Lebanon there are palpable differences between the various ethnic groups. "Muslim villagers are the most conservative element, followed by the Christian villagers, then by the Muslim townspeople, and finally by the Christian urbanites who are the most Westernized element in the country."[20]

Utilizing this ethnic and cultural heterogeneity, and wishing to ascertain whether these cultural differences appeared in early childhood, Prothro administered a Goodenough Draw-a-Man Test to several hundred five-year-old Lebanese children belonging to three religio-ethnic groups: Sunnī Muslim Arab, Greek Orthodox Arab, and Gregorian (Orthodox) Armenian. In addition, each of the three groups was divided into an urban (Beirut) and a village ("Valley") section. The test was used to determine (or estimate) the mental age level of the children and to compare the performance of the three groups. Comparing children of the same class and residential area, it was found "in every case that the Sunnis score lower than the Orthodox, and both score lower than the Gregorians. . . . There were marked differences among the three religious groups, with Gregorians highest, Orthodox next and Sunnis lowest in performance."[21]

Having established the existence of these inter-ethnic differences at the early age of five, Prothro next proceeded to focus on the possibility of a correlation between differences in child-rearing practices and adult achievement. As to the "ethnic differences in the economic sphere," Prothro quotes a number of authorities to the effect that the Armenians in Lebanon are the outstanding innovators in business and show the greatest enterprise in educational and cultural activities. The Christian Arabs rank next in economic enterprise, innovation, and control, while the Muslim Arabs rank third.[22] While "Armenians," "Christian Arabs," and "Muslim Arabs" are more comprehensive categories than the Armenian Orthodox Gregorians, Greek Orthodox Arabs, and Sunnī Muslim Arabs to whose children Prothro administered the test, the identity in the ranking order between these sets of children and the adults of the former three groups is nevertheless significant. With due reservations, it appears that the group whose children scored highest in the Draw-a-Man Test ranks highest in adult achievement as well.

In examining the question of the relationship between achievement and child-rearing practices, Prothro noted differences among his three groups with regard to the frequency of rewards for accomplishing approved tasks. It was found in American studies that the frequent use of such rewards characterizes the child-rearing practices of mothers in high-achieving groups. In Lebanon, a majority of both the Gregorian Armenian and Orthodox Arab mothers said they did systematically reward good behavior in their children, while a majority of the Sunnī Muslim Arab mothers said they did not; furthermore, the latter depended on threats more often than the other mothers. Differences were found to exist also in the mothers' expectation of independent activity and responsibility on the part of their children, with the Orthodox and the Gregorian mothers fostering independence in their young children to a greater degree than the Sunnī mothers—thus confirming the hypothesis that such training characterizes groups of high achievers.[23]

Finally, Prothro found that in the Gregorian Armenian group and the Beirut Greek Orthodox Arab group, the fathers played a lesser role in disciplining the young children than was the case in the Lebanese population in general and in the Sunnī Muslim Arab group in the valley in particular. It thus appears that in the high-achieving group, the father is a more remote figure than in other groups; lower paternal control is correlated, in Lebanon as in America, with higher achievement.[24]

Among the Christian Lebanese, the Armenians are the most urbanized community. They are mostly craftsmen, small traders, and office workers. Culturally as well as linguistically, they have remained in a remarkable state of isolation, preferring the status of a nation in exile to the possibility of becoming absorbed into the Christian Arab majority. They arrived in Lebanon after World War I, came penniless, and have rapidly risen to a state of prosperity. They are characterized by high standards of morality and culture, as well as by energy and persistence.[25]

While it is impossible to say what precisely is the connection between these traits of the Lebanese Armenian modal personality and the child-rearing practices found among them by Prothro, two things seem certain: the specific Armenian child-rearing practices are unquestionably part and parcel of the cultural tradition to which the Armenians tenaciously adhere; and the same child-rearing practices evidently result in the perpetuation of the particular Armenian modal personality.

The other two groups studied by Prothro are both Arab, although one is Christian, the other Muslim. The Greek Orthodox (in Arabic, *Rūm Ortodoks*) Arabs of Lebanon as a whole have a more Middle Eastern orientation than the larger Maronite Christian community. Most of the Greek Orthodox Arabs live in villages (especially in the Koura district of North Lebanon), but a rich and numerically considerable group of them lives in Beirut. The Sunnī Muslims are the largest Muslim group in Lebanon, second only to the Maronites in size. In Beirut they constitute one-third of the population, in Tripoli and its environs they are the majority.

In the villages, especially in North Lebanon, most of them are still dependent on a small upper class of semi-feudal families of "notables"; in the cities they form a great part of the proletariat, although there is also a Sunnī commercial and professional bourgeoisie.[26]

There can be no doubt but that the correlation and interdependence between child-rearing practices and perpetuation of national (or community) character exist among the Greek Orthodox Arabs and the Sunnī Muslim Arabs to the same degree as they do among the Armenians. That is to say—to talk about the Sunnīs only since they are more relevant to the Arabs at large—the specific child-rearing practices which were ascertained and reported by Prothro and which in themselves are a function of their cultural traditions must be responsible, partly at least, for the traits in which they differ from the Greek Orthodox Arabs and the Gregorian Orthodox Armenians. The recall these briefly, the Sunnī Muslim Arab mothers reward successful accomplishment relatively infrequently, use the threat of punishment more frequently (although they often fail to carry out their threats), foster independence less frequently, and let the father predominate over the child.[27] It is in these practices that we must seek a contributing factor to the development of the specific character that the Lebanese Sunnī Muslim Arab children exhibit in childhood as well as in adult life.

One set of features of this national character has been specified by Prothro: the Sunnī Muslims lag behind the two Christian groups "with respect to achievement in the economic, and probably also the educational and cultural, spheres."[28] Since similar correlations between child-rearing practices and achievement have been found in America as well, it seems legitimate to conclude that there is a cause-and-effect relationship between the two.

IV

UNDER THE SPELL OF LANGUAGE

1. ARAB AND ARABIC

WHEN THE INHABITANTS OF TWO OR MORE COUNTRIES SPEAK the same language, the common tongue constitutes a bond among them, an affinity and a sympathy that transcends divisive political boundaries. Thus, the English-speaking peoples on the two sides of the Atlantic and elsewhere feel closer to one another than to other peoples, even though the latter may be nearer to them geographically. The German, Spanish, and Portuguese languages constitute similar bonds among the nations who speak them. However, the sense of affinity created by a common language is invariably limited. It does not blur national considerations and interests, which remain primary in the consciousness of each nation.

Not so with Arabic among the Arabs. In the Arab countries, there is at present a pervading consciousness of being one nation, the Arab nation, irrespective of the number of political units into which this one nation is broken up. This does not mean, of course, that there are no differences, or even enmities and fiery denunciations, among Arab states. But even in the midst of fratricidal wars, the feeling persists that, however painful the conflict, it is merely a temporary disagreement which sooner or later will be settled and which, even while it lasts, in no way infringes upon the

41

principle of Arab brotherhood and the ideal of all-Arab national unity. There can be no doubt but that the Arabic language is the most potent factor in both the creation and the maintenance of this overriding myth of Arab nation, Arab unity, Arab brotherhood. As Jabra I. Jabra, a modern Iraqi critic and novelist, put it, "Such was the unifying force of Arabic that, from the very start, it had become the essence of the Arab ethos."[1]

Moreover, upon closer look it appears that the Arabs not only view themselves as one nation, but consider the far-flung members of this nation as branches of a vastly enlarged single family. Familism, that is the view that the family is central in practically all aspects of life, has been until the present era one of the most important values in Arab tradition, and even today wields considerable power over Arab thought and sentiment. In viewing the "Arab nation" as an Arab family, Arab mentality tends to apply to it the old experiences and rules worked out over the centuries within the family context. One of these rules is aptly summarized in the proverb already cited, current in several variants in many Arab countries: "I against my brothers; I and my brothers against my cousins; I and my cousins against the world." The same proverb is also quoted in reverse order, in which case its intent seems to be a reproach for the proclivity to infighting: "I and my cousins against the world; I and my brothers against my cousins; I against my brothers."

The Arab sociopolitical world view can best be represented by a series of concentric circles. The smaller the circle the greater the sense of belonging, cohesion, and loyalty. In traditional Arab society, the largest such circle which commanded loyalty was that of the tribe, or, among the settled population, that of the village. Beyond the tribe or village loomed the outside world, other tribes or villages, which, by and large, constituted a menace rather than kindred aggregates. Modern Western influences imposed the next larger circle, that of the political nation, which to this day has not completely succeeded in replacing in the Arab loyalty scale the smaller circles of villages, tribes, and other kinship-based units contained in it. Next comes the circle which comprises all Arab states together, or rather all the Arabs wherever they may live and to whatever political entity they may belong. Beyond the Arab world, in the far distance, is the Muslim world, which exists rather faintly in Arab consciousness as comprising, in addition to the "Arab nation," several non-Arab nations. The non-Arab Muslim circle constitutes, to the Arabs, a kind of periphery marking the transition from the Arab world to the rest of the world—which is neither

Arab nor Muslim. However, if an Arab were asked to choose one single dividing line between "us" and "them," between the ingroup of which he feels a part and the outgroup consisting of the alien world, he would in all probability point to the circle within which are found Arabic speakers and outside which are the speakers of all other tongues whatever their religious persuasion.

In the non-Arabic-speaking world, as we have seen, there are several groups of countries in which one and the same language is spoken. However, only in the case of Arabic is the language the factor that defines and determines membership in the national aggregate. A statement such as "A German is one whose mother tongue is German" would be patently false because it would make Germans out of Austrian, Swiss, and other nationals. But in the Arab world the question, Who is an Arab? is usually answered, One whose mother tongue is Arabic. This is the answer many Arabs themselves give; nor has any other valid answer been found. Linguistic identity makes "Arabs" of members of different religions (with certain exceptions). Thus, both Sunnī Muslims and Shī'ī Muslims are "Arabs" in Iraq and Yemen; both Muslims and Christians, if Arabic-speaking, are "Arabs" in Lebanon and Syria; and so on. Language can override even descent traditions, as shown by the general prevalence of a system of dual organization —a dichotomy of society into two opposing halves—all over the Arab world, with members of both groups identified as Arabs.[2] It can make Arabs of descendants of Somali and other African slaves even if they have retained Negroid physical features, and of the descendants of Bulgarian and other European immigrants whose ancestors had arrived in an Arab country often via service in the Turkish army.

Since the Arab world is a living entity, no rule can hold in it a hundred per cent. Thus, while in the overwhelming majority of cases the adoption of Arabic as the mother tongue has meant not only linguistic but also ethnic Arabization, some exceptional groups have retained their ethnic identity despite linguistic assimilation to Arabic. These non-Muslim Arabic-speaking communities, whose members are not considered Arabs, are few and small in numbers but they are conspicuous. The largest is that of the Copts of Egypt, a Christian sect whose members until recently spoke their own old language, Coptic, which they still retain in their church services. Next come the Jews, of whom today only a few remain in Arab countries since most of them immigrated to Israel after 1948. They speak (or spoke) Arabic, but used Hebrew as the language of synagogue, study, and literary expression. There are also members of several smaller Christian sects, who use Arabic as their everyday colloquial language, but Syriac and other languages in their church services. Were it not for the Druzes, who live in Israel, Lebanon, and Syria, one could generalize and say that non-Muslim Arabic-speaking communities which use a non-Arabic language as their religious medium are not considered Arabs. The Druzes, however, constitute a special case. They are the descendants of Muslim Arabs who in the eleventh century seceded from the main body of Islam; although they never ceased being an Arabic-speaking community, and using Arabic in their religious services, they are not considered Arabs, but Druzes and nothing else.

These marginal exceptions, however, are not significant enough to affect in any way the overall validity of our definition: An Arab is one whose mother tongue is Arabic.

2. THE LURE OF ARABIC

The philologist al-Tha'ālibī (d. 1038) said:

> Whoever loves the Prophet loves the Arabs, and whoever loves the Arabs loves the Arabic language in which the best of books was revealed . . . whomsoever God has guided to Islam . . . believes that Muḥammad is the best of prophets . . . that the Arabs are the best of peoples . . . and that Arabic is the best of languages.[3]

What al-Tha'ālibī meant by Arabic being "the best of languages" is not quite clear. But he was right in observing that Muslims in general believe in the excellence of Arabic. However, at least one quality of Arabic, the great eloquence with which it can endow those who become its true masters, has made its impression on Christians as well. A ninth-century Christian writer of Cordova felt it necessary to deplore the fact that Christian laymen were "intoxicated with Arab eloquence."[4]

The high praise of Arabic by early medieval Muslim and Christian authors is echoed to this day in the opinion the Arabs have of the value of their language. Throughout the vast Arabic language area, people hold with relative uniformity that Arabic is superior to other languages because it is beautiful and has a strong appeal, especially for the recitation of classical poetry and for formal or semi-formal oratory. Arabic speakers also hold that Arabic surpasses other languages in beauty because of its inherent qualities. Jabra even talks of the "mystique" of the Arabic language: "Since the language regained its dynamism, its mystique has become even more magical, more operative than ever, lying as it does at the heart of the new political upsurge." He then goes on to say that "Arabic grammar, though complex, is basically as logical as mathematics. This has made the language capable of precision and subtlety." As to the relationship of the Arabs to their language, he comments on "the inherent grandiloquence the Arabs are fond of" and on "the verbal miracle" that is at work within those who speak Arabic.[5]

As an American Arabist remarked, the Arabs take great pride in the logical pattern of the Arabic verb system, while remaining "completely unaware of the near chaos of the Arabic noun system." In fact, the conviction that Arabic is the best and most beautiful language is so strong in many Arabs that when one "pushes" the point of the illogicality of Arabic, the reaction is "strong resentment and hostility."[6]

Other parts of the general set of myths about Arabic, which forms "a fairly well integrated single body of attitudes and beliefs" in the Arabic speech community today, are the notion of the vastness and richness of the Arabic lexicon, and the holiness of Arabic as the language of the Koran. Also, a generally prevalent notion is that classical Arabic is the best of all the existing varieties of the language, and that one's own particular dialect is nearest to classical, easiest to learn, and most widely understood of all the colloquial dialects. Simultaneously, lip service is still being given to the excellence of the Bedouin dialect.[7]

My own inquiries into this subject among Arabs in Jerusalem and Nazareth in 1971 confirmed all these findings. Nazareth Arabs, even highly educated ones (one of them with an American Ph. D. degree in sociology), were convinced that the Palestinian Arabic dialect was the best because it was nearest to classical Arabic, or because it was the most widespread of all Arabic dialects. Among Jerusalem Arabs, the Arabic dialect of Jerusalem (and not of Palestine as a whole) was considered the best because it was believed to be nearest to literary Arabic. In neither Nazareth nor Jerusalem was the Arabic of the Bedouins held in high esteem. It was a pure dialect, but it had remained so limited that it was inadequate as a modern medium of expression.

In each Arab country classical Arabic and colloquial Arabic exist side by side, the latter in many local dialects. Arabs have become aware of the problem presented by this. Many feel that this is an anomaly, which will be eliminated in ten years, or, at the most, fifty. The Arabic of the future will be a unified, standardized, universal language, which will be very close to classical Arabic and which will be the only language used for both speaking and writing in the entire Arab world. It will be appropriate for all kinds of literature, and its spread and universal acceptance will be brought about by increased education, the radio, and the greatly increased mobility and intercommunication of the Arabs.[8]

In order to understand the power of the Arabic language to create and maintain a mythical sense of unity among the peoples of the numerous and widely scattered Arab states, one must cast a brief glance back into history. Until the appearance of Muḥammad, Arabic was spoken only in Arabia, and not even in all parts of that vast, arid, half-uninhabited peninsula. After Muḥammad made Islam the dominant religion in the peninsula, the newly converted Arabs embarked on a conquest of a major part of the world, in a triumphant sweep which has no parallel in history. Within eighty years after the death of Muḥammad (632), the Arabs held sway over Spain, North Africa, Egypt, the Fertile Crescent, and several contiguous areas, most of which have remained both Arab and Muslim to the present day. Successive generations carried the banner of Islam into more remote parts of the world, including, in the east, Central Asia as far as Mongolia, the Indian Peninsula, and Southeast Asia; in the west, the Balkans and Hungary; and in the south, the wide Sudan belt of Africa.

While Islamization and Arabization started out together, and were initially two inseparable aspects of the same process of conquest and conversion, as the distance between the Arabian home base and the newly conquered lands increased, Arabic lagged behind Islam. That is to say, a core area, itself of huge dimensions, within which both Islam and Arabic were established, came to be surrounded by an even larger peripheral zone in which the populations converted to Islam without, however, adopting Arabic in place of their own languages. This is how the Arab world came to occupy a central area within a larger, non-Arab Muslim world.

The Arabic language was able to hold its own only in countries in which the indigenous population had originally spoken a Hamito-Semitic language, that is, a language more or less closely related to Arabic. Thus, Arabic replaced Aramaic, a Semitic language, in the Fertile Crescent (the Palestine-Syria-Iraq area) and Coptic, a Hamitic language, in Egypt. But it did not succeed in supplanting Persian in Iran, Pashtu in Afghanistan, and Kurdish in Kurdistan (all three Iranic languages), nor Turkish in Turkey and Turkic in Central Asia (both Turkic languages). Also, the

Berber tribes of Northwest Africa resisted Arabization quite successfully until the present day, although the Berber language is considered by some scholars a member of the Hamito-Semitic language family.

This still leaves Arabic with a sway over a territory that is larger than the area inhabited by the speakers of any other single language. Arabic is spoken in Southwest Asia, in Arabia and the Fertile Crescent up to the Persian and Turkish borders; in North Africa, from Egypt and the northern Sudan (from the Nile to the Chad) to Morocco and Mauritania, as well as in the northern Sahara. In addition, there are Arabic-speaking pockets in Africa (Djibuti and Zanzibar) and in Europe (Malta). It is a testimony to the largely desert-like character of this huge territory that the total number of Arabs is relatively small: it can be estimated at present (1973) at 110 million.[9]

In that part of the world which was both Islamized and Arabized, and which today comprises eighteen independent Arab states, the Arabic language attained a value second in importance only to that of the Muslim faith. The Koran, the only sacred book of Islam, speaks within the text itself of "this Arabic Koran." Because of the Koran, the sixth-century Meccan dialect of Arabic became the standard language of Muslim religion, as well as the literary form of expression used by Arabs everywhere. Only very gradually, and to a limited extent, was Koranic Arabic allowed to change and to develop into a successively more modern literary Arabic.

Just as the Koran became the holy book of all Muslims, so Arabic became the holy language of all Muslims, including those of the peripheral belt who never adopted Arabic as their colloquial. They read and recited the Koran by heart in Arabic, they prayed in Arabic, and they adopted the Arabic alphabet (with some variations) as the script for their own languages. The few male children who were sent to school in Turkey, Persia, Afghanistan, Bokhara, Turkestan, and the more remote parts of the non-Arab Muslim periphery were taught the Arabic script, they learned to read, and perhaps even to understand, the Arabic Koran, and little else besides. In these countries Arabic played a role not unlike that of Latin in the Catholic Church.

If such was the esteem in which Arabic came to be held in the peripheries, where only a very few scholars attained full mastery of it, in the core area Arabicized after the Muslim-Arab conquest the holy language of the Koran attained a position never approximated by any other language in any other culture. The cultivation of Arabic by those whose mother tongue it had become soon developed independently of its religious foundations into an intellectual endeavor which was pursued for its own sake with increasing intensity and devotion. The best Arab minds considered the Arabic language the greatest treasure possessed by the Arabs and devoted enormous ingenuity to the fullest possible utilization of its potential. In this they were greatly helped by the rich vocabulary of Arabic, the great variability of Arabic verb structures, the ease with which the language lent itself to rhythmic cadences, and its exceptional suitability to rhetoric and hyperbole.

3. RHETORICISM

I suggest the term "rhetoricism" to denote the exceptionally high value Arabs put on their language, their extraordinary attachment to it, and the influence it exerts over them. Rhetoricism is a very important feature in the Arab modal personality.

I myself have on more than one occasion experienced the power of Arab rhetoricism—or at least the incipience of that intoxication with Arab eloquence against which Alvaro warned his Christian contemporaries in ninth-century Cordova. I felt it when attending an Arab theatrical pėrformance, listening to an Arab orator, hanging upon the lips of an Arab storyteller in a café on a Ramaḍān night, or merely following an animated discussion between friends. Being conversant with several languages, I can attest from my own personal experience that no language I know comes even near to Arabic in its power of rhetoricism, in its ability to penetrate beneath and beyond intellectual comprehension directly to the emotions and make its impact upon them. In this respect, Arabic can be compared only to music. For speakers of English, the effect their language has on them is very different from that of great music. Yet the speakers of Arabic react to both language and music in a basically similar manner, except that their reaction to the language is probably deeper, more intense, and more emotional.

I could go on for quite a while giving my personal thoughts and feelings about Arabic. Let me, however, quote a few experts who themselves are Arabs and therefore in the best position to express themselves authoritatively on the subject. This is what Edward Atiyah has to say on the relationship of the Arabs to language: "It is a characteristic of the Arab mind to be swayed more by words than by ideas, and more by ideas than by facts."[10]

The leading Arab-American historian, Philip K. Hitti, elaborates the same theme:

No people in the world has such enthusiastic admiration for literary expression and is so moved by the word, spoken or written, as the Arabs. Hardly any language seems capable of exercising over the minds of its users such irresistible influence as Arabic. Modern audiences in Baghdad, Damascus and Cairo can be stirred to the highest degree by the recital of poems only vaguely comprehended, and by the delivery of orations in the classical tongue, though only partially understood. The rhythm, the rhyme, the music, produce on them the effect of that they call "lawful magic."[11]

Albert H. Hourani, after terming the Arabic language "the flawed mirror in which they [the Arabs] see the world," goes on to say that Arabic carries with it

a certain imagination. Arabs love fine and sonorous words for their own sake, and care for poetry and rhetoric more than other arts. They love heroic gestures and tend to see acts in themselves, as fitting an occasion rather than as links in a chain of cause and consequence. Their vision of the world has a hardness of outline; it is a vision in black and white. Through language and imagination again there enters an ethical system which exalts the heroic virtues: loyalty to friends, family, and tribe; the sense of personal and family honor; hospitality; the magnanimity of the strong man who does not always insist on his rights.[12]

Some writers go so far as to postulate an inner relationship between language and manhood: strong manhood is co-extensive with strong rhetoric. This is the opinion of Aḥmad Ḥasan al-Zayyāt, as expressed in his Difā' 'an al-balāgha or "Defense of Eloquence."[13]

As a conclusion to these brief notes on Arabic rhetoricism, let me add a linguistic observation. The Arabic noun balāgha, eloquence, is derived from a variant from of the verb balagha (which means to achieve something or to attain male maturity), balugha, meaning to be eloquent. Eloquence is, thus, to the Arab an achievement akin to the attainment of masculinity. From the same verbal root is derived the noun mubālagha, which means verbal exaggeration or hyperbole. To the Arab mind, eloquence is related to exaggeration, which is not meant to be taken literally but which only serves the purpose of effect.

4. EXAGGERATION, OVERASSERTION, REPETITION

Rhetoricism and proneness to verbal exaggeration seem to be two related phenomena. Rhetoric leads to exaggeration in other linguistic contexts as well, witness the exaggerated statements, criticisms, demands, and intentions integral to the rhetoric of English-speaking radicals. In Arabic, the greater measure of rhetoricism is accompanied by a correspondingly greater proclivity to exaggeration, *mubālagha*. Next to exaggeration, Arabic speech patterns are characterized also by emphatic assertion or *tawkīd*.

All those who have an opportunity to get acquainted with the speech patterns of Arabs, even of the illiterate majority in the villages and the nomadic tribes, are struck by the extraordinary mastery of the language which characterizes them. This mastery expresses itself in the use of a rich vocabulary, but even more so in a knowledge of and incessant recourse to a very large number of well-rounded and often quite complex phrases. Compared to the eloquence of the simplest illiterate Arab, the use of English by the average American appears as a series of disjointed grunts.

The mastery the average Arab has over his language is accompanied by two related traits. One is stylistic elaborateness, the other stylistic exaggeration and overemphasis. Since we are not dealing here with stylistic elaborateness, two examples will have to suffice to illustrate it. The colloquial Arabic equivalent for the English "Thank you" is *"Katter kheyrak"* (Syrian), which is the abbreviation and at the same time transposition into colloquial of the literary Arabic *"Allāh yukaththir khayraka,"* meaning "May Allah increase your well-being." The colloquial Arabic equivalent of our "Speedy recovery" is *"Ma 'alāk illā 'l-'āfīye in shā Allāh,"* which means "May there be upon you nothing but health, if Allah wills." Even these two examples should be enough to give the reader who does not know Arabic a slight taste of the delicious quality of Arabic style.

It is almost inevitable that people who are used to expressing their thoughts in such (and much more complex) ready-made phraseology, to which must be added the frequent use of innumerable proverbs and sayings, should be led by their language into exaggeration and overemphasis, that is, when measured by non-Arabic, and primarily English, standards. To the English speaker, the two phrases quoted above sound much more emphatic than his own brief and dry "Thank you" and "Speedy recovery." To the Arab, however, such florid expressions sound quite ordinary. To add a third example, in which the element of exaggeration is even more pronounced, the colloquial Arabic equivalent of "We missed you" is *"Awḥashtena,"* which literally means "You made us desolate" (the noun *waḥsh,* from the same root, means wilderness, desert, as well as melancholy, mental agony).

When two Americans meet in the morning, one will say "Good morning" and the other will answer "Good morning." Arab linguistic sensibilities would be offended by such invariant repetition. The general rule is that every phrase of courtesy must be returned by a more elaborate phrase, with interest as it were. The first Arab will phrase his "good morning" wishes as follows: *"Nehārkum saʿīd,"* literally, "May your day be prosperous," to which the other will reply, *"Nehārkum saʿīd wemubārak,"* "May your day be prosperous and blessed."

Examples can easily be adduced to show that both exaggeration and overemphasis intrude even into Arab political statements and discussion. On the eve of the 1948 Israeli War of Independence, Musa Alami, the well-known Palestinian Arab leader, made a tour of the Arab capitals to sound out the leaders with whom he was well acquainted. In Damascus, the President of Syria told him: "I am happy to tell you that our Army and its equipment are of the highest order and well able to deal with a few Jews; and I can tell you in confidence that we even have an atomic bomb. . . . Yes, it was made locally; we fortunately found a very clever fellow, a tinsmith. . . ." In Iraq, the Prime Minister informed him that "all that was needed was 'a few brooms' to drive the Jews into the sea." In Cairo, confidants of King Ibn Saud of Saudi Arabia assured him that "once we get the green light from the British we can easily throw out the Jews."[14] The common denominator in all these verbal assurances was that they were greatly exaggerated statements as to what the Arabs intended or hoped to do, as to what they believed they were capable of doing once they began to fight the Jews; in reality, these statements were not followed by serious or sustained efforts to translate them into action.

Another type of verbal exaggeration is the one which refers as facts to events the speaker wishes to happen. In the fall of 1964, *New York Times* correspondent Dana Adam Schmidt visited Yemen which, at the time, was in the throes of civil war. The Yemeni Royalists were helped by Saudi Arabia, while the Egyptian army participated in the war on the side of the Republicans. Although the military efforts of the Egyptians, says Schmidt,

> were in fact constantly frustrated, the Egyptians persistently ignored all reverses and claimed victories with so much conviction that they convinced themselves and probably some of the Yemenis. I was amazed, for instance, by the easy conviction with which Colonel Hassan Ali Kamal, the Chief of Operations, made statements to me which I knew to be untrue. The statements included the following: that the tribes in the region of Qara had turned against the Imam and had driven him out; that the Egyptian forces could freely travel to the Saudi Arabian border by camel; that the Egyptians had lost only three men during their August offensive from Haradh; and that Prince Abdullah Hassan in the Khawlan had been "knocked out" by the tribes' unwillingness to work with him.[15]

The psychological mechanism which produced all these untrue assertions was similar to the one which produces the typical dream of wish fulfillment: the strong desire that an event should take place, or that a situation should obtain, produces a verbal statement (corresponding to the dream) in which the desired event is represented as an accomplished fact.

This explanation is close to the one given to me in an interview by the Deputy Minister of Health in the government of Israel, 'Abdu 'l-'Azīz Zu'bī, in Jerusalem. As Mr. Zu'bī sees it, one of the bad characteristics of the Arabs is that they like to exaggerate. "Our hearts do the job of our brains" were his words. "We exaggerate in both love and hate. We are emotional rather than coldly analytical. Honor is exaggerated at the expense of the real need. We would *like* to see certain things and we think they *are*."[16]

Much of this predilection for exaggeration and overemphasis is anchored in the Arabic language itself. It is well known that the Arabic verb has various emphatic forms (the so-called *modus energicus*) which consist of the regular imperfect with the addition of certain suffixes denoting special stress. The Arabic verb also has special forms of conjugations which indicate a greater intensity of the activity expressed by the basic verb form. Frequently, sentences are introduced by an emphatic particle, *inna* (literally, behold); for example, the Arabic equivalent of the English "Here is a man" is *"Inna huna rajulan,"* which literally means "Behold, here is a man." The simple interrogative pronoun *mā* (what) is often strengthened by the addition of the demonstrative *dhā* (this); for example, *Mā dhā fa 'alta?* "What did you do?" literally means "What is this you did?" Often the third person pronoun is inserted between subject and predicate, which lends the statement an emphatic character: *Allāhu huwa 'l-hayyu,* "Allah he is the living one."

Especially instructive is the use of the Arabic adjective. This, in contrast to the English adjective with its three forms of positive (great), comparative (greater), and superlative (greatest), has only two forms, a positive and a so-called elative, which can have either comparative or superlative meaning: the positive *ṣaghīr,* young, small, becomes the elative *aṣghar,* younger, smaller, or youngest, smallest. In this respect Arabic is similar to French with its use of *plus* in the sense of more and *le plus* meaning the most (e.g., *plus grand,* greater; *le plus grand,* the greatest). However, in addition to these basic meanings of the positive and the elative, the positive can also mean superlative, and the elative can mean positive; *kabīru 'l-nāsi,* literally, "great of men," means "the greatest of men"; *Allāhu akbar,* literally, "Allah is the greatest," means "Allah is great." The use of the elative in the simple positive sense indicates an inclination to emphatic expression. The intention is to make a positive statement, but to make it emphatically; therefore, instead of the positive, the elative form of the adjective is used. The latter, evidently, can mean not only comparative or superlative, but also what might be termed "emphative." Thus, *Allāhu akbar* can be taken to mean, not only "Allah is great," "Allah is greater," or "Allah is the greatest," but also the emphative "Allah is very great."

The elative form of the Arabic adjective is often used to intensify expression. In such contexts the superlative is used "for the sake of the intensification of the basic meaning of the adjective (and not for indicating the especially high degree of the quality expressed by the adjective). . . ."[17] A passage in the Koran (39:35) reads (in literal translation): "That Allah may cover for them the *worst* that they did, and pay them their reward for the *best* that they used to do." Translated in this manner the verse fails to make good sense. Why should the Prophet foretell that on the Day of Resurrection (which is what he is speaking of), God will cover up precisely the *worst* deeds of the good people, and reward them only for their *best* deeds? What the sentence actually means becomes clear when interpreted as a mere hyperbolic emphasis of the basic sense of the adjective: "That Allah may cover for them the *evil* that they did, and pay them their reward for the *good* that they used to do."

Muḥammad is reported as having said, "I brandished a sword and its edge broke off. . . . I brandished it a second time and it became again *the best* of what it had been." The use of the superlative in sentences such as this serves the purposes of emphasis, hyperbole, affective asseveration, that is, the intensification of a quality per se. In English one would say "as good as." Such a use of the elative strikes us as especially peculiar when it is combined with "as" or "like" (Arabic *mithl*). A passage in Ṭabarī which means "I have never seen a carpet *as* valuable and *as* beautiful *as* this," says in literal translation, "I have never seen a carpet *more* valuable and *more* beautiful *like* this. . . ."[18] It appears, then, that this stylistic device can be considered yet another type of the numerous inducements to exaggeration that the language offers to the Arab mind.

Another is the predilection for repetition. If an Arab wishes to impress his interlocutor with having definitely made up his mind to embark on a certain course of action, he will state several times what he intends to do, using a series of repetitious asseverations, often with increasing emphasis, and always with slight stylistic variations. Take as an example the decision of June 6, 1967, to announce that American and British aircraft were aiding Israel and attacking Egypt. In the brief telephone conversation between President Nasser and King Hussein, in which this decision was reached by the two Arab leaders, Nasser reiterated the point no less than four times, each time with increasing emphasis:

(1) Good, King Hussein will publish a communiqué on this and I'll publish the same communiqué. . . .

(2) So, Your Majesty will publish a communiqué on the American and English intervention. . . .

(3) As God is my witness, I tell you that I shall publish a communiqué and that you will publish a communiqué. And we'll see to it that the Syrians also announce that American and English aircraft are attacking us from their aircraft carriers.

(4) So we will publish this communiqué. We'll really emphasize this point and we'll do it together.[19]

A brief news item broadcast from Cairo in 1957 can serve as a second example of repetitiousness.

Details of the news: The President Gamal Abdul Nasser met today the delegation of Syrian professors and students who are visiting Egypt now for the strengthening of cultural ties between the two countries. And the President delivered a speech to them in which he spoke of the conspirings of the colonialists against the Arab nationalism, and he said, that the Arab nationalism is the protective armor which will defend the Arab nations from the conspiracies of the colonialists and the ambitions of the coveters. And [he further said] that Egypt, while she called upon the Arab nationalism, and while she declared that she is a part of the Arab nation, behold, she felt this with a deep feeling, and she felt that the Arabs, while they are united, they will be able to triumph over the colonialists, and while they are disunited, they will be a choice morsel for the coveters and conquerors. And the President said, This is our aim [to achieve] from the Arab nationalism: cooperative interest, and reciprocal interest, and protection, for whose attainment all of us will work, against the coveters, and the ravishers, and the colonialists.[20]

The repetitive and emphatic character of this "brief" news item becomes more apparent when we analyze it and find that it contains four mentions of colonialists or colonialism; four of Arab nationalism plus two of Arab nation(s) and one of the Arabs; three of "the coveters"; three of "feeling" (two verbs and one noun); and two each of protection-protective interest, and conspirings-conspiracies. Another aspect of the repetitiveness and emphasis is the frequent use of two similar phrases one after the other in order to underline one and the same idea: "conspiracies of the colonialists and the ambitions of the coveters"; "coveters and conquerors"; "cooperative interest and reciprocal interest"; or the use of three expressions: "against the coveters, and the ravishers, and the colonialists," or the repetition of the same expression: "she felt this with a deep feeling, and she felt . . ."

As a third example we can take a programmatic article written by Kamāl al-Dīn Ḥusayn, Minister of Education of the United Arab Republic. The article was printed in a collection of papers dealing with the year 2000 published in 1959 by *Al-Hilāl (The Crescent Moon),* a Cairo publication resembling the *Reader's Digest* in both format and context. The preface to the issue in question was written by President Nasser; Ḥusayn's article follows as the first item. The article is replete with repetitions, as the following sampling from only two pages of the book will show:

"Today the greatness and brilliance of our Arab culture can be seen far and wide" (p. 312).[21] "We already have an Arab civilization whose brilliance and greatness can be seen far and wide" (p. 313).

"Today's Arab culture is somewhat different from what we used to call the 'science of the Arabs' " (p. 312). "It is not the 'Arab science' which was formerly studied" (p. 313).

"Formerly all the Arabs knew what was forbidden and permitted [by God] along with a little literature, philology and history. . . ." (p. 312). "In the past the Arabs were masters of the science of what God has forbidden and permitted and the arts of language, literature and history" (p. 312). "There is a place in it [i.e., Arab civilization] for the science of what God has allowed and forbidden" (p. 313).

"[Arab culture] must advance and must not flag until it has caught up with and surpassed the [European] culture which overtook it. It must catch up with it and surpass it. . . ." (pp. 312–313). "And so we shall overtake Europe. . . ." (p. 313).

Some Arab authors have managed to acquire a true mastery of a European language, including not only its vocabulary, grammar, and style but also its spirit. Most of them, however, have difficulty in ridding themselves of the Arab linguistic tradition of exaggeration even when writing in a European tongue. An example is provided by Mostefa Lacheraf, one of the leaders of the Algerian F.L.N. (Front de Libération Nationale), a leading Algerian publicist, and a professional historian who, of course, writes in French like almost all Algerian intellectuals. But even while writing in French, Lacheraf is unable to free himself of the traditional *mubālagha.* He says, for example: "Here is the drama: most Algerians read and write a little French, hardly any Arabic, and yet claim roots in a culture with a splendid past but one which has become a fiction because of colonization."[22] Knowing very well that "most Algerians" were illiterate (92 per cent at the time he was writing in 1954), what Lacheraf should have said was: ". . . most of that minority of Algerians who are literate, read and write a little French. . . ." But when his attention was focused on making his point, he unconsciously had recourse to exaggeration and wrote instead "most Algerians read and write a little French," although such a statement is patently untrue.

E. Shouby, in an essay on the influence of the Arabic language on the psychology of the Arabs, has some insightful observations on the phenomenology and psychological effects of *tawkīd* and *mubālagha*. In Arabic grammar, special verbal forms exist to express extra emphasis, and there are special connecting words serving the same purpose, as well as other grammatical and syntactic devices. In the stylistic area, metaphors and similes, which are used abundantly, have the same effect, as have the repetitions which are yet another characteristic of Arabic style.[23]

While these grammatical and stylistic features cause no problem in communications between Arabs, they can be a serious handicap when it comes to communication between Arabs and non-Arabs (especially Westerners). Whether the contact between the Arab and the Westerner takes place with the help of an interpreter, or one of them has a "working knowledge" of the language of the other, the difficulty remains the same. The literal meaning of a word or a phrase in every language is one thing, while its true significance can be another. One is reminded of the oft-quoted joke about the lady: If a lady says "No," she means "Perhaps"; if she says "Perhaps," she means "Yes"; if she says "Yes," she is no lady. The point in the first two parts being, of course, that the true meaning of the words uttered by the lady is something very different from the meaning of the same words in ordinary usage.

Similarly, a simple assent from an Arab can be, for him, nothing more than a polite form of evasion, while the same word may mean for his English interlocutor a definite, positive commitment. If the Arab wishes to make such a commitment, he will use *mubālagha* and *tawkīd,* as well as repetition, which to the English speaker will sound strange, to say the least. The same difficulty works in the reverse. A simple "Yes" or "No" is, for the

English speaker, a definitive statement. His Arabic interlocutor, however, conditioned as he is by the exaggeration and overassertion that are the rule in his own mother tongue, is simply incapable of understanding such brief and simple statements in the same sense. For him, "Yes" only means "Perhaps." ("No" has for the Arab a similarly indefinite meaning.) Only if the English speaker had said: "Yes, I am telling you definitely, yes; I assure you positively and emphatically, yes; my answer is irrevocably and permanently, yes!" would the Arab have got the point that what the English speaker *really* meant was "Yes."

Shouby cites a telling example to illustrate the difficulties that can arise in communication between two people conditioned by such different linguistic traditions. An English girl and an Arab youth reported to him about the relationship between them.

> The girl complained that her Arab friend (a) was pestering her with his attentions and declarations of love; and (b) refused to take "No" for an answer when she made it perfectly clear that she was not interested in him at all. The Arab confided (a) that the English girl was encouraging him to make love to her; and (b) that he had so far shown only a little interest and admiration. Both were strictly honest and truthful even to their conscious selves, but they did not know what a contrast could be created between Arab overassertion and British tact and understatement.[24]

Shouby concludes that "Arabs are forced to overassert and exaggerate in almost all types of communication"[25] if they wish to make sure that they are not misunderstood. This conclusion has been subjected to a thorough examination by Prothro, who administered for the purpose a test to some 140 Arab students in Lebanon. The results, which were compared with the responses of American students, led him to the conclusion that "statements which seem to Americans to be strongly favorable or unfavorable seem to Arabs to be more neutral." This bore out the hypothesis formulated by Prothro on the basis of his own studies that Arab students "are more prone to overassertion than are American students," and "that students in the Arab world are either more emotional than those in America, or that they are more emotional with respect to judgments about people." Prothro also has some cogent advice to give to persons interested in presenting the Arab point of view to Americans and the American point of view to Arabs. The first "should keep in mind that statements which seem to Arabs to be mere statements of fact will seem to Americans to be extreme or even violent assertions. Statements which Arabs view as showing firmness and strength on a negative or positive issue may sound to Americans as exaggerated." Those

> interested in presenting the American point of view to literate Arabs should note that a statement which seems to be a firm assertion to the Americans may sound weak and even doubtful to the Arabs who read it. If communications are to take place between peoples of different cultures, then attention must be given not only to problems of language codification but also to problems of culture and cognition.[26]

Arab observers, too, have noted the Arab tendency to exaggerate and have attacked it with sharp words of criticism. Indeed, Salīm al-Lūzī, the editor of the Beirut weekly *Al-Ḥawādith,* in an article published in the June 16, 1972, issue of his paper on the occasion of the fifth anniversary of the Six Day War of 1967, reproached the Arab press and radio with feeding the Arab consciousness with futile imaginings, lies, and exaggerations in recalling what happened in the summer of 1967.

An additional interesting insight into the way in which modern, Western-educated Arabs see the Arab proclivity for verbal exaggeration was given to me in an interview with Dr. Sami Farah Geraisy, probation officer of Nazareth. Dr. Geraisy related this Arab trait to the personal independence that used to characterize the lives of individual Arabs. "Precision," he said,

> is a phenomenon of industrial society. You must be on time for work, you are tied to a machine which will not tolerate imprecision, you live in a world of impersonal relations, you must be precise in what you do and in what you say. But if you are independent, say, you are a fellah who works his field, you come and go when you want, you talk the way you want. Verbal exaggeration, expansiveness, imagination make man more free. When people have more leisure, they fill their time with long discussions, with long greetings, and this leads to exaggerations. As I see it, exaggeration is a cultural phenomenon with socio-economic foundations. Similarly, *mufākhara* ("boasting") is a compensation for what you don't have. As soon as technical know-how enters, precision must come with it. Then much will be changed and lost, including exaggeration.[27]

While leisure and independent working conditions do not explain the tendency to exaggerate, Dr. Geraisy's analysis is valuable because it presents exaggeration as a phenomenon organically connected with the traditional socio-economic conditions of the Arabs. And we can, of course, go along wholeheartedly with his prognostication that the intrusive technological order will, sooner or later, spell the end for the traditional Arab trait of exaggeration.

The sum total of all this seems to me to warrant the following generalizations:

In the course of learning to speak, Arab children acquire not only the Arabic vocabulary and grammar, but also style, including the specific stylistic devices known as *mubālagha* (exaggeration) and *tawkīd* (overassertion). Recourse to *mubālagha* and *tawkīd* soon becomes, and remains throughout life, as "natural" to an Arab as his use of vocabulary and grammar. This means that, when the average Arab uses exaggeration and overemphasis, he actually is either not at all, or only barely, aware of employing these specific stylistic devices. In his mind, as well as in the mind of his Arab interlocutors, exaggeration and overemphasis register as simple statements. This being the case, one must be extremely cautious in reading specific psychological implications into stylistic devices which are exaggeration and emphasis only when viewed from the much dryer climes of the British and American varieties of colloquial English.

5. WORDS FOR ACTIONS

I suggested earlier that a connection may exist between the custom of the nursing mother yielding her breast to her son at his verbal demand and the expectation, formed and reinforced in the mind of the child as a result of this experience, that whenever he utters an emphatic verbal demand it would unfailingly be fulfilled, as well as with the adult Arab's proclivity for emphatically uttering demands and intentions without following them up by actions. Here I want to add one further point to the picture of those Arab child-rearing practices which seem to result in a lasting effect in the Arab personality formation. This additional point is the role verbal threats play in early Arab socialization.

Prothro's study of child-rearing practices in Lebanon showed that among Sunnī Muslim Arabs, mothers frequently used threats in their efforts to control their children but then failed to carry out these threats. In Baalbek, the largest Muslim town in the Beqaa Valley, 88 per cent of the mothers said that "they often used threats which they failed to carry out." Among Muslim mothers in the capital, Beirut, only 52 per cent gave the same reply. Interestingly, among Christian mothers the study showed not only considerably lower percentages but also a reverse relation between the rural town and the capital city: verbal threats were resorted to by only 28 per cent of the valley Orthodox (from the town of Zahle); by 36 per cent of the Beirut

Orthodox; by 16 per cent of the valley Gregorians (from the village of Anjar); and by 35 per cent of the Beirut Gregorians.[28]

It stands to reason that people who in their childhood were frequently threatened with punishment which, however, was not carried out, would in later life resort to the same technique. And this is exactly what one finds as a characteristic pattern of Arab behavior. In fact, the Arab custom of trying to intimidate an adversary by verbal threats is such a prevalent feature of the Arab personality that it could not escape the notice of either foreign or native observers. An example of the latter was supplied in April, 1971, by Egyptian Deputy Foreign Minister Salah Gohar in reply to a question put to him by *Time* Senior Editor Ron Kriss about the meaning of Arab saber-rattling declarations against Israel. " 'When Arabs argue,' said Gohar, 'they start on opposite sidewalks and shout at one another, 'I will carve you into pieces!' and 'You'll never see another sunset!' Then, after ten or 15 minutes, they walk away and nobody gets hurt. This the Israelis don't realize.' " [29] Again, Dr. Sādiq Jalāl al-'Aẓm discusses the phenomenon of Arab self-criticism following the Six Day War between Israel and the neighboring Arab states. He compares the behavior of the Russians before the Russo-Japanese war of 1904 with that of the Arabs in 1967: both indulged in empty threats and frivolous conceit. The Russians threatened that they would "throw these impudent Asiatics into the sea" or "bury them under their own hat," and the like. Similar boasts and threats are found, Dr. al-'Aẓm points out, in the writings of Muḥammad Ḥasanayn Haykal, Egyptian Minister of National Guidance, published in *Al-Ahrām,* Egypt's semi-official newspaper, prior to the Six Day War.[30]

Verbal threats which even while uttered, it is understood, mean that they would never be translated into action, are but one subvariety of the larger category of the substitution of words for acts, of the verbal formulation of an intention or a demand without actually following it up with action. Conditioned by the childhood experience of frequent threats often not carried out, the adult Arab makes statements which express threats, demands, or intentions, which he does not intend to carry out but which, once uttered, relax emotional tension, give psychological relief and at the same time reduce the pressure to engage in any act aimed at realizing the verbalized goal. A few examples follow to show how this propensity intrudes into the political arena. Let us begin with two cases in point described by King Hussein of Jordan.

In discussing the first Cairo summit meeting of January, 1964, King

Hussein states that that conference was "to many Arabs a cruel deception. And for good reason! Everyone had kept insisting: 'if the Israelis divert the waters of the Jordan, the Arabs will immediately take up arms to oppose it.' But no such thing happened: When the Israelis moved to divert the Jordan, everybody turned to Nasser," who thereupon called together the first Arab summit meeting. That meeting was followed by two more summits, without, however, yielding any agreement.

Another example of the Arab over-valuation of words and proclivity for substituting words for actions is found in King Hussein's account of his meeting with Nasser on May 30, 1967.

On that day, despite "the insults broadcast by Radio Cairo over the past year," King Hussein flew to Cairo to meet President Nasser. In the course of the meeting, after some initial tension and distrust between the two Arab leaders had been overcome, Nasser suggested that a pact be drawn up "between our two countries right here and now." Thereupon King Hussein as he later recalled, requested that Nasser send "someone to find the file containing the bilateral defense pact between Egypt and Syria which had bound the two nations together since April. I was so anxious to come to some kind of agreement that I merely skimmed the text and said to Nasser:

" 'Give me another copy. Put in Jordan instead of Syria and the matter will be settled.'

"In an atmosphere of growing relaxation and cordiality, Nasser agreed, and a little later, I signed.' "[31]

Judiciously considered, this signing of a mutual defense pact between two heads of state who up to that very moment were practically at each other's throats could not be interpreted as anything more than a gesture. And the fact that the pact was signed on the spur of the moment, without even a thorough reading by King Hussein, after "Jordan" was substituted in the texts for "Syria," indicated that it was intended primarily as a statement for public consumption. In fact, the effect of the signing of the pact was exactly what it was intended to be. Radio Cairo immediately broadcast the news, and on the afternoon of the same day (May 30), when King Hussein flew back to his capital, Amman, he was greeted by "an indescribable explosion of popular joy." As he emerged from his plane, he "was welcomed by thousands of demonstrators who had rushed in a few hours from every corner of Jordan. To emphasize their satisfaction, they repeatedly lifted his car in triumph." As Zeid Rifai, chief of protocol and private secretary to King Hussein, explained, ". . . to the man on the street it seemed that the

King had overcome the obstacles to Arab divisiveness [Rifai, of course, means obstacles to Arab unity]. At the same time, he had succeeded in organizing Jordan's defense against the Israeli aggression we all considered imminent."[32] As these quotes show, not only the "man on the street" but also the King's private secretary, and even King Hussein himself, accepted a verbal (or in this case, written) declaration in place of an act. The hasty signing of a document was taken to be the equivalent of having "succeeded in organizing Jordan's defense."

In actuality, the Egyptian-Jordanian defense pact resulted in no Egyptian help for Jordan except for the arrival, two days later (June 1), of the Egyptian General Abdel Moneim Riad with his general staff, to take command of the Arab forces on the Jordanian front.

Telling examples of the Arab proneness to substituting words for deeds are supplied by the political history of modern Iraq. In describing the Iraqi claim of 1961 to Kuwait, Majid Khadduri makes this judgment: "[Prime minister 'Abd al-Karim] Qasim [of Iraq] talked loud but made no move to act." And again, "Qasim . . . though continuing to reiterate his claim, made no move to use force. . . ." On several occasions, Qasim stated publicly that he considered Kuwait an "integral part" of Iraq and that it was his intention to bring the sheykhdom under Iraqi suzerainty by peaceful means, although he maintained that he was capable of doing so by force. In his June 25, 1961, press conference, in which he first announced Iraq's claim to Kuwait, Qasim made a statement about administrative measures he *intended* to take in order to effect the annexation of Kuwait. After reviewing Kuwait's historical connections with Iraq and claiming that the area of Kuwait belonged to Iraq as part of the Iraqi province of Basra, he said: "We shall, accordingly, issue a decree appointing the Shaykh of Kuwait as *qaimaqam* [district governor] of Kuwait, who will come under the authority of the Basra province. . . ." The appointment of the hereditary shaykh of Kuwait as an Iraqi district governor would have been, to be sure, a meaningless gesture as far as the shaykh was concerned; but it would have been a step, even if only a declarative one, as far as internal Iraqi politics were concerned. But Qasim did not go even so far as to actually make such a paper appointment. All he did was to state that, at an unspecified future date, he would ("We shall") issue such a decree. This is, indeed, a classic example of substituting words for actions: all that Qasim did was to state that he intended to make a certain statement, which statement, as he and all concerned knew very well, would have remained mere words, in view of the fact that the shaykh of Kuwait had no intention of giving up his British-supported independence.

Another form of this is the Arab inclination to announce an incipient action as if it were already an accomplished fact. The second abortive military coup of 'Ārif 'Abd al-Razzāq, a former Prime Minister of Iraq (1965), against the government headed by President 'Abd al-Raḥmān 'Ārif and Prime Minister 'Abd al-Raḥmān al-Bazzāz in the summer of 1966 supplies some cases in point. No sooner had a group of officers temporarily captured the radio stations at Abu Ghurayb and Baghdad than they broadcast proclamations in the name of Razzāq as head of the new National Council for the Revolutionary Command.

> Another proclamation announced the success of the coup and called on [President] 'Abd al-Raḥmān 'Ārif and [Prime Minister] Bazzāz to leave their offices and retire to their homes. But these broadcasts were interrupted within an hour and denounced in Government counter-broadcasts. President 'Ārif announced that the rebellion had been suppressed and that the rebels had surrendered.[33]

In other words, as soon as the rebels had a mouthpiece under their control, they announced that they had accomplished the overthrow of the government.

The intention of doing something, or the plan of doing something, or the initiation of the first step toward doing something—any one of these can serve as a substitute for achievement and accomplishment. In his article on the year 2000, Egyptian Minister of Education Kamāl al-Dīn Ḥusayn wrote in 1959: "Unity is the road to progress. . . . We have taken the first step along this road and lo! we have arrived. . . ." The Arabist Arnold Hottinger, who quotes Ḥusayn's article, remarks: "The 'plan' plays an inordinate part in nationalist propaganda and in nationalist thinking. What is 'planned' is already as good as achieved."[34]

It is interesting to note in this connection that colloquial Arabic (especially in Syria and Egypt) has a stylistic form which seems to express the same propensity for making an oral declaration of intention rather than embarking upon a definite course of action.

The colloquial linguistic device of using the word "*bidd*" (wish, will), or its abbreviation *b-*, as an auxiliary word or a prefix to make it explicitly clear that the reference is to future action, has a definite bearing on this. When an Arab says, "I want to do this or that," instead of saying "I shall do this or that," he, in effect, substitutes an expression of *intention* for a *description* of future action. When, for instance, he says *"Anā biddī aḍrabek,"* the meaning is "I shall beat you up"; but what he actually says is "I want to beat you up!" By expressing the future act in the form of an intention, he achieves a measure of psychological relief; thereafter it no longer appears imperative to carry out the intended act.

The satisfaction which follows is counterproductive inasmuch as it tends to militate against actually following up the oral declaration by the action described. Once the intention of doing something is verbalized, this *verbal* formulation itself leaves in the mind of the speaker the impression that he *has done* something about the issue on hand, which in turn psychologically reduces the importance of following it up by actually translating the stated intention into action. The psychological pressure to *do* something is reduced by *stating* that one intends to, or will, do it. It is in this sense that in the Arab mentality words often can and do serve as substitutes for acts. Nasser, in one of his early speeches, pointed out and castigated this trait in the Arab character: "I feel in my depths that the tragedy which has befallen all of us in Palestine is but the result of the calm that has descended on our souls after the poetic speeches and the multitudinous gatherings. We listened to the speeches and after them felt a calmness, and this calmness was the primary and basic cause of the tragedy of Palestine."[35] Muḥammad Ḥasanayn Haykal similarly reproaches the Arab leaders for displaying what he calls "enthusiasm," that is, "talk about what is not within the realm of the possible and evasion of acts."[36] Statements such as these seem to indicate that Arab behavior patterns have impressed some Arab observers with the same phenomenon which has led in the West to the formulation of the so-called catharsis hypothesis: Oral display of aggression not only lowers a person's "feeling of tension, but also effectively" weakens "the strength of his aggressive inclinations. . . ."[37]

A slightly different explanation of the influence of the Arabic language on the Arab approach to action and reality was propounded by Shouby, who concluded that the Arabic language itself tends to bring about a "displacement of the perceptual images by the linguistic ones, which for all practical purposes are treated as if they were the real thing and not just a linguistic representation of it." He also noted a "confusion between words and the things they represent."[38]

A similar conclusion was reached three years later by Malek Bennabi, an Algerian writer (who writes in French), in his book *Vocation de l'Islam.* In analyzing the mentality of the *évolués,* that is, the North African Arabs who had had a French education which made them superficially modern and superficially Muslim, Bennabi remarks that "they confuse the word, the symbol, with the reality that once lay behind it."[39]

My own studies have not yielded a confirmation of this view. I have not found among the Arabs a confusion between words and the things they represent, nor a treatment of words as if they were the real thing. What I did find—to restate once more what has been said above—was that verbal utterance, the verbal statement of a threat or an intention (especially when it is uttered repeatedly and exaggeratedly) achieves such importance that the question of whether or not it is subsequently carried out becomes of minor significance. There is no "confusion" between words and action, but rather a psychologically conditioned substitution of words for action.

6. TIME SENSE AND VERB TENSE

In a study of the youth of a Lebanese village, the anthropologist Judith Williams made the observation that the Muslim villagers of Haouch El-Harimi were unable "to order the events of the past." They made "gross transpositions of early childhood events to adulthood and, conversely, of recent occurrences to a long distant past." Moreover, when "they were able to order or date events at all, it was in terms of external markers—a wedding, a holiday, a fight—rather than in terms of any internal orderliness of their growth cycle." One of their stereotyped expressions was "The past does not concern us." Mrs. Williams suspects that the same irrelevance of time finds its expression in "the prevalent indifference to age . . . the very youngest child is 'less than one' or 'more than one' and the older person is 'forty or fifty, maybe sixty.' " "Perhaps more than any other questions . . ." Mrs. Williams wrote, "the few that asked the subjects to view their life from the time perspective imposed an alien and difficult task."[40]

This difficulty may have something to do with the general disinclination or inability of the Arabs to concern themselves with precisely defined timing. As anybody who has lived among Arabs can testify, they are much less concerned with time than Westerners. Western man lives under what amounts to a veritable tyranny of time. He is always conscious of what he will or has to do and where he will or must be at a certain hour in the foreseeable future. Advance planning and scheduling is a basic part of his everyday life. Under the influence of Westernization, some of this has penetrated in recent decades to the Arab world as well. Work schedules, timetables, and the like have become important ordering factors of life in the Arab cities. But even there, and much more so in the villages, the traditional lack of concern with time still obtains in many areas of life. Where a Westerner would say, "May I come to see you tomorrow at five in the afternoon?", the Arab would announce, "I shall come to see you tomorrow afternoon, Allah willing." The "afternoon" referred to may be any time from noon to late in the evening, or, in fact, any other afternoon within the next few days. The phrase "Allah willing"—"*in shā Allāh*"— stamps any advance commitment with a note of uncertainty, in view of which it becomes clearly impossible, and even to some extent improper, to fix the time of a future act with greater exactness.

In view of this unconcern with time and of the behavior pattern in which it manifests itself, it is not surprising to find that the concept of punctuality does not exist in traditional Arab culture, and that the introduction of rigorous time schedules, demanded by modernization, has encountered great difficulties. Nor will it come as a surprise that lateness for appointments or not showing at all has remained to this day a fairly common phenomenon in Arab life, including inter-Arab conferences which, as often as not, open a day or two late, and in which the list of those actually present is rarely as full as, or identical with, the list of participants prepared on the basis of advance commitments.

It may not be too far-fetched to seek a connection between this traditional nonchalant attitude to time and the similar cavalier treatment of time that characterizes the Arabic verb form. In English, there is a rigid correspondence between the form and the meaning of the verb as far as time is concerned. When a verb is put into its past form, its meaning refers to the past. A verb in the present tense means action simultaneous with the time period in which the statement is made. A verb in the future tense indicates something that will take place subsequently to the time in which the statement is made. This correspondence between tense form and meaning is so self-evident that to English speakers it must appear a truism.[41] This, however, is not at all the case in Arabic.

The most outstanding Semitic linguists agree that the semantic study of the Arabic verb is, for the scholar who approaches it from an Indo-European background, extremely difficult.[42] The tenses do not correspond to those in the Indo-European languages. Arabic cannot be considered in isolation from the other Semitic languages; linguists assume that proto-Semitic—the primordial, hypothetical language from which all the known

Semitic languages developed—had only one verbal form, the imperfect, which had a wholly universal function.

In biblical Hebrew Job 3:3 in literal translation, says: "Perish will the day in which I shall be born"; but the meaning actually is: "May the day perish in which I was born." In Arabic the imperfect form can stand for present, future, and past; the perfect can also mean pluperfect, future and, in the most frequently used expressions of everyday life, present participle.[43] That is to say, in addition to the ordinary perfect tense (the narrative tense which talks about an action that was completed in the past, e.g., *Jā'a Aḥmad,* "Aḥmad came"), the perfect form can also have the following meanings:

Action that has reached completion in the present time of the speaker (e.g., *Jā'a Aḥmad hunā,* "Aḥmad has come here").

Pluperfect, that is, action that was completed prior to a point in the past referred to by the speaker (the English sentence "I met two teachers: one of them taught in Damascus, the other had taught in Aleppo" would be expressed in Arabic with the same perfect form used for all three verbs in the sentence).

The present: "*Ikhtalafa 'l–'ulamā,*" "The scholars differed," means "The scholars differ." Or "*Allāhu 'azza wajalla,*" literally, "Allah was mighty and great," means "Allah is mighty and great." Or:"*'alimtu,*" literally, "I knew," means "I know"; "*bi'tuka hādha,*" literally, "I sold you this," means "I sell you this."

In sentences expressing wishes, the perfect form can refer to the future, for example, *La'nahu 'llāh,*" literally, "Allah cursed him," means "May Allah curse him." Or "*Wallāhi lā fa'altu,*" literally, "By Allah, I did not do (it)," means, "By Allah, I shall not do (it)." The perfect can take several more meanings, but these should be sufficient to illustrate our point.

The imperfect form has the basic function of conveying the present continuous and the usual future sense. It can also however refer to timeless general experiences; *Kathratu 'l'itābi tūrithu 'lbaghdhā'a,*" literally, "Too much reproach will produce hatred," means "Too much reproach produces hatred."

In emphatic speech the imperfect can refer to the past; "*Fa'ahwaytu naḥwa 'lṣawti fa'adhribuhu dharbatan bil–sayfi,*" literally, "I rushed toward the voice and shall strike him with the sword," means "I rushed toward the voice and struck him with the sword." The imperfect can express a past action that accompanied another action: "*Jā'ū abāhum yabkūna,*" literally, "They came to their father they will cry," means "They came to their father crying." It can also express a past action that was subsequent to another past action: "'*Atā 'l–'ayna yashrabu*," literally, "He came to the well he will drink," means "He came to the well to drink."

Since the imperfect can have so many different meanings, when the speaker wants to make it unmistakably clear that the intended meaning refers to the future, the adverb *sawfa* (at the end) is put before the verb (e.g., "*Sawfa ta'lamūna*," literally, "At the end you will know," meaning "You will know"). Often the adverb *sawfa* is abbreviated to the prefix *sa-* (e.g., "*Sanurīhum*," "We shall show them").⁴⁴

Thus far our examples have been taken from literary Arabic. However, colloquial Arabic, spoken by the illiterate people who still form the majority in many Arab countries, is characterized by the same extreme flexibility or indeterminateness as far as the time of the action denoted by the verb form in concerned. Consequently, if a speaker wants to make it explicit that he is referring to future action, he places the noun *bidd* (wish, will) with the possessive pronoun suffix in front of the verb. Thus, "He will return" is expressed as "*Huwa bidduh yergi'*," which literally means, "He, his will is, he will return." Most often the word "*bidd*" is abbreviated so that only its first consonant *b-* remains as a prefix to the imperfect verb form, for example, "*baḍrab*," "I shall beat," literally, "I want to beat."⁴⁵

The conclusion from this unavoidably technical presentation of the use of the perfect and imperfect verb forms in Arabic is that for people speaking a language in which the verb has these semantic features, time cannot have the same definite, ordered, and sequential connotation that it has for people speaking a strictly time-structured language. This leads us to a more general consideration.

The existence of a meaningful correlation between culture and language was recognized as early as the 1920's by the linguist Edward Sapir, whose famous statement on the subject is still frequently quoted:

> Human beings do not live in the objective world alone, nor alone in the world of social activity as ordinarily understood, but are very much at the mercy of the particular language which has become the medium of expression for their society. . . . The fact of the matter is that the "real world" is to a large extent unconsciously built up on the language habits of the group. No two languages are ever sufficiently similar to be considered as representing the same social reality. The world in which different societies live are distinct worlds, not merely the same world with different labels attached.⁴⁶

This thesis was subsequently refined by Benjamin L. Whorf and developed into the well-known Sapir-Whorf hypothesis, in which the central idea is that "language functions, not simply as a device for reporting experience, but also, and more significantly, as a way of defining experience for its speakers."[47] As Whorf himself put it, "users of markedly different grammars are pointed by their grammars toward different types of observations and different evaluations of externally similar acts of observation, and hence are not equivalent as observers but must arrive at somewhat different views of the world."[48] Thus, Whorf finds, "the linguistic system (in other words, the grammar) of each language is not merely a reproducing instrument for voicing ideas but rather is itself the shaper of ideas, the program and guide for the individual's mental activity, for his analysis of impressions, for his synthesis of his mental stock in trade. . . ."[49]

The Sapir-Whorf hypothesis has important bearing on our discussion of the influence of the Arabic tempora on perception of time in particular. Of the relationship between the concept of time among speakers of English and the tense distinctions of the English verb, Whorf remarked that "The three-tense system of SAE [Standard Average European] verbs colors all our thinking about time." The concepts of time and matter, which are basic to Western European science, says Whorf, "are not given in substantially the same form by experience to all men but depend upon the nature of the language or languages through the use of which they have been developed." Speakers of SAE "cut up and organize the spread and flow of events . . . largely because, through our mother tongue, we are parties to an agreement to do so, not because nature itself is segmented in exactly that way for all to see."[50] Whorf notes that "a cultural resultant of the Western European view of time is our linguistically conditioned interest in record-keeping, diaries, histories, and concern with the 'past' generally, as well as our emphasis on devices such as clocks, calendars, and time graphs, for the exact quantification of time."[51]

It is necessary to give a detailed presentation of the Sapir-Whorf hypothesis, and especially of what Whorf has to say about time in SAE languages, in order to supply the proper perspective from which we can focus on the relation between Arabic verb tenses and sense of time as manifested by the Arabs. Whorf's thesis can be applied to Arabic and the Arabs in the following manner: Arabic has verb tenses which are semantically vague and indeterminate. This feature should endow Arab culture with a vague and indeterminate perception of time. Arab society, therefore, should be found to be characterized by a relatively lesser concern with time, including quantification of time, consciousness of the relative lengths and positions of past events, and the importance of ordering life according to time schedules.[52]

The observations made by Judith Williams in a Lebanese village which were quoted at the beginning of this section bear out the above conclusion. She found that the task of viewing their life from the time perspective imposed on the people of Haouch was "an alien and difficult task." We now understand that this phenomenon is a manifestation of the relatively greater vagueness about time which the Arabic language imposes in the Whorfian sense upon speakers of Arabic.

In the light of these insights, let us dwell for a moment on one particular feature of the Arabic verb tense which was mentioned briefly above and which seems to explain why the people of Haouch made the "gross transpositions of past events" noted by Judith Williams. Arabic does not easily lend itself to verbal distinction between two different past time periods. Hence, for the Arab mind it is of relatively little concern whether two past actions, events or situations recalled were simultaneous or whether one of them preceded the other. It is almost as if the past were one huge undifferentiated entity, within which time distinctions are immaterial and hence not noticed and which, almost imperceptibly, merges into the present and continues into the future. This particular feature seems to be the consequence of growing up psychologically with Arabic as the mother tongue and as the language which molds the thinking processes.

One can perhaps go farther and relate this grammatical unconcern about distinguishing between the relative time of two past actions to the conflation in early Arab historical tradition of two past events that took place many hundreds of years apart. Mary, the mother of Jesus, lived some six centuries before Muḥammad. The Arabic form of her name is Maryam. Miriam, the sister of Moses, lived some thirteen centuries before Mary. The Arabic form of her name is also Maryam. The two women are represented in the Koran as one and the same person. In Koran 3:35ff., the wife of ʿImrān (i.e., Amram, the father of Moses), is said to have given birth to Maryam, who in turn gave birth to Jesus. Mary, the mother of Jesus, is called "Maryam, daughter of ʿImrān" also in Koran 66:12. In Koran 19:28, Maryam the mother of Jesus is addressed as "sister of Aaron," and a few verses later (v. 53) Aaron is referred to as the brother of Moses. Again, in Koran 23:45–50, the three siblings Moses, Aaron, and Maryam are mentioned together.

Verse 50 reads: "And We made the son of Maryam and his mother a portent, and We gave them refuge on a height, a place of flocks and water springs," which seems to refer to Mary and Jesus. This means, of course, that to the mind of Muḥammad, the Exodus of the Children of Israel from Egypt (thirteenth century B.C.) and the foundation of Christianity were practically simultaneous events.

Similarly, Haman is made a contemporary of Pharaoh in Koran 28:6,38, and there are numerous other indications in the Koran of the absence of a historical perspective which parallels the vagueness of the Arabic language in the temporal area. Since the Koran had an enormous influence on subsequent Arab thinking and writing, it was to be expected that Arab historians would experience great difficulty in shaking off this Koranic ahistoricity which, moreover, was reinforced in the mind of every historian directly by the persisting influence of the language.

This is certainly not the place to embark on a general evaluation of Arabic historiography. But it may be mentioned in passing that Arabic historical writing very frequently took the form of biographies of people of a particular type and that Arabic histories are often replete with anachronisms and confused in detail and chronology.[53] This lack of concern with historical sequence and dates is apparent in the *Ta'rīkh (History)* of the famous traditionist al-Bukhārī (810–870). This work contains biographies of the men whose names appear in *isnāds,* or authorities for traditions going back to Muḥammad: but, less than 7 per cent of the biographies are provided with the dates of death, less than one-half of 1 per cent of them give an indication of the date of birth, and only a little more than one-half of 1 per cent contain, in addition, some date which fixes the time of their subject. Other ancient theological histories are even more sparing with their dates.[54]

In reading the works of Arab historians and critical studies dealing with Arab historiography, one gets the impression of an absence of the awareness of time as a continuous process. Judith Williams found in her Lebanese village that important events, such as a wedding, a holiday, a fight, were remembered, and used as referents for other events which, in recollections, were related to them. This mode of recalling the past in "batches" of simultaneous events without being able to establish the sequences of the disparate batches is characteristic of Arab historians as well. And it is unquestionably the meaning of the definition given to history by that greatest of all Arab historians, Ibn Khaldūn: "History refers to events which are peculiar to a particular age or race."[55] Similarly, to al-Kāfiyajī, the fifteenth-century Muslim religious scholar, the object of historiography was "re-markable happenings which are of interest."[56] Even when Arab historians use the term "time" they use it, not in the sense of a period of duration within whose course a historical process is played out, or, as Spengler put it, "the limitless flight of times," but in the sense of a brief time section centered on a great or remarkable event. As al-Kāfiyajī says, "linguistically, (the words) time-section *(zamān)* and time *(waqt)* are identical."[57] This being the case, Arabic historiography has nothing comparable to the critical method in the study and the writing of history which was introduced into Western historiography (primarily by Leopold von Ranke) nor to the in-teraction of history with other social sciences which has characterized it for the last hundred years.

Let me conclude this section by casting one more glance at Hebrew, one of the few other Semitic languages in addition to Arabic alive today. In its ancient form, Hebrew duplicated the indeterminacy of verb tenses we found in Arabic. In biblical Hebrew usage, as shown by the example from the Book of Job quoted above, the imperfect can refer to the past tense; simi-larly, the perfect can refer to the future, much as in Arabic. However, after the biblical period, the Hebrew language began a process of development whose end result today is a complete elimination of these ancient ambigui-ties. In fact, it can be said that one of the main differences between modern and biblical Hebrew is that in modern Hebrew the verb has past and future tenses as in Western languages, while in biblical Hebrew it had perfect and imperfect forms as Arabic still has to this day.

Before Arabic can become a medium adequate for the requirements of modern life, including those of scholarly and scientific discourse, it will have to undergo a similar development. It will have to become more factual, rid itself of its traditional rhetoricism, its exaggeration and overassertion, and transform its perfect and imperfect verb forms into semantic equivalents of the past and future tenses respectively of Standard Average European.

V

THE BEDOUIN SUBSTRATUM OF THE ARAB PERSONALITY[1]

1. THE BEDOUIN IDEAL

ALTHOUGH TODAY THE BEDOUINS CONSTITUTE PROBABLY NOT more than 10 per cent of the population of the Arab world, many Arabs, in both the villages and the cities, claim Bedouin origin. What is more important than mere numbers is that a very large sector of the settled population still considers the Bedouin ethos as an ideal to which, in theory at least, it would like to measure up. As Jacques Berque, one of the few Westerners who have written about the Arab world with true sensitivity and empathy, put it: ". . . the emotional intensity of the desert dweller has imposed its ideal on the opulent cities."[2] The fact is that the Bedouins are looked upon, not only by the Arab cities, but by the entire Arab world with the exception of its Westernized elements, as images and figures from the past, as living ancestors, as latterday heirs and witnesses to the ancient glory of the heroic age. Hence the importance of the Bedouin ethos, and of the Bedouins' aristocratic moral code, for the Arab world in general.

The heroic age, the period in which the ancestral group performed great deeds with lasting effects, indelibly impresses itself upon the mentality of every people. Looking back upon heroic ancestors, the progeny tends to endow them with almost superhuman traits, transforming them into veritable giants of courage, statesmanship, intellect, or whatever features are most valued in the culture of their descendants. In upholding them as ideal images, the progeny creates for itself prototypes whose words and actions must, and indeed do, serve as exemplars, as powerful influences on value systems and behavior patterns alike.

Among the Arabs, with their typical ahistoricity, the heroic age is actually timeless. It has, of course, existed in the past but, because of the unchanging environment that was its stage, it continues in the present. To put it differently, for the Arab mind there is not so much a heroic age, which left its indelible mark on all subsequent generations, as a heroic environment and a special social form that grew up in response to its challenge. The environment is that of the Arabian Desert, and the society that of the desert people, the nomads. Desert is *badw* or *bādiya* in Arabic, from which is derived the name *badwī* or *badawī*, or "Bedouin" in the customary English form, meaning inhabitant of deserts. Incidentally, another meaning of the noun *badw* is "beginning," which permits the inference that to the old Arabs the desert was the beginning of the world as water was to the Hebrews and to Thales. While the desert and its Bedouins are very far removed from the great majority of the Arabs, who are either town dwellers or villagers and have been for many generations, in ideology and scale of values both still loom large; in fact, they still hold the undisputed first place.

As one of the many indications of this pre-eminence of the desert and the values and mores of the desert people, let me mention that until quite recently it was customary among the best families of Damascus (and of other Arab cities), who had been town dwellers for countless generations, to send their sons for a year or two to one of the *aṣīl* ("noble") camel-breeding tribes of the Syrian Desert in order to expose them to the experience, mentality, manners, and values of the Bedouins, much as the British gentry would send their sons to Eton and Oxford, or aristocratic Japanese families would place theirs in a Zen monastery for a few weeks every year. In each case, the purpose was the same: to enable the youths to absorb as much as possible of what is considered the best and noblest in the national tradition. The young city Arab was supposed, in particular, to learn from his Bedouin hosts their "pure" Arabic and their highly valued manners and customs (the Arabic terms are *"adab,"* literally, good manners or politeness, and *"ādāt,"* customs).

This tendency to look up to the Bedouin as the "ideal" Arab was reinforced by the practice of many generations of Muslim jurists who in their legal decisions relied heavily on Bedouin precedents,[3] and by the reliance of Arabic philologists on Bedouin usage in deciding on fine points of grammar.[4]

If time has cast a veil of oblivion over the Bedouin origins of a village population, social or political circumstances occasionally bring back the awareness of Bedouin ancestry forcefully, compellingly. Such was the case, for instance, in Egypt, where under the influence of the Egyptian nationalist movement led by Aḥmed 'Urābī ('Arabī) Pasha (1839?–1911), the Bedouin ideal was brought back into the villages. It is still dominant especially in the Ṣa'īd (Upper Egypt), where "patriarchal hierarchies and vendettas and the proud attitudes" of the nomadic Bedouins have "oddly and dangerously influenced" the mentality of the fellahin.[5] More recently, a psychologically oriented Arab analyst of the contemporary scene has criticized the Arab countries for adhering to Bedouin values and glorifying them. The Shī'ite Iraqi author 'Alī Ḥasan al-Wardī takes exception to the entire trend of thought and emotion which looks up to the Bedouin virtues as something to be emulated. He criticizes even Arab nationalism because, while it combats imperialists with the sword, it breeds imperialism within itself in glorifying the Bedouin ethos. Closely related to Wardī's criticism of the Bedouin ethos is his attack on the traditional values of Arabic literature, including those of the greatest classical writers, whose works, he says, abound in panegyrics of authority, Bacchic exaltation, amorous sensuality, and verbal decoration. All these features—which incidentally stem from the Bedouin ethos—are uniformly denounced; Wardī does not hesitate to declare that the very idea that classical Arabic literature was "noble" is nothing but a fable, a legend, without any foundation in reality.[6]

The preservation in many families of a tradition of or claim to tribal ancestry is another common form of nostalgia for the Bedouin virtues. Such traditions and claims are found quite frequently among the inhabitants of small towns and large cities alike, even in families who have been town dwellers for many generations. People of humble circumstances, such as artisans and workers, preserve the tradition of their Bedouin descent carefully and jealously, for it supplies them with the one and only claim they have to a semblance of status and social importance. A case in point is the descent claimed by the parents of 'Abd al-Karim Qasim, the revolutionary leader of Iraq from 1958 to 1963. His father, Jasim Muḥammad Bakr, was a poor carpenter who lived in the Mahdiyya quarter on the left bank of the Tigris, inhabited by poor and hard-working Sunnī Muslim families. He claimed descent through his father from the Zubayd (or Zubēd) tribe, and through his mother from the Bani Tamīm, both well-known tribes of Arabian origin.[7]

In general, even in the poorest suburbs of Baghdad, where swarms of uprooted people live in frightful congestion in primitive huts, people take great pride in keeping up their tribal traditions and divisions, their old loyalties, their own customary law, in a word, their Bedouin heritage.[8] In Damascus, each constituent group of the population used to uphold "its own interests and virtues according to a partriarchal code of honour which owed much to the Bedouin model; the latter, both through its poetic tradition and its geographical importance, forced itself on the city."[9]

What kind of person is this Bedouin to whom relationship is claimed by high and low alike in settled Arab society? We may begin by stating that he is son and master of the desert, whose way of life has changed very little from the time he domesticated the camel in the eleventh or twelfth century B.C. until the penetration of his ancestral habitat by modern technology in search for oil. For three thousand years, the desert was his impregnable stronghold: here the Bedouin could preserve undisturbed the way of life he had developed in close symbiosis with his camel, the "ship of the desert." In the desert he was able to guard his sacred traditions, the purity of his language and his blood, and develop a unique social and cultural adaptation to one of the harshest environments known to man on earth. In the process he himself became, like his hunting falcon, tense, keen, quick-tempered, a bundle of nerves, sinews, and bones. His life alternates between periods of lethargic inactivity and outbursts of frenzied activity and almost frenetic effort. Except for a few festive occasions when he gorges himself on the meat of a slaughtered sheep or young camel, the Bedouin subsists on dates, sour camel's milk, and a mixture of flour or roasted corn. His long belted shirt *(thawb)* is covered by an equally long cloak *('abā)*, which gives him an uncommonly dignified and aristocratic appearance. His head is covered by a shawl *(kūfiyya)* held in place by a crown of thick cord *('iqāl)*. Trousers are not worn and footwear is rare. The trying, often cruel, conditions of his life endow him with a mentality to which passive endurance seems preferable to all effort to change his lot. At the same time, he is a rugged individualist who refuses to bend to authority and whose loyalty is limited to family and tribe. The desert itself is such a hard taskmaster and demands so much discipline that the Bedouin has no patience left for any imposed by outside authority.

A discussion of those Arab values which go back to Bedouin origins, or belong to the Bedouin substratum, must begin with a brief indication of the nature of Bedouin society itself. This society, where it still exists today, has remained essentially unchanged since pre-Islamic times in many basic aspects: it is still organized along the same structural lines, exhibits the same internal dynamics, upholds the same values, and has preserved even in its religious life many pre-Islamic features.

The Bedouins were, and are, a patrilineal and patriarchal society, kin-based and strongly kin-oriented. The functional social unit in Bedouin society is the wandering group—a number of extended families, all of whom usually trace their descent to one common patrilineal ancestor. Such a unit camps together, wanders together in search of pasture for its animals, practices endogamy (ingroup marriage), and has a strongly developed feeling of cohesion. In the world of the Bedouin, subsisting in the forbidding physical environment of the Syrian, Arabian, and North African deserts and steppes, social development until recent times has never grown beyond the stage of tribal organization. In practice, this meant that several related wandering units formed a subtribe, several of these a tribe, and some of the tribes occasionally constituted a tribal confederation. The larger the social aggregate thus produced, the smaller the cohesion among its constituent groups, and the rarer the cases in which it was able to join forces for common action. This also meant that beyond the extended family and the next larger kin group to which it belonged and which made up the wandering unit, there was no power structure, no authority, and no protection on which the individual could count. In the desert it was literally each man and his kin group against the rest of the world.

The effect of this situation was to develop a number of interlocking social measures, each backed by similarly interlocking values. Or perhaps it would be more correct to say that nomadic life in the desert was made possible by the development of certain values and by the measures in which they were embodied and expressed. In any case, the challenge of the desert was met, and met by a very specific set of values, structures, and dynamics. The interlocking nature of these can easily be demonstrated while analyzing them from the point of view of their responsiveness to desert conditions.

First of all one must recognize that the desert, at least until the discovery of oil and the digging of artesian wells for water, was capable of supporting barely more than a subsistence economy. Hence only the tribe and no larger, more complex political structure could be erected, because the latter would have required the production of surplus food to be used to support administrators, soldiers, and other economically non-productive sectors. Given this limitation, the first order was to protect the individual from attack by others stronger than he. This was achieved primarily by the emphasis on the kin group and kin cohesion, and by instilling into each member a commitment to group solidarity and mutual responsibility as supreme values. Such values can develop and function as mandatory guidelines only in a small society, in which interpersonal relations are based on personal contact and social life takes place in a milieu where people are all personally known to one another and most are related by blood or, at least, by a fiction of common descent. In such a small society there are considerable pressures to conform, to uphold the group values, and to live by the unwritten but inevitably well-known moral code of the group. To put it in the simplest form, without the effective support and protection of the kin group, the individual would be lost. The price he has to pay for this support is conformity to the group's code and values and their internalization to the extent of emotionally identifying his own interests with those of the group, a conformity, that is not felt to do violence to individuality.

2. GROUP COHESION

In most general terms it can be stated that those personality traits which tend to strengthen group cohesion are considered positive values, are encouraged and rewarded in childhood, and approved and upheld as ideals in adulthood. Conversely, those personality traits which can in any way be detrimental to group cohesion are considered faults; their manifestations are discouraged and punished in childhood, and met with strong disapproval and censure throughout the individual's life. In childhood, those who exercise this control over the individual are father, mother, aunts, uncles, siblings, cousins, and other members of the extended family. Later, the control group becomes co-extensive with the functioning social unit, that is, the group which camps and wanders together.

Here there is no anonymity. Everybody is personally known to everybody else, and this in itself makes for very effective social control, which is reinforced by the age hierarchy. In other words, the younger one is, the smaller is the number of those who, being even younger, do not wield the double-edged sword of approbation and reprobation. The older a person gets, the smaller the number of those to whose judgment he must defer, and the larger the number of those who must defer to his. On the other hand, the older a person gets, the more he feels a different kind of pressure: that of serving as an exemplar, a status that can only be achieved by scrupulous conformity to the moral code and value orientation of the group.

What are the personality traits most approved or censured in Bedouin society? They come in pairs, directly juxtaposed. At the positive end is the trait or value which aids and abets group cohesion, and hence group survival; at the negative end is its opposite. Bravery *(ḥamāsa)* and cowardice are one set of such pairs, and an elemental one at that: it needs no special explanation to understand that in a society in which each group is fair prey to the others, only that group can survive whose members are brave and willing to defend the group no matter what the personal risk.

Related to bravery and cowardice are the traits of aggressiveness–peacefulness, or manliness *(muruwwa)*[10]–meekness. Yet there is an important difference between the two sets of pairs. Bravery is an absolute value; brave behavior is expected of a man in every context. Its opposite, cowardice, is absolutely contemptible: in no context must a man show himself a coward. Aggressiveness, on the other hand, is expected of a man only outside the social group to which he belongs. Within it, it would be met with reprobation, and the man guilty of ingroup aggression would be judged a troublemaker, a man not fulfilling his supreme duty as a group member, which is to support and strengthen the social aggregate. Again, peacefulness is judged a negative trait only if because of it a man refrains from defending the rights of his group against another. Otherwise, the peaceful and peace-seeking man is valued, and is often called upon to mediate in intergroup disputes. Within the group, where aggressiveness is condemned, peacefulness is always considered desirable and laudable; the peaceful man tends to maintain peace in his group and thereby strengthen it *vis-à-vis* other groups.

An oft-recurring situation in Bedouin society in which both the aggressive and the peaceful members of the group are expected to play out the roles to which their natures predispose them is the blood feud. If a member of a group is killed by a member of another group, the relatives of the victim have suffered because their group strength has been diminished. The overt emotional reaction of the injured group is that its honor has been blemished. Revenge is called for, which becomes the duty of all the male members of the victim's kin group, all the men within his *khamsa*. (The *khamsa* is a man's kin group, composed of all those male relatives who are removed from him by no more than five male links. The exact composition of the *khamsa* varies from tribe to tribe, but its function is largely identical everywhere: it serves as the group on whose support a man can always count in any feud with an outsider in which he gets involved.[11]) If the avengers cannot find the murderer, any member of the murderer's *khamsa* is a legitimate target for blood revenge. In this effort it is, of course, the aggressive members of the victim's *khamsa* who play an active role. They will go after the murderer and make plans to revenge the murder in a manner prescribed in detail by the tribal law. In the meantime, or after a certain period, the peaceful members of the victim's family (usually the older men) will begin a parallel effort to find one or more respected leaders, equally distant in kinship from both feuding groups, and persuade them to undertake the difficult but highly honorable task of mediation.

The duties of blood revenge and mediation are features of the Bedouin ethos which have been passed on almost unchanged into village life and which survive in Arab urban society as well. The persistence of blood revenge makes the work of the police and the judiciary difficult in capital cases or other offenses for which tribal law demands blood revenge: even if a murderer is sentenced to death and executed, the duty of the victim's *khamsa* to avenge their kinsman's death will not be fulfilled; it will be fulfilled only if they actually kill either the murderer or one of his relatives. *Dam buṭlub dam,* "Blood demands blood," says the oft-quoted Arabic proverb. The honor of the victim's family is restored only if its members themselves retaliate, or a reconciliation *(ṣulḥa)* is arranged and appropriate damages paid.

Because of the inexorability of the law of blood revenge, raiding—which until recently was a favorite pastime as well as an economic necessity among the Bedouins—used to be carried out with circumspection and caution so that no member of either side was killed. The spilling of blood would transform the raid (in Arabic *ghazw,* whence *razzia*) into a blood feud in which both sides would inevitably suffer. The purpose of the raid was to rob another group of as many of its animals as possible, without actually clashing with the men who tended them. A successful *ghazw* achieved two aims at once: it strengthened one's own group by augmenting the numbers of its herds and flocks, and it weakened the enemy by reducing its herds and flocks, which are the basis of livelihood, even survival, in the desert. As Hitti put it,

Since the days of Ishmael, the Arabian's hand has been against every man and every man's hand against him. . . . In desert land, where the fighting mood is a chronic mental condition, raiding is one of the few manly occupations. . . . The poet al-Quṭāmī of the early Umayyad period has given expression to the guiding principle of such life in two verses: "Our business is to make raids on the enemy, on our neighbur and on our own brother, in case we find none to raid but a brother."[12] . . . According to the rules of the game—and *ghazw* is a sort of national sport—no blood should be shed except in cases of extreme necessity . . . . These ideas of *ghazw* and its terminology were carried over by the Arabians into the Islamic conquests.[13]

However, the game of the *ghazw* must be played according to rules as strict and as confining as those of chess. If it were simply a matter of robbery, the weaker tribes, deprived of their animals by the raids of the stronger ones, would have long disappeared. Obeying the rules, which carry with them the sanction of loss of honor, raiding can take place only between tribes, or tribal sections, which are each other's equals or near-equals in both status and strength. For a noble tribe to raid an inferior tribe (everybody in the desert knows the distinctions between the two) would be so shameful that the noble tribe would rather starve than do such a thing. Similarly, a strong tribe would only heap shame on its head if it raided a tribe patently weaker than itself.

If happens, of course, that these rules of the raiding game are not obeyed and that a group of young men from a noble camel-breeding tribe sometimes undertakes a predatory foray against an inferior tribe or a settled community. While these excursions are not considered to be up to standard according to the ethos of a noble tribe, not much opprobrium attaches to them because the booty they bring home improves the economic situation of the tribe, and because they provide something like training exercises for the tribal youth. In order to preclude such incursions, the non-noble tribes and the settled communities which lived within raiding distance from a powerful noble tribe used to enter into a client relationship with it, paying it an annual *khuwwa* ("brotherhood"), that is, protection money.[14]

Since these norms and arrangements leave only a relatively small number of tribes as potential targets for a tribe intent on raiding—tribes equal to it in status, and near it in strength—the outcome of the *ghazw* game depends not on sheer numerical superiority or the physical strength of the two sides as measured in manpower, but on their relative daring, skill, and endurance. It is in this light that a raid assumes the character of a supreme test of all the manly virtues subsumed under the concept of *muruwwa*.

Enough has been said of the Bedouin ethos to make us understand one additional juxtaposition which it impresses upon the Bedouin mind, and which found its way from there into the Arab mind in general. This juxtaposition is that of activity–passivity. The typical Bedouin's life alternates between relatively long periods of passivity, of spending all day in what the Italian mind, with a similar appreciation and inclination, considers the "dolce far niente" "the sweet doing nothing," and brief spurts of frantic activity best exemplified by the *ghazw*. The Bedouin temper is characterized by sudden flare-ups, which can easily lead to violence and even murder, followed by remorse and long periods of tranquility, inactivity, almost apathy. This alternation between two poles has been observed and commented upon by numerous students of the Arabs, for it is characteristic not only of the nomads but also, although to a lesser degree, of the settled people, villagers and city dwellers alike.[15] Even in semi-Westernized Arab society, in a generally friendly gathering, such sudden, violent outbursts of temper occur not infrequently, but they cause only a momentary flurry, since everybody knows they mean nothing serious, and that the even flow of give-and-take will return after what normally proves to be but a short interruption.

In the Arab method of introducing changes into the social order, economic structure, and political life, one notices the same phenomenon: sudden, sporadic advances followed by periods of quiescence in which what was achieved in the brief stage of activity either gradually erodes or becomes set into a new pattern of tradition. This new tradition, in turn, becomes an impediment to further gradual advance, and can be overcome only by a new outburst of changes.

George Antonius remarks in his well-known book *The Arab Awakening* that the Arabs approach any undertaking in successive and isolated spasms, rather than in a continuous and sustained effort and endeavor. It is to this trait that (following Antonius) Fāris and Husayn attribute the "intermittent and violent explosions interspersed with periods of repose and inactivity" which, they find, characterize the history of the Arab national movement.[16]

The same point is repeated almost verbatim, although based on quite a different set of observations, by Leila S. Kadi in her study of the Arab summit conferences. In commenting on the failure of the individual Arab governments to implement the resolutions of the conferences, Miss Kadi remarks: "It is much easier, it would seem, to plunge into *immediate* action, envisaged as a 'one-shot' action, than it is to embark upon a protracted action which, it is recognized in advance, would necessitate continuous implementation and patient sacrifice over a long time."[17]

It is, of course, a far cry from the juxtaposed Bedouin activity–passivity to the alternating pattern one can observe in the conduct of affairs in Arab government circles and other echelons of leadership. But there are connecting links between the two phenomena. One must not forget that the leaders of the Arab world today, or at any rate their parents, were brought up in an environment where Bedouin values were upheld and Bedouin influences strongly felt.

VI

BEDOUIN VALUES: HOSPITALITY, AVERSION TO PHYSICAL WORK, AND HONOR

1. HOSPITALITY

THE HISTORY OF NOMADIC HOSPITALITY GOES BACK TO BIBLI-cal times and further. The greatest reward Abraham reaped was given to him by God because of his exceeding hospitality—or so it would appear from the context of Genesis 18, in which the meal Abraham prepared for his divine visitors is described in considerably greater detail than the conversation between him and God and God's promise of a son to him and his aged wife Sarah. The hospitality of the Bedouins, the modern-day heirs of Abraham, has been often described. It is a noble trait, exhibited proudly even by the poorest Bedouin, and impressive even in the modified and reduced form in which one encounters it among Arab city folk. But the role of hospitality in strengthening the group which extends it has been largely overlooked. Quite apart from the prestige which accrues to the lavish host, his generous behavior secures for him a potential client and political ally in tribal disputes. In other words, hospitality, like other Bedouin values, ultimately serves the one great goal of Bedouin life: the strengthening of the group.

Only conjectures can be made about the origins of Bedouin hospitality. In the desert, it probably developed in response to a dire need: without it an individual undoubtedly would have lost his life as soon as he left behind the protective circle of his kin and tribe. If the desert itself did not kill him, the very first human group he encountered would have done so. The kinless, unprotected individual's anguish is mythically projected in the outcry of Cain: "My punishment is greater than I can bear . . . I shall be a fugitive and a wanderer in the earth . . . whosoever findeth me will slay me." Without the protective shelter of hospitality, every Arab in the desert would be a fugitive and a wanderer. With the rules of hospitality, the fugitive becomes an honored guest whom the host must protect even at the risk of his own life.[1]

Soon a refusal to offer hospitality to a stranger or harming him after having accepted him as a guest became an offense not only against the established mores and honor of the group, but against God Himself, the real protector.[2]

The rules of hospitality can be so exacting and uncompromising that they occasionally demand the greatest sacrifice from the host, and may force him to forego what otherwise would be a sacred duty: the duty of avenging the murder of a kinsman. The laws require a man to receive into his tent and protect anyone who comes and asks asylum, even if the guest may otherwise be a legitimate victim of the host's blood revenge.[3] Another sacred duty which, at least in some remote parts of the Arab world, must give way to the more important obligation of hospitality is the preservation of the sexual inviolability of women. From Southern Arabia come reports of the custom of sexual hospitality which used to be observed until recent times and which will be discussed in Chapter VIII.

Poverty, even in the extreme form in which it is encountered among the weak tribal splinter groups in the desert, does not excuse a man from fulfilling the sublime duty of hospitality: to shelter and feed a guest, stranger or friend, for three days. Stories are current among the desert folk that to the uninitiated Western ear sound like tales of a prodigal son who squanders away his last pennies but to the Bedouin exemplify true virtue. One of them tells of Bu Zaid, the mythical hero of the Bani Hillal tribe, who, in fulfilling the duties of hospitality, slaughtered his camels one after another to serve their meat to his uninvited guests, until he remained without any camels and was himself faced with starvation. His tribe, recognizing the character of their kinsman, presented him with a few camels but only after exacting a promise that he would not sacrifice them on the altar of his hospitality. Having no choice, Bu Zaid agreed; but ere long his uncontrollable addiction to hospitality reduced the number of his animals to one last milch camel. A few days later, as he was sitting in front of his tent, the figure of a stranger appeared on the distant horizon. In order not to see the stranger approach and not to have to invite him to become his guest, Bu Zaid hid in the depth of his tent, but could not refrain from asking his wife, "Has the guest been called into one of the tents yet?" After three or four negative answers while the stranger came closer and closer to his tent, Bu Zaid, no longer able to restrain himself, ran out toward the stranger, bid him welcome to his tent, and then took his last camel and slit its throat to fulfill the supreme duty and privilege of Bedouin hospitality.[4]

Among the settled population, hospitality has undergone certain modifications. The village and urban home is not as open to strangers as the nomadic tent in the desert, and the strict segregation between the sexes practiced in the conservative sectors of the settled population can make visits awkward. While hospitality remains a general custom that one is expected to practice throughout one's life, there are special added occasions in the individual's life cycle on which an extraordinary show of hospitality is required. These occasions include marriage, burial, circumcision, and the completion of housebuilding; during the holy month of Ramaḍān, village-wide visiting and sharing of meals, particularly with the poor, is common.

Whether among nomads or settled people, hospitality is organically tied to honor, or, better, to the concept of "face." By practicing hospitality lavishly, one "whitens" one's "face," that is, increases one's reputation; contrarywise, a show of inhospitality can blacken one's face. If a visitor is not received hospitably, the failure reflects on the entire tribe or village and blemishes its reputation. Therefore, compliance with the noble custom of hospitality is motivated not only by the desire of the individual host to "whiten his face," but also by pressure to uphold the reputation of the larger social aggregate of which he and his family form part.

In the Jordanian village of Kufr al-Ma, located in the denuded eastern foothills of the Jordan Valley, "visitors who pass through and wish to spend the night there, are always referred to the richest men in the village, men who can offer good meals and proper sleeping accommodations. . . . It is on the rich man that the onus of preserving the name of the village falls."[5]

The value of hospitality is impressed upon Arab children from an early age. Only recently I had an opportunity to see just how effectively it is inculcated into the youngsters—even among semi-Westernized urban Arabs. In the summer of 1971 I visited the home of an old Arab friend on the outskirts of East Jerusalem. He had no phone, so I was unable to call for an appointment. When I arrived, neither my friend nor his wife nor any of their older children were at home. But his youngest daughter, aged ten, and his little son, aged thirteen, were playing in the garden in the back of the house. Since it had been some two or perhaps three years since I last visited the family, I was quite sure that the children would not remember me. I told them that I was a friend of their father, and that I would come back another time. But the children would not let me go. They insisted that I go into the house and wait, since their father would be back shortly. I hesitated, then complied. They made me sit down in the living room, and without asking me whether I wanted any refreshment, brought in pistachio nuts, a bowl of fresh fruit, some homemade cookies, and a bottle of Coke, and offered me cigarettes. While it was I who had to keep the conversation going by asking them questions about their school work and the like, as far as the forms of hospitality were concerned, they had completely mastered, and, I would venture to say, internalized them.

2. GENEROSITY

Hospitality is the most specific and characteristic expression of the more general value, again traced back to the Bedouins, of generosity. Lavish generosity in traditional Arab society counterbalances the accumulation of wealth and the development of inordinate extremes of riches and poverty. It entails a certain dispersion of wealth by redistribution, and thus takes its place next to the Muslim duty of paying a "poor due" or *zakāt* (the annual distribution of 2½ per cent of one's wealth to the poor), which is one of the "Five Pillars of the Faith" in Islam, and the only religio-legal financial obligation imposed upon the "haves" *vis-à-vis* the "have-nots."

Although this Islamic rule is but a pale reflection of the older Bedouin value of generosity, it nevertheless reinforces it and ensures its general acceptance among nomads and settled people alike. It is tied directly to a belief in, and affirmation of, God's rule over the fate of each and every individual. As the Koran (16:71) puts it, "Allah hath favored some of you above others in provision," that is, the unequal distribution of wealth is a manifestation of God's will. Such tenets constitute a strong pressure on the wealthy to use some of their God-given assets for the support of the poor.

Miserliness is decried and is one of the favorite subjects of Friday mosque sermons.[6]

Hospitality is so closely connected with generosity that occasionally the same term is used to designate both. Thus in Sudanese Arabic, *karam* means both hospitality and generosity and, in actuality, there is no sharp distinction between the two. Hospitality is the most readily available means of obtaining the approbation of one's community, of earning its respect, and thus of increasing one's self-respect. A man "is judged largely on the basis of the manner in which he receives his guests," and "a reputation of being hospitable is very valuable to an Arab, who therefore tries to show off before his guests, knowing that they will spread the news of his generosity."[7] This being the case, a very elaborate and detailed set of rules has grown up around the single act of receiving guests, compared to which the Japanese tea ceremony is simplicity itself.[8]

Nowhere is a man in as good a position to show his generosity as in his own home, where he can lavish his attention, his polite pleasantries, and his offerings of food and drink, smoke and flowers, on his guests. However, the truly self-respecting man takes his generosity with him wherever he goes. Should he, by chance, meet a friend in the street, he will insist on inviting him to his home, or, if they are too far away, to a café or restaurant. Should the friend plead that he is due to go somewhere, the self-respecting generous man will offer to take him there in a taxi. If he rides in his car and sees a friend walking in the street, he will stop and insist on giving him a lift, even if the friend is heading in the opposite direction. If two friends meet on a bus, each will try to prevail on the other to let him pay the fare for him.[9] The offering of gifts and a lavish spending of money is an integral part of the same pattern.

Since hospitality and generosity are such important values, folk custom had to make sure that a man is not frustrated in trying to live up to the ideals they represent. Should the person to whom an invitation is extended refuse to accept it, or should he decline a gift, this would frustrate the intentions of the host or the donor. Therefore, the traditional mores require that one must comply with an invitation and, equally, that one must accept a gift. Refusal in either case would be tantamount to an offense, a slight, a show of disrespect. As we can see from these few remarks, such rules go far beyond the Koranic injunction to help those who are in dire need and to pay the *zakāt*.

3. COURAGE

It is rather difficult to distinguish between the Arab concepts of bravery and courage. It would seem that bravery is expressed primarily in a man's willingness to risk his life for the benefit of his group. Courage, on the other hand, means essentially the ability to stand physical pain or emotional strain with such self-control that no sound or facial expression betrays the trial one is undergoing. Among the Arabs of the Sudan, a number of games are voluntarily engaged in by adolescent boys in which their courage is tested. Lashings are administered to them, or their arms are burned with pieces of durra cane or cigarettes or cut with a knife.[10] It is with a similar aim of inuring adolescent boys to physical pain that the preferred form of punishing a son of fourteen to sixteen years of age among the Rwala Bedouins is for his father to cut him with a saber or stab him with a dagger. "By cutting or stabbing them, the father not merely punishes the boys but hardens them for their future life." In Egypt, corporal punishment in the form of beating, striking, whipping, or slapping is common. Brutal physical punishment of boys is not uncommon in other Arab countries either.[11]

In this context, the various forms of the circumcision of boys practiced in the Arab countries, which are everywhere considered a test of the boys' courage, must be mentioned. Occasionally this occurs as a direct preliminary to marriage, with the bride looking on. The most painful form is the operation performed among some Arab tribes in the Hijāz and in 'Asīr in Saudi Arabia, where the skin of the entire male organ is removed, as well as the skin of its environs on the belly and the inner thigh. While this is being done, the youth must show unflinching courage, standing upright, shouting "with a mighty joy," and brandishing a long dagger! Throughout the operation, his bride sits before him, beating a drum, and trilling the traditional shrill, sustained cry of joy. Should the youth as much as whimper, she has the right to refuse to marry him. In other Arab countries less drastic forms of circumcision are practiced, but the element of testing courage is discernible everywhere. (Girls, who are not supposed to be "courageous," can cry and shriek as much as they please during their circumcision.)

The courage which is expected of the Arab youth and man is primarily a matter of outward appearance. One is almost inclined to say that the Arab boy child is socialized to be able to *act* courageously, to display a show of fortitude, without any consideration to his true feelings. As long as he does not betray by any outward sign that he is afraid or that he suffers under the pain that is being inflicted upon him, he *is* courageous. However, "not conscious of any role-playing, the Arab does not know that he is hiding some weakness behind this facade. He believes in himself and is not aware of the internal weakness that may be driving him into such bombastic behavior."[12] Where his internal weakness does become manifest, at least to the psychologically aware observer, is when any allegation that he might be afraid causes a most vehement reaction. A person who is truly unafraid shrugs off accusations of fear. One who merely hides his fear or his weakness is seriously wounded by such an accusation and reacts by hurling back challenges and menacing invectives. Also, it has been pointed out that it is because of this externality of his courage that the Arab "has a passion for performing fantastic *beaux gestes* that appeal to the imagination" and "on many occasions performs feats that are not commensurate with his abilities; but the momentary intensity of his feeling empowers him to attain extraordinary achievements."[13]

4. HONOR

Much has been written on the subject of honor *(sharaf)* among the Arabs.[14] What has not been emphasized, at least as far as I am aware, is that there is a strong correlation between honor and group survival. Honorable behavior is that which is conducive to group cohesion and group survival, that which strengthens the group and serves its interests; while shameful behavior is that which tends to disrupt, endanger, impair, or weaken the social aggregate.

Honor in the Arab world is a generic concept which embraces many different forms. To mention only a few: there is the kind of honor a man derives from his virility as manifested in having numerous sons; another comes to him from engaging in certain types of work and refraining from others: hence, it is honorable for the Bedouins to tend their camels, dishonorable to engage in artisanship or agriculture. A third type of honor used to be associated with the sword—the ability to defend oneself against enemies and with bravery in general. To buy protection from a more powerful tribe by paying *khuwwa* (protection money) seriously diminished one's honor. To undertake a raid, within the prescribed rules, is honorable. To refuse participation in a raid is dishonoring. To defend one's livestock against raiders is honorable. To own livestock is honorable. Hospitality and generosity are matters of honor. To be inhospitable or ungenerous is shameful. It is honorable to have pure Arab blood, on both one's father's and one's mother's side. It is honorable to exhibit a strong sense of kin group adherence. It is honorable to behave with dignity and always to be aware of the imperative of *wajh* ("face"): under all circumstances a man must beware of allowing his "face" to be "blackened"; he must always endeavor to "whiten his face," as well as the face of the kin group to which he belongs. Cost what it may, one must defend one's public image. Any injury done to a man's honor must be revenged, or else he becomes permanently dishonored. And, of course, there is the sexual honor of the woman, through which her entire paternal family is constantly and dangerously exposed to the possibility of becoming dishonored.

The honor concept is easily extended from the individual, the family, and the tribe to the nation as a whole. Thus, a *fatwa* (religious decree) issued on July 11, 1952, by the Commission of Fatwas of al-Azhar in Cairo chastises those who argue that Egypt should modernize its attitude on women and do what others do in the twentieth century. That, the *fatwā* states, would be aping others in a way which is against the honor of Egypt.[15]

All these different kinds of honor, clearly distinguished in Arab life and operative at various times and on various occasions, interlock to surround the Arab ego like a coat of armor. The smallest chink in this armor can threaten to loosen all the loops and rings, and must therefore be repaired immediately and with determination. There are those who see as paranoid the extreme sensitivity of the Arabs to any infringement of their honor. Others judge it positively as an expression of pride and uncompromisingly high moral standards. We cannot take a position on the issue, but must cite it as an important characteristic of the Bedouin mentality which has left its mark on the Arab mind in general.

Two components of the honor syndrome which have most to do with group survival are virility and kinship spirit. In the Bedouin hierarchy of values it redounds to the honor of a man to have many children, and especially sons. The usual explanation for this is that many children are a tangible proof of a man's virility.[16]

Virility is one of those overriding qualities which a man will uphold even if he must in the process sacrifice other values. Any aspersion cast upon virility is considered such a great dishonor that a man will make extreme efforts to remove every shadow of a doubt about it, even at the price of taking the onus of other dishonors upon himself. Impotence in a husband is one of the few causes for divorce which can be claimed by a wife. If true, the husband will usually consent to a quiet divorce so as not to be exposed to the shame of publicity. However, if untrue, his sense of honor is cut to the quick, and he will insist on proving it, even though this may mean the performance of the sexual act—*horribile dictu*—without the customary and obligatory privacy. Reports about how exactly this is done (e.g., among the Awlād ‘Alī of Egypt’s Western Desert) are vague, but it involves the use by the couple of what is termed a *bayt al-shan‘a,* or “house of abomination,” which seems to be simply a tent so constructed that one or more respectable neighbors can see and hear what is going on in it between husband and wife. The neighbors’ observations and conclusions decide the fate of the marriage.[17] It can be assumed that a man will submit to this ordeal only if he is potent, and if he has no other means of proving his wife’s accusation false. In the process he is forced to violate the lesser, but still very important, value of sexual privacy.

As this case shows, virility is indeed a supreme value, and what could more eloquently attest to a man’s virility than fathering numerous offspring? In this sense, then, to have many children redounds to a man’s honor. But there is a deeper meaning behind the honor and respect a man acquires by having many children. Both his numerous offspring and the sexual potency to which they testify serve quite directly the group of which he and they are parts. In Bedouin society, other things being equal, the safety, and therefore the chances of survival, of each group are directly correlated to the number of its male members (only the males participate in and defend against raids; this contributes to the much higher valuation accorded to male offspring). The value of female children from the point of view of group survival or group safety asserts itself only a generation later: when the male offspring *they* bear grow up to augment the manpower of the group.

The same considerations supply at least one of the reasons for the general Bedouin preference for endogamy: the child-bearing capacity of its women must be preserved for the ingroup in order to make sure that all the natural increase or replacement thus obtained will take place within its own ranks rather than those of another, potentially hostile, group. Were exogamous marriages permitted (these, in fact, occur in Bedouin society only in exceptional cases), under the prevailing patrilineal rules of descent a child born to a woman of one group would belong to his father’s group and would thus grow up a virtual stranger to the group in which his mother belongs. By

carrying the same principle one step further, the most preferred marriage
is that between children of two brothers; such a marriage means that all the
children will be members of the same extended family and thus increase its
numbers, power, prestige, and honor. A young man has both the right and
the obligation to marry his father's brother's daughter (the so-called *bint
'amm*); indeed, his honor depends to a considerable extent on his fulfilling
this obligation. Again, the tribal mores consider action which strengthens
ingroup cohesion honorable, and frown upon acts that tend to weaken the
group.

The same consideration underlies power relationships within the extended family. The honor of the patriarch depends to a great extent on his
ability to impose his will upon the members of his family. A man who is
respected by the members of his family and commands their loyalty has
honor both inside the family and outside it, in the larger social aggregate
—tribe or village—of which the family is part. A loyal and obedient family
is strong and united when it comes to defend family interests against other
competing families, and such a family is one on which the larger aggregate
can count in *its* external relations. Thus, the concept of honor again proves
to subserve the strengthening of the group.

Historically, the sense of honor was so much tied to the group spirit that
both were (and still are) referred to by one and the same term, *"'aṣabiyya,"*
which means primarily "family spirit" or "kinship spirit" (it is derived from
the root verb *'aṣab,* meaning to tie together). Although Muḥammad condemned *'aṣabiyya* as contrary to the spirit of Islam, this could not eliminate
it from the consciousness of the Arabs. Ibn Khaldūn, the great fourteenth-
century theoretician of Arab history, even went so far as to uphold *'aṣabiyya*
as the fundamental bond of human society and the basic motivating force
in history.[18]

The primary meaning of the term refers to tribal cohesion, or the spirit
which holds together a tribal or subtribal group: the secondary meaning—
of "sense of honor"—was assumed because to be devoted to one's kin group
was considered in Arab tribal society the most essential expression of one's
sense of honor. *'Aṣabiyya* implies boundless and unconditional loyalty to
fellow tribesmen. "Be loyal to thy tribe," sang a bard; "its claim upon its
members is strong enough to make a husband give up his wife."[19] This
ineradicable tribal particularism assumes, of course, that the tribe is a unit
by itself, self-sufficient and absolute, and regards every other clan or tribe

as its legitimate victim and object of raiding and plunder. These unsocial features, which inevitably accompany 'aṣabiyya, remained imprinted into the Arab character after the rise of Islam, and, as Hitti observed, "were among the determining factors that led to the disintegration and ultimate downfall of the various Islamic states."[20]

While 'aṣabiyya is thus, in the first place, a Bedouin tribal trait, it was carried over from nomadic to settled Arab society in the form of family and lineage cohesion. Kinship ties, and primarily family bonds, are extremely strong in all sectors of traditional Arab society. They remain an influential factor even after members of a group have moved away from the family home and lived for years in a faraway city or even overseas. Illustrative of the persistence of these ties is the well-known fact that Lebanese emigrants regularly send financial contributions to their families back home, not merely to their immediate, but also to their extended families.[21] One of my Arab friends, who happened to have read a news item in *The New York Times* to the effect that a first cousin of President Nixon was receiving social welfare benefits, remarked to me with utter incomprehension that such a thing would be unimaginable in his country: to support a cousin or any other relative is as much a moral duty as supporting one's own children.

The extent to which family ties remain effective even after emigration overseas is illustrated by the Lebanese economy. In 1961, when the total merchandise exports of the country yielded an income of 231 million Lebanese pounds, the income from emigrants' remittances was 92 million pounds, or almost 40 per cent as high as export income.[22]

As a broad generalization one can say that the 'aṣabiyya of the old Arab tribal society survives in practically the same form and with the same intensity among those Bedouin Arabs whose life forms have changed little in other respects. Where modernization intrudes, tribal and family cohesion must gradually give way. The same gradual weakening of the traditional intensive forms of group cohesion can be observed in the settled Arab society as well. Since modernization is more advanced in the cities than in the villages, more of the group cohesion is preserved in the rural than in the urban sectors. Nevertheless, even in thoroughly Westernized upper-class urban Arab families, the claim of kinship is still much stronger than anything known in the West. Arab culture can still be termed "kinship culture," and is still characterized by "familism" as it has been in the past.[23]

5. SELF-RESPECT

Honor is so close to self-respect that it can almost be confused with it. At any rate, all actions, words, happenings that are not in accordance with the accepted mores of the society result in diminishing a man's honor, or even in bringing about its loss. These, in turn, diminish or destroy the respect he enjoys in the eyes of others and, therefore, ultimately have the same effect on his self-respect. Once honor is impaired, great efforts are needed to restore it. If lost, it is almost impossible to regain. Honor is the collective property of the family: if any single member of the family incurs dishonor, the whole family is disgraced. It is like a life-raft designed to carry the family over the dangerous waves of the inimical sea which is the social environment. As long as all members of the family obey the rules of conduct, the precarious raft enables them to survive. However, the slightest uncontrolled move by any member of the family can knock a hole into the fragile craft and, if that happens, the whole family must drown.

It is therefore up to the adult males of the family to see that no member becomes guilty of any act that would spell disaster for all. They must make sure, first of all, that their own behavior is impeccable, in the sense of preserving at all cost the outward appearances imposed by the code of honor. Then there is the even more difficult task of protecting the honor of the family's womenfolk, which the men must shoulder, or at least scrupulously supervise, since women are too weak to be relied on when it comes to such heavy responsibilities. This important and highly sensitive subject will be discussed in Chapter VIII.

If honor is lost, it causes the loss of *karam* or *karāma,* which can best be translated as dignity. The relationship between these concepts, as well as between them and *iḥtirām al-nafs* (self-respect), can best be made tangible by the domino theory. If a woman loses her honor, this causes her menfolk to lose theirs, which causes them to lose their dignity, which, in turn, causes them to lose their self-respect. What, then, can a man do if threatened by the loss of his *karam?* For one thing, if it was threatened (or even if actually lost) by a woman's loss of honor, the folk mores had their traditional remedy: her menfolk (brothers and father) must kill her. By killing her they demonstrated for everybody to see that they had cut off the offending limb from the body of the family, thus enabling the body to recover and survive. Next, they would try to kill her paramour, because they must take blood revenge on him for bringing about the death of a member of their family.

Since *karam* depends on the respect accorded to a man by others, if a man is insulted his *karam* is damaged. To restore it, one must put up a great show of reaction. By hurling back a greater insult than the one sustained, one shows that one does not acquiesce in the insult, that one "rebels" against it, that one rises up and musters all one's resources to repel the attack. The man who has self-respect does not allow anybody to insult him with impunity. By rising to the defense of his dignity, he compels others to respect him, and thus restores his self-respect.

Because one's self-respect is so vulnerable to treatment by others, the Arab is extremely wary of being slighted and sees personal insults even in remarks or actions which carry no such intent. Nordenstam reports that an ironical or critical comment addressed by a teacher to a student is interpreted as an insult, while the promotion of a junior official may be taken as an insult by his senior.[24] When the commander of the Jordanian army, Glubb Pasha, suggested to his orderly that he take his wife to view a military parade, the orderly's retort was: "Do you think I am the kind of person to sit with women?"[25] By putting his commanding officer in his place, the orderly "rebelled" against the insult and saved his honor.

To sum up: Arab ethics revolve around a single focal point, that of self-esteem or self-respect. The one most important factor on which the preservation of this self-esteem depends is the sexual behavior of the women for whom the Arab is responsible: his daughters and sisters. Because of this central position of the women's honor or 'ird, the preoccupation with female sexual chastity has grown to a veritably obsessive intensity. Other factors on which Arab self-respect depends are the two syndromes of courage-bravery and hospitality-generosity. Beyond the immediate purpose of maintaining self-respect, all these features have been found to serve the larger aim of promoting the interests and, ultimately, the survival of the community.

VII

THE BEDOUIN ETHOS AND MODERN ARAB SOCIETY

1. KORANIC AND FOLK ETHICS

NOTHING POINTS UP MORE EMPHATICALLY THE SURVIVAL OF Bedouin values in the Arab world today than an inquiry into the ethics upheld by the Arabs as supreme values in their lives.[1] Such an inquiry soon reveals that the virtues which figure foremost in the Arab mind have little in common with the teachings of the Koran, but rather reflect the largely pre-Islamic ideals of the nomadic Arab tribes. The distinction between the two sources is not always clear-cut; certain pre-Islamic Arab ideals have been incorporated into the Koran and Muslim tradition. There is, for instance, a *ḥadīth* (tradition) to the effect that Muḥammad said: "Look to those moral practices you had in the *jāhiliyya* [the time of pagan ignorance which preceded Islam], and apply them in Islam: give security to your guest, be generous toward the orphan and treat the stranger who is under your protection with kindliness."[2] In fact, the same three moral precepts are found in the Koran itself (4:36).

The major features that predominate in the Arab ethics of virtue can be summarized by three syndromes, which are themselves related: (1) the courage–bravery syndrome; (2) the hospitality–generosity syndrome; and

(3) the honor–dignity syndrome. These syndromes are found everywhere in the Arab world, and everywhere they constitute the bulk and body of Arab ethics. Tore Nordenstam, who made an intensive study of Sudanese Arab ethics, found that its dominant elements are "the ideals of courage, generosity and hospitality, and a cluster of subtly interrelated notions of honour, dignity and self-respect." He emphasizes that these features are not specific to the Sudanese Arabs but constitute the ethical system of Arabs in other countries as well.[3]

There are no similar systematic studies of the ethics of other Arab groups, but whatever comments are made on the subject by students of Arab life in various countries indicate that everywhere bravery, hospitality and generosity, honor and self-respect (occasionally described as dignity or proper behavior) are the most highly prized personal qualities.[4]

There is even some statistical evidence to indicate that the Arabs consider values of this type, and especially hospitality and generosity, friendliness and pride, honor and honesty, as the best traits in their personality. This was shown in a study carried out among Arabs in the city of Nazareth and surrounding villages in Israel, in which 41 per cent of the 464 respondents stated that they thought the Jews should learn from the Arabs hospitality, friendliness, and generosity; while 19 per cent answered that they should learn from the Arabs pride, honor, and honesty. Only a very small percentage of the respondents felt that the Jews should learn from the Arabs other things, such as tolerance and nondiscrimination (4 per cent), honor for parents and modesty (2 per cent), customs and details of traditions relating to foodstuffs, style of building, etc. (3 per cent), and agriculture (2 per cent).[5] The insight afforded by the results of this study is especially valuable because the question was formulated in such a way as to avoid provoking the respondents to boasting *(mufākhara)*. It did not ask "Which are the finest features of the Arab personality?" but merely, in a purposely vague formulation, "What do you think the Jews should learn from the Arabs?" When, in reply to this question, 60 per cent of the respondents answered as they did, this showed that hospitality, friendliness, generosity, pride, honor, and honesty were the features which they not only considered to be the Arab *ideal,* but which they sincerely believed were the finest traits *actually* characterizing them. The context within which the study was carried out (among Arabs who constitute a religio-national minority in Israel) explains, I believe, the absence of reference in the responses to bravery and manliness. Still smarting under the repeated Arab defeats by the Israelis, the question of Arab bravery and manliness, they must have felt, was better left untouched.

Bravery and manliness, hospitality and generosity, and the honor syndrome, all pre-Islamic concepts of Bedouin origin, are the dominant concerns. Yet, with one exception, none of them is part of the ethical system of the Koran; and conversely (again with the same exception), none of the ethical teachings of the Koran have developed into a dominant feature in the actual Arab ethics of virtue.

The Koran stresses chastity, except for lawful intercourse with wives and concubines (70:29); the guarding of trusts and covenants, and honest testimony (70:32–33); giving full measure and full weight (55:8–9; 11:85); kindness and gratitude to parents (29:8; 46:14; 31:14); kindliness toward kinfolk, orphans, the poor, the stranger who is under one's protection, fellow workers, wayfarers, and slaves (4:36); establishing worship; enjoining kindness; prohibiting iniquity; perseverance; and modesty (31:17–19). Instead of the imperative of revenge, which was part of the pre-Islamic ethic, the Koran teaches that true nobility lies in forgiveness and that he who restrains his anger and pardons men shall receive paradise (3:133–134); it admonishes the Muslims to be patient in tribulation and adversity (2:177). Equity and just dealing come next to the fear of God (5:8). The Koran also enjoins the Muslims to pay the poor due or zakāt (2:43, 177; 5:12); not to misappropriate the possessions of the orphan (17:34); to give food on the day of famine to the orphan who is near of kin or to some poor wretch in misery; to free a slave; to believe, and to urge patience and compassion on one another (90:10–18; 2:177). It commands them not to squander (17:27; 25:67), but not to be miserly either (25:67); not to slay one's children in fear of poverty (17:31); not to commit adultery (17:32; 25:68) or engage in homosexual intercourse (26:165–166); not to kill unjustly (17:33); not to make false accusations (25:72); not to take usury (3:130); and not to be scornful (31:18), nor proud and boastful (4:36; 31:18).

Special commandments addressed to women are: to be modest and steadfast in prayer, to give alms, obey God and His apostle (33:32–33). Both sexes are admonished to be truly "resigned" (i.e., Muslims), devout, truthful, patient, humble; to give alms, be punctilious in fasting, guard their sexual modesty, and be constant in remembering God (33:35; cf. 24:30–31).

While these commandments all are, of course, known to the average Arab, who on occasion may obey them or let his conduct be guided by them, only one item in this long list is considered by him a pivotal tenet in his present-day system of ethical virtues: the one which enjoins sexual modesty on women. If it is true, as indicated in the Koran itself, that this command-ment was given by Muḥammad in order to make the women give up the immoral customs of the Time of Ignorance ("And stay in your houses. Bedizen not yourselves with the bedizenment of the *jāhiliyya*," 33:33), then in this respect at least the Muslim mores succeeded in bringing about a total reversal.[6] In addition, there is some relationship between the Koranic teach-ing of "kindness" toward orphans, the poor, relatives, strangers, and slaves (4:36) and the great Arab ethical imperatives of hospitality and generosity. But the two are by no means identical, and the Koranic injunction is much weaker and much more limited in scope. All the other major components of the modern Arab ethical system are pre-Islamic, and as such impose a code upon the Arabs which, on occasion, actually contradicts the laws of Islam as laid down in the Koran and subsequently developed in the *sharī'a*, the traditional law. The traits extolled by the pre-Islamic Arab poets in their songs of praise as the supreme virtues of the Arabs were *ḥamāsa* or bravery, *muruwwa* or manliness, *sharaf* or honor, and *ḍiyāfa* or hospitality[7]—precisely those traits which still occupy a central position in Arab ethics.

The second thing that strikes us in comparing the Koranic ethical rules with the code of the Arab world today is that in place of the large number of ethical imperatives contained in the Koran one finds only a handful, five or six, actual functioning major demands which, among them, fill the entire horizon of the Arab ethical world. Moreover, even these five or six can be reduced to a single issue which appears to be the one overriding moral aim of the Arab: the preservation of his self-respect.[8]

However, in contrast to what one would expect from its name, this ultimate Arab moral imperative of self-respect *(iḥtirām al-nafs* or *iḥtirām al-dhāt),* this all-important value of the Arab personality *(shakhṣiyya),* depends not so much on the behavior of the individual himself as on the attitude and relationship to him evinced by others in the society of which he is a member. Of course, it goes without saying that the individual must always act in an honorable way. But over and above his own behavior, his self-respect depends on whether or not others respect him, that is to say, whether they show a respectful attitude toward him, whether they treat him with the respect he feels is due to him. Therefore, the code of behavior followed by the individual is primarily calculated to impress others with those qualities of his personality that will induce them to respect him. As

Pierre Bourdieu puts it, in the Kabyle society of North Africa (which in this regard, as in many others, faithfully reflects the Arab mores), "the man of quality, i.e., the man of self-respect must continually be on his guard; he must watch his words. . . . A man lacking in self-respect . . . is a man who exposes his inner self with all its errors and weaknesses. . . ."[9] Subsequently, Bourdieu remarks that "the fear of reprobation and shame, the negative aspect of the point of honour, is such that it compels a man most lacking in self-esteem to conform, with constraint and of necessity, to the dictates of honour. . . . A man of honour is his own honour."[10]

The same code is observed among the Bedouins of Egypt's Western Desert. The honor of the group depends on whether outsiders relate to it with due respect. "A slight offence inflicted against a lineage or a lineage-segment is taken as an unforgiveable humiliation requiring immediate retaliation to wipe out the shame, regain honour and restore the same relations as formerly between the groups."[11] On the basis of his observations among the Sudanese Arabs, Nordenstam even goes so far as to say that "self-respect depends entirely on the respect from others."[12] This, in turn, leads him to the conclusion that their systems of virtues are predominantly other-determined, that is to say, that they emphasize the importance of being respected by others, and that the Sudanese Arabs (and, by extrapolation on the basis of references to studies carried out in other Arab countries, the Arabs in general) are clearly outward-oriented. This latter term means that motives, intentions, feelings, attitudes, and so on are of no importance as long as one's outward behavior conforms to expectations. Because of this overriding motivation, the Arabs are largely conforming: they accept the ethics of their society to a high degree.[13]

2. WAJH OR "FACE"

The other-determined, outward-oriented character of honor finds emphatic expression in a concept which we have mentioned so far only in passing: the concept of *wajh*, or "face." We quoted the Arabic phrase which refers to a diminution of a man's honor as "blackening his face" (see above, p. 86). Since we have the concept of "face" in our Western vocabulary as well, and we, too, speak of "loss of face," the Arab term rings a familiar bell. In both Western and Arab culture, "face" is the outward appearance of honor, the "front" of honor which a man will strive to preserve even if in actuality he has committed a dishonorable act. As long as such an action remains unknown, his "face" is saved; once it becomes known, "his face is lost" as the English phrase has it, or "his face is blackened," as it is phrased in Arabic. The "blackening" of the face, of course, means that "black" is dishonorable, while "white" is honorable. Therefore, when a man does something that redounds to the honor of his kin group, the latter's elders will say to him, "You have whitened our face."

There is a considerable difference between the intensity with which the concept of "face" affects the thinking and the conduct of people in the West and in the Arab world. In simplest terms one can say that in the Arab world, "face" is a much more powerful consideration in weighing one's acts and words than it is in the West. The difference is so great as to amount to one in kind. Hence a more detailed discussion of *wajh* and its working in the Arab psyche is helpful here. Let us begin with an illustration.

On Monday, June 5, 1967, in the early morning hours, the Israeli air force destroyed practically all the combat planes of the U.A.R. (United Arab Republic) with negligible losses to itself. At about 9 A.M., Marshal Abdel Hakim Amer, commander of the Egyptian forces in Cairo, sent a coded message to General Abdel Moneim Riad, the Egyptian officer in command of the Arab forces on the Jordanian front. The message, according to the account given by King Hussein of Jordan, read as follows:

1. Israeli planes have started to bomb air bases of the U.A.R. and approximately 75 per cent of the enemy's aircraft have been destroyed or put out of action.

2. The counterattack by the Egyptian air force was under way over Israel. In Sinai, U.A.R. troops have engaged the enemy and taken the offensive on the ground.

3. As a result, Marshal Amer has ordered the Commander in Chief of the Jordanian front [i.e., General Riad] to open a new front and to launch offensive operations, according to the plan outlined the day before.[14]

A few hours later, in a second message, Marshal Amer informed the Jordanian front

that the Israeli air offensive was continuing. But, at the same time, he insisted that the Egyptians had put 75 per cent of the Israeli air force out of action. The same message said that U.A.R. bombers had destroyed the Israeli bases in a counterattack, and that the ground forces of the Egyptian army had penetrated into Israel by way of the Negev![15]

King Hussein concludes his account of Marshal Amer's messages with an understatement that bears the stamp of Harrow and Sandhurst rather than that of the impassioned eloquence of his Hashemite forebears: "These reports—fantastic to say the least—had much to do with our confusion and false interpretation of the situation."[16]

It is not often that one encounters such a telling example of both the overriding imperative of saving one's face and the price it can exact. While nobody can tell what would have happened had the Egyptians frankly and without procrastination notified Jordan that on the morning of June 5, 1967, they had suffered a serious setback, it is almost certain that Jordan would either have refrained from entering the fight or could have extricated itself from it with fewer losses. But both peoples and their leaders are, as a rule, the prisoners of their cultural values. Given the traditional Arab value of "face," it was impossible for the Egyptian military leadership to act differently. Before having a closer look at *wajh* and the hold it exercises on the Arab mentality, let us first conclude the story of the Egyptian-Jordanian exchange in the Six Day War of 1967, since it allows some additional insight into this tyrannical hold of the *wajh*.

On the same fateful day of June 5, Nasser phoned King Hussein and told him the same story: "Israel bombed our air bases. We answered by bombing hers. We are launching a general offensive in the Negev."[17]

Next morning, when the damage done by the Israeli air attack could no longer be kept a secret, Nasser in a telephone conversation with King Hussein suggested that a communiqué be issued by the Jordanians, as well as by the Syrians, to the effect that American and British aircraft were collaborating with Israel and attacking Egypt from their aircraft carriers.[18] This at the time seemed a perfect plan to save face. It was no longer little Israel that had dealt the blow to Egypt, but the great powers, the United States and Great Britain, to whose combined strength it was not shameful to have succumbed. Yet in the very same telephone conversation in which he suggested this face-saving device to King Hussein, President Nasser could not resist the temptation to continue trying to save his own (that is, Egypt's) face *vis-à-vis* Hussein, and said:

> We will fight with everything we have. We fought on all fronts, all night. If we had a few problems at the beginning, so what? We'll come out of it all right. God is on our side. . . . We dispatched our planes against Israel today. Our planes have been bombing the Israeli airports since early morning.[19]

A few hours later, at 12:30 P.M., King Hussein sent a personal telegram to Nasser in which he informed the Egyptian President in simple and matter-of-fact language (we are again reminded of the King's British education) that the situation on the Jordanian front was desperate.[20] This frank admission of defeat by Hussein finally broke the hold *wajh* had on Nasser, and he was able in his reply (which he sent after a delay of eleven hours, at 11:15 P.M.) to admit that he, too, had been defeated. His long cable speaks of "critical moments that nations are sometimes called upon to endure," of a situation that "demands courage beyond human capacity," and of the necessity to "face up to our responsibilities without fear of consequences." Then Nasser ties the admission of his own defeat to that of Hussein: "We are fully aware of your difficult situation as at this very moment our front is crumbling too." Finally, he is able to come to the point: "Yesterday, our enemy's air force inflicted a mortal blow on us. Since then, our land army had been stripped of all air support and forced to withstand the power of superior forces." Thereafter, Nasser continues to talk about matters quite extraneous to the issue at hand: "When the history books are written, your courage and tenacity will be remembered. They will not forget the heroic Jordanian people who went straight into battle without hesitation, and with no consideration other than honor and duty." After suggesting that the Jordanians evacuate the West Bank, and expressing the hope that the Security Council will order a cease-fire, Nasser remarks philosophically, "The histories of nations are full of reverses, victories and defeats . . ." and that "It is Allah's will—and maybe something good will come of it. We trust in Allah and he will not desert us. Perhaps, thanks to him, the days ahead will bring us victory." Then, after repeating the compliment already paid to the courage and heroism of Hussein and the Jordanian people, Nasser closes his telegram with the traditional blessing, "Peace be with you and may Allah bless you." In reproducing the full text of Nasser's telegram, Hussein caustically remarks in a footnote that "the Jordanians had to wait 48 hours to learn what had really happened in Egypt at the start of the conflict which determined the war's outcome."[21]

The Arabic noun *wajh,* while it means face, outer side, outward appearance, surface, and the like, has also the further meanings of first place, place of honor, advantage, pre-eminence; personal satisfaction; outstanding personality, prince, nobleman, person of honor; beginning, intention, purpose (of speech); cause, ground; respect, regard, manner, style, means; payment, wages; rental; essence, substance, individuality; and more of the like. While this long list of meanings may be somewhat confusing, it certainly indicates, even to the non-Arabist, that for an Arab to "save one's face" is a much weightier matter than for an English-speaking person. For the latter, loss of face does not at all mean loss of honor: the various meanings of the English noun "face" all pertain to the surface, the outward aspect. For the Arab, on the other hand, "face" and "honor," while separate and distinct, are nevertheless closely related concepts. "Honor" always verges dangerously near the "face," and "loss of face" always impinges on honor to some extent. Therefore, in the Arab world, much greater efforts will be made to prevent "loss of face." One is considered justified, for instance, in resorting to prevarication in order to save one's face. If it comes to saving somebody else's "face," lying becomes a duty.

The code of proper behavior requires an Arab to go to great lengths in order to save his face. Physical discomfort, even danger, will be accepted readily if necessary to prevent loss of face. This attitude underlies several proverbs—those eloquent expressions and, at one and the same time, molders of folk mores: "Let my left hand not need my right hand," and "I'd rather die of starvation than ask for help."[22] Many other sayings admonish people to preserve appearances when in the company of others, whether friends or enemies.[23] In his attempt to "save face," a hungry Arab will often refuse an invitation to a meal, pretending that he has already eaten, for fear that the host may suspect that he was too poor to have enough food. Instead of seeking help, the Arab will rather pretend that "thanks to Allah, I am fine and have enough," because to ask for, or even to accept, help offered would mean a loss of face.[24] Because of this tyranny of the "face," the Arab will make great efforts to hide his troubles from friends, let alone enemies.

The phenomenon known in the American business community and political world as "projecting one's image" is present in a greatly intensified manner in the Arab world. As Professor Carleton S. Coon, a lifelong student of the Middle East, has remarked, among the Arabs "two kinds of personality are at play; that which your man presents to the outside world, and that which is known to his kin."[25] This cogent observation needs a slight emendation: in both the behavior toward the outside world and that in the kin or family group, the Arab obeys rules or laws, albeit different ones, imposed upon him by the necessity to "project an image," that is to say, to save face. While a man will relax somewhat in the company of his kin, his true personality remains hidden even from them.

To come back to the incident described above, it is now clear that President Nasser and Marshal Amer were not able to behave differently from the way they did. Their cultural conditioning left them no choice but to "save face."

One may go one step further and note the difference between the simple and relatively brief statements in which Amer and Nasser notified Hussein of the Egyptian "victories" over the Israelis, and the effusive, repetitious, and emphatic language Nasser used when impressing Hussein with his decision on announcing the imaginary participation of the British and American air forces in the war. Had Hussein not lost, during his formative years spent in England, the ear for catching the meaning behind the words which is an indispensable prerequisite of true communication among Arabs, he would have understood that a *real* victory over Israel would have been announced by Amer and Nasser in a long tirade of repetitious and emphatic assertions, and that the brief and, for Arabs, totally unusual factual form of the statement betrayed it for what it actually was: a face-saving device, a reference not to a real, but to an entirely imaginary victory.

3. SHAME

"Face" is one example of the other-determined, outward-oriented character of the Arab personality. The role that shame plays in the Arab consciousness points in the same direction. Shame must, of course, be carefully distinguished from guilt. "Shame" has been defined as a matter between a person and his society, while "guilt" is primarily a matter between a person and his conscience. A hermit in a desert can feel guilt; he cannot feel shame.[26]

One of the important differences between the Arab and the Western personality is that in the Arab culture, shame is more pronounced than guilt. We have discussed the Arab concepts of honor, self-respect, and face in sufficient detail to show that the referents of all these are primarily external. What pressures the Arab to behave in an honorable manner is not guilt but shame, or, more precisely, the psychological drive to escape or prevent negative judgment by others. Sania Hamady has very adequately discussed that aspect of Arab life which she calls "Shame Society," and come to the conclusion that the main concern of the Arab in performing an action or refraining from it is "whether he would be ashamed if people would know about it. 'What would people say' is the main criterion for his choice."[27] The feeling of shame is inculcated into the young generation by shaming techniques, for example, by comparing one child with another, which are widely used in childrearing in Lebanon, in Egypt,[28] and probably in other Arab countries as well.

4. THE *FAHLAWĪ* PERSONALITY

Precisely because shame is such a menace and danger for the Arab, and the fear of shame represents such an ever-present psychological pressure, his response often takes the form of merely outward conformity with ethical demands whose substance is largely neglected. The one overriding concern of such a personality is to save face, to appear as a person who adheres to the ethical norms of his society. Such considerations, if they become dominant in the psyche of the individual, can turn him into what a well-known Egyptian sociologist, Dr. Ḥāmid 'Ammār, has defined as "the Fahlawī personality."[29]

The term *"Fahlawī"* is derived from a Persian word meaning a sharp-witted, clever person. However, Dr. 'Ammār's portraiture of the Fahlawī as the Egyptian modal personality consists, as he himself admits, mostly of negative character traits. After laying the theoretical foundations for his discussion, Dr. 'Ammār asks: "What is the present social mode of the Egyptian's personality[30] in whose formation the elements of time and place and the way of life have combined?" He explains that what he means by "mode" (or "norm") is the fixed responses which recur in well-known situations, and which the society expects and prefers over any others . . ." and that "social mode" is a concept similar to the statistical "mode" (he uses the Arabic term *"wasṭ,"* which can mean average, mean, or mode).

The first trait of the Fahlawī personality described by Dr. 'Ammār is "ready adaptability." The Fahlawī has "the ability to adapt rapidly to various situations, and to understand what responses these require." He is able to adjust "his behavior to these requirements to the extent which he deems appropriate." However, Dr. 'Ammār observes, this ready adaptability has two facets: one is a genuine flexibility and aptitude for digesting and assimilating the new; the other, "a readiness to express superficial agreement and fleeting amiability which is meant to conceal the situation and hide the true feelings." He goes on to explain that this inclination to simulated, insincere, external agreement has been instilled in the Egyptian personality by the long series of rulers, governors, sultans, and kings to whom the people had to submit or else risk severe punishment. "This superficial adaptation became, under such conditions, a matter of utmost necessity for survival. . . . In effect, the people had to rejoice when it was desired [by the rulers] that they rejoice, and to be sad when mourning ceremonies were imposed upon them." When the turn of Western imperialism came, this tendency to superficial assent was reinforced.

Another trait of the Fahlawī personality is quick wit *(nukta)*. One of the reactions of the Egyptian people to the successive misfortunes that befell them was to respond with bitter, ironic, or sarcastic comments. They derived personal satisfaction from these witticisms, found them soothing and "diverting from reality." In the *nukta* the people gave vent to the resentments they felt; it made their life bearable. While other nations, too, have their equivalents of the *nukta,* the Egyptians alone developed it to a veritable art and came to value it as a desirable personality trait. At the same time, "one of the most important functions of the *nukta* is to cover up the problem, to make light of it, to pass over it in a way which protects the personality from having to think seriously about reality, as if the 'punch line' [*farqa'a,* lit. "explosion"] of the *nukta* would settle the question or in itself were a solution to it."

Self-assertion is the next trait of the Fahlawī personality discussed by Dr. 'Ammār. This manifests itself in an "exaggerated assertion of the personality, and the persistent tendency to demonstrate one's superior powers and to dominate things." This, 'Ammār says, is not the kind of self-assurance which results from self-confidence and the proper understanding of the relationship between personal capabilities and external situations. It is, rather, "the result of a loss of confidence and a lack of desire to assess situations objectively." The adaptability of this type of exaggerated self-reliance

> takes at times the form of recklessness, and at others that of scorn for others, or else that of outstanding and exceptional ability in solving and discharging issues, "either with [the movement of] a finger or by a pen-stroke." Excess and exaggeration *(mubālagha)* and embellishment *(tazayyud)* are of the characteristcs of the Fahlawī. The question of outward appearance and "the size of the barn" also belong to that kind of self-assurance which becomes manifest even in buildings and edifices whose external appearance very often detracts from their interior structural arrangement and their quality. This also becomes manifest in what is known as the habit of "flourish" *(kanzaḥa)* in behavior and speech.

This overriding drive to self-assertion, Dr. 'Ammār surmises,

> is at the bottom of much of the conspicuous display *(badhakh)* at banquets *('azā'im),* of the emphasis on first impressions and on questions of personal dignity *(karāma),* of the concern with public rites at weddings and funerals,

and with everything connected with the domain of the "front of the personality" either individually or communally.

Therefore, Dr. 'Ammār finds it not at at all strange that "the sweet word"
is "among the most important means regarded by the Egyptian as unfailingly establishing a kind of personal and immediate relationship between
himself and others." On the other hand, self-assertion leads to the inclination to disparage, insinuate, and slander, to belittle the value of others and
their activities, and to scorn them; he who practices these arts is greatly
admired and esteemed. The favorite character of Egyptian folklore,
Guḥā (Juḥā), personifies and illustrates this negative side of the self-asser-
tive personality.

The next feature to which Dr. 'Ammār turns his attention is the romantic
view the Fahlawī personality takes of equality. This view, "one of the
important values of Egyptian society," is the outcome of the bitterness felt
toward the conditions in the country which have led to inequality and
discrimination. Related to it is

> the refusal to accept authority or leadership and its disapproval from the
> depths of the consciousness; and this despite the external veneer which people
> display toward the leaders and which consists of expressions of respect and
> rites of respect. The latter, in most cases, masks hidden feelings of resentment
> as indicated by the phrase "So-and-so plays the boss." The Fahlawī does not
> look upon authority or leadership as something necessary . . . but rather as
> an irresistible power to which the individual resigns himself submissively
> when it implants fear and dread in his soul.

At this point, Dr. 'Ammār adduces historical examples to show that circumstances imprinted the Egyptian personality with a fear of authority to
such an extent that the fellahin only respected the ruthless tax collector
while ridiculing and despising one who showed them mercy. Nevertheless,
the idea of equality remained a motivating force in the Egyptian's behavior
and "one of the captivating values that fascinated him."

Thus, Dr. 'Ammār continues, one of the most important psychological
resources with which the Fahlawī personality is endowed is the technique
of "removal and relegation."

> By means of removing the responsibility from himself to others or by its
> relegation to an area outside his own sphere, it becomes easy to justify any
> embarrassing situation in which the individual might find himself, or derelic-
> tion in his social responsibilities. "Fahlawism" increases with the increase of
> the ability to perfect these techniques of removal and relegation.

What motivates the Fahlawī is not dedication to duty, nor a wish for self-realization, but rather the desire for reward or the fear of punishments.

> One of the most important manifestations of this relegation is the oft-recurring verbal complaint about misfortune and dissatisfaction with dismissals, and the constant placing of the responsibility on the "government," "the town which has no head *('omda),* " the "administration," or any outside factor which can serve as an excuse for the outcome.

While this tendency to blame others for one's own shortcomings is a general human failing, the specific social and political circumstances in which the Egyptians have lived for thousands of years have developed it in them to a very great extent.

Yet another characteristic of the Fahlawī personality is "reliance on individual activity and preference for it over group activity." This tendency results from the wish to assert one's personality and to avoid friction with others. Contributing factors are the system of individual rewards, the fragmentation of property, and the remnants of tribal solidarity *('aṣabiyya)*. The preference for individual activity is also the response to the numerous rules and regulations which circumscribe Egyptian life. Moreover, it is possible that "the pressures of society with its various institutions and its emphasis on formal compliance with its demands, has in actuality created a counter-inclination manifested in the tendency to defiant individualism. . . ." This is expressed in proverbs such as "The shared kettle does not boil," or "Better a mat of my own than a house shared." However, "if group activity is unavoidable, there is no objection to formal compliance of an amicable kind without the genuine commitment which group-responsibility demands."

The inclination to rely on individualism is related to the endeavor to reach a goal by the shortest possible route. Occasionally, this leads to enthusiasm, boldness, and a disregard of difficulties which enable the individual to overcome obstacles successfully. When, however, perseverance and patience are called for, the Fahlawī personality's enthusiasm wanes, his eagerness and determination falter. This search for the quick and easy achievement is characteristic of many Egyptian students: instead of seriously studying for their examinations, they try to "succeed without the necessary toil." Even the work of the Egyptian artisans, "despite their skill and ability, lacks something of care in its finish."

In concluding his analysis of the Fahlawī personality, Dr. 'Ammār refers briefly to some of its other aspects, such as the emphasis on virility *(rajūla)* and honor *(sharaf)*, and its attitude to innovations, productivity, and work; he justifies his dwelling on "the weak points rather than the strong ones" in the Egyptian character by expressing his belief that such an analysis is "an indispensable necessity and a basic step in the rebuilding of society."[31]

Dr. 'Ammār's findings on the "Fahlawī" personality were partly recapitulated and partly amplified by Dr. Sādiq Jalāl al-'Aẓm, a left-oriented Arab thinker who served as Lecturer in Philosophy at the American University of Beirut and the University of Amman. He emphasizes that the Fahlawī personality always tries to use all the short-cuts to achieve his goal without any exertion. If he must perform a task, he will not make an effort to execute it in the best possible way, but, on the contrary, will only try to impress others with his ability to perform it, lest people say that he is incompetent. The Fahlawī student is interested only in formal success in connection with his studies, in the external impression, and will often resort to illicit means to achieve it. He will flatter his teacher or try to bribe him, will cheat in his exams, will try to find out in advance what the questions will be, and his great dream is to be able to lay his hands on a copy of the test material. What the Fahlawī personality dreads most is not failure in itself, but the shame and disgrace in case his failure becomes known. Therefore, many students who do fail in their exams take great pains to hide the fact from their families and friends. When such a Fahlawī student finishes his course of studies and becomes a high official in a government department, or an officer in the army, then disaster strikes, because he will continue to use his Fahlawī methods in his new responsibilities. Because of these traditional traits, the Arab people are unable to accept facts with the speed and flexibility required by serious situations, but are forced to hide shortcomings and failures in order to preserve appearances and save their self-respect.

The Fahlawī personality is inflated, full of self-importance, always ready to demonstrate his superior knowledge and mastery, and his control over a situation. This is accompanied by a contempt for others, especially for those who really make an effort to work hard and to produce a well-finished job.

Such an individual actually suffers from a feeling of inferiority, but is unable to divulge it because he is dominated by the concept of shame and

111

the fear of shame more than he adheres to reality and objectivity. For this reason, says Dr. al-'Aẓm, the Fahlawī personality excels in superficial accommodation and ephemeral courtesy, which are calculated to mask the real situation and to hide the true feelings, and are expressed in such stereotyped phrases as "Doesn't matter, everything is all right, we are all brothers." The same features characterize the relationships among the Arab countries: formal agreement expressed in politeness, accommodation, and brotherhood without, however, any real faithfulness to the demands of the group responsiblities, even though there may be dire need for conscientious, concerted group action.

When the Fahlawī personality finds himself in a situation in which there is no escape from the exposure of all his weakness and failings, he tends to disclaim all responsibility and to blame external forces for the negative results of his activities. Just as the Fahlawī student blames for his failure in the exams not himself, but bad luck, the teacher, the difficult questions, the country, the system, and God, so the Arab nations blame the enemy, imperialism, betrayal, bad luck, and everything else, instead of penetrating to the roots of the evil and extirpating it.

It is clear, says Dr. al-'Aẓm, that this Fahlawism is directly connected with the Arab concepts of chivalry, manliness, honor, courage, and prowess. For it is a fact that the Fahlawī personality flourishes in tradition-oriented societies in which the eyes of the individuals are focused on old and deeply entrenched traditions and customs. These circumstances tend to develop conservative personalities, people who plod along slowly, conform to the characteristic rhythm of their environment, and are disinclined to seek new solutions to old problems. This is also why such a society values old men more highly than young ones, without weighing the individual talents of each, and assigns certain rights to people without taking their actual qualifications into account.[32]

While the picture of the Fahlawī personality as painted by Drs. 'Ammār and al-'Aẓm is certainly one-sided and exaggerated, and especially so since Dr. al-'Aẓm's purpose is to arouse the Arabs to extraordinary efforts to remedy the failures he describes, there can be no doubt that the great force of the "face" and shame concepts does channel people of a weak and conforming character into the direction of "Fahlawism." When the individual's attention is focused on the externals of his behavior, true values are apt to be pushed into the background.

5. AVERSION TO PHYSICAL LABOR

Aversion to manual labor, in particular work that involves dirtying one's hands, is another Bedouin attitude that has widely influenced the Arab mind. Among the nomads to this day there is a notion that engaging in agriculture or any craft is dishonoring. This preference for a life of leisure, or, if that is impractical, as it is for the overwhelming majority of Arabs, then at least for work that does not involve the use of muscle power bears importantly on both the historical development of the Arab culture and the processes of its Westernization.

Let me begin with an example that will, at the same time, also illustrate the difference in attitude in this respect between Arabs and Americans. Many middle-class or working-class Americans quite willingly engage in tinkering around the house. If they have a garden, they will mow and water the lawn, trim the hedge, spread fertilizer, rake the leaves, transplant bushes, and do whatever else they think necessary. Many will paint or paper a room, lay down tiles on a floor. Most will wash and polish the family car and take pride in being able to carry out minor automotive repairs. This American readiness to "do it yourself" contrasts sharply with the Arab unwillingness to engage in any activity of this kind, or, in fact, to undertake any type of manual work. True, in Arab countries it is possible to hire laborers for a few pennies to take care of such tasks while in America the cost of calling in an expert in every case would be prohibitive. But the point is not the cost or saving involved, but the fact that the Americans *like* to do such work, while the Arabs of similar socio-economic status not only dislike it, but consider it actually demeaning.

Among the many observers who have commented on this trait let me quote one at random. Dr. William A. Darity, who had extensive experience with health programs in the Middle East, tells that in one country he was approached by six students with the request that he help them obtain work so that they could attend the university. "Arrangements were made for them to work with a construction company, helping a foreman at a site." One accepted the job, but the other five informed Dr. Darity that "they were looking for office work, this despite the fact, also, that the construction work paid considerably more than the office jobs they desired." Years later, when Dr. Darity again met two of those who had refused the work offered (since they had been unable to study at the university, they were still "working as clerks for a very minimum [*sic*] salary"), and they still maintained that "we just couldn't accept that type of work."[33] The low status of manual work in Egypt, a management expert observed, "fosters class consciousness and inhibits cooperation, communication, and opportunities for advancement."[34]

If the work in question has to be performed out of doors, the aversion to it is even stronger. Speaking of the Arab countries near Iran, a British Middle Eastern labor expert said: "In these countries, the local populations eschew outdoor labouring . . . so the work is done mainly by Iranians."[35]

What are the psychological motivations that make physical labor unacceptable to Arabs above the working classes? Why are most Arabs, unless forced by dire necessity to earn their livelihood with "the sweat of their brow," so loath to undertake any work that dirties the hands? One answer is found in the very passage from Genesis which contains the phrase quoted in the sentence above. The full text of the biblical curse of Adam pronounced by God after the ancestor of mankind had eaten of the forbidden fruit of the tree of knowledge reads:

> Cursed is the ground for thy sake; in toil shalt thou eat of it all the days of thy life. . . . In the sweat of thy brow shalt thou eat bread, till thou return unto the ground, for out of it wast thou taken; for dust thou art and unto dust shalt thou return. (Genesis 3: 17–19.)

This ancient and venerable myth not only answers questions such as: Why must man toil all his life? Why must he die and be interred? It also, and for our present considerations more importantly, expresses, codifies, and validates an attitude to work which to this day characterizes the Arab personality in the area in which the myth arose. This attitude can be expressed very succinctly: Work is a curse. It represents the diametrical opposite of the Protestant ethic, which considers work as a good, as something that ennobles man. In the Middle Eastern ethic, from pre-biblical times down to the present, the ideal has always been to escape the curse of work, to earn, or rather to acquire, riches through a stroke of luck, by finding a treasure, by finding favor in the eyes of a king, by buying something cheap and selling it at a high price, by being helped by a jinni. The *Arabian Nights*—that priceless collection of medieval Arab folklore and faithful mirror of medieval Arab life, beliefs, values, and intrigues—contains numerous examples of this ethic. One story in the *Nights* begins: "Once upon a time there lived in Baghdad a wealthy man who lost all his fortune and became so destitute that he could earn a living only by hard labor." Evidently, for both the authors of the *Nights* and those who enjoyed listening to their recital, to have to earn a living by hard labor was one of the worst fates that could befall a man.

This ethic considers all work a curse, but especially work that makes you sweat. Above all, tilling the soil, fighting its thorns and thistles, toiling and sweating in order to make it yield—this is the curse, the yoke of life and livelihood. When God cursed Adam, He condemned him to become a fellah —this is how any Arab would read the sad ending of the story of the Fall. Lucky the one in a hundred who manages to escape the curse, who can make a living without sweating his life away, in the comfort of an office or store, sheltered by roof and walls and floor from the burning sun, the stinging, dust-laden wind, the dirt of the soil.

Although working with one's hands is the inescapable fate of all villagers (except the teacher, the guard, and the imām), the aversion to such work is so much a part of the village atmosphere that it influences the feelings of young children. A striking example of this was supplied by the answers given by the majority of adolescent boys in a Muslim Lebanese village to the question: "If there were things about your life that you could change, what would you change?" Twenty out of thirty five boys answered: "Not to have to work with my hands," or words to the same effect.[36] Since the adolescent boys of the village had, in actuality, to work on the family lands, "not to work with the hands" in effect meant not to engage in farm work. Nevertheless, it may be significant that the desire to be released from agricultural work was expressed in this more general form: not to have to work with the hands. It is in this generalized form that the aversion to manual labor remains a characteristic Arab trait even in the long-urbanized sectors of the population.

Some 90 per cent of all Arabs are either villagers or townspeople, and their way of life is far removed from that of the nomads. But the *ideal* of the nomadic mores remains, however great the gap between it and the realities of life. Now, one of the basic features of the Bedouin ethos is a contempt for all physical labor with the exception of the tending of the livestock and raiding, which are considered the only fitting occupations for free men. Among the despised varieties of work, agricultural labor is the one most emphatically rejected: to engage in cultivation would inevitably result in an irreparable loss of status; in fact, it would dishonor the Bedouin. Because of this disdain for agriculture, the attempts in several Arab countries to sedentarize the Bedouins have met with only indifferent success. When, nevertheless, such settlement does take place, it takes many years to complete; the settled nomads retain their tribal organization for many generations and never tire of pointing with pride to their desert origins.[37]

Group consciousness is a general human phenomenon, along with the high valuation of one's own group and the deprecation of others'. "We" are almost everywhere better than "they." The Arab fellahin form a remarkable exception to this general rule. So strong among them is the spiritual heritage or pervasive influence of the Bedouin ethos that they unquestioningly accept a status lower than the Bedouins', and acquiesce in it as in one of the unalterable facts of life. The fellahin, like the Bedouins, consider working the soil an inferior occupation, if not quite a degrading one. This being so, those who can escape the slavery of the soil gladly seize any opportunity to do so.

In the past, such an escape could be accomplished only rarely. The fellah, typically, grew up illiterate. He learned from his father one work only: how to till the soil. He also learned that while to be a fellah meant to occupy a low rung on the social ladder, his state was the will of Allah, and man must obey God. Allah made him a man of the soil, and a man of the soil he must remain.

The attraction of the town, of course, was there. Rare visits to its busy streets and bazaars taught the fellah that he was looked down upon by the townspeople as much as by the Bedouin. Occasionally, nevertheless, a fellah managed to find work in the town. He may have been driven to seek employment there because there was no room for him on the land. The usual way out of this economic squeeze was to seek work as a hired hand with a relative or, failing that, another villager. This possibility was far from attractive; besides involving loss of face within the fellah society of the village, the wages were minimal. Therefore, the young villager's thoughts would first turn to the town. True, there too he could not hope to be more than a day laborer, with low wages; but at least, being among strangers, he would incur no loss of face. He might even make good.

For many generations, the village-to-town movement contributed to a slow and gradual growth of several urban centers. The village, which always supported about as many people as it could given its traditional and unchanging methods of cultivation, remained by and large stationary in population. But particularly during the last three or four generations, some increase was caused by the settlement of nomadic tribes no longer able to maintain themselves as pastoral nomadic breeders.[38] These nomads, for lack of choice, had to settle in agriculturally marginal areas: as a result the crops they raised were quite unreliable. Eventually, some of their young men too had to go to the cities to seek a livelihood there. Sometimes the move to the city occurred within the lifetime of one generation. The moving on from village to city had an emotional as well as an economic motivation. By proceeding to the city, the nomad-turned-fellah felt he improved his lot so far as presige was concerned; he escaped the most degrading of all types of manual labor: that of the "slavery of the soil."

The contempt in which the townspeople hold the fellahin has two main sources. One is the lingering influence of the Bedouin ethos. The other is the cultural gap that separates the city dweller from the peasant. The urbanite finds the fellah ignorant, backward, primitive, and uncouth.[39] Since the villager who has moved to the city must normally engage there in the simplest types of unskilled labor, unskilled labor as well as agricultural work have become associated in the mind of the townsman with fellah primitiveness. In Arab countries the manual laborer has, for the time being, acquired class consciousness in one sense only: in becoming aware that he is a member of a low class, with many disabilities. He does not yet try to remedy the situation by bettering the position of his class or trade as a whole[40] (as is done in the West), but by escaping individually from the class to which he belongs into the higher class of non-manual laborers. Needless to say, very few are successful in doing so.

Against this background it becomes understandable that young townsmen prefer to be clerks for inadequate wages rather than helpers to a construction foreman with considerably more pay. In fact, not only is the first choice preferable, but the second is totally impossible given the hold traditional values have over the Arab mind. One can foresee that a great and patient effort will be needed before the Arab mind can accept the concept of the dignity of labor.

VIII

THE REALM OF SEX

THE ISSUE OF SEX IN THE ARAB WORLD REMINDS ME OF THE
old story about the sorcerer's apprentice and the pink elephant. The master
of alchemy, after explaining to his apprentice the complex steps to be
followed in making gold, added: "And, most importantly, throughout the
entire process you must not think of the pink elephant." Having been duly
impressed by this warning, the apprentice tried desperately to heed it, but,
of course, was unable to keep the forbidden subject out of his thoughts. At
last he had to give up his attempts at making gold and sadly reproached
his master: "Why, O my master, why did you have to tell me not to think
of the pink elephant? If you had not, I would never have thought of it."

The "pink elephant" in the alchemy of Arab life is the sex taboo. Parents
and other authority figures imbue the Arab child with the notion of the
sinfulness of sex, and the culture as a whole surrounds the individual with
an atmosphere which constantly reminds him of the same subject. The
segregation of the sexes, the veiling of the women where it is practiced, and
all the other minute rules that govern and restrict contact between men and
women, have the effect of making sex a prime mental preoccupation in the
Arab world. The very taboo of sex creates a kind of fixation on the subject.

1. SEXUAL HONOR

The general Arab concept of honor is one that the average Westerner has no difficulty in understanding. After all, honor, even in its more concretely defined form as *wajh* or "face," is operative in Western society as well. Where the Westerner becomes truly baffled is in his attempt to understand the special Arab concept of one's own honor depending on the sexual conduct of the women one is connected with. The Westerner, too, suffers a certain loss of face if his wife—and to a lesser extent if his daughter— commits adultery and it becomes public knowledge. But a divorce is, as a rule, all that is required for a husband to regain his "face" as well as his poise; and as far as a father is concerned, he will in most cases demonstratively display sympathetic understanding for his daughter as she goes through a crisis in her life. In the Western view, a person can neither legally nor morally be held responsible for the acts of another, and consequently the dishonorable deed of even a very close relative casts only a pale shadow, if any, on the honor of an individual.

In the kinship culture of the Arab world, the situation is very different. Family bonds are so strong that all members suffer "blackening of the face" after the dishonorable act of any one. However, within this general context, there is for the Arab mind a sharp distinction between those shameful events that do involve women and those that do not. In the Arab world, the greatest dishonor that can befall a man results from the sexual misconduct of his daughter or sister, or *bint 'amm* (one's father's brother's daughter). The marital infidelity of a wife, on the other hand, brings to the Arab husband only emotional effects and not dishonor.

The roots of this particular view of male honor go deep into the structure and dynamics of the Arab kin group. The ties of blood, of patrilineal descent, can never be severed, and they never weaken throughout a person's life. This means that a woman, even though she marry into a different kin group, never ceases to be a member of her own paternal family. Her paternal family, in turn, continues to be responsible for her. This has beneficial effects for the married woman, especially during that difficult period in her life which precedes the time when her sons reach maturity and become her supporters and defenders. Prior to that time, the young wife, who is considered something of an outsider by her husband's family, can always count on the aid and sympathy of her own father and brothers. The very knowledge that these men are lined up solidly behind her, and are ready, if need be, even to fight for her, puts a restraint on her husband's family in their treatment of a young daughter-in-law.

Whatever credit or discredit a woman earns reflects back on her own paternal family. This continuing responsibility comes powerfully into play if a woman becomes guilty of a sexual indiscretion, or if her behavior arouses as much as a suspicion that she may be tempted to do something forbidden by the traditional code. The most powerful deterrent devised by Arab culture against illicit sex (which means any sexual relations between a man and a woman who are not married to each other) is the equation of family honor with the sexual conduct of its daughters, single or married. If a daughter becomes guilty of the slightest sexual indiscretion (which is defined in various terms in various places), her father and brothers become dishonored also. Family honor can be restored only by punishing the guilty woman; in conservative circles, this used to mean putting her to death.

That the sexual conduct of women is an area sharply differentiated from other areas of the honor-shame syndrome is reflected in the language. While honor in its non-sexual, general connotation is termed *"sharaf,"* the specific kind of honor that is connected with women and depends on their proper conduct is called *" 'ird."* *Sharaf* is something flexible: depending on a man's behavior, way of talking and acting, his *sharaf* can be acquired, augmented, diminished, lost, regained, and so on. In contrast, *'ird* is a rigid concept: every woman has her ascribed *'ird;* she is born with it and grows up with it; she cannot augment it because it is something absolute, but it is her duty to preserve it. A sexual offense on her part, however slight, causes her *'ird* to be lost, and once lost, it cannot be regained.[1] It is almost as if the physical attribute of virginity were transposed in the *'ird* to the emotional-conceptual level. Both virginity and *'ird* are intrinsically parts of the female person; they cannot be augmented, they can only be lost, and their loss is irreparable. The two are similar in one more respect: even if a woman is attacked and raped, she loses her *'ird* just as she loses her virginity. Where the two differ, of course, is in the circumstance that the legal, approved, and expected loss of virginity during the wedding night has no counterpart in the *'ird:* a good woman preserves it, guards it jealously until her dying day.

What is even more remarkable is that the *sharaf* of the men depends almost entirely on the *'ird* of the women of their family. True, a man can diminish or lose his *sharaf* by showing lack of bravery or courage, or by lack of hospitality and generosity. However, such occurrences are rare because the men learn in the course of their early enculturation to maintain at all cost the appearances of bravery, hospitality, and generosity. Should a man nevertheless become guilty of an open transgression of any of these, he will, of course, lose his honor, but this is not accompanied by any institutionalized and traditionally imposed physical punishment. Over crimes which are outside the focus of the code of ethics, such as killing, stealing, breaking promises, accepting bribes, and other such misdeeds, Arab opinion is divided: some say such acts would affect a man's *sharaf,* others feel they would not. But as to the results of a woman's transgression of the *'ird* there is complete and emphatic unanimity: it would destroy the *sharaf* of her menfolk. This led one student of Arab ethics to the conclusion that the core of the *sharaf* "is clearly the protection of one's female relatives' *'ird.* "[2] To which we can add that this attitude is characteristic of the Arab world as a whole, and that, moreover, a transgression of the *'ird* by a woman and by her paramour is the only crime (apart from homicide) which requires capital punishment according to the Arabic ethical code. Since any indiscretion on her part hurts her paternal family and not her husband's, it is her paternal family—her father himself, or her brothers, or her father's brother's son—who will punish her, by putting her to death, which is considered the only way of repairing the damage done to the family honor.

It is not difficult to see that the rule demanding punishment of an adulterous woman by her paternal family and not by her husand ultimately serves to maintain group cohesion. It is in keeping with the jealous claim of control over the life of its members exercised by the patrilineal family that it does not abdicate this right even in the case of a married daughter. To allow her husband, who is not a member of the woman's paternal family, to punish her would give control to an outsider, and thus weaken the control the family has over its members. Since, however, the woman must be punished, her paternal family undertakes the unequestionably bitter task of killing her, in accordance with the principle that the honor of the family must be protected even at the cost of a member's life.[3]

On the other hand, it is primarily up to the wronged husband to seek out the seducer and kill him. In the relationship between the husband and the seducer, another set of values comes into play. While the husband's honor has not been materially impaired by his wife's indiscretion (in this respect Arab mores differ markedly from the South Italian in which the cuckolded husband is derided as a *"cornuto"* and sustains great loss of face), his property rights in the exclusive sexual services of his wife have suffered irreparable damage which calls for blood revenge. French legal sentiment tends to be on the side of the husband who finds his wife *in flagrante delicto* and in his moral outrage kills her and/or her lover. Arab sentiment goes farther: it exonerates the husband who kills his wife's lover even years after the deed, and, moreover, it demands that he do so.

All this indicates that the Arab man who engages in an extramarital affair runs great risks indeed, which are usually sufficient to discourage any person able to weigh logically the possible consequences of his acts. (Even if he manages to escape the wrath of the injured husband, there is another risk; in some of the conservative Arab countries, which punish a theft with the chopping off of the right hand, sexual transgression is punished by the cutting off of the corresponding offending member.) All of which means that the average Arab, unless he happens to live in a larger town where prostitutes are available, or where, as in Beirut, Western sexual mores have begun to penetrate, has no sexual experience with women until he marries. If we add the fact that the average Arab does not marry until his middle or even late twenties (what with the necessity of paying a bride price to the father of his chosen), we find that usually years pass between sexual maturation and the beginning of licit heterosexual activity.

The Arab sensitivity to the *ird* is so great that an entire way of life has been built around it, aiming at the prevention of the occurrence of a situation which might lead to a woman's loss of her sexual virtue, or which might enable a man to cause such a loss. Even before the onset of puberty, and from then on until the very end of her life, a woman must be protected by societal arrangements decreed by the men. These measures, designed to protect the women's chastity, take many forms, some merely restrictive, others extremely painful and harmful to health. To the former belong such measures as the veiling and seclusion of women and the keeping of girl children out of school; to the latter, female circumcision. Occasionally, the fear that a wife or a daughter might lose her *'ird,* whether voluntarily or not, can be so strong that it leads to putting her to death: her death is deemed preferable to the loss of *sharaf* which her loss of *'ird* would mean for the menfolk of her family. Fulanain tells the story of a shaykh of a noble tribe, a refugee among the Marsh Arabs of Southern Iraq—who were considered ignoble according to the prevailing status hierarchy because they were sedentary and not nomadic camel-herders. Haddam, a young chieftain of the Marsh Arabs, fell in love with the shaykh's daughter, but, of course, the shaykh refused him because of his ignoble blood. One day, however, the shaykh noticed that his daughter was looking with interest toward the young chieftain as the latter passed by in the distance poling his reed-boat. Thereupon, the old shaykh took his daughter to a deserted place and killed her so as to prevent her *'ird,* and hence his *sharaf,* from being destroyed by her wanting to marry the young chief.[4] From the southern end of the Arab world comes the report that during the Mahdist uprising, some Sudanese Arabs "killed their wives and daughters for fear that they would be attacked by soldiers from the Khalifa's army who were considered as slaves."[5] Such extremes are, of course, becoming more and more rare, and today, even among the Sudanese Arabs, a girl who is discovered to have lost her virginity prior to her marriage "may no longer be killed." An adulteress, on the other hand, may be subjected to the fire ordeal, and if she does not pass it, she is killed. The seducer, too, would traditionally be killed by the woman's relatives.[6]

As far as female circumcision is concerned, its rationale is that it either prevents the girl from wanting to engage in illicit premarital sex (in the case of clitoridectomy), or makes it altogether impossible for her (if infibulation is performed), until her vulva is again cut or forced open. The custom is pre-Islamic and, in fact, was practiced in Hellenistic Egypt. In pre-Islamic Arabia, the operation used to be executed by a woman-specialist called a *mubazzira.* Even in early Islamic times, it was considered among some Arab tribes as an indispensable prerequisite for marriage.[7] Female circumcision is still customarily performed (or was until recently) in the following Arab countries: among some townspeople and Bedouins of Jordan; in Mecca; in Southern Arabia (the Zufar area, Oman, etc.); in the Southern Iraqi tribes, as well as in the city of Basra; in Egypt (among both Muslims and Copts); in the Sudan (where infibulation is practiced despite the objection of the *'ulamā* or conclave of religious scholars); in some parts of the Sahara; and so on.[8] This list is certainly not complete, and the wide diffusion of the custom makes it probable that it is practiced also in those Arab countries from which it has not been reported.

While numerous observers have commented on the function of male circumcision as a test of manliness, bravery, and courage which fills the boy who passes it with a feeling of self-importance and achievement, very few have raised the question of what is the psychological effect of female circumcision on the girls who are subjected to it. It goes without saying that nowhere is female circumcision considered a test of courage, since courage is not a quality associated with, or expected of, women. Since, moreover, female circumcision, in contrast to male, is typically carried out in privacy and surreptitiously, the operation is calculated to impress the girl with her own inferiority in relation to boys. While the male circumcision serves the assumed purpose of increasing the man's virility, the female operation is performed in order to reduce the woman's femininity in terms of her sexual desire, to intimidate the girl's sexuality.[9] One observer remarks that female circumcision, expecially in the cruel form in which it is performed in the Sudan, "causes a shock so severe that those responsible for female education say that girls are often permanently dulled.[10]

One last question remains in connection with the concept of *'ird:* what is the explanation of this enormous sensitivity to female sexual honor displayed by Bedouin society in particular, and by traditional Arab society in general? Why should the folk mores demand capital punishment for an infringement by a woman? The answer can only be attempted by referring to several factors in traditional Arab culture.

Capital punishment for adultery committed by a woman is a pre-Islamic heritage. In fact, it goes back to biblical times, together with the notion that adultery causes sterility, and is such a grave sin that it can cause the whole people or group whose members are guilty of it to "perish from off the good land."[11] Since Arab society, like the ancient Near Eastern societies out of which it sprang, was patriarchal, patrilineal, and polygynous, a man had great sexual freedom. His own marital status in no way put a limitation on his sexual activity. This situation still obtains. Even if married, and even if he has four wives—the legal limit according to Muslim law—he can have sexual relations with concubines (slave girls whom he owns), with prostitutes, or with any woman who is not under the jurisdiction of another man. When a man marries he is not expected to refrain from extramarital sexual activity. He becomes guilty of a sexual offense only if the woman with whom he has sex relations commits thereby an act of sexual dishonor.

For the woman, the situation is profoundly different. She is supposed to have sex relations only with her legally wedded husband. Her sexuality is his exclusive property as long as they are married. Moreover, a woman must preserve her sexuality (i.e., her virginity) intact until her first marriage. To make sure that this is, indeed, the case is the supreme duty of her paternal family. For a woman to allow her sex to be enjoyed by anybody except her husband is the gravest offense she can commit.

In Bedouin society strict sexual segregation was impracticable. It could be imposed neither in the nomadic encampment nor during the long treks from one grazing ground to another. Men and women of different families knew, saw, and met one another. Under the prevailing system, the young men would marry girls within their own tribe, subtribe, or family. In such a situation, the ever-present temptation of illicit contact had to be powerfully discouraged by severe rules.

To these must be added the relatively lesser concern with individual human life which is a further consequence of the extremely strong emphasis placed by the Bedouin ethos on group cohesion. The life of any member of the group is valued primarily in terms of his contribution to the group's welfare. This means that the group, whose will is embodied in, and expressed by, its male elders, will always consider the life of a member expendable if the honor of the group is at stake. Insofar as women are considered inferior to men—this is a pre-Islamic concept confirmed by the Koran (4:34)—and insofar as the main value of a woman from the point of view of the group is in her capacity as potential or actual mother of male group members, if she commits a transgression which makes her unfit for this supreme task of womanhood, she seals her own fate: she must die. The grave sin of female sexual transgression was surrounded by a wide perimeter of forbidden behavior patterns, to all of which the concept of 'irḍ was extended, and whose infringement also came to be punishable by death.

The all-encompassing preoccupation with sex in the Arab mind emerges clearly in two manifestations that suffuse the entire Arab world (with some local exceptions). One is that men and women see members of the opposite sex primarily as sex objects, and are convinced that they themselves are so regarded. The second is that all activities of women are considered by the men *sub specie sexi* and, in particular, from the point of view of whether those activities infringe on the traditional rules of female segregation.

It is characteristic of the tenacity of traditional convictions that even Arabs who favor certain improvements in the position of women continue to believe that a man and a woman alone will inevitably engage in sexual intercourse. In Algeria, the question was put to Arab men in a remote oasis village and in the casbah of Algiers: "What would you do if you came home and found a strange man in your house?" The responses were most characteristic: "Every Arab interpreted the presence of a man in his house as indicative of adultery. The response was usually immediate, clipped and emotional: 'Kill him.' "[12] According to an Algerian Arab student, young men could "only see a woman, in actual confrontation, as an object of pleasure":[13] while Mouloud Feraoun, an Algerian writer and rebel leader, put it bluntly: "To date, social life, manners, customs had as their essential objective the jealous safeguarding of the woman's sex. They [the men] consider this as inalienable, and their honor was buried in the vagina as if it were a treasure more precious than life . . . "[14] The corresponding stereotype of women sees in them creatures in whom one cannot have confidence, who are "like animals, highly sexed and willing to have intercourse with any man. That is all they care about."[15] Or, as a Sudanese Arab saying has it, "Whenever a man and a woman meet, the devil is the third."[16]

The women themselves cannot help being influenced by, and reacting to, such male views. They recognize that

> the women is an erotic object to be pursued and, if conquered, then condemned. Men are raised to be possessive toward women and to have a wholly erotic attitude toward them. . . . Because of the primitive attitude toward sexuality in which they are raised, women think there is something shameful about sex.

At the same time, they are convinced that the men are "sex haunted."[17]

These few indications, which could easily be paralleled by many more from the rest of the Arab world, should suffice to show how the preoccupation with sex influences the total view that men and women have of the opposite sex, and thus, inevitably, of their own sex. To sum up: the two sexes are irresistibly drawn to each other, see each other primarily as sex objects, and must be kept by stringent rules and "fences" from engaging in illicit sexual enjoyment.

The second manifestation of this preoccupation is that no female activity can be viewed without reference to the overriding consideration of female segregation. Thus, for instance, the entry of the Arab woman into the world of business is opposed by traditionalists not on the basis of her abilities or inabilities, but on the assertion that in the world of business a woman could not retain her chastity.[18] The same considerations motivate the traditionalists to prevent the entry of women into political life. The 'ulamā (conclave of religious scholars at the famous al-Azhar in Cairo, Islam's supreme theological school) rejected in 1952 a demand for the right of women to vote and serve as deputies in Parliament, basing their argument on the admonition in the Koran (33:33) which tells women to stay in their homes; therefore, "it is the duty of the woman to do everything to safeguard her honor and reputation. . . . Woman must be kept from temptation and prevented from being a temptation to others." Women must be excluded from meetings, such as would be involved in voting, elections, Parliament, and the like, because on such occasions they would mix with men, which would arouse promiscuity. This argument is supported by a secondary one which also goes back to Koranic tradition: women are particularly influenced by emotion. "In truth, the woman, because of her femininity, is tempted to abandon the path of reason and measure."[19]

Although subsequently the 'ulamā of al-Azhar had to go along with the changing times (women received the vote in Egypt in 1956, as they did in Syria in 1949, in Lebanon in 1952, and in Iraq in 1967), the views expressed in their 1952 *fatwa* on the innate differences between the male and the female mind are still current among many Arabs, men and women, educated and ignorant alike. Even among emancipated Arab women engaged in occupations outside the home, one often notices a certain self-consciousness expressed either in a degree of residual embarrassment at being unveiled or in a subtly defiant attitude about it. The natural ease with which Western educated men and women, boys and girls, behave in each other's company is in most cases noticeably absent.

2. SEXUAL REPRESSION

Two stereotypes about the sexual life of the Arabs are often encountered in the Western world. One depicts the Arabs as victims of severe restrictions in the sexual area, with veiled women strictly segregated from the men. The other portrays the Arabs as "dirty old men" even while young, enjoying the sinuous contortions of voluptuous, half-naked belly-dancers in public, and indulging in private orgies in their harems at home. As is usual with stereotypes, these bear only the faintest resemblance to reality.

The sexual life of the Arabs comprises at least as many variant forms as that of the peoples of the West. Hence it is extremely hazardous to venture any generalization about Arab sexuality, unless it be the statement that, to the Arab mind, the realm of sex is a more personal and more sensitive area of life than to the modern Westerner. Because of this attitude, the study of this area of Arab life is beset by greater obstacles than any other. Difficulties are encountered not only in the field work of anthropologists and personal interviews, but also in extracting information from published literature, where data dealing with sexuality are scanty.

Like many other aspects of Arab life, the sexual aspect is now in a state of flux. Under the impact of Westernization, traditional sexual mores have begun to change. As Western mores are being accepted by more and more people in the Arab world, the centuries-old reservoir of traditional Arab sexual attitudes begins to drain. The vast majority of the Arabs still adhere to their old traditions, but the number of those who follow the Western ways is increasing daily.

As far as the traditional Arab sex mores can be observed without penetrating into the secrets of the bedchamber, the impression is gained that they are the product of severe repressions. The avoidances observed in public between men and women, the existence of two separate societies, male and female, each with its own customs, language, and religious obligation,[20] and many other factors indicate, even to the psychologically untrained observer, behavior patterns developed in response to early repression.

According to both Freudian theory[21] and experimental psychologists, there is a definite linkage between aggression and sexuality. Not only is aggression more prominent in males, but its intensity is correlated with the intensity of the male sex drive.[22] Although these aggressive tendencies are repressed from earliest infancy and throughout the life of the individual, they remain part of the unconscious, as is shown by the fact that "the production of infantile desires and fantasies of a sexual nature continues right into old age."[23] The instrument of repression in early childhood is the moral influence of the environment:[24] in the first place, the dominant figure of the mother.

The unrelenting demand of the parent that the child conform with her or his wishes is the primary factor in creating frustration in the child. Occasionally, the child finds the frustration too much to bear, refuses to accept it or the domination by the parent, and displays an aggressive temper outburst, which is but a vigorous attempt at self-assertion.[25] While some researchers have argued that "aggression is, primarily, an expression of vitality,"[26] most psychologists assume that aggression is synonymous with hostility and destructiveness, and argue that it arises always as a consequence of frustration.[27] It is in this second sense that we shall use the concept of aggression in this chapter in our endeavor to understand the sexual repression–frustration–aggression syndrome of the Arab personality.

To begin with, we must try to find out what attitude toward sex is inculcated into the Arab child. There is some documented evidence to the effect that Arab child-rearing practices in this respect, at least after the second or third year of life, are extremely repressive. In the typical Arab home, the existence of infantile sexuality is either ignored or denied. The repressive attitude of the mothers with reference to sexual manifestations in their children is so strong that 75 per cent of the mothers questioned in a study on the subject stated that their children had never handled their own genitals. This is interpreted by the investigator as possibly reflecting the strong opposition of the mothers to such behavior rather than its actual incidence:

> the mothers are so firmly opposed to such behavior that they refuse to admit, even to themselves, that it could occur. Moreover, of the 25 per cent of the mothers who admitted having seen their children handling their genitals, almost all (90 per cent) expressed strong disapproval.

Arab mothers were not only found to be much more restrictive in sexual matters than American mothers, but also much less permissive of aggression toward parents, more severe in their toilet training and in their use of corporal punishment.[28]

The result of such child-rearing practices within the context of a religiously oriented culture, as Arab culture is, is to create a close association in the child's mind between sex and sin. Elsewhere I have shown that in biblical Hebrew and Talmudic Jewish societies, fornication (i.e., any kind of illicit sexual activity) "was looked upon as the arch-sin, the sin most hateful to God, the one sin that He can never forgive.[29] This ancient view has been retained completely by the Arabs to this day. As Edward Atiyah expresses it in his autobiography, there were many sins against which, as a child, he was warned by his parents; but

> there was one that overshadowed them all, the One, the Sin of Sins, Sex. Sex, I gradually imbibed the notion, was altogether something to be ashamed of, a thing to be kept in the dark. In the bonds of holy matrimony it might become just permissible, a sort of legalized offence; but outside those precincts, even a kiss was a pretty scarlet affair, unless with a view to immediate marriage. . . . The net result of all these influences had been to develop in my mind a general and acute feeling of shame about the whole subject of sex, sex in all its aspects, legitimate and illegitimate. It had seemed to me that even when you were married you could not approach the matter save in an apologetic manner. In my first days at school I was too shy even to mention girls.[30]

The attitude toward sex described by Atiyah is precisely what one would expect as a result of the severe repression demanded by Arab parents. By the time the child reaches five or six, the repression is sufficiently internalized to determine or at least influence thenceforward the adult attitude toward sex. Repression and inhibition show their effect in the delay in the onset of sexual activity. A small-scale study among Arab university students from Lebanon, Syria, Jordan, and Iraq in the form of a questionnaire to which responses were, of course, given anonymously supplies some information on the subject. The respondents, 113 male students, seventeen to twenty-eight years of age, had experienced nocturnal emissions at about the same age as the male American students studied by Kinsey, which indicates that they had matured sexually at about the same age. This in itself is an important finding because it refutes the oft-encountered notion that Arabs mature sexually earlier than members of more northern ethnic groups; as far as men are concerned, this does not seem to be the case. Nevertheless, the Arab students had their first experience in sexual activity (whether masturbation, homosexual intercourse, or heterosexual intercourse) about a year later on the average than did American male college students. This is interpreted by the authors of the study as "likely to be a result of the repression of sex in the home." One more finding points to the lasting effect of early sexual repression: the students estimated the incidence of various kinds of sexual activity among male friends and members of their community to be lower than the data showed them to be, and also "estimated the number of women in their community who had engaged in premarital sex activity to be quite low. Median estimate was 4 per cent, and mean estimate slightly higher than 10 per cent. Yet 34 per cent of those students had had heterosexual experience with women other than prostitutes."[31]

This gap between belief and actuality is paralleled by a similar discrepancy between public behavior and private conduct. Public behavior in the area of sex creates the impression that the repression experienced in childhood carries over into adulthood. Any and all public display of sexuality is abhorrent to the Arab. The traditional Arab garb, with some exceptions, effectively conceals the outlines of the human figure, covering it from neck to foot. In middle- and upper-class urban society, it was traditional for women to wear a veil over their faces; while a headcloth covered the head and hair of both men and women. Consequently, one of the first reactions of the Arabs to the appearance of Westerners was to judge them immodest and hence immoral. This was the impression made on them by the European women's tight and often short skirts, fitted blouses with open necks and short sleeves or no sleeves at all, their elaborate and uncovered hairdos, their painted and unveiled faces; as well as by the men's tight trousers which outline the legs and buttocks, their short-sleeved and open-necked shirts, their clean-shaven faces, and their effeminately long and unconcealed hair.

In traditional Arab society, a man and his wife would never dream of walking together in the street, side by side, let alone arm in arm or hand in hand.[32] Such behavior would be considered an indecent public display of intimacy whose proper place is at home, in the privacy of the bedroom. Even at home in the presence of children, siblings, or parents, the contact between husband and wife evinces the same restraint. This is carried so far that it is considered utterly bad form for a man to inquire about the well-being of a friend's wife. The very word for "wife" *("zawja")* in Arabic is felt to be too indelicate to use, because of its sexual connotations (it is derived from the verb meaning to couple), and is replaced by various euphemistic expressions or circumlocutions, such as *"imrā'atī"* or *"mad-damtī"* ("my lady"); *haram* ("woman," "that which is forbidden," and "that which is sanctified"); *"umm Ḥasan"* ("mother of Hasan," if Hasan is the name of the firstborn son); *"bint 'ammī"* ("my cousin," used by the husband even if the wife is not a cousin); *"yakhtī"* ("O, my sister"); or *"yā bint al-nās"* ("O, daughter of people"). The wife, in return, calls her husband *"yā sidī"* ("O, my master"); *"Yā ibn 'ammī"* ("O, my cousin"); or *"yā abū Ḥasan"* ("O, father of Hasan").

The same very restrained attitude is expressed in the behavior of young men prior to marriage, at least in tradition-dominated evironments. The boys want to see the girls and will go to great lengths to catch a glimpse of them. But the mores of the village hold that it is unseemly for young men and girls even so much as to look at each other across a street or square. Therefore, the following scene could be observed every afternoon in one Lebanese village studied: the young men would stroll up and down in front of the village well in the afternoon, about half an hour before they knew the girls would come to fetch water. The purpose of this parade was, of course, to catch a glimpse of the girls. But as soon as they approached to draw water, the young men would retire. The very sight of the girls, for whom they had waited half an hour, triggered in them the internalized reaction to an unrelated woman: you automatically move off, because it would be improper to stand around ogling her.[33]

3. SEXUAL FREEDOM AND SEXUAL HOSPITALITY

While restraint is found in many parts of the Arab world and in many sectors of Arab society, there is quite a range of local variants as to what is considered within the bounds of proper sexual behavior. In nomadic and village society, as well as among the lower classes in the towns, the exigencies of life are such that women must engage in certain activities outside the home. Among the nomads they gather brushwood and dung, tend the flocks, fetch water, and the like. Among the villagers they take food to the menfolk working in the fields, help them in the agricultural work, especially at harvest time, fetch water, take produce to the market, and so on. In the towns they go to market to buy food, go to work as household help in the homes of the well-to-do, and, with the advance of Westernization, engage more and more in income-producing occupations outside the home. In all these activities unmarried girls have opportunities to see men and be seen by them, and eventually to meet them and form friendships. Even before the onset of Westernization, the relative freedom enjoyed by young men and girls even among the most noble Bedouin tribes often led to love affairs between them, and many a girl became pregnant, frequently with tragic consequences.[34]

In settled society, there used to be a traditionally sanctioned participation of both men and women in religious festivities in mosques, which provided opportunities for flirting and jesting, and for the men to lay their hands upon the women very freely.[35] Especially on the peripheries of the Arab world, in areas remote from the urban Muslim centers, old pre-Islamic traditions survive which allow a much greater latitude in relationships between the sexes, and approve of sexual mores which evoke horror and disgust in the traditional Muslim. Reports of great sexual license come in particular from two areas, both marginal to Muslim Arab culture: from the Tuaregs of the West-Central Sahara, and from the inhabitants of the southern edges of the Arabian Peninsula. Since the Tuaregs are not Arabs,[36] we shall not deal with them here, but confine our remarks to South Arabia.

The Arab traveler and geographer Yāqūt (1179–1229), author of the most comprehensive geographical dictionary in Arabic, the *Mu'jam al-Buldān,* in describing the town of Mirbāṭ on the coast of Southern Arabia says that the men have little jealousy which is the result of the customs of the country. Every night their women go outside the town, entertain those men who are not forbidden to them [because of first-degree blood relationship] and play with them and sit with them until most of the night passes. And a man may pass by his wife or sister or mother or paternal aunt, and if she plays with another, he lets her do so, and goes on to another woman and sits with her as one does with one's wife. . . .[37]

More than a century later, a similar report is given about the mores of another town in Southern Arabia. The author of this report is Ibn Baṭṭūṭa, one of the most famous travelers of the time, who visited most of the known world of the fourteenth century. He reports of the women of Nazwa, the main town of Oman, that they "are very bad in their mores" but that their menfolk neither become jealous nor disapprove of their behavior. The women are under the protection of the prince, give themselves up to immorality, and even their own fathers cannot prevent them from doing so.[38]

Sexual laxity, or at least the rumor of it, has survived. The most remarkable form this license took was the practice of sexual hospitality. Johann Ludwig Burckhardt, the well-known Swiss Arabist and traveler, reported in the early nineteenth century that in one tribal group in Southwestern Arabia, it was an old custom that a guest had to pass the night with his host's wife. If the guest rendered himself agreeable to the woman, he was treated next morning with great honor; if not, he found the lower part of his cloak ('abā) cut off by her, as a sign of contempt, and was driven away in disgrace by the women and children of the encampment.[39]

Sexual hospitality and other manifestations of sexual laxity were reported in the late nineteenth century from various tribes in Southern Arabia, where a girl was free to engage in sexual affairs with strangers from the age of fifteen until she was married. Even after marriage, she would refrain from entertaining strangers only "if her husband is in the camp and if the secret cannot be guarded." The custom has its local variations, but the common denominator is the great sexual freedom it affords to women, including one-night encounters with unrelated men within the tribe and with strangers.[40] This license must have been a residual fertility ritual, whose purpose was to ensure fruitfulness for mankind, animals, and vegetation.[41] While several recent authors make reference to the survival of sexual hospitality among certain Arab tribes, others deny it, at least in those parts of Arabia with which they are familiar.[42] However, all reports agree that in certain groups in South Arabia, the men wear only a loincloth and walk about

133

without any covering on the head, and that the women wear no clothing above the waist, are unveiled, wear no headkerchief, and are free and easy in their contact with the men. They take part in the service of guests and greet and chat with them. Both marriage and divorce occur with great ease.[43]

4. VARIETIES OF SEXUAL OUTLET

Such details are interesting mainly because they constitute exceptions to the rule of great decorum and restraint in public in all matters of sex characteristic of the Arab world in general. However, public behavior is one thing and private conduct another. In private, it has been found that sexual activity is more intensive among Arab students than among Americans. Once the Arab students overcame the sexual inhibitions drilled into them in childhood, more of them had heterosexual relations, and homosexual relations, than the American students with whom the authors of the study mentioned above compared them. The number of those who masturbated was about equal in both groups. However, the American students practiced masturbation about twice as frequently as the Arab students, which may have had something to do with the fact that masturbation among the Arabs is condemned more severely than in the United States. On the other hand, more than twice as many Arab (59%) as American (28%) students had visited prostitutes within a year before the study, which seems to be considered the best release since "it involves little romance, it does not reduce the partner's [i.e., the girl's] chance for marriage, it does not violate a family's code of honor, etc."[44] All these considerations are well known to those who are familiar with the mores of Victorian England. They cannot therefore be considered as throwing light on the Arab mind in particular, except to attest to a general attitude that has long been overcome in the West.

In contrast, the attitude to homosexuality is more liberal among the Arabs than it was in the West until the "gay liberation" movement of the last few years. The taboo on homosexuality is not so strong as it was in America in the 1950's when this study was carried out, and "the active homosexual role in particular is thought of by the Arab students as compatible with virile masculinity."[45] In this respect, the Arab attitude coincides with that of the Turks, among whom the performance of the active homosexual act is considered as an assertion of one's aggressive masculine superiority, while the acceptance of the role of the passive homosexual is considered extremely degrading and shameful because it casts the man or youth into a submissive, feminine role.[46]

In most parts of the Arab world, homosexual activity or any indication of homosexual leanings, as with all other expressions of sexuality, is never given any publicity. These are private affairs and remain in private, especially since homosexual relations are forbidden in the Koran (26:165–166). Popular opinion, however, takes no stand against them, and despite the warnings of the Muslim schools of jurisprudence, the practice seems to be common to this day.[47] Only in outlying areas, such as the Siwa Oasis in the Western Desert of Egypt, has homosexuality come out into the open with the shaykhs and the well-to-do men lending their sons to each other.[48] It is interesting that even in a place like Siwa where homosexuality is the rule and practiced completely in the open, the passive partner in the relationship is derided as a woman. An informant said: "There is not one man in Siwa; they are all women," and explained, "Don't you see, if a man has done it when a boy, he has played the woman; and when he does it when a man, he is still playing the woman."[49] That is to say, even where it is a generally practiced custom, it is felt degrading for a man to play the female role.

The same evaluation of the sexual act as the assertion of aggressive male dominance comes through in the Arab view that masturbation is far more shameful than visiting prostitutes.[50] With a prostitute a man performs a masculine act. Whoever masturbates, however, evinces his inability to perform the active sex act, and thus exposes himself to contempt.

There is one situation in which the customary public restraint on sexuality is broken through. When provoked to anger, both men and women are apt to let loose a verbal barrage of obscene sexual abuse. The readiness with which Arabs burst into such abuse was observed in the early nineteenth century in Cairo and described by the incomparable Edward William Lane: "From persons of the best education, expressions are often heard so obscene as only to be fit for a low brothel."[51] To this day, the slightest quarrel or disagreement can easily provoke angrily hissed references to "quṣṣ ummak" (your mother's vulva"), followed by an exchange of even more explicit and therefore more damaging and more infuriating obscenities.

The Arab attitude to sex has one additional aspect that must be touched upon. This is the extreme matter-of-factness with which sexual desires and functions are referred to or even discussed in great detail and with gusto, especially in either all-male or all-female company. This phenomenon has always been perplexing to the Western observer, who is at a loss to reconcile it with the extreme modesty and bashfulness that charactizes Arab sexual conduct in public. On the surface, it would seem that one has here to do with a striking manifestation of the contrasting trends, the bipolarities and ambivalences exhibited by the Arab mind in so many areas. Before trying to reach an understanding of this baffling paradox, let us first have a closer look at the way and the contexts in which this matter-of-fact approach to sex expresses itself.

For one thing, in popular literature which has served as a source of entertainment for both literate and illiterate Arabs for many centuries (such as the famous *Thousand and One Nights,* better known in the West as the *Arabian Nights),* incidents of illicit sexual exploits are frequently described with an explicitness which is not equaled in the comparable European erotica. While there can be little doubt that the point was to titillate the reader or listener who was most unlikely to encounter any of the lurid adventures described, there is in them at the same time a remarkable absence of moral judgment. The sexual conquests of the hero of the story are (like the attainment of riches, another favorite theme of this type of Arabic literature) the result of his perseverence and cunning, or else of a stroke of good luck. As a rule, no retribution or punishment overtakes him, despite his obvious violation of the moral code.

The same moral indifference is evinced in the freedom which characterizes the discussion of sexual matters, even in the presence of children. Such discussions are recorded as early as the tenth to twelfth centuries when the *Arabian Nights* were collected,[52] and were overheard in nineteenth-century Cairo by Lane, who felt constrained to remark: "Things are named and subjects talked of, by the most genteel women, without any idea of their being indecorous, in the hearing of men, that many prostitutes in our country [i.e., England] would probably abstain from mentioning."[53] A hundred years later, the same observation was made by Winifred Blackman among the women in an Upper Egyptian village. "Sexual matters," she writes, "form the chief topic of their conversation." Even before children, adults "discuss the most private matters without the slightest reserve," with the result that children from their earliest years hear discussions and jokes about sexual matters.[54] As a result of this, children early acquire the same matter-of-fact attitude toward sex. As one observer noted: "Even girls playing with dolls enact [sexual] scenes of complete realism. But this calm

136

animal shamelessness is not alarming and has nothing to do with obscenity. Fundamental morality is not affected by it."[55] Evidently, the fellahin see no contradiction between this free talk and behavior and the strict sexual restrictions under which both boys and girls are placed as soon as they reach puberty. Arab children rarely have to be told "the facts of life" by an embarrassed father or mother: long before adolescence, they learn all that is known to their parents about sex, including all its licit and illicit varieties.

In trying now to understand what can be termed the sexual paradox in Arab life, we must be aware that much as the traditional mores insist on female chastity and sexual segregation outside marriage, within marriage the practice of sex is encouraged. The Ḥadīth—that great storehouse of originally oral religious tradition which regulates all aspects of Muslim life —states that the best member of the Muslim community is the man who contracts the most marriages, while celibacy is considered to be against religious tradition.[56] Accordingly, a man may make reference to his own sexual desires or activities without any embarrassment, in much the same manner in which he would talk about being hungry or enjoying a hot bath. Examples of this abound in both the highest and lowest reaches of Arab society. Of the late King Ibn Saud it was reported that, after a rich luncheon in the company of numerous male guests, he would often excuse himself by saying to those who sat next to him something to the effect that he was going into the *haram,* only to return a little while later to rejoin his friends without the slightest embarrassment.[57]

In all-male company, friends will on occasion boast of their sexual prowess, no doubt intermingling fact with exaggeration.[58] The same unabashed attitude to marital sex is illustrated by an episode related by the American student of Arabia, Richard H. Sanger. In the home of an important Saudi Arabian government official, a group of women attended a private showing of a motion picture. At 11 P.M. a recently installed telephone rang.

> It was the husband of four of the women guests, who asked that one of his wives be sent home to him; it did not matter which one. Four plump and slow-moving ladies promptly got up and left, begging the hostess to allow them to come back the next night to see how the picture ended.[59]

The lines between "bashful" and "unashamed" behavior now begin to emerge. There is, first of all, a severe taboo on all public contact between men and women, including anything even faintly suggestive of such contact.

137

Only the anonymity provided by a crowd can lift this ban. In private, on the other hand, everything is allowed; there all the inhibitions are shrugged off. The knowledge that nobody sees what is being done, and that therefore anything can be done with impunity, breaks through the repressions and inhibitions.

As for verbal manifestations, the situation is different. In the monosexual company of friends, the interest in sexual matters can be freely expressed and, in accordance with the Arab proclivity to oral expression and verbal elaboration, almost as much pleasure is derived from talking about sex as from the actual performance of the sexual act. Some restraint is exercised only in references to one's own wife or husband. As far as the oral discussion of sexual matters is concerned, a monosexual company is considered a private circle; only if members of both sexes are present does talk about sex become taboo.

Viewed thus, it appears that there is, in actuality, no paradox in Arab sexual behavior. There are only polarities. There is the polarity of licit and illicit sex: the former encouraged, the latter prohibited. There is the polarity of private and public attitudes: in private, sex is freely indulged; in public, it must not be even alluded to. A third polarity is that of acting and talking: one can talk, in monosexual company, about sex as much as one likes; the acting out is surrounded by numerous limitations. And within the realm of talk, there is the polarity of controlled and uncontrolled language, one of which allows only decorum and restraint while the other, provoked by anger, bursts into obscenities.

5. AMBIVALENCE AND CHANGE

Enough has been said of the sexual mores instilled into Arab children and adolescents, and about the atmosphere which surrounds the realm of sex, to make us suspect that the typical Arab attitude toward sex must be ambivalent. And this, indeed, is the case. The constant reminders of the sinfulness of sex are at one and the same time constant reminders of its desirability. The enculturation of both boys and girls consists of an incessant sequence of admonitions against sex, until awareness is instilled into them that no transgression they could commit would be a calamity of such magnitude for their entire family as one in the sexual area. As they grow up, they find that almost all the social arrangements which circumscribe the life of their community are centered on the single issue of preventing the possibility of a sexual transgression. All this cannot fail to create a definite image of themselves in the minds of both men and women, as well as a definite image of the opposite sex. The youth grows up believing that were it not for the segregation of the sexes and the capital punishment that would be meted out to him if caught in a sex offense, all the prohibitions hammered into him would be unable to inhibit him from having intercourse with the first woman he encounters. And he comes to consider his own sex drive so strong that only the physical impossibility of making love to the women of his social circle (because of their segregation, supervision, etc.) prevents him from consummating his desire. The image the youth has of girls and women complements this self-image. Their sexual drive is equally strong, and should he but manage to corner one of them alone, she might put up a wild show of resistance at first, but once he as much as kissed her, her "eye would be broken" and she would readily become his. In fact, as the popular view has it, a woman's lust is greater than that of a man.

The self-image of the woman is practically identical with this. She is brought up to believe that once she found herself alone with a man, she would be unable to resist his advances; therefore, she must never allow herself to be found in such a situation. She has been taught to believe from childhood that the mere sight of a woman is sufficient to arouse a man sexually, and only external circumstances can prevent him from having his will on her. These views and expectations are, of course, self-fulfilling. In a society in which everybody believes that, unless prevented by circumstances, a man and a woman will inevitably make love, both of them will behave accordingly.[60]

Thus sex is both prohibited, and therefore feared, and desired, and therefore sought after. Both emotions are experienced with considerable intensity, which can be taken as an indication of the intensity of the childhood repression of the sexual interest. After adolescence this repression creates a strong sense of frustration. If, however, the social controls break down, or are eliminated, the repressed aggression engendered by the frustrated sex drive breaks through to the surface and seeks its expression in sexual as well as other aggression. In one such situation, anger produces strongly aggressive verbal sexual abusiveness. Another occurs with an individual's removal to a new social milieu, such as a big city. In an environment where he is unknown, the individual feels that the old taboos with their built-in threat of punishment can be infringed with impunity. A third type of occasion in which inhibition ceases to function is at the accidental encounter between a man (or several men) and a woman in a place where there are no witnesses. In such a situation, and especially if the woman is not a member of the ingroup, or is a member of a hostile group, her sexual abuse is quite likely to occur. And if there is a possibility that she can identify her attackers, they may proceed to kill her in order to protect their own lives.

Before concluding this chapter let us touch, albeit briefly, upon the question of whether there is *any* truth at all to the stereotype which sees the Arabs as addicted to sex to a greater extent than peoples who live in more northerly climes. Are they more sensuous, more prone to indulge in sexual activity for the sake of the pleasure it affords? Does sex play a more important role in the Arab mind than it does in, say, the British or the German? In the early nineteenth century, Lane, who was a keen observer and meticulous reporter, answered these questions with an unqualified Yes. "In sensuality," he said, "as far as it relates to the indulgence of libidinous passions, the Egyptians, as well as other natives of hot climates, certainly exceed more northern nations. . . ." The women of Egypt especially, Lane reports, "have the character of being the most licentious in their feelings" and, what is most significant, he adds that "this character is freely bestowed upon them by their countrymen, even in conversation with foreigners."[61] We, for our part, would hesitate to give such an unequivocal answer. From the much stricter sexual code that is part of the traditional culture of the Arabs, one could conclude that all the taboos contained in it are indeed necessary because of the greater enticement sex offers to them than to members of other cultures mentioned. But then, one could argue that the obviously greater preoccupation with sex which characterizes the Arabs is the result of those very codes which circumscribe and inhibit their sexual activity.

In any case, it is safe to conclude that in comparison with the West, the realm of sex constitutes more of a problem for Arabs and hence elicits more concern and more preoccupation. The contrast has become especially noticeable since the so-called sexual revolution of the 1960's in the West, which resulted in the disappearance of many socially and culturally imposed sexual taboos. The new mores accepted in the large urban centers of the West have by their very libertarianism reduced the problematic aspect of sex and turned sexual activities into something strangely reminiscent of athletics in which all young people participate as a matter of course. Where in the past young people were called upon to devote all their energies to their studies and sports, and engaged in sexual activities only clandestinely, today it has become accepted that there are three areas in which a young person must achieve proficiency before he is fully prepared to take his place in society, and they are (in alphabetic order): sex, sports, and studies. No such three S's can be said to exist in the Arab world. There, while study has been fully recognized as of overriding value, and sports are more and more coming into their own (nationalism is a powerful impetus for both), sex is still under the shadow of the ancient taboos.

At least one influential modern Arab thinker, 'Alī Ḥasan al-Wardī, has come out with a condemnation of traditional Arab (or Muslim) sexual ethics. He even goes so far as to ascribe the ruin of Muslim society and the sapping of the vitality of the younger generation to the elaborate sex taboos which have had the effect of creating inhibitions and suppressed drives, forcing Arab youth to find outlets in homosexuality and other unnatural sex practices. He urges a total acceptance of Western sexual behavior (of the pre-1960 type) by Arab society: Let the women discard the veil, the two sexes intermingle freely, engage in social dancing and even in flirting. (Incidentally, for flirting he uses the Arabic noun *mughāzala,* literally, "love talk," derived from the Arabic verb which means to court a woman, or to talk sweetly to her.) Needless to say, Wardī's advocacy of sexual liberation has provoked strong condemnation from various quarters and a rejection of his proposals, often within a sweeping opposition to Westernism in general.[62]

The tenor of the arguments on both sides reminds one of the tone that characterized the discussions on the sexual emancipation of women that preceded the sexual revolution of the West in the 1960's. The issue, in final analysis, comes down to the question of whether or not women should enjoy the same sexual freedom as men; or, to put it differently, whether or not the double standard of sexual morality should be maintained. Since traditional sexual mores are a focal concern in Arab culture, one can anticipate protracted struggles around the issue. The innovators will be accused, as Wardī already has been, of trying to introduce into the Arab world fallacious notions and vices from the Western lands of moral darkness.[63] A point will probably be reached where the West will be accused of an entirely new type of "sexual" imperialism, which will denote to opponents of innovation perhaps the most vicious, because most insidious, attempt of the West to impose itself upon the Arab East. However, just as all the protests against Western cultural imperialism are of no avail, as will be shown later, one can expect that ultimately the Arab mind will have no choice but to accept Western sex mores; and its innate ingenuity will find a way to modify and mold them until it will create, after the example of "Arab socialism," a special Arab subvariety of the new sexuality.

IX

THE ISLAMIC COMPONENT OF ARAB PERSONALITY

1. RELIGION EAST AND WEST

THE ISLAMIC COMPONENT OF THE ARAB PERSONALITY IS best approached by comparing the role of religion among the Arabs and among Westerners.

The normative function of religion is manifested in the extent to which it regulates everyday behavior through positive and negative commandments, all of which, ideally, must be observed. In the West, at least since the onset of the Industrial Revolution, this function of religion has shrunk considerably. Religious doctrine and ritual, even for those who follow religious precepts meticulously, cover but one area of life, separate from most of the everyday pursuits. Religion has thus become divorced from the essentially secular goals and values which constitute the bulk of modern Western culture. Moreover, most people, especially in the large metropolitan centers, do not feel religious or, at the utmost, are quite lukewarm in their attitude to religion. Religion does not regulate their lives. Indeed, in the West religion has largely lost its normative function.

In the Arab world, on the other hand, before the impact of Westernization, Islam permeated life, all of which came under its aegis. Religion was not one aspect of life, but the hub from which all else radiated. All custom and tradition was religious, and religious do's and don'ts extended throughout all activity, thought, and feeling. Most importantly, all the people in the Arab world were religious in the double sense of unquestioningly believing what tradition commanded them to believe, and obeying the ritual rules with which religion circumscribed their lives. Religion was—and for the traditional majority in all Arab countries has remained—the central normative force in life.

In the West, religion has largely lost its function as an inner sustaining force. The most obvious expression of this loss of power is that most people no longer believe that man is protected by God. Despite the unceasing efforts of valiant evangelists to persuade Western man that "Jesus saves," most Westerners do not feel the need to be saved, although they certainly feel insecure. Toynbee speaks of "the spiritual vacuum which has been hollowed in our Western hearts by the progressive decay of religious belief that has been going on for some two-and-a-half centuries."[1] What Islam can impart, in contrast to this, has been observed by Rebecca West. Speaking of a Christian youth who acted as her guide in Yugoslavia, she remarks: "The lad was worse off for being a Christian; he had not that air of being sustained in his poverty by secret spiritual funds that is so noticeable in the poverty-stricken Moslem."[2] In the Arab world, and in the entire Middle East, all religions have such spiritual sustaining power. All share with Islam the "characteristic of being able to generate a psychological certainty of possessing the Truth, of following the Right Path, and of wielding the Perfect Key to the gate of the Great Beyond." They all impart

> the feeling that one does what is right because one observes the commandments of one's religion, and that one is inwardly protected from serious harm because God, in whom one trusts, keeps an eye on each individual and ultimately metes out just retribution. These convictions give the true believers of every faith, creed, and sect an extraordinary sense of security, an ability to preserve their calm and dignity and detachment, without depriving them of the ability to seek and enjoy whatever pleasures can be wrung from this world.[3]

As far as the supernatural component of religion is concerned, both official Christianity and official Islam paint a similar portrait of the deity. Both agree that God can be described in the same way: He is eternal, the creator of the universe and of man, omnipotent, omnipresent, omniscient, benevolent, and merciful. They differ in that Islam insists, like Judaism, that God is invisible and that therefore it is sinful, and hence forbidden, to represent Him in a painting or a statue. Christianity, especially Catholicism, while also maintaining that the deity is invisible, permits, and in fact encourages, artistic representations of God. Another significant difference is that, at least according to the Muslim view, Christianity is not strictly monotheistic since it believes in three persons of the deity, while Islam insists on the strictest oneness of Allah. To the Muslim, the Christian concept of a God who became man and, while man, suffered and died, smacks of outright idolatry, as does the Catholic veneration of statues of Christ, Mary, and the saints.

Beneath the thin veneer of official doctrine are old popular beliefs, held by the masses who know little of the theological tenets of their religion. In the West, little of this popular religiosity has survived. A belief in the existence of the Devil, which, incidentally, is also part of the official doctrines of both Islam and Christianity, does survive on the popular level; but in order to find a living belief in demons, spirits, the evil eye, and other supernatural forces, and an actual worship of local saints, one has to go to the Mediterranean, a region transitional between the West and the Arab world. In the Arab world itself, popular religion places even more emphasis on demons. There is belief in innumerable demons and spirits, jinn, ghouls, 'ifrīts, the evil eye, and the like, as well as belief in, and ritual worship of, numerous saints who, especially at their tomb-sanctuaries, wield great supernatural power. With the inconsistency characteristic of religious thinking and feeling on this level, the believers are unaware of any incompatibility between their belief in Allah the only God, and these numerous superhumans who people their world of the unseen.

There is a marked similarity between Christianity and Islam in their exclusivity. Both are characterized by religious jealousy, intolerance, the conviction that only the doctrines of the faith, or rather the sect, to which one belongs are true and valid and that all other faiths are in error. While Christianity has recently begun to modify its position on these issues, in the past it was considered the duty of the Church to impose, by force if necessary, its faith on unbelievers. This had a Muslim counterpart in the doctrine of *Dīn Muḥammad bi'l-sayf* (literally, "The religion of Muhammad with the sword"), which required all Muslims to spread Islam by the force of arms. When two such doctrines met, as they did many times in the Middle

Ages, clashes were bound to ensue, and the number of those massacred in the name of "gentle Jesus" and "Allah the compassionate" was legion.

The days of religious wars between Christians and Muslims (although not between Muslims and Hindus) are gone. Christianity is struggling to work out a compromise between its old religiocentrism and the new ideal of ecumenism. Islam has not yet come face to face with this problem. The issues it is grappling with are rather similar to those Western religions tackled a century to a century and a half ago: primarily the problems of adjusting an antiquated religious law (the *sharī'a)* to the changing conditions of modern life.

Both Christianity and Islam (as well as Judaism, their fountainhead) present man with a balanced teleology. The ultimate aim of human life, they maintain, is twofold: to achieve moral stature and live a good life in This World, and to obtain salvation in the Other. This dual purpose is given classical expression in the popular Arab saying: *"Ta'mal li-dunyatika ka'annaka ta'īshu abadā; wa-ta'mal li-ākhiratika ka'annaka tamūtu ghadā"*—"Labor for This World of yours as if you were to live forever; and labor for the Other World of yours as if you were to die tomorrow." The recurrent theme in the prayers offered up to God by the faithful of both religions (as well as of Judaism) is the request that God provide the "daily bread," that is, the material wherewithal man needs to continue living in This World. Curiously, the blessings one strives for in the afterlife, in the World to Come, are also conceived in material terms, in both Christianity and Islam. In Christianity, somewhat vaguely, the spiritual existence of the just in the heavenly paradise is described as a perpetual pleasure derived from God's radiance in a glorious realm; while in Islam, it is described more robustly as the enjoyment of a well-watered, shady garden, in which the pious will have everything, including the services of houris, those eternally young, beautiful, and virginal black-eyed maidens.

To sum up, the main differences between Islam and Christianity lie in their normative and psychological functions; in their view of the supernatural, their exclusiveness, and their teleological orientation, the two are more similar than different. This means that the crucial difference is not doctrinal but functional; what Muslims fear from Westernization is not that it will cause their co-religionists to abandon Islam in favor of Christianity, but that it will bring about a reduction of the function of Islam to the modest level on which Christianity plays its role in the Western world.

146

2. PREDESTINATION AND PERSONALITY

In the modern West, the "spiritual vacuum" left behind by the "progressive decay of religious belief " which Toynbee bemoaned has, at least partly, been filled by an attitude of self-reliance and a drive to know and understand the world. It is no coincidence that the great urge to explore the universe methodically, which is a unique characteristic of the modern West, arose as religion began to wane. Whatever the shortcomings of the scientific approach, it implies a firm belief in man's ability to understand and improve things around and within him, and expresses the conviction that it is his moral duty to make every effort to do so. This, ultimately, is the intellectual, moral, and, if you will, spiritual foundation of modern Western culture.

It is interesting in this connection to note how a Muslim Arab author views the changing interrelationship between religion and science in the modern Western world. The Abū 'l-Ḥasan 'Alī al-Ḥasanī al-Nadwī (1913–   ) devotes several pages to this subject in his book *What Has the World Lost Through the Decline of the Muslims?* Nadwī admits that Europe is unsurpassed in its inventions and discoveries and that there is nothing wrong with technical progress as such. What is wrong with Europe is that, because of her irreligiosity, she has nothing to guide her, and so confuses means with ends. This being the case, power and science are ever growing in Europe, while ethics and religion are ever declining. "This is why all progress leads Europe nowhere but to suicide. As European civilization is corrupt in its roots, no wholesome fruit can come of it. Its dominant role is merely the consequence of the decline of Islam."[4] There is no need to comment on the shortsightedness of a view which sees Western technological advance as nothing but an increase in mechanical aptitude and which is totally unaware of its ideational and ideological bases.[5]

In contrast to the West, the Arab world still sees the universe running its predestined course, determined by the will of Allah, who not only guides the world at large, but also predestines the fate of each and every man individually. The very name of *Islām* indicates that the one overriding duty it imposes upon man is to obey God; it is derived from the verb *aslama,* which means "to submit, to surrender oneself wholly, to give oneself in total commitment."[6] Hence, *Islām* means primarily "submission [to the will of God]."

The Muslim belief in predestination is at least as old as Islam itself. It is found in the Koran as a firmly entrenched doctrine. According to the Koran, not only were all things created by Allah ("Lo! We have created everything by measure," Koran, 54:49), but He also "createth, then measureth, then guideth" (87:2–3). "Every small and great thing [that men do] is recorded [in advance in God's books]" (54:53). Even though God may delay the punishment of the wicked, "verily on the day when it cometh unto them, it cannot be averted" (11:8). Therefore, Allah commanded Muḥammad: "Say: Naught befalleth us save that which Allah hath decreed for us. He is our Protecting Friend. In Allah let believers put their trust" (9:51). When Muslims meet unbelievers in battle and vanquish them, "Ye [Muslims] slew them not, but Allah slew them. And you [Muḥammad] threwest not when thou didst throw, but Allah threw. . . . Lo! Allah is Heaver and Knower! . . . Allah maketh weak the plan of disbelievers. . . ." (8:17–18). Even human will is subordinated to and controlled by God's will: the very will to "walk straight" does not exist in man's heart "unless it be that Allah willeth, the Lord of Creation" (81:29). Moreover, "Allah verily sendeth whom He will astray, and guideth whom He will" (35:8). While doctrines such as those underlying these verses gave rise to much philosophical discussion, analysis, and controversy within Islam,[7] their import filtered down to the level of the common folk in the form of simplified generalizations: Whatever man is or does and whatever happens to him is directly willed by Allah.

Such a deterministic view of human existence had become an ancient Judeo-Christian heritage by the time Muhammed lived.[8] However, in the course of their development, both Judaism and Christianity in the West have considerably modified their original determinism, allowing human will to play a more and more decisive role. Not so Islam, where absolute will is still considered as one of God's attributes operating in the manner of an inexorable law. Some students, in fact, see a parallel between the Muslim doctrine of God's will and the way in which Oriental despotism has worked: in both, there is no objective measure of what is good and what is evil.[9] "What God has called good is good, and the doer virtuous; and similarly, what God has called evil is evil and the doer of it is a sinner."[10]

In like manner, and with similar arbitrariness, God is said to determine the character of each person. This is the dominant belief among villagers and other simple folk in all parts of the Arab world to this day. Neither the individual himself, nor external factors, can change a man's God-given character, which remains with him throughout his life and which destines him to a certain way of life. Events in a person's life are likewise determined from the very beginning. Man has no choice but

> to go through the course of events which have been written down for him in God's Book[11] to the smallest detail. Not even in everyday life can a man do anything either to hasten or otherwise influence events . . . it does not pay and is not even possible to try to do anything to procure an advantage.

Such an attempt would only carry its own punishment. Each person receives the lot that is his: that and nothing else.

> He himself can do nothing either for or against it. In small things as in great, man is absolutely subject to Fate . . . even his deeds and the way in which he acts are decided beforehand. The logical consequence of such a view is that man has no free will, and further is not personally responsible for his morality and his deeds.[12]

The views above were expressed in those words by the people in the Muslim Arab village of Arṭās, near Bethlehem, about forty years ago. A hundred years or so earlier, Edward William Lane made very similar observations in Cairo. The Muslim, he says, is expected to "believe in God's absolute decree of every event, both good and evil." Belief in predestination, Lane found, predisposed the men

> to display, in times of distressing uncertainty, an exemplary patience, and, after any afflicting event, a remarkable degree of resignation and fortitude, approaching nearly to apathy; generally exhibiting their sorrow only by a sigh, and the exclamation of "Allah kereem!" (God is bountiful!)—but the women, on the contrary, give vent to their grief by the most extravagant cries and shrieks. . . . The same belief in predestination renders the Muslim utterly devoid of presumption with regard to his future actions, or to any future events. He never speaks of anything that he intends to do, or of any circumstance which he expects and hopes may come to pass, without adding, "If it be the will of God." . . .[13]

Elsewhere, Lane quotes the special prayer recited by the Egyptians on the night of the fifteenth of the month of Shaʿbān, when the fate of every man is supposed to be confirmed for the ensuing year. The prayer reads, in part:

> O God, O Thou Gracious . . . if Thou have recorded me in thy abode, upon the "Original of the Book," miserable or unfortunate, or scanted in my sustenance, cancel, O God, of thy goodness, my misery, and misfortune, and scanty allowance of sustenance, and confirm me in thy abode, upon the Original of the Book, as happy and provided for, and directed to good. . . .[14]

An omnipresent manifestation of the Arab belief in predestination and the consequent reliance on God is the invocation of God's name on every conceivable occasion. To this day, whenever an Arab does anything, or tells anything, or hears of anything, he accompanies it, or receives the news, with phrases such as *"bismi 'llāh"* ("in the name of God"), or *"Allāhu akbar"* ("God is great"), or *"al-ḥamdu li-'llāh"* ("Praise be to God"). All references to the future, to what one plans to do or hopes will happen, contain the expression *"In shā'a 'llāh"* ("If God wills"), contracted in the colloquial to *"Inshallah."* The most usual exclamation at hearing or seeing something surprising or exciting is *"wa'llāh"* ("by God"). The simple Arabic phrase for "thank you," *"Katter kheyrak"* in the Syrian colloquial, is an abbreviated form of the full phrase which in literary Arabic has the form *"Allāhu yukaththir khayraka,"* "May God increase your well-being!" And, of course, every good wish similarly invokes God: *"Allah-isalmak"* (colloquial), from the literary *"Allāhu yusallimak,"* meaning "May God give you peace!" and many more. The omnipresence of God in the mind of the simple folk is amply attested by frequent pithy references to Him in sayings such as "God will provide," "God spreads His benefits," "God brings the harvest," "God is with the patient," "To everyone the fate God gives him," "Verily we are from God, and to God we shall return," "God is there," "The day is God's and He provides," "Man proposes, God disposes," and "God cuts the cold to the size of the blanket."

On the other hand, the name of God is invoked with the same readiness in the course of quarrels. The stronger the quarrel, the larger the group which God is asked to curse. From "May God curse you!" one soon proceeds to "May God curse your father!" then "May God curse your ancestors!" and finally, "May God curse your religion!" or even "May God curse your Muḥammad!"[15] Even the refusal to give alms to a beggar is couched in such terms as "May God give you!"[16] There can certainly be no doubt that God is present in the Arab mind at all times, and that the smallest everyday event or activity is believed to be determined by His personal decision.

3. IMPROVIDENCE

A character trait closely related to fatalism is improvidence. It is inevitable that people who rely on providence should themselves not be provident. For the tradition-bound Arab mind, there is even something sinful in engaging in long-range planning, because it seems to imply that one does not put one's trust in divine providence. While most Arabs do not conceptualize their improvidence to the extent of relating it in this manner to their belief in divine providence, they manifest it in many areas of life. The improvidence of the fellahin has been for centuries a contributing factor to their impoverishment. In innumerable cases, the poor fellah was unable to exercise control over his habits of consumption and put by enough seed for next year's sowing, so that when sowing time arrived he had to borrow the seed from the landowner or a wealthy neighbor. This loan, of course, had to be repaid at harvest time with an exorbitant interest, which left even less of the crops for feeding the fellah and his family during the ensuing year.

The same improvidence made it possible for the *mushā'a* system to maintain itself for centuries among the Arab villagers of the Levant coast. This system consisted of the communal ownership of land by all the established families in the village, and the periodic reapportionment of plots, every year or every two years, by means of casting lots. The *mushā'a* led to a deterioration of the land because the fellah who merely had the usufruct of a piece of land for one or two years was not willing to make any effort to improve it; instead, he exploited the land to its maximum capacity and left it utterly exhausted to the next man, who did the same during his term of tenure.[17] Any measure of foresight would have induced the villagers to abolish this system and effect *ifrāz* (permanent apportionment), which would have enabled each owner to improve his land and make it produce richer harvests. Instead, the fellahin waited until the Ottoman government took the initiative and introduced what it termed *"tatwīb"* or "betterment," in the 1860's. But even thereafter the progress of the *ifrāz* was so slow that by 1917 about 70 per cent of the village land was still held under the *mushā'a* system.[18]

The improvidence of the Arabs is expressed in their disproportionate and inordinate spending on feasts and festivities, such as those accompanying a circumcision or a wedding. These lavish expenditures show that even the hoarding of money, which is practiced by many, cannot be considered as a sign of being provident. It is rather a matter of habitual frugality, a series of momentary decisions to save rather than spend, without the thought of laying aside a nest egg for rainy days. This feature was observed as long ago as the fifteenth century by the great Arab historian Maqrīzī (1364–1442), who stated that "one side of the Egyptian's character is that he never concerns himself with the future. He does not store up provisions like the inhabitants of other countries; each of them goes to the market every day, in the morning and in the evening, to search for victuals."[19] While Maqrīzī speaks in this passage about the Egyptians, the Arabs of other countries largely share the same characteristic. "History and literature are full of tales of flamboyant generosity and stupendous prodigality."[20]

Numerous proverbs current in all parts of the Arab world express the conviction that it is futile for man to make plans and efforts to provide for the future. A Syro-Lebanese proverb states explicitly, "The provision for tomorrow belongs to tomorrow," while another advises, "To each moment its decision." In a similar vein it is said in Southern Arabia, "Caution does not avert the decree of fate."[21]

Arab improvidence, in turn, is bolstered by the traditional Muslim view which considers worldly possessions dangerous because they lead to greed and because wealth is accompanied by temptations.

> Together with *silence, humility,* and the *remembrance* of God, *poverty* is of great help toward the attainment of salvation. . . . The rich man is tied to this world with much stronger cords than the poor. To be given a share in this world is likely to entail a threat to one's share in the next. Poverty, especially if voluntarily preferred to security, perfects man's confidence in God. It is not for man to fret about his sustenance. He who created him will also provide for him.[22]

While only few Muslims aspire, and even fewer actually attain, to complete renunciation of the world, most of them have absorbed enough of the teachings of Islam to view human life as consisting of two parts: life in the *dunya,* or This World, and life after death in the *ākhira,* the Other World. Trust in God therefore means that one believes that God dispenses material blessings in this life, and compensates the unfortunate but deserving with His blessings in afterlife. Hence, while ordinary mortals cannot help wanting a good life in this world, they must and do keep in mind that worldly goods are actually worthless encumbrances, and that the only real achievement of man is righteousness, purity of the soul, and reliance on God. The supreme good man can acquire is of a moral quality, although the road to attaining it leads primarily through the observance of the rituals, and especially those subsumed under the Five Pillars of the Faith: The pronouncement of the Oneness of God, Prayer, Fasting, Almsgiving, and the Pilgrimage.

For the great masses of the Arab poor, many of whom live in a poverty unknown in our Western world, Islam with its moralistic and spiritual tenets and its great promise of future reward is an asset of inestimable psychological value. Protected by religion, life with all its vicissitudes and deprivations is assessed from a wider angle, from a long-range perspective: sojourn on this earth appears as a lesser half of a great totality of existence, whose essentials and ultimates lie in the Beyond. This spiritual outlook provides a composure and a peace of mind, preserved even in the face of great adversity, which often astonishes Western observers.[23] But belief in predestination is a basic and indispensable element in all this.

As far as the Arab personality is concerned, there can be no doubt that the same belief in predestination or fate (referred to variously as *qisma*—hence "kismet,"—or *naṣīb,* or by the Persian-derived term *"bakht,"* or by merely saying *"maktūb,"* "it is written") exerts considerable formative influence. It endows the Arab mind with a calm and equanimity in the face of adversity, with patient resignation to whatever occurs, and with an acceptance of one's "place" and circumstances, which make the hardships, hazards, and deprivations comprised in the narrowly circumscribed life of the average Arab easier to bear. On the other hand, it engenders an attitude of passivity and of disinclination to undertake efforts to change or improve things. It especially discourages long-range efforts which require advance planning, because any such activity might come dangerously close to rebelling against Allah and His will as manifested in the existing order of things.

This deterministic orientation inclines the Arab to abdicate responsibility for improving his lot or providing for his future. As Sania Hamady remarked,

> He attributes the ills of his society, his mistakes and failures either to fate, to the devil, or to imperialism. Whenever he is blamed for passivity or corruption, the answer to the accusation is that he is forced by an uncontrollable factor about which he can do nothing. This refusal to assume responsibility in the issues of his life and environment increases the Arab's weakness and encourages his surrender, as if fate were bound to act against him and not for him.[24]

Of course, this attitude causes considerable difficulties when it comes to industrialization and modernization. And yet, alongside the view that there is something intrinsically improper in taking action lest one go against the will of Allah, one finds in daily life all sorts of efforts to change an existing situation, to prevent something one fears might happen, to bring about events one wishes for, and to act in many ways which appear to us as being logically irreconcilable with the belief in predestination. Efforts are constantly made to influence people to show mercy, to bring about reconciliation, to make those insulted be generous, and so on—all this despite the constantly reiterated belief that every act of man is predetermined, indeed, written down in the Book of God forty days after the individual is conceived.[25] Not surprisingly, it appears that the generally upheld theory of predestination is believed in on one level of consciousness, while everyday behavior is determined on a different level.

Of special interest in this connection are the magic beliefs and practices frequently found among the villagers in all Arab countries. To the outside observer, it appears that the omnipotence of Allah is greatly circumscribed and reduced by the belief in a rich variety of superhuman beings and forces, which constantly endanger man and which can be dealt with only by resorting to magic. Simple magical means and practices are known to everybody: if more effective action is required, magical specialists are available in the village or near it, and their services can easily be obtained for a fee. Thus, quite oblivious of predestination, the Arab villager will resort to magic for the purpose of realizing a wish, curing an ailment, causing harm, casting a spell, counteracting the evil eye, and the like. These practices and the folk beliefs on which they are based occupy a more important place in the life of the Arab masses, and especially of women, than do the officially sanctioned doctrines and rituals of Islam. In many cases, they are of pre-Islamic origin, and while official Islam frowns upon them, it tolerates them with a resignation that befits those who put all their trust in Allah alone. As for the simple folk, the very fact that these magic beliefs and practices survive among them is eloquent testimony to the persistence of the age-old human readiness to engage actively in actions that promise a fulfillment of needs as old as humanity itself. The patent contradiction between these practices and the Islamic imperative of believing in and relying on Allah alone strikes them no more than the Catholic villagers in Italy or Spain are aware of the equally great incompatibility between their "superstitious" doings and the doctrines of their Church. Both would be equally confused if the contradictions were pointed out to them.

The fact remains that under traditional Islam, efforts at human improvement have rarely transcended ineffectuality. In general the Arab mind, dominated by Islam, has been bent more on preserving than innovating, on maintaining than improving, on continuing than initiating. In this atmosphere, whatever individual spirit of research and inquiry existed in the great age of medieval Arab culture became gradually stifled; by the fifteenth century, Arab intellectual curiosity was fast asleep. It was to remain inert until awakened four centuries later by an importunate West knocking on its doors.

X

EXTREMES AND EMOTIONS, FANTASY AND REALITY

1. POLARIZATION

SEVERAL WESTERN SCHOLARS HAVE BEEN STRUCK BY THE pronounced Arab tendency to take a polarized view of man and the world, to see everywhere stark contrasts rather than gradations, to note opposites rather than transitions, to perceive extremes and be oblivious of nuances. As Lawrence of Arabia put it,

> Semites had no half-tones in their register of vision. They were a people of primary colours, or rather of black and white, who saw the world always in contour.... This people was black and white not only in vision, but by inmost furnishing: black and white not merely in clarity, but in apposition. Their thoughts were at ease only in extremes. They inhabited superlatives by choice.[1]

I myself could not help making the same observation repeatedly when, for instance, after an Arab theatrical or motion picture performance I heard the loudly voiced comments of the audience as they converged in the aisles and moved slowly toward the exits. Almost invariably the opinions expressed were in black and white; the play or film was judged to have been either "excellent," "magnificent," "great," or "terrible," "disgusting," "stupid." Very rarely could one hear any qualification, anything less than either total, enthusiastic affirmation or total condemnation.

In searching for the origins of this phenomenon, some Arabists have tried to explain this inclination to extremes by relating it to the contrasts which, they maintain, characterize the desert. According to Léon Gauthier, a foremost exponent of this school of thought, the desert "left a profound imprint on the Arab soul *(âme)*." On the elevated plateaus of the central Arabian desert, "a torrid summer is followed by a rigorous winter, and even in one and the same season an icy night comes after a burning day. . . . " The landscape, too, offers such sharp contrasts, which are re-echoed not only in the Arab soul but also in the most diverse aspects of Arab culture. According to Gauthier, a "race" (the study was written at a time when scholars still used the term "race" for what we prefer today to call "people")

> formed in such an environment, although ordinarily calm and apathetic, is subject to sudden and violent outbursts of passions, to momentary but irresistible upsurges of energy, to alternatives of chivalrous generosity and savage ferocity. At the same time rapacious and hospitable, greedy and generous, deserving of both blame and admiration, the Arabs exhibit a disconcerting mixture of the most contrasting tendencies. The extremes meet and mix in them, or follow each other abruptly: there are no transitions, no degrees, no nuances in feelings and ideas.[2]

Gauthier expatiates on the "juxtaposition of extremes" which, he finds, characterizes both Arab sentiments and ideas. In a rapid survey, he shows this juxtaposition of contrasts in cuisine (as a true Frenchman he would, of course, start with food), clothing, language, architecture, decorative sculpture, music, literature, poetry, the history and social organization of the Arab countries with their Muslim institutions, and in "the contrast resulting from a juxtaposition of the *autocratic* families in an *anarchical* tribe or state." His conclusion is that "a singular mixture of democratic mores and governmental autocracy characterizes Muslim society."[3] While not all the examples here adduced by Gauthier can bear close scrutiny, the idea of extremes as a characteristic of the Arab mind is one that seems to have a solid factual basis.

Winifred Blackman, who spent a number of years in an Upper Egyptian village, comments on the sharp contrast between the fertile Nile Valley and the arid waterless desert arount it. This contrast, she finds, is reflected in the character of the Egyptian peasant. "It is a remarkable fact," she writes, that the most divergent traits of character can be found in a single individual. The Egyptian peasants . . . are as a whole a wonderfully cheerful and contented people. They are very quick of comprehension, of ready wit, dearly loving a joke, even if directed against themselves, usually blessed with a retentive memory, lighthearted, kindly and very hospitable; they are also very hard-working.

This is one side of the picture. The other side, as Miss Blackman sees it, is that "at the same time they are very emotional, highly strung, most inflammable, generally very ignorant, and nearly always conspicuously lacking in self-control." Especially "under the influence of jealousy, which often becomes a raging passion, a man or a woman is rendered capable of committing any violent crime." And Miss Blackman adds that a quick, gentle, peaceful man, on the spur of the moment may commit brutal murder.[4]

Other manifestations of the contrasts in the Upper Egyptian fellahin's character are, according to Miss Blackman, that while "they are not a military people . . . in their intervillage fights, which are not of infrequent occurrence, they sometimes display surprising ferocity." The attitude displayed toward outsiders, that is, people from other villages, is characterized by a peculiar contrast. They are "treated with hospitality and courtesy as visitors," but "are, in some cases, looked upon with as much suspicion as if they were positive aliens."[5] As to the women, their temper is even more given to contrasts. "Most of the women have unfortunately a dangerous and difficult temperament."[6]

Father Henry Habib Ayrout, who has had intimate knowledge of the Egyptian fellahin and was himself an Egyptian, adds several traits to the portrait of the mixed fellah personality. The Egyptian fellahin, he writes, "are both credulous and mistrustful, individualistic and gregarious, miserly and thriftless, long suffering and fiery tempered." In money matters, "the more the fellah has saved up in the secret hiding-place of his home, the more likely he is to be carried away by the sight of the crowd at a holiday feast and squander it—as much for show as for enjoyment. . . . " He is mild, peaceful, patient, and indifferent; "his mind is passive and fatalistic: he accepts things as they are." But, on the other hand, "he acts on the impulse of the moment, without discrimination or sense of proportion, without considering the importance of what has happened or the consequence of what he is doing." If something happens that "strikes him as intolerable . . . he reacts violently, and infects the others with the same passion. Human life at such a time counts for little." Especially the "fellahin of the Said

[Sa'īd, the southern part, or Upper Egypt] are like a volcano that will erupt when least expected." However, "their outbursts do not last for long, and are succeeded by resignation which, being habitual, is a much more noticeable characteristic."[7]

Sania Hamady, another modern Arab scholar, comments on the contrasts in the Arab temperament. She finds them polarized between quick temper and self-control:

> The very same Arab whose character is hostile and quarrelsome, who shows extreme emotionalism in easily aroused anger and sorrow does not ordinarily demonstrate his joys, fears, and weaknesses. These feelings are not given vent, they are checked from positive overt expression. . . .[8]

In general, as we have already suggested, Arab emotional life revolves around several interlocking syndromes, each one of which is juxtaposed between two contrasting extremes. There is, first of all, the polarity between unity and divisiveness. Then there are the polarities of shame and honor; of aggression and submission; of vengefulness and forgiveness; of competitiveness and mutual help; of prevarication and honesty; of pride and humility; of rudeness and politeness; of bursts of activity and lethargic passivity; of modesty in sexual matters and resort to obscenities.

Some of these syndromes are complementary and mutually reinforce each other. Thus, for instance, conduct is almost constantly directed and controlled by the dual endeavor of trying to avoid what is harmful and trying to do what is honorable. Other bipolarities, also constantly present, work at cross purposes and pull the individual in two opposite directions. The unity-divisiveness syndrome is an example of this. The desire to achieve or maintain unity on a large scale runs counter to the divisive desire to achieve or maintain small, provincial, ingroup advantages. Most of the juxtaposed syndromes referred to, however, belong to neither of these two types but to a third. They fight for predominance in the Arab breast, with the result that the individual frequently veers from one extreme to the other: at one moment he evinces an outburst of uncontrolled emotions, in the next he regains self-control; in one he is aggressive, in the other submissive.

Still another polarity is that between the divine and the human, which Nuseibeh found to be akin to the "schizophrenia in [Arab] thought and emotion" between "two separate planes of reality," namely, the Arab-Islamic tradition and the secular, mundane reality expressed in the actual pattern of government derived from European models.[9]

2. CONTROL AND TEMPER

For the Western mind, the strangest and most fascinating of all these contrasts is undoubtedly that between self-control and uncontrolled outbursts of emotionalism, or the related opposites of lethargy and upsurges of activity. This is something quite foreign to the Western outlook, which expects each individual to steer an even course rather than veer from one extreme to the other. If, in exceptional circumstances, a Westerner is provoked to doing something that is contrary to his usually controlled behavior, he is excused, or excuses himself, with having momentarily lost his head; and he usually makes a firm resolve never to let such a damaging thing happen to him again.

In the Arab world, no such onus attaches to loss of self-control or outburst of temper. Quite the contrary: such seizures are expected to happen from time to time, because in the Arab view of human nature no person is supposed to be able to maintain incessant, uninterrupted control over himself. Any event that is outside routine everyday occurrence can trigger such a loss of control and turn the docile, friendly, and courteous Jekyll into a raging, dangerous, and maniacal Hyde, who will return to his former self as soon as the seizure of temper passes.

Particularly interesting is the frequency with which self-control gives way to temper, the ease with which the flood of anger, violence, or other intense emotion sweeps over the dam of self-control and in an astonishingly short time transforms the entire personality. If I were inclined to seek a correlation between the Arab temperament and the natural phenomena found in the environment, I would refer to the wadis, those rocky, narrow ravines in the desert which for most of the year are dry and dead, and then, on a few occasions when rain falls, possibly miles away, are suddenly transformed into tearing, raging torrents, rolling down big rocks and destroying everything that happens to lie in their way, only to subside again a few hours later as quickly as they rose. In any case, I must admit to having been reminded of a wadi on more than one occasion on seeing a usually quiet and calm Arab become suddenly enraged.

Observations of this quick change from quiet self-control to uncontrollable outbursts of temper abound. Sania Hamady discusses the subject in some detail, showing how Arab emotionalism expresses itself in many areas. "The Arab communicates by shouting accompanied with signs of anger."

When bargaining in the market place, he yells and squabbles. When hurt, he "expresses his pain freely by words, sounds, and gestures. He talks and complains about it openly, manifesting his sufferings by groaning, moaning, and crying." When death occurs, "his culture allows him outbursts of emotional behavior. Even more, he is supposed to show his emotions and his sorrow openly—he must weep and exhibit his pain and misery." The women wail in loud cries, and men also lament. A demonstration of feelings under heavy affliction is not considered unmanly. As to anger, the Arab is intensely susceptible to it. He flares up easily, and does not refrain from outbursts; and, once aroused, his wrath has no limits. Quarrels in the family are everyday occurrences. "At each meal a quarrel, with each bite a worry," says a Syro-Lebanese proverb.[10]

Emotionalism can crop up on the most unexpected occasions. Mohammed Neguib (Muḥammad Najīb), the first President of Egypt from 1952 to 1954, who headed the group of young officers who forced King Faruk to resign, relates that when Faruk left the royal palace, "the palace servants, in accordance with Egyptian custom, set up a wail of lament that could be heard a quarter of a mile away." When Neguib himself had his final meeting with the deposed king, all of whose small last requests he had denied, he records: "We were both gripped by a mixture of emotions that brought us close to tears."[11]

Especially in a crowd situation are emotions apt to break loose. The emotionalism of the Iraqi populace, which makes it easily incitable and inclined to participate in violent street demonstrations, is described by Majid Khadduri:

> . . . the rank and file supplied the mass of manpower and the outflow of emotionalism which inundated the capital's [Baghdad's] streets whenever a popular uprising occurred. In the past (prior to the 1958 revolution), though popular uprisings caused damage to life and property . . . they were like the floods of the river Tigris, capable of destruction but short-lived and quickly exhausted. The ruling Oligarchy well understood the nature of these outbursts and learned how to cope with them by letting the flood pass swiftly, and the police often tried merely to channel it and clear the wreckage. . . . [But in the July 1958 Revolution] once the police were not in evidence, the unchecked energy of the mob wrought havoc the like of which Baghdad had not witnessed before. . . .[12]

Even Fayez Sayegh, a staunch defender and avowed propagandist of the Arab cause, describes the Arab masses as prone to a "somewhat excessive display of emotional vitality," and in the very next paragraph as "over-emotional," and characterized by a "heated and somewhat blind enthusiasm."[13]

3. HOSTILITY

Once aroused, Arab hostility will vent itself indiscriminately on any and all outsiders. On November 2, 1945, when the leaders of Egypt called for demonstrations on the anniversary of the Balfour Declaration, the demonstrations not only developed into anti-Jewish riots, but led to attacks on a Catholic, an Armenian, and a Greek Orthodox church. On January 4 and 5, 1952, in the course of anti-British demonstrations in Suez, a Coptic church was looted and set on fire and some Copts killed by demonstrators. Bernard Lewis sees in these acts the survival of the attitude expressed in an old Muslim-Arab tradition: *"al-kufru millatun wāḥida"*—"Unbelief [or rather, the realm of the unbelievers] is one nation"; that is to say, just as all the Muslims (and, within them, all the Arabs) constitute one nation, at least in theory, so do the unbelievers.[14]

Wilfred Cantwell Smith tries to explain the Arab proclivity for mob action by referring to a number of psychological factors: Arab society, or Egyptian society, he says, "has deteriorated to a point where violence is almost inevitable." The program of the Ikhwān al-Muslimūn (Muslim Brothers)

> is the expression of the hatred, frustration, vanity and destructive frenzy of a people who for long have been the prey of poverty, impotence and fear. All the discontent of men who find the modern world too much for them can in movements such as the Ikhwān find action and satisfaction. It is the Muslim Arab's aggressive reaction to the attack on his world. . .the reaction of those who, tired of being overwhelmed, have leapt with frantic sadistic joy to burn and kill. The burning of Cairo [on January 26, 1952], the assassination of Prime Ministers [Maḥmūd Fahmī al-Nuqrāshī assassinated on December 28, 1948], the intimidating of Christians [based on personal conversations with Egyptian Christians], the vehemence and hatred in their literature—all this is to be understood in terms of a people who have lost their ways, whose heritage has proven unequal to modernity, whose leaders have been dishonest, whose ideals have failed. In this aspect, the new Islamic upsurge is a force not to solve problems but to intoxicate those who cannot longer abide the failure to solve them.[15]

What emerges from these and other such scenes is the picture of a human type which readily and frequently throws off the restraints of discipline and, especially in mass situations, is likely to go on a rampage. Why one group is characterized by such oscillation between the extremes of self-control and uncontrolled outbursts of emotion, while the life of another runs its even course, is one of those tantalizing questions to which no satisfactory answer has yet been found.

4. THREE FUNCTIONAL PLANES: THOUGHTS, WORDS, ACTIONS

In attempting to recognize correlations between various aspects of the Arab personality, it is helpful to examine the discrepancy that exists among the Arabs between the three planes of existence that can be distinguished in each individual and group. All of us engage constantly in action. Our actions express our intentions, but, at the same time, are influenced by external factors, such as the control the social and physical environment has over us. The world of action and activity is the first plane of our existence. The second is that of verbal utterance. We often express verbally intentions that we cannot carry out because of external impediments. In this respect, verbal expression corresponds more closely to intentions than actions. But even in words we do not express all our intentions. We refrain from uttering certain things because of the realities of the environment in which we live. The third plane is that of the intentions themselves, that is, of the thoughts we entertain, the wishes we have, the ideas we believe in, and so on. The world of the mind, as this plane can be called, is the one most independent of the limiting influences of the environment. Yet, while thoughts cannot be censored, thought is to a considerable extent related to reality. A normal person will not entertain thoughts which are in overt conflict with reality. He may engage in "wishful thinking," or even "day dreaming," but he will always be aware of the difference between such idle thoughts and reality.

As to the control of the reality factor over ideas and words, there are unquestionably significant differences between individuals and groups. In a pragmatically oriented community, the modal personality is strongly influenced by reality and his verbal expression even more so. At the other end of the scale we find societies where reality does not exercise a high degree of influence on thinking and speech. Western peoples stand at one end of the scale, the Arabs near the other end. In the Arab world, thought and verbal expression can be relatively uncorrelated with what the circumstances actually allow.

Y. Harkabi found that among the Arabs both thought processes and verbal utterances enjoy a high degree of autonomy. Thoughts, wishes, and their oral expressions develop in freedom from the control of reality. Since the thought processes are generally hidden from the eye, it is in particular the discrepancy between the verbal utterance and the acts that is apparent. The verbal utterance, which expresses such mental functions as feelings, aspirations, ideals, wishes, and thoughts, is quite divorced from the level of action. Harkabi goes on to show that numerous Arab observers are themselves aware of the discrepancy between Arab wishes, desires, imaginings, and the words expressing them, and the reality to which their actions must conform. While a certain discrepancy between ideology and verbal formulation on the one hand and actions on the other is a general human phenomenon, among the Arabs the difference is considerable, although even here there is no absolute break between the ideal and reality.[16]

Related observations were made some years earlier by Morroe Berger, who speaks about "the Arab's infatuation with ideal forms" to which he clings "emotionally even while he knows they are contradicted by reality." While a "distinction between ideal and real exists in other societies too," in them there is a greater awareness "of the gap between the two, and the ideal is more consciously held up as a basis upon which to *judge* the real." The Arabs, on the other hand, "confuse the two, professing to believe against reality that the ideal is carried out in conduct and is identical with practice. . . ." One modern manifestation of this tendency is the Arabs' love of adopting a plan which "can be a perfect thing, like a work of Arab calligraphic art," with "emphasis upon appearance and not meaning," and without considering their capacity to carry out such a plan. "There is also the feeling that one need not go beyond the plan, for the ideal picture is sufficient, and is in any case esthetically far more pleasing than the uncertainty and disorderliness of reality."[17]

It would seem to me that there is a psychological connection between the two phenomena discussed in the foregoing pages. The oscillation between controlled and uncontrolled behavior can be connected with the insufficiently strong hold that factual realities have on the Arab psyche. A psyche that has well internalized reality factors does not have to indulge in emotional outbursts which bear no relationship to reality, outbursts qualitatively akin to the "impotent rage" expressed in infantile temper tantrums. It will instead try to deal with the inevitable frustrations of life by rational and purposive reactions. Similarly, the gap between thought and speech, on the one hand, and action, on the other, can be seen as the result of the failure of reality to penetrate sufficiently. A person who entertains thoughts and makes utterances which cannot be translated into action indulges in a flight into a fantasy world for the sake of its emotional satisfaction. While this satisfaction is not as intense as that obtained from an emotional outburst, it is of longer duration and fulfills a basically similar function: both obliterate the objectionable world of reality, and allow the individual to live, for a shorter or longer spell, in a world that is the creation of his wishes.

All this, however, does not mean, as has been alleged by some Arab and Western scholars, that there is in the Arab mind a "confusion" between the ideal and the real.[18] Far from it. What the Arab mind does is to elect purposely to give greater weight in thought and speech to wishes rather than to reality, to what it would like things to be rather than to what they objectively are. I, for one, do not see that this indicates confusion. There is at least one area of life in which the Western world behaves in a very similar manner: that of religion. We purposely elect to give greater weight in our thought and speech to the workings of a deity, which is how we would like things to be, than to the objectively verifiable causality of human suffering. To an informed Buddhist or adherent of another non-theistic religion, we may appear to be "confusing" the ideal with the real. We are saved from a similar "confusion" between the ideal and the real in realms other than religion primarily because we have managed to relegate religion to one remote corner of our existence.

Arab cultural development has not divorced religion from other aspects of life. Therefore, it is to be expected that the Arab preference for thought —wishes, ideas, ideals, aspirations, and the like—over factual reality should not be confined to the area of religion, but should penetrate, together with religion, all other aspects of life. Far from representing a confusion between reality and ideality, this view considers ideality a major aspect of existence both in This World and in the Beyond, while reality, whose very existence is confined to This World, and even here to only one segment, is of relatively less significance.

The way we judge disregard of reality and adherence to the ideal depends to a great extent on our general impression of the person or group in whom we observe it. Many great historical figures have been admired for heroic determination in pursuing ideals, disregarding reality. On the other hand, if we speak of a person or people who have earned our disrespect, we are inclined to reproach him or them for being out of touch with reality.

We are as yet far from knowing the outcome of the historical course on which the Arabs have embarked since their independence from Western domination. The forces that propel them forward are many, but by and large they all fall into two categories: those that were set in motion by Westernization; and those that have existed in the Arab personality for many centuries but have gained a new scope since independence. The latter comprise the character traits discussed in this chapter: thinking and seeing in extremes; oscillation between controlled and uncontrolled behavior; divorce between thought and speech on the one hand and action on the other; inclination to prefer the ideal to the real. Each of these features can be viewed positively, with sympathy, or negatively, with condemnation. What is more important, each of them carries within it the seeds of fruitful growth as well as of decline and decay. Only future historians will be in a position to judge the way in which these seeds reach fruition.

XI

ART, MUSIC, AND LITERATURE

WE HAVE DISCUSSED THE ARABS' DISREGARD OF REALITY AND
inclination to adhere to ideal constructs. Now we will see the way in which
this tendency is expressed in the Arab visual arts, and how the salient
features that characterize Arab art occur also in music and in literature.

1. DECORATIVE ARTS

One of the fields in which the Arab neglect of reality in favor of the ideal
most strikingly expresses itself is in the decorative arts. Actually, the term
"decorative arts" when applied to Arab artistic endeavor is something of
a tautology, because all Arab visual art is decorative, never, or extremely
rarely, representational.[1] It is as if all reality appeared to the Islam-
dominated Arab mind as being of so ephemeral a nature that its representation in artistic form would needs be an exercise in futility. True, there is a
traditional Muslim prohibition of the representation in visual form of any
living being, and especially man. But had Arab artists deemed this type of
art worthy of their attention they would have blithely ignored this injunction, as their colleagues did in Turkey, Persia, and other non-Arab Muslim
countries. Wherever there was a special reason to disobey the *ḥadīths* which
warn against image-making,[2] they were disregarded with complete uncon-

167

cern, or at the utmost with some very superficial indication that the figure made or painted was not really intended to be a true representation of an animal or a human being. Thus in the Arab shadow theater or puppet shows, a few holes in the bodies of the figures were considered sufficient to pay formal respect to tradition.[3] Had it not been for their disdain of reality, Arab artists would undoubtedly have found a similar way to circumvent or ignore the tradition and would have created a great Arab representational art.

Speculation about what might have been aside, the fact is that Arab artists chose to express their creativity in the decorative field. Here the artist was free from what he must have perceived as the encumbrance of reality. His task was not to imitate a small portion of the ever-fleeting forms that surrounded him but, ignoring them, to give free play to his imagination and create forms and patterns which expressed nothing but an idea he had conceived in his mind, an ideal he wanted to become manifest, a concept which in its complexity, symmetry, and, yes, perfection was incomparably superior to anything found in nature. Such an ideal concept merited perpetuation in stone or tile or wood or metal or any other medium, to endure while the imperfect and ephemeral forms found in nature perished.

Another point in which the Arab artist went against nature was in his constant recourse to repetition of the units used to achieve his total artistic effect. In nature, while the combination of identical elements into a large pattern is not unknown (a flower can consist of a circularly arranged pattern of identical petals), the typical phenomenon is the existence of the most diverse shapes and parts side by side without any formal correlation or repetitious arrangement. The Arab artist saw in this another manifestation of the imperfection of physical nature and proceeded in a diametrically opposite way. He chose what did not exist in nature as the cornerstone of his art: the repetition of a relatively small, albeit complex, unit or motif, and its arrangement into a large decorative pattern according to certain geometric principles. Thus, a piece of Arab decorative art has two separate but intertwined aspects: as you approach it, it first impresses you with the total arrangement, which gives you the feeling of an organized whole; when you look closer, you become aware of the basic unit or units of which this whole is made up, and you are drawn almost magnetically to immerse yourself in the interplay between identical parts, between variant parts, and between the parts and the whole.[4]

Having foresworn the use of the animal and human figure even as a decorative motif, Arab art was left with only three elements on which to build its infinite constructs: the plant motif, the geometric motif, and the Arabic script. Among plant motifs, the vine tendril was the dominant element, used in many variations including wave, spiral, and loop forms. The forked-leaf vine tendril was the original "Arabesque," although many students of Muslim art use this term to designate a large number of other Islamic decorative motifs as well. As if dissatisfied with the "natural" origin of the plant motif, in medieval Arab art stylization was soon carried to a point of almost total abstraction: all similarity to actual plants was eliminated, to be replaced by geometric forms.

In the utilization of geometric motifs, Arab decorative artists reached the height of their accomplishment. Starting out with a number of basic geometric forms—the circle, the square, various polygons, and a few simple patterns such as the swastika, the meander, the checkerboard, and the zigzag—they reached such heights of complexity and richness, and developed such ever-varying designs based on abstract principles, that one is filled with admiration for their extraordinary achievement in artistic creativity within the rigid framework of logical geometric patterning.

Perhaps even more remarkable is the artistic use to which the Arabic script was put. The Arabic alphabet itself betrays something of the artistic skill expressed in the utilization of a few basic design elements for the requirements of a language built on quite a large number of phonemes. Arabic script uses no more than twelve basic signs (ا, ـﺤ, ح, د, ر, ص, ﻛ, ع, ﻚ, ر, ﻻ) for twenty-eight consonants, and manages to accomplish this feat of graphic economy by the use of combinations of two of the signs (س, ﻃ, ل) and of so-called diacritical points (ﺐ, ﺖ, ﺚ, ﻦ, ﻲ, ﺝ, ﺡ, ﺥ, د, ﺬ, ر, ز, ﺲ, ﺶ, ص, ﺾ, ﻃ, ﻇ, ع, ﻍ, ﻑ, ﻕ). Each of the several script styles (the angular and massive Kufic script, the round and readily changeable Nakshi style) was used in many variations and in varying degrees of further stylization, as a decorative device, especially in the form of horizontal bands in architecture to frame doors, to serve as a frieze around the top of walls or on the base of domes; or for the decoration of all kinds of objects such as vases, bowls, and so on. The texts used for these decorative inscriptions are in most cases verses from the Koran; to my taste at least, the most beautiful examples are those executed on tiles, with the white characters set off against a blue background. In contrast to a geometrically designed frieze with its regularly repeated pattern units, the script-frieze, because it reproduces actual Arabic sentences, has no such recurrences at fixed intervals but presents the few basic characters of the Arabic script in a constantly varying pattern of repetition. The pattern nevertheless has its inner rhythm, in contrast to the outer rhythm of the geometric pattern, and is not altogether unexpected to those who contemplate it and who are familiar with the Koranic verse it presents. The seemingly endless horizontal chain constituted by most characters of the Arabic alphabet is interrupted, again rhythmically but at indefinite intervals, by the letters ﺍ, ﻁ, ﻅ, ﻙ, ﻝ whose vertical strokes are emphatically elongated, and by the ﺭ, ﺯ, and ﻭ whose dip beneath the line is also given special stress.

In all this, the Arab artist achieved a triumph of thought, idea, and imagination over the mundane reality of form observable in nature. He created a great artistic tradition which was, and remained, completely divorced from nature and which was purely the product of the mind, of the artistic fiat. And since the Arab artist worked and lived within a religious context, and the prime purpose of his endeavor was to provide an esthetic embellishment and enrichment for the channels through which the Muslim sought to approach God, no wonder that the artistic creativity was considered not only a service to man and God, but an *imitatio dei* on a small and modest scale, a work like that of God's not copying nature which God created, but using the God-given thought, the idea, to create something out of nothing.

2. MUSIC

Arab decorative art shares a number of its characteristics with other Arab artistic endeavors. The repetition of the same small-sized element in an unchanged form or with minor variations which is a part of the Arabs' decorative art is also found in their music. A typical Arab musical piece will begin with one or more instruments playing a brief melodic line, then repeating it several times with or without variation; then the vocalist takes over and does the same; after him, it is again the instruments' turn; then again the vocalist; and so on several times until the conclusion. This is the heritage of the Arab folk song, which consists of one solitary phrase that is repeated with each verse or even each hemistich. This structure is, of course, reminiscent of the structure of an ornamental frieze; it comprises a long sequence of one, two, or perhaps three, motifs, alternating, but without change in either the rhythm or the amount of emphasis, without reaching a point of culmination or a dramatic turn, and without the coda which so typically brings the Western musical piece to a formal close at a point well signaled in advance. Just as the decorative frieze has no beginning and no end, but simply starts and ends according to the space to which it is applied, so the Arab musical frieze fills the available stretch of time and is characterized throughout by the same level of emotion sustained unchanged from beginning to end.

The Arab's disregard of time, his refusal to let his life be structured and cut up by the tyranny of the clock, finds creative expression in the traditional world of Arab music. Jacques Berque has remarked that the Arab musician, while playing at a concert, may feel himself possessed,

> step aside from the orchestra, and improvise for an hour or even two. It was thus, they say, that the future star 'Abd al-Wahhāb first shone in an orchestra at Tanta, some twenty or twenty-five years ago; he began to improvise, to modulate in that manner which disconcerts the Western listener but which brought the singer his fame.[5]

Music is, of course, as far removed from the world of physical reality in which we live as an art form conceivably can be. Except where he uses folk tunes and bases his composition upon them, or relies on some other source, the melody is the pure creation of the composer's mind. It is, as some philosophers of art have pointed out, the most mysterious process of artistic creativity because it has absolutely no point of departure in observable nature.

The creative process of the Arab composer is not as different from the creative activity of the visual artist as it is in the West. Arab decorative artists, especially if they utilized geometric patterns, could nowhere in nature observe anything that would give them a basis for the development of, say, a new design of interlacing bands and polygonal star configurations; they had neither kaleidoscopes nor microscopes to observe the forms of snowflakes. All they had were the works of artists who preceded them, whom they studied, and upon whom they tried to improve. The Arab composer worked within a very similar frame of reference. Probably, even if it had been possible to reproduce natural sounds musically, he would have refused, like his colleague in the decorative arts, to "copy" nature, which was ephemeral, imperfect. The new melody he wanted to compose had to be the creation of his own imagination. Where he did go for both inspiration and raw material was—in analogy to the work of earlier decorative artists

—to the musical heritage of his culture. This musical heritage was as highly formalized as the tradition of geometric patterns, and much more minutely organized, classified, and categorized. To understand its nature, a few words must be said about the characteristics of Arab music in comparison with the music of the West.

To begin with, the tonal raw materials used in the two musical traditions are utterly different. The tonal material of Western music is the tempered system of equal semitones, twelve of which make up an octave. Arab music is not tempered, and is based on quarter-tones, twenty-four of which constitute an octave. This means that Arab music has a richer and finer raw material at its disposal than Western music. Because Arab music is built on quarter-tones, it impresses the Western listener as being plaintive and sensuous, while Western music creates the impression on the Arab listener of being crude and rough (since it inevitably jumps in its melodic line notes that would be utilized by an Arab composer), as well as loud and confusing (because what Western music considers as harmony is regarded in Arab musical tradition as dissonance). In the course of the centuries the Arab tonal scale has undergone gradual changes, but since the eighteenth century the most generally accepted Arab scale divides the octave into twenty-four equal parts of fifty "cents" each.[6] This means that each octave in Arab music contains twice as many notes as the European octave, and that the difference in pitch or interval between any two neighboring notes in the Arab scale is a quarter-tone.

Secondly, while in Western music there are only two modes—major and minor—Arab music in its entirety is modal and possesses dozens of modes (called ṭibaʿ, nature; naghamāt, notes; or maqāmāt, places).[7] The compass of an Arab mode may be as few as five notes, or as many as ten. Basically, the modes consist of scales differing in their series of intervals, in which the fixed element is the sequence of tones of varying pitches.

> Each mode gives birth to fixed "motives," and this latter is the most interesting phase of the Arabian modal system, because these "motives" are traditional. Many of them carry in their structure the clear features of folk origin. . . . It is this folk element in Arabian music that makes its appeal universal. . . .[8]

On the other hand, the fact that all Arab music is modal means that the composition of a new piece of music must be executed within the narrow frame represented by the particular mode the composer chooses for his opus.

Thirdly, Arab music is homophonic, that is to say, the modal melody is carried purely in unison; usually a single voice carries the melody or, at the utmost, two tonal sources present the same melody at a distance of an octave. This contrasts sharply with Western music, which is polyphonic and combines a number of individual harmonizing melodies. As the Israeli musicologist Edith Gerson-Kiwi put it, in Arab music

> the elements of harmony and counterpoint are not known . . . and the whole of the creative forces concentrate around the evolution of melody and rhythm. Melody in Oriental practice, especially in singing . . . is not "composed" of single clear-cut notes, but proceeds in larger entities, tone-groups or tone-movements which are interwoven with intrinsic ornaments—leading to a somewhat spiral like procession. These ornaments are not additional as in European music, where they may or may not be observed, but constitute the very body of the music itself.[9]

These ornaments, or "gloss," as they have been termed, represent the fourth characteristic of Arab music. They are of supreme importance in it, are improvisations (as indicated above), and correspond in the musical field to the Arabesque and other decorative ornamental patterns in Arab architecture and visual art in general, to the filigree work in the gold and silver decorative objects, and to the colorful embroidered patterns on pieces of clothing. In all these visual art forms the same general patterns are reproduced again and again, but each time with some slight individual variation which is equally important for the artist-craftsman and the connoisseur. In music, no performing artist reproduces a musical composition in exactly the same fashion as he has heard it performed by the master under whom he studied and from whom he learned it; he must add his own ornamental improvisations, which is the way he demonstrates his own virtuosity.

Fifthly, Arab rhythm is different from traditional Western rhythm. Without becoming too technical, all we can say on this aspect of the difference between Arab and Western music is that for the Western-trained ear it is as difficult to respond to the Arab rhythms as it is to enjoy the Arab melodies built on quarter-tones. There are in Arab music eight rhythmic modes, each of which comprises several species.[10] To these difficulties can be added the specific traditional Arab musical instruments, which produce tone qualities that sound strange and often unesthetic to the Western ear. However, it should be stated emphatically that we cannot and must not judge Arab music by Western standards. It has its own standards and only after having thoroughly familiarized oneself with them—which for an outsider is an extremely difficult and lengthy process—can one judge the quality of Arab music, let alone enjoy it.

The question inevitably arises, What is the place and role of originality in Arab music? If it is based on fixed modes or motives, it could be (and, indeed, has been) argued that there can be no place in it for originality. This argument can be answered on two levels. One is that, given the purely homophonic nature of Arab music, it allows of a set melodic progression by means of fixed motives, which is "no different in unoriginality from the stereotyped sequences of Occidental harmonic music. . . . With a scale which furnished a wider selection of notes and modalities, the Arab *virtuosi* were able to furnish more subtle moods for their auditors. . . . "[11] As to the performer, he is, in fact, allowed and even required to evince a much greater degree of "originality" than his Western colleague. The Arab musical performer (as mentioned above) is expected to produce improvised modulations and it is by the quality of these that his virtuosity is judged.

While technically the Arab musician thus has considerable leeway for originality within the framework of the traditional modes, there is quite a different ideational, or, more precisely, teleological, consideration in approaching the question of originality in Arab music. For, despite the richness of the Arab musical modes and rhythms, the composer working in the traditional idiom could introduce only relatively minor innovations in a composition of his own. He had to prove his mettle within one of the modes which he thought would best suit the musical idea he wanted to express, and this in practice meant that he had to work within the rather narrow confines of a fixed sequence of tones. Therefore, the main objective of the Arab composer is not originality (what his Western colleague strives for), but rather a significant refinement or improvement on the existing melodies within the modal framework—just as the decorative artist working in a geometric "mode" does not strive for originality but likewise for refinement, improvement, and perhaps an additional elaboration.

3. LITERATURE

Only a few words can be added here to show that the traits characterizing Arab visual arts and music can be found in Arabic literature as well. We have found that both the visual and musical expressions of the Arab artistic inclination are characterized by small units used as basic building blocks; in both, the whole work of art contains a seemingly endless repetition of one, or occasionally two, elemental units. Moreover, just as time is an undifferentiated continuum for the traditional Arab mind, so in his works of art the Arab does not strive for a crescendo which reaches a culmination, after which the creative surge diminishes and subsides, but finds his satisfaction in repetition, with minor modulations filling equally and evenly a physical space or time span. Occasionally—especially in the largest-scale works of art ever produced by Arabs, their architectural masterpieces—the single units which are repeated again and again to combine into an overwhelming whole can be quite complex in themselves; but the principle of many identical or almost identical units making up the whole is adhered to unfailingly.

A very similar set of features characterizes Arab literary expression, as has been noted by both Western students of Arabic literature and those Arab critics whose familiarity with Western literary forms has sensitized them to the phenomena. Among the former, Sir Hamilton A. R. Gibb expressed the observation succinctly when he stated that the Arabs' "physical environment has moulded their habits, thought, and speech, impressing on them those repetitions and abrupt transitions which are reproduced in nearly all aspects of Arab life and literature."[12]

With repetitiousness goes standardization. The early Arabic *qasīda*, or complex ode, for example, whose "final object . . . is self-praise, eulogy of the poet's tribe, satire directed at rival groups or individuals, or panegyric of a patron" starts with a conventional opening theme, technically called *nasīb*, in which

> The poet is supposed to be travelling on a camel with one or two companions. The road leads him to the site of a former encampment of his own or a friendly tribe, the remains of which are still visible. He beseeches his companions to halt for a moment, and sorrowfully recalls how, many years ago, he spent here the happiest days of his life with his beloved. Now life with its constant wanderings has separated them, and over the deserted scene roams the wild antelope.[13]

Fourteen centuries after these early *qasīdas,* the poets of the Bedouin tribes still compose poems which are still called *qasāyed* (sing. *qasīde*), and many of these still begin with a description of the deserted camping grounds of the poet's former beloved.[14] Since the tribal poets are still illiterate, no definite version of their poems is available in a written form. When a poet composes a poem, his friends learn it by heart, and then others learn it from them. This method of oral transmission has two consequences; one is that each poem, or each couplet in a poem, is known in different versions; those who recite them change the wording of the verses, or even substitute new verses for the original ones. This procedure, of course, is quite similar to that of the musical performer who changes the original form of a musical composition by introducing into it variations of his own. The second consequence of oral transmission is that poems, and especially long ones, are not recited by different people in exactly the same order as far as the verses are concerned.[15] Such variations in verse order are, of course, only possible because there is no logical connection between one verse and the next, or procession from the one to the other, but each verse or couplet is an independent unit which expresses a separate thought; couplets can be arranged in many different orders. Here again we have an analogy between the structure of poems and that of musical pieces or elements in an overall decorative pattern.

The same phenomenon was observed by Professor Elie Salem, a foremost Arab literary critic, who has remarked of Arabic prose literature that "thought comes to the Arab in flashes . . . not in an unfolding, exhaustive, and full rational order," and that even in Arabic books dealing with political history there is little or no relationship between successive paragraphs.[16] Each paragraph here corresponds to the basic unit in decorative art and in music. The effect of the whole is based on the serial presentation of one piece after another. As to repetitiousness, without which neither Arab visual art nor Arab music can be imagined, its presence in Arabic verbal expression, whether oral or written, is too well known to need documentation.

Yet another similarity between the Arab visual and vocal arts and Arabic literary expression is that in both the major aim is not originality but the restatement of a well-established theme, preferably with some elaboration and refinement. One only has to read the medieval Arab authors to see that this trait is part of an old Arab literary tradition; and one only has to read modern Arab authors to observe to what extent repetition of what others have already said, and of what the writer himself has already said in an earlier part of his book, are common.

4. TOWARD WESTERN FORMS

Westernization is inexorably spreading in the Arab world. This means that the days of the old Arab artistic and musical tradition are numbered. Young Arab art students learn Western art forms in academies of fine arts such as the one in Cairo, founded as early as 1908, and aspiring Arab musicians study in Western-style musical academies. Both types of institutions teach Western forms, Western standards, Western techniques, and Western artistic trends. Most teachers at these schools consider the traditional arts and music backward and primitive, and instill into their students a hostility toward them, and contempt. Add to this the impact of Western magazines, books, films, radio, and television programs, exhibitions of the works of Western artists, and concerts given by Western musicians and orchestras, and you have an atmosphere suffused with the simplistic dichotomy which holds that Western art and music equals good, while traditional Arab art and music equals bad. This, in turn, leads to a total estrangement in these important aspects of culture between the tradition-bound rural majority of every Arab country and the Westernizing urban upper and middle classes. The upper and middle classes neglect native artistic traditions. As a result, native arts and crafts have generally declined. Deprived of their richest and most discriminating customers, the traditional craftsmen-artists no longer had the incentive to bend their best efforts in the execution of a piece of work. There followed a vulgarization and deterioration of the traditional skills, thus seemingly justifying the contempt for the traditional product entertained by the Westernized élite. The vital cultural arteries running between the top and the bottom of the social pyramid were severed.

Many music-loving Arabs who have had a European education despise traditional Arab music. The young Westernizing generation is captivated by jazz. In the Egyptian review al-Majalla, the Egyptian music critic Dr. Fū'ad Zakarīyā "writes despairingly of Arab music, judging it inferior to Western music as regards composition, performance and audience," and comes to the conclusion that "we need a new generation of musicians."[17] Dr. Ḥusayn Fawzī, a physician, oceanographer, and musicologist, goes so far as to see in Western music the substance of a universal humanism, while denouncing the traditional music of his own country as nothing but a "titillation of feeling."[18] A survey of listeners to the Cairo radio showed that almost all the cultured class ("muthaqqafīn") approved of Western classical music.[19] Similarly, most musicians and music critics incline toward Westernism. Some, like Rajā' al-Naqqāsh, see in the inferiority of traditional Arab music an expression of the sickness of which the Arab people suffer in general. Only general progress in all spheres can eliminate the "underdevelopment" in the musical realm. Others, like a young Alexandrian journalist, find that "Eastern [i.e., Arab] music is nothing but languor, the lowest form of sexuality. Western music describes, represents, makes reference to intellectual movements and schools. Many critics feel that while "everywhere else music had developed . . . with us it has remained stationary." Nevertheless, there is also an increasing interest in the traditional source of Arab folk music, as demonstrated by the efforts to make recordings of the work songs that accompany all or most activities in the rural areas, and even such songs and drumbeats as are used in exorcising ceremonies.[20] There can be little doubt, however, that this endeavor to record and save Arab folk music and to use its melodies as a basis for musical compositions is in itself a Western-inspired development.

In the visual arts, the impact of the West wrought a much more revolutionary change than in music. For one thing, entering in the field of sculpture meant for the Arab artist entering a completely new realm which had simply not existed in his artistic traditions. And even in painting, the very use of canvas and oils was something quite new. To these must be added the basic tension between art as decoration and art as representation; between art that was always a part of something else—a building, a piece of furniture, a book, a utensil, a piece of clothing—and art that is produced independently, solely for its own sake. The Westernized Arab painter and sculptor thus cannot find any roots in his own cultural tradition, and has no choice but to relate his work to Western traditions, with which he must first become well acquainted.

Under these circumstances, it is small wonder that the work of the first- and even second-generation modern Arab painters and sculptors was derivative, and in many cases nothing more than imitative. Within these limitations, every major Western school of art soon had its followers in the capitals of the more "advanced" Arab countries, in Baghdad, Damascus, Beirut, Cairo, and Alexandria, and in the lands of the North African Maghrib. The task of absorbing simultaneously all schools which the West itself had developed in the course of two centuries or more was not an easy one, and often proved confusing for the Arab artist. Interestingly, abstract art, which on the surface would seem to have more in common with traditional Arab geometric decorative art than any other Western school, has attracted relatively few Arab artists and has so far failed to stimulate them to the production of anything truly original or important. In traditional Arab art, originality in its full Western sense of creating something entirely new, without precedent or antecedent in past artistic development, simply did not exist. If the term "derivative" had been used in traditional

Arab art criticism, it would have been an accolade, an expression of the highest praise. But the artists are no longer working with these values. In adopting a Western art style, we now understand, the Arab artist is forced to adopt, among other things, criteria of good and bad which are the direct opposites of what traditional Arab connoisseurship has taught him or his predecessors. He must unlearn the old values, and accept new and contrary values in their stead. To be pronounced derivative has suddenly become a criticism of the strongest opprobrium; to be recognized as original, the greatest compliment.

XII

BILINGUALISM, MARGINALITY AND AMBIVALENCE

PROBLEMS OF MARGINALITY AND AMBIVALENCE BESET THE educated minority in the Arab world. Bilingualism and cultural marginality usually go hand in hand, and frequently give rise to an ambivalent attitude to both European language and culture and the traditional Arabic language and culture. While all three —bilingualism, marginality, and ambivalence —are confined to the educated classes, which are still relatively small in the Arab countries, their effect extends far and cannot fail to have an impact upon the rest of the population.

1. BILINGUALISM AND PERSONALITY

Alienation from the culture of their native land has been common among educated people outside Western Europe in certain periods of their history. Side by side with this alienation there developed a fascination with—even an immersion in—one of the Western cultures. In the seventeenth, eighteenth, and nineteenth centuries, French was the language spoken by the élite in many countries lying to the east of France, even as far off as Russia. In the nineteenth century, German assumed a similar, albeit more limited, role in Central Europe. With the French language went French culture, French furniture, French clothes, French manners; and often an actual or feigned ignorance of the language of one's own country, and a contempt for it and for the culture of which it was the medium.

By the twentieth century, this phenomenon was a thing of the past as far as Europe was concerned. The prestigious French or German had everywhere been replaced by the national language, which had come into its own partly because of developing nationalistic sentiments and partly because of the emergence of a native literature and press. But in the last third of the twentieth century, this emancipation from a foreign tongue has not yet taken place in the Arab world.

There is a peculiar, almost pathetic, element in the dependence of the educated on a foreign language in several Arab countries, especially North Africa and Lebanon. Educated Arabs share admiration and love for Arabic with their unlettered countrymen. In fact, appreciation of the beauty, the esthetic value, and all the other exquisite qualities of Arabic is greater among the educated Arabs, if for no other reason, then simply because one must be literate and familiar with the treasures of Arabic literature and poetry in order to appreciate fully their richness. And yet it is precisely many of the educated Arabs who display the same attitude toward Arabic as the Russian noblemen did toward Russian in the eighteenth century. The language which lures most of these Arabs is the same as the one which earlier lured the Central and East European nobility: French. There is one important difference, however. The eighteenth-century East European élite had assimilated to French culture wholeheartedly. For them the French language was, apart from its value as a mark of education, the key to the French way of life. Polish, or Russian, nationalism was as yet unknown.

In the Arab countries in which French plays a similar role, today nationalism is a potent force, embraced in particular by that educated class which considers French superior to Arabic, whose members know French better than Arabic and in some cases know no Arabic at all, or almost none. Moreover, these French-speaking educated Arabs are usually strongly anti-French, and anti-Western in general, in political orientation and sentiments. In fact, especially in North Africa there is almost a direct correlation between the degree of cultural and linguistic assimilation to the West and the intensity of anti-Western feelings. The massive majority of the population has no acquaintance at all with the West, it does not know what Western culture is, speaks no Western language, and has no anti-Western feelings, apart from the vague antipathy that most conservative Muslims have against non-believers. This majority constitutes one end of the spectrum; at the other end we find the Westernized élite, which has learned to designate itself by the French term *"évolué"* (i.e., a person who has "evolved" from a lower state of existence to a higher one by adopting the French language and way of life). From this group came most leaders of the anti-French revolt in North Africa after World War II.

The psychological toll taken by such an ambivalence can easily be imagined. Few situations are more devastating to the integrity of the personality than to be a hanger-on in an alien culture, while at the same time hating the very people who are its creators, carriers, and undisputed masters. Yet this exactly is the situation in which many educated Arabs find themselves.

Their linguistic dependence on the West is both a result and an expression of the cultural dependence that developed in the period in which most Arab countries were controlled by France or England. The three former French territories in North Africa were subject to the full impact of the French colonial policy of educating native élites to speak and think like Frenchmen. After achieving independence, the Arab countries of Morocco, Tunisia, and Algeria experienced a nationalistic upsurge. One manifestation of this was the elimination of French as a language of instruction in the schools and the substitution of Arabic. But before long the impracticability of this changeover became evident, and bilingual—French-Arab—instruction was restored. The story of the language problem in Morocco, Algeria, and Tunisia since independence is a long and intricate one, and it had many local variations. But all revolve around the same basic theme: willy-nilly, French has remained to this day the language of modernity; it is used most widely in the administrative apparatus of the three countries, in their universities, and by most writers.[1]

More than that. In Tunisia, according to the bilingual system of national education adopted in 1958, instruction began in Arabic in the first and second grades of elementary school. In the third grade, French was introduced and gradually received more and more emphasis at the expense of Arabic. As a result of this system, the more education a Tunisian received, the more he veered toward French. What was most remarkable in this connection was that the French language became more popular in Tunisia after independence that it had been before. As a result in 1969 the teaching of French was introduced in the first year of elementary school. Nevertheless, the Tunisians regard Arabic as their national language, and as the vehicle of Tunisian nationalism; because of this, "most Tunisians . . . make it a point of honor to learn at least a few phrases [in Arabic]."[2] No observation could more clearly show the linguistic alienation of the educated Tunisian from his Arabic matrix than this statement. Responsible political leaders in Tunisia have, since the 1960's, felt that it is their duty to make efforts for the spread of Arabic among the country's élite and in administration; but at the same time they have given due recognition to the importance of French as a medium of communication with the world at large.[3]

The ruling Socialist Destourian Party of Tunisia, which publishes a French language newspaper, *L'Action,* has argued in it that "the French language makes it possible for Tunisia to maintain the rhythm of its progress by separating it to some extent from the more traditional Arabic speaking world." As against these views, some Tunisian deputies strongly advocate the total elimination of French from the educational system and the administration, because they consider the presence of French as a vestige of colonialism, and because they feel that Arabization is required to infuse Tunisian youth with a sense of national identity.[4]

Neighboring Algeria is faced with the same problem and manifests similar attitudes. After independence (1962), there was at first a general determination to eliminate French as rapidly as possible. By the mid-1960's, however, this position was modified and the necessity of retaining French as the channel of modernization was recognized. Consequently, here too a bilingual educational system was introduced, relying increasingly on French as the pupils advanced into the higher grades. By 1971, more than 2 million Algerian students were learning French, a figure never even remotely approached during the period when Algeria was an integral part of France. At the same time, as in Tunisia, many members of the Algerian educated class, who themselves speak better French than Arabic, condemn the alienating effects of French. The undeniable fact is that there is a widening cultural dichotomy—created primarily by the use of the two languages—between the French-speaking élite and the Arabic-speaking masses.

To what extent the Francification of the Algerian bureaucracy had already advanced can be gauged from the new rule introduced in 1971, decreeing that government officials and employees of state institutions must "pass an examination demonstrating a minimum level of competence in Arabic in order to be eligible for promotion."[5] If one did not know that Arabic is the native language of Algeria, one would conclude from this newly introduced regulation that the government insists that its employees should master a foreign tongue in addition to their own.

In Morocco, also, the initial post-independence commitment to Arabization gave way to a bilingual approach. In 1966, the Moroccan Minister of Education declared that Arabization had reached an impasse due to a shortage of qualified Arabic instructors at the intermediate and secondary level, and a slowing down of Arabization was decreed. This step was strongly opposed by the Istiqlal Party and the Union Marocaine de Travail (UMT), the largest Moroccan labor union; but it received strong support from Prime Minister Ahmad Laraki and the Minister of Administrative Affairs as late as in 1970.[6]

There are indications that cultural alienation develops on the village level as well as as a result of the bilingual instruction in elementary schools. This was clearly established by a survey conducted in the Tunisian village of Tadjerouine. The spoken language in the village is, of course, dialectal or colloquial Arabic, an idiom very different from the classical or literary Arabic taught at school. In addition to being taught in the classroom, French also penetrates the home through radio and television, and is used in the regular film showings. As a result of these influences, parents understand that a knowledge of French is essential for a good job.[7]

In the village school, during the first two years the children receive only fifteen hours of instruction weekly, all in Arabic. From the third grade on, the total number of hours is increased to twenty-five, of which, however, only ten are in Arabic while fifteen are in French. After the fifth or sixth grade, the students learn little Arabic. Testing of reading comprehension of sixth graders (most rural students do not go past the primary level) suggests that about one-third can understand the Arabic newspaper, and that their probability of retaining this skill is about 0.5.

Knowledge of French is "a major key to the doors of higher education, social prestige, and political responsibility." Those who do not do well in French are thereby relegated to second-class status. In secondary school, success depends more on French achievement than on Arabic, "at least in the minds of the students if not in the actual weight given to the grades in the several subjects. And as a corollary of this, further higher education and more prestigious jobs depend more on French ability than Arabic." In the academic secondary school, students who did not gain proficiency in French soon dropped out.[8]

The survey showed a number of significant differences between the students who did well in French and those who did not. Those who did well (and they were in the minority) tended not to participate in organizational and club activities. They did not like their schoolmates. Unlike most of their classmates, they denied that they were influenced by their fathers. The less the influence of their siblings on them, the better was their French score. Therefore, "the greater the alienation that a boy feels, the better he will score on French reading and comprehension tests." To this must be added that the higher the socio-economic status level of the student's family, the higher his French achievement. All of which adds up to suggest that the French achievers are deviant members of their communities. The village community itself is "culturally split, and schooling deepens the split."[9]

This situation has further serious consequences. One can assume that the best rural French achievers go on to secondary school and possibly to college, and eventually rise into the urban élite. If this is the case, the urban élite is being replenished by precisely those village boys who felt alienated in their childhood from their village environment, an experience which may supply one of the root factors to "the snobbism of the urban élite toward the rural folk."[10] Thus, a dichotomy that was originally introduced into the village by the urban policymakers contributes in turn to the deepening of the cultural distance between the urban élite and the rural masses.

A second type of bilingualism is also found in all parts of the Arab world and, like the Arabic-French or Arabic-English bilingualism, it has weighty psychological consequences. This is the bilingualism represented by the presence side by side, in every Arab country, of literary Arabic and local colloquial dialects.

Literary Arabic is the language in which books, newspapers, and magazines are written, the language which educated people try to employ in delivering speeches and lectures, and which is used in serious plays and films, as well as in most of the radio and television news broadcasts. This language is one and the same in all parts of the Arab world, although some variations are present in it, for example, between the Syrian and the Egyptian pronunciation. The Koran forms the basis of literary Arabic, as far as grammar is concerned. The vocabulary of the Koran also exists in unchanged form in modern literary Arabic, which, however, employs a much richer vocabulary developed in the course of the centuries. Thanks to the use of literary Arabic, a book or newspaper published in any part of the Arab world can be read and understood in all other parts of the Arab world with the same ease as if it had been produced locally.

However, and here is the rub, literary Arabic can be understood only by those who have studied it or acquired a knowledge of it through repeated and prolonged exposure. The unschooled, who form the majority in most Arab countries,[11] speak a local, colloquial dialect which is so different from literary Arabic as to make it appear almost a foreign language. Needless to say, these dialects also differ from one another to such a degree that those spoken in two remote countries are mutually unintelligible. Differences between the literary language and the dialects, and between one dialect and another, occur both in vocabulary and in greatly disparate pronunciations of the same words.

Uneducated people may be unable to understand news broadcasts emanating from the capital of the country in which they live, or can understand them only partially. Since they cannot read or write, they are not bothered by the problem of being unable to understand the literary Arabic of the newspapers. They have their own language, which is adequate for all their needs and which is the only tongue they know, apart from a few verses from the Koran which are in literary Arabic, and which make them aware of the existence of a literary language that is greatly different from their own idiom. They therefore know nothing of the technical problems of bilinguality.

Educated Arabs, on the other hand, live throughout their adult lives in two language-worlds. One is the world of their own families and of childhood friends, the world represented by workers, shopkeepers, and the majority of the population. With these people the educated Arab will speak in the colloquial dialect which is the only one they know and which was the only one he himself knew in his childhood. This is the language in which he can express himself with ease and which he would use in situations of emotional stress.

The other is the literary Arabic which he had acquired with no small effort in the course of his later school years. Even among the educated Arabs, the knowledge of the literary language is primarily a passive one. They know it well enough to understand it, enjoy it, come under its magnetic influence; but they do not know it well enough to speak it with any degree of fluency, let alone eloquence, or with a faultless observance of all its intricate grammatical, syntactical, and stylistic rules. Nevertheless, they are constantly aware of the existence of literary Arabic, and proud of whatever proficiency they have attained in it: and they have the feeling, whenever they use colloquial Arabic, that they, as it were, are slumming. On the other hand, when those who can use the literary language actively, in speaking, do so, they cannot get rid of the feeling that they are resorting to a language which is something artificial. The young actor who on stage declares, in literary Arabic, "I love you," uses words and forms very different from the words he would use off-stage when actually declaring his love.

To make matters more complicated, many educated Arabs find it too difficult to maintain the mental effort needed to use literary Arabic for any length of time. Actually, the only occasion when oral literary Arabic is used exclusively over a period of time is when a person reads aloud. In extemporaneous speaking, various dialectal features are usually mixed in. Moreover, speakers tend to pass from literary to dialectal Arabic and back, as they proceed from one sentence to the next: the two are even mixed within a single sentence. The public speeches of President Nasser were well-known examples of this intermingling. One of his speeches that has been analyzed from this point of view began in standard classical; after the first three sentences, it switched to colloquial; then it went on in a sort of modified classical, then back to standard classical, then again back to colloquial, and so on throughout the speech.[12]

Quite frequently in conversation one party uses classical Arabic while the other answers in colloquial, as was observed in the course of the trial of Fāḍil al-Jamālī in August, 1958, in Baghdad.[13] Such exchanges can, of course, take place only between people who know classical Arabic. Otherwise a situation can develop like the one described in the anecdote I heard many years ago from a clerk in a British Mandatory district court of Palestine. A Bedouin was hauled before the judge of the court, who addressed him sternly in literary Arabic: "You are accused of having stolen ten goats. Do you plead guilty or not guilty?" Whereupon the Bedouin answered in his own dialect: "O judge, don't talk to me English, I only know Arabic." The clerk was not sure whether the judge had understood the Arabic dialect of the Bedouin.

The psychological problem represented by the existence side by side of the literary and colloquial varieties of Arabic is a different one for the uneducated masses and the literate, educated élite. The former, although they may know practically no literary Arabic at all, in most cases have a knowledge of the existence of a literary, classical version of Arabic which, however, they are unable to speak. They also know that literary Arabic is superior to the colloquial Arabic they speak. The Arabic term for literary Arabic is "*naḥwī,*" "grammatically correct," or "*fuṣḥā,*" "beautiful and clear," or "*lughat al-muta'allimīn,*" "the language of the educated." A dialectal Arabic colloquial is called *"basiṭa,"* "common" [i.e., language]. These terms, which are known to the uneducated as well, imply value judgments: a derogation of dialectal Arabic and a recognition of the higher value of classical or literary Arabic. This means that the uneducated Arab, who is unable to "speak correctly," must consider himself, on this count as well as several others, inferior to the educated Arab who, as a rule, is a city dweller and, even more important, a person *not* making a living by manual labor.

The educated élite, too, is saddled with psychological problems resulting from the two Arabic tongues. A member of the élite knows, of course, that literary Arabic is superior to dialectal Arabic, and is convinced that, by dint of having acquired a knowledge of it, he is superior to 90 per cent of the population of his country. This conviction reinforces his consciousness of being part of the élite, and strengthens his feeling that his country owes him a living without obliging him to dirty his hands with physical labor. At the same time, he must admit to himself that, despite his many years' studies of literary Arabic, he still feels more at home in the "common" colloquial which was his mother tongue, and which he still uses much more frequently than the "beautiful" or "clear" language of the educated, when talking to his wife, children, and close friends. This factor implants in him a seed of doubt as to his own superiority.

Since most Arabs who have received a thorough grounding in literary Arabic also have acquired at least a smattering of a European language, they are beset, in addition, with the problems of Arabic-Western bilingualism which were discussed earlier. Thus, whatever feelings of superiority they may have *vis-á-vis* their own illiterate countrymen are more than nullified by the feelings of inferiority they often acquire when they are forced to recognize that they have, after all, managed to acquire only a marginal mastery of one of the great languages, and only a peripheral participation in one of the great cultures, of the West.

2. MARGINALITY

"Marginality" denotes the state of belonging to two cultures without being able to identify oneself completely with either.[14]

An individual becomes "marginal" if, after having been born into a culture and enculturated into it in a more or less normal fashion, he becomes exposed to another culture, is attracted to it, acquires a measure of familiarity with it (including its language), and strives to become a full-fledged carrier of it—an endeavor which, in most cases, never completely succeeds. The marginal man suffers from his inability to feel completely at ease or "at home" in either culture, although exceptional individuals may acquire a broader horizon and become more immune to ethnocentrism.

The problem of marginality is undoubtedly most acute in the three North African Arab countries of Morocco, Algeria, and Tunisia. It is present to a similar extent in Lebanon, and to a lesser extent in Syria and Egypt. These six countries are inhabited by some 77,000,000 people, almost two-thirds of the total population of all Arab countries.

All the six Arab countries in which the problem is present were under French control, the length of which varied from the brief three-year period of the military occupation of Egypt by Napoleon's forces in 1798 to 1801 to the 132 years of colonial rule over Algeria from 1830 to 1962. Throughout, French policy was to make it as desirable as possible for members of the élite to acquire the French language and the French way of life. The French pursued this policy with relentless consistency, even in places and at times where they were not actually in control, as long as local governments enabled them to continue with their *"mission civilisatrice."* That they did their job well, nobody can doubt. Nor can anyone doubt that the French, in their intense cultural ethnocentrism, could never have conceived that their efforts would result in the creation of an Arab population element marginal to both French and Arab culture and evincing an ambivalent attitude to both.

The marginality of the Frenchified Arab (and especially the North African Arab) has been studied by a number of Arab, European, and American social scientists so that his characteristics are quite well known.[15] As a rule, he is either the scion of an upper-class family or an individual who showed promise as a child, and was enabled to go on to high school and, in many cases, to college as well. As a result of this higher education he has acquired a good working knowledge of French, and became habituated, to a degree, to French manners, the French style of life, and French ways of thinking. As to the last, the foremost Moroccan nationalist writer, Allal al-Fassi, who himself did not receive a Western education, attested that his French-educated countrymen "usually were better able to organize their ideas and their work," and that he considered "the scientific approach as one of France's great gifts to Morocco."[16] Another Moroccan intellectual and nationalist leader, Mohammed Lyazidi, stated that the four men who, together with al-Fassi, constituted the leading echelon of the nationalist movement were "the most Westernized from the standpoint of regular, organized habits of work and thought." As Halstead concludes: "It was in French schools that Moroccans learned the Cartesian methods of ordered thought and exposition, and acquired a taste for rational criticism as well as a Gallic clarity of expression."[17]

However, methods of ordered thought and exposition and the like are matters of intellectual activity and it is not in this area that marginality expresses itself. Marginal man is marginal, not because he is unable to acquire the intellectual thought processes of the culture to which he wants to assimilate, nor because he is unable to free himself of the thought processes of the culture on which he has turned his back. He is marginal because *emotionally* he is unable to identify with either of the two cultures. It is this aspect of marginality which the Lebanese writer and editor Georges Naccache must have had in mind when he wrote: "We Orientals with western culture live in a perpetual state of internal division."[18]

The emphatic emotional overtones of marginality date from early school age, when the Arab child is impressed with the superiority of Western (in most cases French) culture and the indispensability of a European language (usually French, but at present increasingly English) as the medium of contact with the advanced world. After the completion of high school, young members of the North African élite would usually be sent to study in France where these early impressions would often harden into unshakable convictions. As a result, in the 1970's, years after the French language and culture have lost their pre-eminent position in the world, almost all the Arab leaders of North Africa (and many in Lebanon and Syria as well) still believe that French must be the language of communication with the cultured world, and justify the retention of French in many areas of activity and organization in their own country with the argument that without French they would become isolated from the world at large.

Arab marginality is thus heavily weighted in favor of the French language and culture. Until the achievement of independence, many marginal North African, Lebanese, or Syrian Arabs would have gladly assimilated to French culture completely and irrevocably if it had been practicable. Circumstances made this virtually impossible, except for those few who managed to settle in France and thread their lives into the fabric of French society. For most marginal Arabs French culture, the French language, and the French way of life have remained shrouded in the mist of nostalgia. While living in an Arab country, their heart was in France. Their entire orientation was geared to demonstrating their affinity with France and the French. They wanted to be what they were not and what they could not be—Frenchmen. They acquired and used the trappings of French civilization (language, clothing, food, social forms), without ever acquiring the feeling that they were indeed integrated into French life. The *évolué* did not become a Frenchman; he became an *évolué* Arab.

This concept of *évolué,* introduced by the French into all the overseas territories under their control, had quite a devastating effect on the self-esteem of the peoples native to *"France Outre-Mer."* The term itself, heavily laden with French ethnocentrism, is anchored in the typical nineteenth-century view of cultural evolutionism which held that the contemporary culture to which the exponent of the theory happened to belong represented the highest development of which human culture was capable, and that the more another culture differed from it the lower it stood on the evolutionary ladder. Whether or not this was justifiable at the time among the French who arrived in North Africa almost bursting with the notion of the *"mission civilisatrice"* (which was quite different in kind from, and much more intense than, the British idea of "the White Man's Burden") is beyond the scope of the present study. But for the Arab élite, which became exposed to the full force of French civilization, backed as it was by the prestige of the conquerors, its impact was too strong to resist. Before long the Arab upper class had adopted the French view. And for this they had to pay the price of becoming "cultural hybrids."[19]

The marginal Arab is forced by the very circumstance of his marginality to oscillate several times a day back and forth between the two worlds on whose margins he lives. At home, with his wife and children, with whom he, of course, speaks the colloquial Arabic of his locality, he exhibits the authoritarian attitude that is normal in all sectors of traditional Arab society. If he is jocularly inclined, his jokes will be of the robust, often ruthlessly teasing kind which is a characteristic expression of the traditional Arab sense of humor, and which, for example, prompted President Nasser of Egypt to say to King Hussein when they met at the Almaza air base in Egypt on May 30, 1967: "Since your visit is a secret, what would happen if we arrested you?" or, later, to King Hussein in the presence of Palestinian leader Ahmed Shukairy: "You may take Shukairy with you. If he gives you any trouble, throw him into one of your towers and rid me of the problem!"

While in a Western society such a joke would have been greeted with a pained silence as tasteless and brutal, on that occasion, "everybody burst out laughing."[20]

The traditional Arab world (as we have seen) is divided into two hemispheres, that of the men and that of the women, which meet only in the privacy of the home. If a woman happens to enter the company of men among whom conversation takes place in Arabic and in the Arab mode, they will ignore her and it will occur to none of them to try to draw her into the discussion. The tradition-directed Arab when meeting a friend will never inquire about the well-being of the latter's wife, and will consider it undignified to show any sign of affection or consideration for his own wife outside the home, including walking or sitting next to her in public. Reference has already been made to an incident reported by John Bagot Glubb ("Glubb Pasha" of Jordan), which shows that even the most experienced non-Arabs may have difficulty in gauging the depths of the Arabs' sensitivity on this score. The day before a ceremonial review of the Arab Legion was to take place, Glubb said to his orderly: "I don't really want you tomorrow. You can have the day off and take your wife to the review, if you like." Whereupon the deeply insulted orderly replied: "Do you think I am the kind of person to sit with women?"[21]

This conversation took place several years ago, in Arabic, and in an Arab atmosphere in which even Glubb, the British commander of the Arab Legion, regularly wore an Arab *kūfiyya* (head-kerchief) as part of his uniform. In a North African country under strong French influence, such a conversation would have taken place, of course, in French, and the semi-Frenchified orderly would have tried to impress his commander with being sufficiently *évolué* to exhibit an attitude to his wife which resembled what he gathered was the commander's attitude to his. It has, in fact, been observed that when a marginal North African amuses himself in the company of his *évolué* friends, his entire personality, at least as far as can be gauged from his overt behavior and mannerism, changes. In such a situation, for instance in a *salon de thé,* if a woman enters, the men, far from ignoring her, will pay attention to her in the manner expected from people who know French etiquette. The jokes will assume a refined character in which the purpose is not to embarrass others or cause acute discomfort, but to demonstrate one's own *esprit,* refinement, and ability to give and take light banter. The sum of it all is that the marginal person actually tries to conform to two different, often contrasting codes of behavior, with the result that he remains uncertain of some of the most basic values of his life.[22] Or, as Albert Hourani put it:

> To be a Levantine is to live in two worlds or more at once, without belonging to either; to be able to go through the external forms which indicate the possession of a certain nationality, religion or culture, without actually possessing it. It is no longer to have a standard of values of one's own, not to be able to create but only able to imitate; and not even to imitate correctly, since that also needs a certain originality. It is to belong to no community and to possess nothing of one's own. It reveals itself in lostness, pretentiousness, cynicism and despair.[23]

3. CULTURAL DICHOTOMY: ELITES AND MASSES

The Frenchified, or semi-Frenchified, Arab is often looked upon askance by the majority of his countrymen, who feel that he has set himself apart from them. They sense that his contact with French culture has put an unbridgeable distance between him and the majority. They cannot help resenting his attitudes, his speech, his manners, his very being. He, on his part, reciprocates this feeling of estrangement with the conviction that he is superior to the majority of his countrymen, that he is *évolué* while they are not.

In general, one can observe all over the Arab world that as the non-Arab education of the élite progresses, the distance between the élite and masses increases. In the past too, there was, of course, a considerable distance between the upper and lower classes in Arab lands. But the distance in those days was of the kind that exists in many places between people who enjoy the best that their culture has to offer and those whose lot it is to have to put up with that variety of the same culture which Oscar Lewis has called "the culture of poverty." The rich and the poor, the educated and the ignorant, however great the distance between them, occupied in the past positions at the two extremes of the same cultural continuum.

With the introduction of French education in North Africa, and French and English education in Lebanon and Egypt, an entirely new cultural dimension emerged. From then on, the rich and the poor, the educated and the ignorant, became increasingly separated by an additional element which created an alienation between them.

The common cultural denominator between the upper-class, Westernized Arab and his illiterate or semi-literate countrymen is minimal. While this factor creates a sharp cultural dichotomy between the urban élite and the urban and rural masses, it alone would not turn the Western-educated Arab into a marginal person. True, it can alienate him from the traditional culture of his country, isolate him to a greater or lesser extent from its old-established social structure, and makes him feel an outsider. The factor of marginality enters at the point where the Western-educated Arab is forced to recognize that he is unable to achieve total assimilation to the culture and values of the Western nation toward which he has been gravitating. Since the most striking case in point is that of the French-educated Arab élite in North Africa, let us comment on it in particular.

The North African *évolués* are the product of a French education. They are deeply imbued with French culture. They have a great admiration for France, its language, literature, civilization, values. Many of them believe that the French system of education "provides the finest humanistic training in the world and is the bearer of the highest expression of Western humanistic culture."[24] The attitude that France succeeded in inculcating into the North African Arab *évolué* is strikingly illustrated by an article entitled "France—That's Myself" written and published by Ferhat Abbas in his own paper, *L'Entente,* on February 23, 1936. In this article Abbas, who later was to become President of the Algerian National Assembly, stated: "There is no such thing as an Algerian Fatherland. I have not been able to discover it. I have examined its history; I have questioned the living and the dead; I have walked through cemeteries; nobody talked to me about it. . . . We are children of a new world, a creation of the French mind and of French energy." Ten years later, in a speech in the French National Assembly, Abbas openly admitted that he had changed his mind on the issue of Algerian nationalism; "The Algerian personality, the Algerian fatherland, which I was unable to discover among the Moslem masses in 1936, I have discovered today. . . . " And on the eve of Algerian independence he had completely identified himself with the nationalist view, denouncing colonialism for "preventing us from learning our own language" and for having destroyed "our national culture."[25]

While the case of Ferhat Abbas is not a typical example of marginality —because it manifests a clear-cut change from total commitment to French culture to a total identification with Algerian nationalism—it nevertheless illustrates the bipolarity of the *évolué*. When France still ruled North Africa, many *évolués* actually wanted to become as French as the French, but could not because they were unable to tear themselves completely away from the traditional Arab culture of their childhood, and because, as long as they continued to live in an Arab land, they were simply unable to become Frenchmen. Since the North African states have achieved independence, in the struggle for which the *évolués* had played a leading part, the nationalistic enthusiasm that has been engendered in the process has made it psychologically impossible for any native Algerian, Moroccan, or Tunisian to aspire to Frenchhood. Even the most *évolué* North Africans (that is, even those who had attained a remarkable degree of mastery of, and assimilation to, French culture) have become too closely identified with Algerian, Moroccan, or Tunisian nationalism to entertain any thought of becoming Frenchmen.

This, however, does not mean that the *évolué* is willing, or able, to effect any radical change in his attitude to French culture. His admiration for it continues, and he has to find an adjustment to the new situation in which, while admiring French culture and perhaps even contributing to it, he must be severely critical of what the French did to his country in the name of that very same culture. Thus, the new *évolué* is often anti-French politically, while being pro-French culturally; or, to put it in more general terms, he is anti-Western politically and pro-Western culturally.

When it comes to his relationship to his own country, a reverse situation obtains. The Westernized Arab, generally speaking, is a fervent patriot of his country. He identifies, for instance, wholeheartedly with his country's struggle against Israel, against Western, and most recently Soviet, imperialism, against any other Arab state, and so on. But culturally he cannot identify with his country and with the great majority of its population. Having tasted Western culture, he has become tainted by it, in the sense of being unable to look at the culture of his country and countrymen with anything but Western eyes. And to the Western eyes of the Westernized Arab the culture of the majority of his country must needs appear as backward and primitive and its carriers as ignorant and superstitious. They are people with whom he could not identify even if he wanted to: the very idea that he could be part of them appears to him absurd and abhorrent.

This leads us to what is perhaps the most damaging feature of the emotional marginalism in which many educated Arabs in North Africa are caught up: the all too frequent adoption by the marginal personality of the French stereotype of the Arab. This projects an image of an Arab who is dirty, lazy, indolent, sticking to his old-fashioned, primitive, and superstitious ways, untrustworthy, treacherous, devoid of self-control, ruled by

195

passions and emotions; in brief, an individual who needs protection from both himself and others, and from whom, in turn, others had better protect themselves.

Even in Arab countries which were exposed to Western influences to a much lesser degree than Morocco, Algeria, and Tunisia, such stereotypes of the uneducated Arabs have been current among the members of the middle and upper classes. The views of the supervisors in a large Egyptian textile company about the workers employed in the plant can serve as an illustration. These supervisors (five hundred in number) were all graduates of Egyptian trade schools, and most of them worked as foremen and charge hands. Although some 20 per cent of them had spent some time abroad in technical training, their position, in general, was only somewhat superior to that of the workers (who numbered nine thousand), and there was a considerable gap between them and the upper management of the plant. The workers were young men with no previous industrial experience. The policy of the company was to hire fellahin (i.e., agricultural laborers from the villages), who could be easily satisfied and who would constitute a docile, submissive, obedient work force.

> The supervisors, so the top management claimed, did not like to get their hands dirty and preferred white-collar jobs; they had exaggerated notions of the worth of their trade-school education and too great a feeling of superiority over the workers they supervised. . . . For their part, members of supervision criticized the indolent, slothful, lazy and untrained workmen whom they had to supervise. . . . [26]

Although undoubtedly there were workmen in the plant who actually manifested these traits, the supervisors' criticism of "the workmen" as a generalized blanket statement strongly smacks of stereotyping. It would seem that the foremen latched onto this stereotype of the workmen in order to establish and maintain a distance between themselves as educated (and partly European-educated) persons who did not have to engage in physical labor, and the workmen who, because they were uneducated, could never rise into supervisory positions. Trade-school education was the privilege of a very few among the Egyptian youth, and this circumstance in itself, together with the influence of that 20 per cent of their colleagues who had supplementary training in Europe, seemed to have been sufficient to taint the typical foreman with some marginalism. The real marginals in the company were, or course, the thirty members of the top management, all of whom had had college education and the vast majority of whom had spent at least one or two years in Europe or the United States studying at company expense. This managerial élite was able to speak English; it was socially homogeneous, professionally oriented, and "stood more or less isolated from the lower echelons of the salaried workers and laborers." One of the ways in which this top-level group emphasized the distance between itself and the supervisory staff was to be critical of the latter and to place the blame on it for the deficiencies of the labor force.[27]

Nor is it only the individual educated Arab who falls victim to the marginal man's perpetual state of internal division. Institutions, too, can become caught between the two worlds represented by the Arab and Western cultures. An example of such institutional marginality is supplied by *El-Moudjahid,* the official weekly paper of the Tunisian Front de Liberation Nationale (FLN). Originally this paper was published in French only, but subsequently it was issued in two separate editions, one in French and one in Arabic, each selling about 25,000 copies. The two editions, however, differ in content and, what is more significant, in the political line they follow. "The Arabic version tends to appeal to opinion and sentiment among Arab nationalists. The French version tends to be oriented toward liberal and radical opinion in the West."[28] In its French edition of June 22, 1963, for instance, *El-Moudjahid* denied that the use of French by Tunisians was unpatriotic because, the paper argued, "French had been used as a weapon against France herself in the Revolution"; and in another issue it printed a statement which referred to the Arabic language as "that other Don Quixote."[29]

Neighboring Morocco supplies a very similar example. The Istiqlāl ("Independence") Party of Morocco is strongly opposed to any slowing down of Arabization in education, in the bureaucracy, and so on. This is in line with both the nationalistic character of the party and its position as the major opposition party since 1963. However, despite its energetic advocacy of total Arabization, the party itself is guilty of fostering French: it publishes two large circulation national daily papers, one, *Al–'Ālam,* in Arabic; the other, *L'Opinion,* in French.[30]

To give one more general example of institutional marginality, one can refer to the continued use (discussed in the preceding chapter) of both French and Arabic as languages of instruction in North African schools.

4. AMBIVALENCE

This, then, is the tragedy of marginality: to be caught in the vise of a double ambivalence. Toward the West, in whose culture the marginal Arab desperately wants to participate, he feels admiration and envy, love and hate; he is irresistibly attracted to it and at the same time he fears it and distrusts it. He wants to acquire as much as possible of Western culture, yet he wants to eliminate Western influence from his country as far as possible. Toward his own country and its society and culture his feelings are similarly ambivalent. He loves it with a patriotic fervor, yet hates the backwardness of its people. He is proud of his great "Arab heritage," yet bemoans the inadequacy of its traditional culture as it survives at present among the ignorant masses. He enjoys the mellifluous rhetoricism of the Arabic language, yet admits and emphasizes that Arabic is an inadequate medium for modern communication, thought, science, and scholarship. He upholds the value of the Bedouin ethos, yet tries to avoid personal contact with the unkempt and uncouth Bedouin. He knows that the villager is the mainstay and backbone of his country's economy (and, incidentally, often the basis of his own relative affluence); but he has contempt for the backward, ignorant, dirty fellah. He knows that the salvation of his country lies in increased productivity, because his Western education has taught him something of the value of work and efficiency (being Westernized, he has long given up the habit of thinking of salvation in spiritual terms); but his upper-class status, anchored as it is in the traditional value-hierarchy of his country, demands that he never dirty his hands with physical labor and that his work consist of nothing more or less than supervising others, or of handling papers.

As this sampling of the Westernized Arab's marginality shows, his ambivalence differs considerably from the Freudian concept according to which the prohibition of doing something is known, is in the forefront of consciousness, while the desire to perform the prohibited act is unconscious, the individual knowing nothing of it.[31] Or, to put it differently, Freud considered ambivalence as the conflict between subconscious attraction and conscious repulsion.

The ambivalence in which the Westernized Arab finds himself caught up is of a different character. In his case, both the attraction and the repulsion are conscious. The Arab is aware of both his positive and negative feelings, although not necessarily of the conflict they engender. Analytically inclined minds among the Arabs, as we have seen, occasionally give verbal formulation to this conflict and complain of the internal division it causes in their psyches. Others, unable to bring the issue into sharp focus, manifest the psychological wear and tear of conflicting attitudes in their thought processes and behavior patterns.

An additional circumstance aggravates the issue. Ambivalence coupled with marginality results, as indicated above, in a doubling of the psychic stresses. One set of ambivalences is directed toward the traditional culture and its carriers, from which and from whom the individual has grown away; another set centers on the new foreign culture and its carriers, toward whom his growth processes have led him. A young Syro-Lebanese novelist, Ḥalīm Barakāt, gave salient expression to this double ambivalence in the character of his hero, Ramzy, who has an ambivalent love-hate relationship toward both his own Arab country and the United States.[32]

Fortunately, as far as the populations of the Arab countries are concerned, only a small proportion of them labor under the double stress and strain of this twofold ambivalence. The great majority of the people in every Arab country live in villages more or less remote from the turmoil that often characterizes Arab city life, and know nothing of the trials and tribulations of such marginality and ambivalence. Yet even the most remote villages or nomadic Bedouin tribe cannot entirely escape their effects. With the introduction of some hygiene and preventive medicine (itself a result of Westernization), the number of children born to village mothers who survive the formerly hazardous years of infancy has grown to such an extent that the villages experience what in the Western world is referred to as a population explosion. Since most villages cannot support many more people than they did in former generations, surplus sons upon reaching young manhood are forced to move to the city to try to eke out a living there. They return from time to time, bring back word of what is going on in the city, and subtly influence the entire atmosphere of the village in the direction of the city. Coming as this does on top of the emanation of urban influence through the newspapers, radio, and most recently television, the village is being exposed to the world of the city as never before throughout its long history.

Thus, the values of the city seep down into the village, including the values of the Westernized upper class. In the course of this process, the village cannot help becoming aware of the cultural *apartheid* displayed by the urban leadership. In the past, the enormous social distance between fellah and pasha notwithstanding, the fellah could on rare occasions approach the pasha, kiss his hands, and understand whatever kind or unkind words the great lord deigned to address to him. The common language indicated to the fellah that those on top of the social pyramid, and he himself at its bottom, were still parts of the same community sharing a common religion, a tradition of common genealogy, and common values.

Today, if a Moroccan peasant or tribesman is fortunate enough to own a radio and tunes it in to a broadcast by his King, on occasions such as a press interview, he will hear the King speak in a foreign tongue which he will not understand and which he may not even be able to identify as French.[33] This alone is sufficient to reduce considerably the common element between the peasant and all those Europeanized newspapermen who address questions to the King in the foreign tongue. The knowledge that his leaders literally do not speak the same language as he does makes the peasant or tribesman feel that they do not speak the same language in a figurative sense either, that they do not belong to the same community.[34]

While this situation creates a sense of alienation among the élite, in the masses it produces a feeling of resentment. In a society such as that of the Arabs, in whose culture family spirit and kinship are all-important, resentment of alien domination becomes especially strong. The Westernized élite tends to be regarded by the traditional masses with almost the same intense resentment that the Arabs have always felt toward aliens in control of their lands.

This resentment is especially strong among the urban working classes. An urban proletariat, in the Western sense, has come into being out of the surplus village population only relatively recently, as a result of Westernization. Living as it does in the immediate proximity of the upper classes, this proletariat witnesses the signs of Westernization much more closely than the rural population. As a result, it evinces an ambivalence toward Western cultural traits and values which rural people have no opportunity to develop. The rural population and the urban poor had always felt a traditional resentment at the display of wealth and waste by the idle rich. When this display came to include a growing number of new-fangled Western traits objectionable to the more tradition-bound outlook of the poor, resentment increased. Simultaneously, there developed a strong attraction for the glitter of Western cultural trappings which, while highly visible, remained mostly unattainable for the poverty-stricken masses.[35] It is against this background that one must view, and can understand, the readiness with which the proletariat in an Arab urban setting can turn into a raging, uncontrollable street mob—looting and burning, attacking anybody who appears not to belong to it, sustaining several wounded and dead at the hand of the police or militia—and, a few hours later, its fury spent, subside again into its wonted lethargy alternating with brief but harmless flare-ups of short temper.

5. *IZDIWĀJ* — SPLIT PERSONALITY

A number of modern Arab thinkers and writers have recognized and analyzed the dangers of marginality for the Arab personality. 'Abdallāh 'Alī al-Qaṣīmī, in his book *These Are the Chains,* published in Cairo in 1946, diagnoses marginality much as we have done above, describing a personality torn between two powerful opposing forces. We identified these forces as two opposing emotions: attachment to the traditional Arab culture on the one hand, and attraction to modern Western culture on the other. Al-Qaṣīmī sees them as the desire to adhere to the old ways (or, as he expresses it elsewhere, the desire to "see perfection in the ancients"), which entails a rejection of progress, and the "forward moving development" of "the stream of life." Al-Qaṣīmī goes on to describe the individual caught between these two forces as becoming "divided against himself." Thus, he not only recognizes the phenomenon of Arab marginality, but appears to have sensed the ambivalent attitude the marginal Arab displays toward the forces of progress, which he himself has identified as emanating from the West. On the one hand, he tries to deny progress, to reject Westernization; on the other, he has internalized these trends sufficiently to make them a powerful agent in his breast, a force which attracts him as strongly as the force that pulls him to traditionalism. Having thus diagnosed the problem, al-Qaṣīmī does not hesitate to prescribe the remedy: the wholehearted adoption of progressive humanism, the ridding of the Muslim lands of the "crushing heritage" of the past, and the realization that "all human existence and all human civilizations are predicated on the idea of development. . . . "[36]

A few years after the publication of al-Qaṣīmī's book, a related study appeared in Baghdad by 'Alī Ḥasan al-Wardī. Although, as its title, *The Personality of the Iraqi Individual,*[37] shows, it purports to deal with the Iraqi Arab personality in particular, its findings are true of the Arabs in general.[38] In this study Wardī comments upon the marginality of the Iraqi Arabs, but a marginality of a different kind from the one discussed above. Wardī notes that the Iraqi personality, and the psychology of Arab countries in general, is characterized by a deep-rooted duality, which he terms *"izdiwāj,"* that is, "split personality." Especially in Iraq one finds manifestations of two value systems contending for the people's loyalty: the ancient values of a sedentary population on the one hand, and the values of the nomadic Bedouin on the other. The sedentary or urban mores exalt such qualities as endurance, hardship, submission, and cunning: while the Bedouin mores stress courage and pride, show and rapaciousness. This Bedouin-sedentary split is basic to the Iraqi personality, but it is not the only split in it. There are several more dualities: segregation of men and women; colloquial versus classical Arabic; innovation and conservation; sincerity and hypocrisy. There are, moreover, quarrels between Sunnīs and Shī'īs; between the revolutionary tradition, with its heroic, democratic ideal, and complacent moralism, mercantilism, and greed.[39]

Although Wardī presents his observations in a way which makes them seem applicable only to town dwellers, a very similar marginality characterizes the Iraqi and Arab villager, except that in the villages the stress on hardship and endurance, submission and cunning predominates, while the nomadic-tribal values of courage and pride definitely take second place. This particular dividing line, therefore, runs between the nomadic-tribal element on the one hand and the settled population on the other. Marginality between settled and nomadic values is present in both the town and the village; it is absent only among the nomads, who are still committed to their traditional values and have not yet begun to absorb those of the settled population. Both Arab townsman and villager look down on the nomads because of their primitive way of life, but they also admire them for their courage and pride, their hospitality, generosity, keen sense of honor, ingroup loyalty, and so on.

Hisham Sharabi, another Arab author, touches on the painful issue of the marginality of this new Arab generation destined to supply the leadership of tomorrow. Sharabi acknowledges that the young Arab intellectual derives his "inspiration and strength from another [i.e., Western] culture whose methods and values he has not yet fully assimilated."[40] Then he goes on to state that

> there is no turning away from Europe. This generation's psychological duality, its bilingual, bicultural character are clear manifestations of this fact. It has to judge itself, to choose, and to act in terms of concepts and values rooted not in its own tradition but in a tradition that it has still not fully appropriated.[41]

He sees the resolution of the problem created by the psychological, linguistic, and cultural duality of these young intellectuals in a more complete assimilation of Western values and concepts.

Arab novelists and fiction writers have also recognized ambivalence and its attendant features as a widespread malaise. The Syro-Lebanese Ḥalīm Barakāt has one of his characters say:

> ... we are a people who have lost their identity and their sense of manhood. Each of us is suffering from a split personality, especially in Lebanon. We are Arab and yet our education is in some cases French, in some cases Anglo-Saxon and in others Eastern-Mystic. A very strange mixture. We need to go back and search out our roots. We're all schizophrenic . . . [42]

The facile use of such Western psychological terms as "split personality" and "schizophrenic" combined with such traditional Arab concepts as "manhood" and historical "roots" indicates clearly that this protagonist in Barakāt's novel, and possibly also the author himself, indeed suffers from marginality and ambivalence.

According to Freudian psychoanalysis, the first step in ridding a patient of an ambivalence and its damaging effects is to enable him to become aware of its psychological roots. *Mutatis mutandis,* the problem of Arab ambivalence can be resolved only after its psychological bases have become known to the Arabs themselves. The work of Arab writers and thinkers such as Barakāt and al-Oaṣīmī shows that this primary step has been accomplished. Once their approach becomes known to the Arab intelligentsia and, what is more difficult, internalized, there is a good chance that the phenomenon itself will gradually subside. What started out as an emotional conflict, tearing the individual apart in two opposite directions as al-Qaṣīmī put it, can then be transformed into a synthesis of two cultures. This should combine in the minds of its carriers to form a new and felicitously fecund cultural configuration, liberating talents and energies to embark on new ventures in many areas of cultural advancement.

XIII

UNITY AND CONFLICT

1. THE IDEA OF ARAB UNITY

MANY OBSERVERS OF THE CONTEMPORARY ARAB SCENE HAVE
noted the contradiction between the reiterated asseverations of Arab unity
and the incessant quarrels that characterize inter-Arab relations. The idea
of unity is expressed, among other things, in the constitutions of several
Arab states—Syria, Iraq, Kuwait, Yemen, Egypt, Libya, Tunisia, and Algeria—all of which include a proclamation to the effect that their country
is part of "the Arab nation," "the Arab homeland," "the Arab family," or
"the Arab world." The same proclamation is emphatically reiterated with
almost monotonous persistence by the leaders of all the Arab countries in
speeches and in writing, and is epitomized in the concept of Arab *qawmiyya*
(literally, nationalism), which always refers to the national unity of all
Arabs. Many Arab authors, in speaking of Arab countries, state that they
are parts of the "Arab fatherland."

This idea of the national unity of all *Arabs* is a very new concept.
Historically, the Arab world view was wrapped in the Islamic outlook,
which considered all *Muslims* one nation. Although national states have
been in existence within the domain of Islam for centuries, the traditional

Muslim religious law, the so-called *sharīʿa*, recognizes only one indivisible Muslim entity, the *umma Muḥammadiyya* or "Muḥammadite nation."[1] The same view is expressed in the often-quoted old saying," *Lā umam fi'l-Islām*" ("There are no nations in Islam"), which has its counterpart in the similarly monochromatic view of the non-Muslim world: *"al-kufru millatun wāḥida,"* literally, "Unbelief is one nation," meaning that all of non-Muslim humanity constitutes something like one national unit. The opposition between these two large sectors of the world is expressed even more succinctly in the juxtaposition of the *Dār al-Islām* ("House of Islam") and the *Dār al-Ḥarb* ("House of War") which, ever since the foundation of Islam, have stood arrayed against each other.

Islamic unity is the theme of numerous articles, pamphlets, and tracts, among which let us mention Muḥammad Abū Zahra's pamphlet, *Al-Waḥda al-Islāmiyya* (*Islamic Unity*). Abū Zahra argues that all the Muslims are one nation (*umma*), tied together by the religion, belief, worship, and moral principles of Islam. Therefore, he says all Muslims should strive to unite their countries into an Islamic League of Nations or Commonwealth of Nations. He goes on to outline the principles which should be binding on all member states of this federation: Since all Muslims are brothers, they should solve all disputes among themselves. Aggression against any individual Muslim or any one Muslim country is aggression against all Muslims. All Muslim lands must cooperate in fighting for the liberation of brethren who are under the yoke of the enemies of Islam. Muslims must be ruled by Muslims. And finally, all planning and other activities in the economic, financial, and commercial spheres must be carried out exclusively by Muslims.[2]

Many modern Arab thinkers agree with this view. Thus Fatḥī Yakun, in a tract entitled *The Mission of Arab Nationalism,* disputes language, history, law, destiny, feeling and so on, as the bases of Arab nationalism, and argues that the religion of Islam is the sole foundation of this nationalism. Since, moreover, religion and politics are inseparable, the mission of Arab nationalism is the liberation and unification of 500 million Muslims into one state which will be based on the teachings and principles of Islam.[3]

Nevertheless, under the impact of Westernization, the idea that the Arabs form a "nation" gradually gained acceptance among the younger generation of Arab intelligentsia. The concept of political nation, as distinct from the aggregate united by the faith of Islam, began to make headway in the Arab lands only during the last century, and it did so under European influence.

To express the notion of ethnic nationalism, a new word had to be coined in Arabic, *"qawmiyya,"* derived from the old Arab word *"qawm,"* which means people, followers, group, or tribe, and especially the group of kinfolk mobilized for mutual support.[4] In the printed version of the proceedings of a meeting held by Arab students in Brussels, in 1938, the term *"qawmiyya,"* coined only a few years earlier, is defined as "sensitivity to the existing necessity of liberating and unifying the inhabitants of the Arab lands in view of the unity of the *waṭan* (territory) and language and culture and history, and the necessity of improving those things which are of common concern." The "Arab movement" is defined as "the new Arab renaissance which is always astir in the Arab nation; it is animated by the impulses of its glorious history, its unique vitality and its legitimate interest in the present and the future."[5]

According to this statement, Arab unity is based on a common Arab homeland, language, culture, and history, and undefined common Arab concerns and interests. As against these five elements of Arab nationalism, the Lebanese Muslim author 'Abdullāh al-Alāyilī discerns six features on which Arab "national feeling" is based. They are language; common interests "within the great Arab fatherland"; the geographical environment, which has "great influence on mentality and temperament"; ties of blood; common history; and similarity of customs.[6]

Analyses such as these have become commonplace in Arab writing, and new formulations rarely represent radical departure. However, variations on the theme of Arab unity have been many. The Lebanese Christian Arab author Nabīh Amīn Fāris (b. 1906), in his book *The Living Arabs,* criticizes those pillars on which, according to the views of many, Arab unity rests. Racial unity, he says, is not a genuine pillar of Arab unity, because many Arabs, including Arab kings, have mixed blood, while being "Arabs to the core with regard to language and the educative power of history." Nor is geographical situation, because many foreigners have lived for centuries in Arab lands without becoming Arabs. Religion is not, and has never been, a pillar of *'urūba* ("Arabism"), because many non-Muslims were true Arabs and contributed importantly to Arab culture. Fāris then proceeds to expound his own view, according to which the pillars of authentic Arab unity are two only: the Arabic language and "the formative force of history." The latter, Fāris explains, includes not only historical events and their memories but also traditions, customs, tales, stories, legends, fables; that which moved the hearts of the people to compassion, grief, delight and sorrow; and that which awakened in them the spirit of initiative and drove them to the fore. This education through history must tend to prepare individuals to assume, consciously or unconsciously, responsibility for this history, and to cultivate it.[7]

A few years later, Fāris co-authored a book with Mohammed Tawfik Husayn, a Muslim Arab. In this new study, two additional factors are discerned which may gradually make the Arabs into one nation: one religion (i.e., Islam), and one mentality. Of special interest for us in the present context is the second, on which the gist of the two authors' observations is that "Arabs differ little in their attitude towards the various problems of life, and in their response to external influences," including such issues as the dignity of the individual, human effort, time, women, honor, manliness, loyalty, generosity, hospitality, and neighborliness. They explain this uniformity by referring to the similarity of "the economic, social, and spiritual bases upon which Arab society rests." Arab society, they say, has been since remote times agricultural for the most part, and "organized along feudal, tribal, and religious lines." Religion, "involving first and foremost belief in the unseen and surrender to fate—has dominated the lives of Arabs for centuries." In the cities, a few powerful "feudal lords exploit the labors of the majority," while nomadic and semi-nomadic Bedouin tribes "leave the imprint of their nomadic and tribal mentality upon the entire population." The governments have always been theocratical and/or despotic. Arab literature has always been "saturated with the all-important spirit of Islam." The specific character of Muslim religion, Fāris and Husayn observe, tends "to cripple their [the Arabs'] creative will, driving them to dream of past glories, oblivious of their urgent current problems."[8]

The attitude of the Pan-Arabists on religion as a unifying factor in the Arab world has been ambiguous. They were, on the whole, proud of the Arab role in giving Islam to the world and in converting to it one-sixth or one-seventh of mankind. They felt no doubt that there was a common factor among Muslims, accepting the dictum that "There are no nations in Islam." Yet at the same time, undoubtedly as a consequence of absorbing ideas of nationalism from the West, they felt that the bonds uniting Arabs are stronger than the bonds between them and the non-Arab Muslim countries. If the Muslim world constituted one "House," the Dār al-Islām, the Arab world within it represented the inner sanctum. This feeling of Arab unity as primary brought some opposition from the Pan-Islamists. For them, religion was the strongest, holiest bond. For the Pan-Arabists, it was merely a historical, or divine, instrument which played a role in shaping Arab unity. And, since they thus relegated Islam to a secondary place among the pillars of Arab unity, they seem to have felt the need for additional pillars, over and above those of language and common historical background.

According to the Pan-Arabists, *'Arabiyya,* or "Arabdom," comprises the community of Arabic-speaking peoples, inhabiting a large area stretching from the Atlantic to the Persian Gulf, which is characterized by considerable geographical similarities. The Arabs are "a young race that has its origin in the harmonious fusion of various human strains which Islam has brought together in one crucible." The intermixture has resulted in a great similarity of intellectual and moral aptitudes, even though a variety of physical types has been preserved. This Arab "race" recognizes no distinctions of color, is extremely "prolific, courageous, enthusiastic, enduring, patient, and guided by the spirit of fairness." Its language, Arabic, is superior to all other languages, and enables the Arabs to play a great civilizational role. Islam, the religion of almost all Arabs, confers on Arabism a sense of spiritual values which sets it off against the materialism of the West. Whatever internal divisions exist among the Arabs, such as tribes and religious sects, are but the result of ignorance or of foreign interference.[9] Additional elements of Pan-Arabism are supplied by the claim that the most outstanding features in Western civilization were originally contributed by Arabs (or Muslims), and by "the peculiar feeling of being a chosen people" derived from the Arabs' central position within Islam.[10]

These, then, are considered by Arab analysts to be the main features making for Arab unity. A vague and amorphous feeling that the Arabs are one people, and that in the not too distant future they will become one in actuality, is everywhere part of the Arab consciousness. Arab political leaders find it expeditious to reiterate their conviction of Arab unity on every possible occasion, and especially when they are embroiled in a fight or dispute with another Arab country. As far as the simple people are concerned, they do not know much of inter-Arab relations, but the word "Arab" has an almost magic power over them, and news about Arabs in trouble, even thousands of miles away, can easily provoke them to violent manifestations of solidarity. That the Arabs are brothers is for them axiomatic, a tenet of faith which, like other credos, neither requires proofs nor is capable of being refuted or even as much as shaken by specific instances of Arab disunity, or fratricidal wars, or other manifestations of Arab dissension, strife, or enmity.

2. FIGHTING: SWORDS AND WORDS

However, neither the old idea of Islamic religious oneness nor the new one of Arab cultural and national unity was able to overcome the divisiveness, or conflict proneness, which is a much older pre-Islamic heritage of the Arabs. One of the most important features in this heritage was the ancient Near Eastern *lex talionis,* or law of retaliation, which not only left it to the individual and his immediate kin group to take revenge for any injury suffered, but made it their duty under penalty of forfeiting their honor. As a result of this law, epitomized in such pithy statements as the biblical "An eye for an eye" or the still current Arab saying, *Dam buṭlub dam* ("Blood demands blood"), blood feuds among families and larger kin groups were the order of the day for many generations before the appearance of Muḥammad.

It should be pointed out that blood feuds were and are not confined to the Arab world, they feature in other Mediterranean cultural traditions as well. But it is among the Arabs that the blood feud has remained a most important and emphatic value.

The blood feud is an organic part and inevitable consequence of the intensive group cohesion which characterizes the Arab ethos. A society in which great emphasis is placed on the kin group, in which individual interests are subordinated to the interests of family and lineage, and in which, in addition, honor is given the highest priority, it is inevitable that every homicide, premeditated or accidental, should give rise to blood revenge and trigger a chain reaction that soon involves an increasing number of men and groups.

The blood feud, moreover, can be considered as merely the most explicit manifestation of a general Arab propensity for fighting and conflict. Just as the taking of blood revenge was considered a value and redounded to one's honor, so was fighting in general. The fighting spirit expressed itself in many different ways throughout the thirteen centuries of Muslim Arab history. There were times when it propelled great armies to victorious battles against the infidels in the three continents. At other times, the fighting spirit pitted

Arab against Arab. And there came a period, following the onset of the Arab stagnation which is bemoaned by so many Arab scholars and historians, when the fighting spirit expressed itself more in verbal abuse and vituperation, in threats and shouting matches, than in actual hand-to-hand combat.

Fighting among the Arab tribes in pre-Islamic times was such a permanent feature of life that the Prophet Muḥammad found it necessary to proclaim a period of "holy truce" for four months every year, during which all fighting was forbidden and which were set aside for religious observances and trading. An important contributing factor to Muḥammad's success in rallying the people of the Arabian Peninsula around the banner of the new religion he preached was the fact that widespread feuding had weakened the Arab tribes and made it impossible for them to unite against him. The blood feuds, we are told by Arab historians, were so intense that practically every tribe was involved in hostilities against one or more other tribes. While the actual number of men killed in these feuds was probably not large, intertribal animosity was such that the tribes were unable to put up serious resistance to the Muslim army led by the Prophet.

In pre-Islamic times, intertribal and interfamilial feuding among the Arabs consisted of more noise than action. It has been observed by students of the *Ayyām al-'Arab (Days of the Arabs)*—that old romantic chronicle of the "days" of Arab battles—that a number of the events celebrated in it were not true battles at all, but rather insignificant skirmishes in many of which only a few families or individuals took part, while numerous so-called battles were limited to the throwing of stones and beating with sticks. Many of the "days" follow a typical pattern: a few men come to blows with one another, mostly in consequence of some dispute or insult; then the quarrel grows into hostility between entire tribes, who meet in battle. No sooner are a few men killed than a neutral family intervenes and peace is restored, with the tribe that lost fewer men paying blood money to the other side for the surplus of dead bodies.[11] This pattern seems to indicate that even in the old, heroic days of early Arab history, the major weapon of intertribal fighting was verbal: actual combat was engaged in only when things somehow got out of hand, and then it was stopped as soon as possible.

The same pattern survives to this day. Among the Kabyles, Berber tribes in Algeria who were profoundly influenced by the intrusive Arab culture, the political and warlike leagues used to pursue their hostilities "in the form of a strictly regulated game, of an ordered competition." Intertribal fights sometimes took the form of a proper ritual: insults were exchanged, then blows. During the fight the women would encourage the men with their shouts and songs which exalted the honor and vigor of the family. The purpose in these fights was not to kill or crush the opponent, but to show, generally through a symbolic act, that one had the upper hand. . . . It was only as a result of an unfortunate accident that somebody was killed in these fights, or because the stronger group threatened to burst into the living quarters, the last refuge of honor, of the besieged faction, which then felt forced to resort to the use of firearms. This was often enough to stop the fighting. The mediators, the *marabouts* and the wise men of the tribe, would then ask the aggressors to withdraw, and give them a pledge that they would not be molested during their withdrawal. In this and other ways the *marabouts* acted as mediators, sanctioning the end of a fight without dishonor and shame recoiling on either of the contestants. In this manner, the moment the fighting threatened to assume a bloody character, the mediators arrived and put an end to it. Nevertheless, a state of war between tribes and factions could last for years, so that in a certain sense hostilities were a permanent condition, to which repeated truces, sealed and guaranteed by honor, put only a temporary end.[12]

Whatever our opinion of the manliness (*muruwwa*) evinced in this brand of conflict, one thing is certain: it is more humane conduct than the kill and overkill patterns developed by the Western world in its recent armed conflicts. For the Arabs themselves, whether the fighting took the form of armed clashes or the use of sticks and stones or oral attacks, the aggressive propensity manifested in it was considered an honorable expression of manliness.

Since the Arabs were always a poetic nation, bravery in standing up to one's enemies was a favorite subject of poetic praise. Many of the old Arab poems were composed in praise of the bravery exhibited by the poet's tribe. In others, the poet sings of his own prowess in fighting. In fact, some of the best known and most admired early Arab poets left behind little more than odes celebrating their own character and achievements. In addition to bravery in battle, the old Arab ideal of *muruwwa* comprised such traits as patience in misfortune, persistence in seeking revenge, protection of the weak, and defiance of the strong. Complementary traits of *muruwwa* were loyalty, fidelity, and generosity.[13] All these features together added up to a man's honor, which he was supposed to defend no matter what sacrifice it required. Compared to the value of honor that of a human life was minor —an attitude exemplified by numerous stories, both old and new, telling of how the hero fulfills a pledge, which is a matter of honor, or protects or restores his honor, even though it requires that he sacrifice the life of his own son or of one or more of his subordinates.[14] As a widely read Arab friend of mine once remarked in a critical vein, both the Japanese and the Arabs are ready to kill in order to regain their lost honor; but the Japanese will kill himself, while the Arab will kill somebody else.

In pre-Islamic Arabia, at fairs and on other occasions, representatives of tribes and especially tribal poets used to engage in *mufākharāt*—competitions for glory, which consisted of boasting of all that constituted their honor and abusing vehemently their adversaries. These competitions, which remind us of the potlatch of the northwest coast American Indians made famous by Ruth Benedict,[15] took place between tribes and clans, and occasionally between families and individuals. They were literary tourneys, which contributed a great deal to the development of poetry and oratory; but, on the other hand, they stirred up such unbridled enthusiasm that they frequently ended in violent quarrels or even bloodshed which, in turn, led to wars. The competitions continued in Islamic times and were occasionally held in the presence of the caliphs, who were not ashamed to take part in them.[16]

The old Arab tradition which considered exaggerated self-praise and boasting an acceptable and even commendable method of enhancing one's honor can be regarded as the basis of a similar feature characterizing Arab behavior at the present time. The inclination to such exaggerated self-praise can be observed especially in the writings and speeches of Arab leaders which, whatever the subject matter, frequently contain references to various aspects of the Arab grandeur. An Arab orator addresses his audience as a "noble and proud people" and tries to evoke a positive or even enthusiastic response from it by praising it as part of the great Arab nation in exaggerated and repetitious terms, referring to its heroism, manliness, steadfastness, and the like. This tendency is so strong that it appears even in official announcements, which in most parts of the world use a matter-of-fact language. Thus, one can hear in Arab radio broadcast references to "our heroic soldiers," "our heroic pilots," and the like.

The same tendency finds expression also in political-ideological writings. Dr. 'Abd al-Raḥmān al-Bazzāz, for instance, in his massive volume on Arab nationalism, considers several traits, all of which he believes are derived directly from Arab nationalism and bound up inseparably with it. They are democracy, Arab socialism, progressivism, revolutionism, positivism, and activism.[17] Quite a lengthy eulogy of this type is found in the writings of Nāṣir al-Dīn al-Nashāshībī in answer to the question, Why are we Arabs?

We are Arabs because we believe in God and not in matter, we sanctify the prophets and not the gun, and because our strength is the basis of our existence. . . . We are Arabs because we have a human mission which calls for the good of all, for social justice, and for mutual help among the classes. We are Arabs because we love the independence of our lands and the independence of all nations together with us. Because of this we do not attack anybody and we do not rob anybody's right to life. We are advancing and we shall take the hand of anybody who wants to advance with us. We are Arabs because we maintain a bond with our past, and are proud of our traditions and pride ourselves on the heritage of our fathers. Our generation guards this heritage in order to pass it on, whole and pure, to our children and grand-children. We believe in eternity, the eternity of the spirit and the eternity of the fatherland. We are Arabs because the spiritual values are dear to us; we shall not exaggerate them and not exchange them for others. Because the foundations of these values are the true, the beautiful, and the good. In these values there is something of God, the attributes of God. We are Arabs because we do not adhere to a view of social philosophy taken from outside our own horizon, outside our borders, outside our great fatherland, because such views would shatter our existence and injure everything that is sacred to us. We are Arabs because we relate to the Arab nationalism and are built up by it. It is of us and we are of it; we are a part of it and it is a part of us. In it are our common language and our common history, the common sentiments; in it is the fixed definition of our past days and our present, in it is the clear revelation of our roots which reach back far into past generations, in it are the strong and evident and real ethnological and anthropological ties which confirm our belonging to the Arab race all of whose special characteristics, culture and ideational heights are embodied in us.[18]

The opposite of such self-praise is verbal attack on the adversary. In the past, oral abuse and invective, in the form of a *hijā* (an insulting poem or diatribe), used to be an important part of the struggle with an enemy. The earliest instance of such verbal attack in a poetic form, as Goldziher pointed out, was what Balak, King of Moab, wanted his prophet-poet Balaam to pronounce over Israel (Numbers 22:6).[19] One could add as another early example the insults hurled by Goliath, the Philistine giant, against his Israelite adversaries, which were returned in kind by David (I Samuel 17:10, 43, 46). The origins of these pre-battle invectives go back to the primitive belief in the power of the word, the effectiveness of utterance, and especially of the insult which, once it finds its mark, must cause great damage. In ancient Israel, the *hijā* fell into disuse long before the end of the biblical period. Among the Arabs, it remained in vogue in both pre-Islamic and Islamic days. The belief persisted that once a *hijā* was uttered, even if totally defamatory and calumnious, it had a powerful effect and lasting conse-quences. Therefore, the more violent the insult, the more the adversary was

213

brought low, without regard to the amount of truth in the words hurled against him. The insults had to be clad in poetic form, or at least in rhyming prose, and therefore composed by poets. The usual insults, when directed against an individual, and whether they did or did not have any basis in reality, consisted of accusations of avarice, refusal to provide hospitality for travelers, lack of intelligence, cowardice, timidity, failure to keep one's word, lack of *ḥilm* (i.e., dignity, justice, forbearance, leniency, etc.), obscurity of forebears, mixed blood, and so forth. A group, such as a tribe, would be charged with smallness and weakness, mediocrity of its poets and orators, defeats suffered, undistinguished ancestors, falsification of the chiefs' genealogies, the abandoned conduct of its women, and various detestable habits such as eating the flesh of a dog or man. The grosser the insult, the more effective the *hijā*.

Reactions to the *hijā* were usually violent. Woe to the wretched poet who fell into the hands of the tribe against which he had let loose in his *hijā*. He would be killed, or his tongue cut out. Not infrequently, if a *hijā* was uttered by a poet while there was no actual fighting in progress, armed conflict was provoked by the very gravity of the oral insults.

A time came, from the ninth or tenth century on, when poets turned their poisonous pens against their own patrons, whom they held to be too miserly, and accused them of avarice, meanness of spirit, lowly origin, homosexuality, and other deviations. Like many another old cultural feature, the *hijā* survives to this day in the Arab world. Its general tone, it is true, has become more moderate; gross insults are no longer fashionable. The targets of the *hijā* have also changed. They are no longer enemy tribes but rather hostile political parties, the governments of Arab states, foreign governments, colonialism, imperialism.[20] However that may be, the *hijā* supplies one more example of the survival of archaisms in Arab culture and the persisting influence of ancient modes of thought on the modern Arab mind.[21]

While the Arabs appear to have been more bellicose than belligerent, more pugnacious and contentious than martial and militant, the usual state of affairs between and within Arab social aggregates was one of conflict. There was, as a result, an almost perpetual tension, a feeling of being threatened and, consequently, of having to threaten. In order to survive in such a social situation, the aggressive qualities of the individual had to be upheld as a value, and the culture had to develop techniques to maximize whatever aggressive tendencies existed in his psyche. The *mufākharāt*, or boastful oral competitions for glory, the *hijā,* or oral invective, the imperative of preserving or restoring one's honor, the ideal of *muruwwa* or manliness, and many more were all institutionalized features which made it possible to exist and thrive in such a social environment. There was only one ideal which all these cultural traits could not achieve: that of unity, which throughout Arab history remained unattainable and which today is still far from realization.

The general impression conveyed by all these considerations requires one addition or qualification. It was primarily when Arabs fought Arabs that the emphasis was placed on oral invective, boasting, and the use of weapons that were less than deadly. Intertribal fighting most typically took the form of raiding in which armed clashes were avoided as far as possible. However, when it came to fighting non-Arabs, which in the heyday of Arab expansion meant non-Muslims, the religious fervor instilled by Islam changed the concept of battle radically. It then became a matter of killing or be killed, the only proviso being that if the pagan enemy submitted and accepted Islam, his life was spared. The Arab heroic spirit in these wars was fanned by the Muslim promise of paradise to all those who fell in a *jihād*—a holy war waged by Muslims against non-Muslims—and by the Muslim doctrine that the fate of man was *maktūb*, "written," that is, predetermined.

3. DUAL DIVISION

While the blood feud, the keen sense of honor, and the great emphasis on group cohesion are undoubtedly the three main sources of the conflict–proneness that characterizes all areas of Arab group life, one more factor throughout the ages intensified the Arab feeling of distrust and dislike for people outside the group. This factor, an integral part of the descent tradition which goes back to the days of paganism, holds that the Arabs are the progeny not of one single ancestor but of two, who lived at two different times in two different places: within the Arabian Peninsula and at its northern perimeter. They therefore constitute to this day two separate groups. This dual descent tradition is, of course, not capable of historical verification. It is a myth, but a powerful and potent one, which imbues the mind of each group (or moiety, as it may be termed after the generally accepted anthropological usage) with a favorable self-stereotype and a corresponding stereotype of the other moiety that is in most cases unfavorable, derogatory, and inimical. Wherever such a dual system exists (and it exists in many places outside the Middle East), it always involves tension between the two moieties, competitiveness and hostility. Outside the Middle East, the two are always exogamous; men of moiety A must marry girls from moiety B, and vice versa. In the Muslim Middle East, it is the other way around; the two moieties (as well as smaller sections within them) are always endogamous. This results in a greater alienation between the groups.

According to the tradition, one of the two original ancestors was Qaḥṭān, progenitor of all the South Arabian tribes, and the other was 'Adnān, ancestor of all the North Arabian tribes. This tradition of the division of the Arabs into a northern and a southern moiety is definitely pre-Islamic. The sixth-century Byzantine historian Procopius refers to it.[22] There was a pre-Islamic tribal confederation called Qaḥṭān or Yaman (meaning south), and Qaḥṭān tribes still occupy a sizable area south of Mecca. Yaman (or Yemen), in the southwestern corner of the Arabian Peninsula, is considered the original home of all these southern tribes.

Learned Arab genealogists identified Qaḥṭān with the biblical Yoqtan (Genesis 10:25), a son of 'Ēbher (Arabic 'Abar), and 'Adnān as the son of Ishmael, son of Abraham. Since in Arab genealogical tradition the older a family tree, the nobler it is, Qaḥṭān who was five generations removed from Noah is nobler than 'Adnān who was twelve generations removed from Noah. Thus, the Qaḥṭān or southern tribes are considered the true aboriginal Arab stock, while the younger 'Adnān or northern tribes are considered merely Arabized peoples. To complicate matters, the two moieties are often referred to not only as 'Adnān and Qaḥṭān but also as Qays and Yaman; and the northern group is also called Ma'add, Nizār, or Muḍar.[23]

Two points in this genealogical myth are significant for our consideration of the Arab mind today. One is that all the peoples conquered by the Arabs adopted this genealogical scheme and came to believe, not only that they were Arabs in a generalized sense, but that they were either of 'Adnān (Qays) or Qaḥṭān (Yaman) descent. The other is that once they adopted these eponymous ancestors as their own, they also arrayed themselves in ethnic, dynastic, political, and military struggle against the opposing moiety. In other words, they became Arabs of one or the other moiety and thus transformed whatever internal rivalries had existed among them into a re-enactment under local conditions of the ancient Arab rivalry of 'Adnān and Qaḥṭān, or Qays and Yaman.

Since genealogy and, in particular, pride in ancestry and purity of line is a fundamental value in the Arab ethos, the acceptance of Arab ancestry by the conquered peoples of Southwest Asia and North Africa stamped them as true Arabs as soon as the fictitious character of the claim was forgotten, that is, within a few generations. This is how it came to pass that Aramaeans in Iraq, Hamites in Egypt, Berbers in Morocco, and the natives of Spain were transformed into scions of the same noble ancestors from whom the Arabian Arabs themselves claimed descent. Hand in hand with the claim of northern or southern Arab ancestry went the adoption of the combative spirit that filled members of one moiety *vis-à-vis* the other; and within a short time after the conquest by the Arabs, bloody battles between the newly grafted twigs of the two great old branches of the Arab ancestral family tree occurred in distant lands. The smallest incident was sufficient to trigger protracted warfare between the two parties. The district of Damascus became the scene of a relentless two-year war because a "northerner" stole a melon from the garden of a "southerner." In Murcia, Spain, blood flowed for several years, because a "northerner" picked a vine leaf from the garden of a "southerner"; and early in the ninth century there was a seven-year war between the two groups. Toward the end of the same century, the Arabs almost lost their control of the province of Elvira in Spain because of the rivalry between the two parties.[24] As summed up by Hitti,

> Everywhere, in the capital as well as in the provinces, on the banks of the Indus, the shores of Sicily and the borders of the Sahara, the ancestral feud, transformed into an alignment of two political parties, one against the other, made itself felt. It proved a potent factor in ultimately arresting the progress of Moslem arms in France and in the decline of the Andalusian caliphate.[25]

The strife between the two groups has continued down to the present time in all parts of the Arab world. In many places, the tendency to divide into two competing factions has led to the emergence of local moieties which trace their descent back to two ancestors, one of whom belonged to a Qays (or 'Adnān) tribe, the other to a Yaman (or Qaḥtān) tribe. In other cases, which are even more frequent, two brothers or other related individuals are considered the original progenitors of the two factions, which are nevertheless lined up in hostility against each other. In the Palestine-Syria area, the fighting between the two factions (here called Qays and Yaman) was so pronounced and incessant that C. F. Volney remarked in the late eighteenth century: "This discord, which has prevailed throughout the country from the earliest times of the Arabs, causes a perpetual civil war. . . . The mutual devastations of the contending parties render the appearance of this part of

Syria more wrecked than that of any other."[26] Sporadic fighting between Qays and Yaman continued well into the twentieth century, as did the display of the white southern flag and the red northern flag on all formal occasions.[27] It is not unlikely that these flags originally go back to ancient Egypt, in which the color of the crown of Upper Egypt (the southern region) was white, while the crown of Lower Egypt (the north) was red, and where the two moieties used the red and the white flags as their emblems even in recent times.[28]

In the course of modern developments in several Arab countries, this originally genealogical division was gradually transformed into two rival political alignments, each centered on one of two leading feudal families. Once such a transformation took place, the principle of descent was gradually less and less emphasized, and individuals or even groups could change their allegiance and ally themselves with the opposite group if it attracted them for some reason. An early example of such a switch was that of the Caliph Hisham (eighth century), who at the beginning of his rule was a Yamanī but later declared himself to be a Qaysite for what seemed purely financial reasons.[29] To take a modern case as a second example, in modern Oman, whatever the original descent of a weaker tribe living in the proximity of a powerful tribal federation, it has to place itself under the protection of its powerful neighbors, and must ultimately affiliate itself with their political faction, which in popular view is still considered a single, large descent group.[30] But whether the two moieties are considered descent groups, or make the transition to political parties, the forms of rivalry and enmity remain unchanged, as do the negative stereotypes in the mind of the opposing side.

The myth of Arab dual descent and the dichotomy correlated with it are important for a study of the Arab psyche primarily because they create a predisposition to internecine strife and rivalry on many different levels. In all likelihood, neither the average Arab nor the leadership in any Arab country knows much about the age-old rivalry between the two historical moieties or, for that matter, about their very existence. But the tradition of fighting, of one's own group being arrayed over and against another group occupying a parallel position within the social structure, of the incessant pressure to promote and prove the superiority of one's group is, so to speak, in the Arab bloodstream. This tradition, without doubt, is a major contributing factor to the conflict-proneness which still characterizes Arab relations on all levels of kinship, social, and political organization.

218

4. CONFLICT PRONENESS

The people of Yemen and 'Asir are still savage; not one of them would trust his brother. They live in perpetual fear and anxiety. . . . They are like wild beasts which fear everything and everybody that may come near them. As to the Yemen . . . all our people are armed, all fight, and all kill for the least thing. We are very jealous of our rights. . . . If in this village two houses should suddenly engage in a fight, the entire population would split into two parties and join in the fight. War could break out in the village. When it subsides, and only then, would the people ask what the cause of the fighting was. They fight first, and then inquire as to the cause of the fight. This is our way of life in Yemen. We fight our own relatives. The brother would fight his own brother, the son his own father. . . .[31]

While this description by a Yemenite noble is undoubtedly colored by the upper-class man's disdain for his lower-class countrymen, as well as by the Arab propensity for exaggeration, internal fighting is so abundantly attested in all parts of the Arab world that one must accept the truth of the general situation described. For it is a fact that the internal history of each Arab country consists in the main of struggles between two opposing parties on all successive levels of social organization. In many cases, two neighboring villages belong to two opposing moieties and this alone is reason enough to pit them against each other. In Upper Egypt, for instance, two villages on opposite sides of a canal frequently engage in fighting, armed with stout and heavy sticks, and sometimes with even more dangerous weapons. The men of one village will cross the canal, enter the market place of the "enemy" village, and start a fight. On the next occasion, the visit will be repaid by the men of the attacked village.[32] In recent years these traditional antagonisms have been channeled into the political area.[33] Examples illustrating the fighting mentality within and between villages are so numerous that to cite them would soon become monotonous.

Apparently, the closer the two groups, the greater the hostility. Closeness is most frequently a matter of spatial proximity. A village will relate to a neighboring village, rather than to a remote one, with the greatest hostility. The proximity between a pair of "favorite" enemies may be as close as two sections or quarters in one village or town. Two such factions, fighting with each other and deeply hating each other, are found in the towns of Ma'an and Karak in Jordan,[34] in Laghuat in Algeria, in the town of Siwa in the center of the oasis of the same name in the Western Desert of Egypt, in the village of Silwa in Upper Egypt, and in the village of Bir near Jerusalem.[35]

Occasionally, the leading families of the antagonistic factions manage to transform their followers into political parties. This development can be observed on the village level as well as in the cities, and even on a national scale. For instance, in Sirs al-Layyan in the Nile Delta, a village with 22,000 inhabitants, there used to be an old traditional factionalism between the northern and southern parts of the village, headed by two shaykhs who belonged to the two major families. Each of the factions consisted of several large descent groups, and both included Muslims as well as Copts. When, in the nineteenth century, the office of 'omda (village headman) was instituted, a leader of one of the same two families was selected. After the Wafdist revolution of 1919, the village became interested and involved in politics, and the old genealogical factionalism was transformed into political rivalry, which manifested itself in events that the scholar who reported on the village glosses over as "too terrible to be related."[36]

A very similar development could be observed in the city of Jerusalem during the British Mandatory period. In the Arab population of the city two families, the Khālidīs and the Ḥusaynīs, had been the leaders of the traditional Qays and Yaman moieties respectively, for several generations. Under the influence of the politically oriented atmosphere during the Mandatory régime, the Khālidīs and the Ḥusaynīs became the main competitors for political leadership in the city, which also meant political leadership of the whole Arab Palestine.[37]

Lebanese social structure is characterized by a dual division of each territorial or ethnic community, which is but the local outcropping of the old traditional Arab division into two competing moieties. Lineages, villages, city quarters, and sometimes even extended families manifest this dichotomy. Political effort invariably makes use of this duality, an interesting feature of which is that it cuts across confessional lines, despite the great importance otherwise attached to religious affiliation in the Arab world in general and in Lebanon in particular: groups belonging to different religious sects or even to altogether different religions often form parts of the same moiety; and, conversely, members of the same sect or faith belong to both moieties.[38] In the 1958 Lebanese "civil war," for instance, each religious sect was represented on both sides, the side of the government as well as the side of the rebels. Of course, on the occasion of such widespread fighting, many an old internal feud burst out into the open and numerous hostile clans tried to settle old scores or carry out a long-planned revenge against a favorite nearby enemy.[39]

Civil disobedience, taking the form of armed resistance to the government, is a possibility that is always close to the surface in Arab countries. Internal wars such as the Yemenite struggle between the Royalists and the Republicans, or the conflict between the Palestinian guerrillas and the Jordanian army, seem, from the historical point of view, to be manifestations of characteristic fratricidal tendencies. But even when these tendencies do not surface, the view that the world is an inimical place where a man must be ready and able to defend himself and his family by force of arms, even against his next-door neighbor, is shared by the majority of the population in every Arab country. The governments are well aware of this fact and therefore they hesitated, at least until the most recent times, to impose their will on the people in matters that the latter opposed. For example, the Iraqi government was unable to carry out a program in 1932 because the people had no less than 100,000 rifles as against the 15,000 owned by the government.[40]

Hostility can be positively correlated, not with spatial but with ideological proximity. Since in the Arab world to this day religion is one of the most important ideological factors, one would expect greater hostility between Muslim Arabs and Christian Arabs than between Muslim Arabs belonging to two different sects of Islam. But in fact the correlation of greater proximity-greater hostility holds good here too. This was demonstrated in a study carried out by the psychologists Prothro and Melikian among students at the American University of Beirut. The main instrument of their study was an old questionnaire which had been given to students in 1935. The repeat study showed that, in the intervening sixteen years, hostility between Sunnite and Shī'ite Muslims had increased to such an extent that the Sunnites expressed greater hostility toward Shī'ites than toward several Christian denominations. It also found that frequently there was greater enmity between two related groups having the same goal but advocating different means, than between two groups seeking entirely different goals: only one of forty-nine Muslim respondents stated that he wished someone would kill all Maronite (Catholic) Christians; but five of fifty-four Christians expressed this intense hostility toward Maronites.[41]

Arab conflict proneness is nowhere frought with more dire consequences for the Arab nations than in the political area. Despite the ideal of Arab unity, to which lip service is constantly being paid by Arab leaders in all their public pronouncements, the fact is that ever since World War II, which marked the beginning of full Arab political consciousness and intense Arab political activity, the relationship between governments and parties has been dominated by bitter rivalry. At best, this rivalry lay dormant for a while; at worst, it burst into the open in the form of fiery denunciations, plotting of assassinations, attacks or threats of attacks across borders, and, every few months, a *coup d'état* followed by the execution or imprisonment of ousted leaders. In between the two extremes, there were long series of meetings convened for the purpose of ironing out differences and formulating resolutions on issues of common interest to all Arab states, but ending in most cases with more disagreements than they started with. In fact, the Arab League, which was created to serve as an instrument for Arab unity, has often become a stage on which the particularistic interests of the individual member states clashed.

This inability to avoid disunity, discord, and mutual denunciations has, of course, not remained unnoticed by Arab observers. Gamal Abdul Nasser even went so far as to denounce the Egyptians for the hostility they showed toward fellow Egyptians. He had never heard, he wrote, an Egyptian speak fairly about another Egyptian, nor seen an Egyptian who had "opened his heart to pardon, forgiveness and love for his Egyptian brethren," or who did not "devote his time to tearing down the views of another Egyptian."[42] Other leaders usually confine their criticism to Arab governments beyond the borders of their own countries, and bemoan the disunity and intrigue that characterize inter-Arab relations at the top level. The following quotations from King Hussein's book *My "War" with Israel* can serve as illustrations:

"Following the 'Es Samu affair' some of my Arab allies, instead of going after Israel, turned against me!" Thereafter, "I learned by way of the international press and 'The Arab Voice,' the Cairo radio and that of Damascus, that 'before liberating Tel Aviv, we must liberate Amman!' " Since he had come to the throne in 1952, King Hussein says, he "had to cope" twelve times "with plots hatched beyond our borders!" On May 21, 1967, the Syrians sent "us a car which exploded on our border at Ramtha . . . Result: 14 Jordanians killed. . . . The incident filled Jordan with unease. In such delicate circumstances, we no longer knew who was less trustworthy: Israel or our Arab allies!" Considering that unity was essential to Arab survival, King Hussein says, "That is why I tried—disregarding the persistent hostility of some of our allies toward Jordan—to restore the ties that were supposed to bind us."[43]

Observations made by a foremost Arab political scientist show that even when faced by a common enemy, the Arabs find it difficult to put aside internal dissension and suspicion. In his book *Republican Iraq*, Dr. Majid Khadduri discusses at one point the relationship between Iraq and Syria. In 1956 there was an Iraqi force stationed in Jordan to aid that country in case of an Israeli attack. However, the Syrians considered the Iraqi force inadequate for defense against Israel and interpreted its presence in Jordan as threatening Syria rather than Israel. In another context, Khadduri refers to the criticism that has been leveled against the Arab leaders "who had been dissipating their manpower in inter-Arab conflicts" in the Yemen war.[44]

Arab analysts of the modern Arab world have often commented on the factors which prevent the Arab countries from achieving in practice the unity they all believe in and desire. Fāris and Husayn, in their book (to which reference has been made repeatedly), isolate and discuss eight such factors: Dynastic rivalries; Foreign powers; Religious minorities; National minorities; Diversity of political aims; Disparity in political development; Economic and social disparity; and Cultural disparity.[45]

While one can take no exception to this classification of the divisive factors in the modern Arab world, two comments seem in order. First, the entire approach is ahistorical. The divisive elements are all sought in contemporary developments (with the exception of the presence of minorities, which is incontestably a minor issue in the Arab world with its solid Muslim Arab majority). Moreover, the authors give the impression that it was the impact of the West which dismembered the Arab world, introduced kings and presidents and various forms of government, and thus created local patriotisms and nationalisms, bringing about disparate economic and social developments as well as great disparities in cultural attainments. They disregard the numerous roots of Arab disunity, which go deep into the historic subsoil of pre-Islamic and early Islamic Arab life and which still nourish the present-day divisiveness in the Arab world.

Secondly, Fāris and Husayn say nothing about the kin-based Arab divisiveness which pits members of two neighboring groups against each other, in many cases for no other visible reason but that they constitute two branches of one and the same larger descent group between whom rivalry, antagonism, and competitiveness are centuries-old traditions. These rivalries between social aggregates which are otherwise completely homogeneous (e.g., two villages on the opposite banks of the Nile) would remain a powerful divisive factor in the Arab world even if all the other factors discussed by Fāris and Husayn were eliminated.

A more politically oriented analysis of the divisive factors among the Arab states and, more particularly, among their ruling circles, is given by Leila S. Kadi in her book on the Arab summit conferences.[46] Miss Kadi, writing some twelve years after Fāris and Husayn, finds that in the 1936–50 period, "the rivalries and conflicting ambitions of the big colonial powers in the Middle East area were to a great measure passed on to the regimes governing the Arab states after independence." Furthermore, the former colonial powers still retained "enough power to influence the various Arab rulers to act according to the interests of the ex-colonial powers." Secondly, "the divergence of interests among the Arab States could be traced back to the personal ambitions of some of the Arab rulers (Iraq, Jordan, Saudi-Arabia) to extend their influence as much as possible at the expense of the other Arab States. . . . This expressed quite well the medieval tribal mentality of their rulers. . . ." A third reason was that, in some Arab states, such as Syria, Lebanon, and Iraq, the governing régimes represented not only the traditional feudal institutions, landlords, local chieftains, and aristocratic families, but also a newly arisen middle class or bourgeoisie, which had supplied the leadership in the struggle for independence. This new middle class, backward in its outlook, methods, and practices, was concentrated in the cities, engaged primarily in trade with the former colonial power, and was thus dependent on them.

In the period between 1964 and 1966, Miss Kadi finds that while many of the old conditions still prevailed in the Arab world, one important new factor was added. This was

> the division of the Arab world into two camps, a revolutionary camp calling for the adoption of more or less extreme socialist measures to cure the basic ills of under-development, and a reactionary camp calling for the maintenance of the prevailing conditions accompanied by the introduction of mild social reforms.

This dichotomy, the author notes, can be found within single Arab states as well: "Large segments of the population of an Arab state might have more loyalty and feel stronger affinity to the revolutionary regime and policies of another Arab state than they do to their own conservative governments." And she warns that the "two systems," that is, the revolutionary and the reactionary (or conservative) camp, "are quickly moving towards the point at which the survival of one can be achieved only at the expense of radical modification (if not liquidation) of the other." The divergence of interests between the two camps is expressed in their separate calls for two different sets of Arab conferences, and the alliances they maintain or seek in the international arena. "The interests of the reactionary camps are closely tied to the Western capitalist powers, whereas the interests of the revolutionary camp have become more and more associated with the Eastern communist powers."[47]

Again, while there can be no doubt that the conservative-revolutionary dichotomy is a serious problem in the Arab world, it is simplistic to attribute the lack of unity among the Arab countries and within them to this single factor.

My own conclusion from the foregoing analysis is that Arab disunity is a manifestation of a tendency that has been part of the Arab personality since pre-Islamic days. At every level discord has always been present, either actually or potentially. At the slightest provocation the fighting propensity surfaces, a quarrel ensues and easily degenerates into physical violence. In this connection, it appears that the readiness with which Arabs break into violent verbal abuse and threats is, in effect, a mechanism whose ultimate function is to prevent an oral dispute from leading to physical action. As long as what can be called the oral phase of a conflict lasts, there is always hope that the aroused passions will exhaust themselves in words and the swords remain in their hilts. The more vehement the abuse, the greater the likelihood that it will provide sufficient satisfaction and thus will not be followed up by physical violence. Once, however, the second phase, that of physical fighting, starts, different and even older psychological mechanisms come into play, making it practically impossible for either side to stop fighting, unless totally and hopelessly defeated, or unless mediation can bring about a settlement of the dispute.

All in all, the tension between unity and conflict can be taken as a most telling example of the Arab's infatuation with ideal forms (in this case, unity) to which he clings emotionally even while he knows that they are contradicted and vitiated by reality (in this case, conflict). As Morroe Berger put it, "Arabs confuse the two, professing to believe against reality that the ideal is carried out in conduct and is identical with practice rather than merely constituting the criterion by which practice is to be judged."[48] The situation is complicated by the fact that "unity" is merely a very abstract and remote ideal, while strife has its historical antecedent and underpinning in the age-old Arab virtues of manliness, aggressiveness, bravery, heroism, courage, and vengefulness, which have been extolled by poets for more than thirteen centuries and survive in the Arab's consciousness, predisposing him to conflict even though he believes in Arab unity and brotherhood.

Two of the sources of Arab conflict proneness can readily be isolated. One is the competitiveness and sibling rivalry instilled by Arab mothers into their children. A favorite device used by mothers is to make the children behave by provoking a jealous reaction from them. For instance, if a child refuses food, the mother will say to him: "If you don't eat it, I shall give it to your brother," and make a motion as if she were indeed about to give the food in question to one of her other children. In most cases this is sufficient to change the mind of the unwilling child. Or, if a child cannot or does not want to do something the mother wants him to do, she will say to him: "Look, your brother can do this, why can't you?" Frequent repetitions of such scenes lead the child at an early age to consider his sibling his arch rival, and, of course, the closer the age of two siblings the stronger the feeling of competition between them. In some parts of the Arab world sibling rivalry is considered an essential incentive in the process of growing up, and it is purposely provoked.[49] The residue of such child rearing techniques in the adult Arab mind is a keen sense of rivalry especially between those individuals and groups who occupy similar positions in the prestige hierarchy, or are located in each other's proximity.

The preference for close in-family marriages is another contributing factor to the Arab conflict proneness. In an exogamous society every man has affinal ties to the outgroup which supplied him with a wife, and the women are the natural links between the two groups to which their husbands on the one hand, and their paternal families, on the other, belong. In case of tension or disagreement they tend to prevent it from deteriorating into a conflict. The men themselves will be reluctant to take up arms against a neighboring group of which their wives' fathers and brothers are members or into which their daughters and sisters have married. As against this, the entire Arab social structure is calculated to reinforce ingroup isolation. Patrilineal descent means that a man is considered a descendant of only his father, his paternal grandfather, and so on, but not of his maternal grandfather and the latter's ancestors. Thus even if his mother comes from an outgroup (e. g. a neighboring village or town) he belongs only to his father's group which claims his entire, undivided loyalty. When his father and mother are paternal cousins (which is the ideal), this loyalty to the father's line is reinforced by the fact that his paternal and maternal grandfathers are brothers, and that one generation farther back there is one single ancestor who is both his paternal and maternal great-grandfather. A man growing up in a society in which the ideal is such a self-contained family tends to view the successively larger social units as genealogical extensions of the family: whatever the size of the social unit, it is in theory the patrilineal progeny of one single original ancestor. The larger the unit, the more generations ago its common ancestor lived, the weaker the bonds of loyalty within it. By the same token, the smaller the unit, the closer the patrilineal relationship, the stronger the feeling of kinship and the greater the readiness to fight for its interests against more remote kin formations.

Be this as it may, the fact is that conflict proneness is an outstanding characteristic of the Arab mind.

XIV

CONFLICT RESOLUTION AND "CONFERENTIASIS"

1. CONFLICT RESOLUTION

A SOCIETY IN WHICH CONFLICTS ARE FREQUENT MUST DEVELOP mechanisms for settling differences which, if allowed to get out of hand, can destroy the entire social fabric. In the Arab world, mediation on the tribal and village level has for centuries been the traditional method of settling disputes, and the same method has, in modern times, been adapted for settling political and military issues within and between Arab states.

In tribal and village society, the role of the mediator *(wasīṭ)* or mediators in resolving conflict has been, and still is, a crucial one. In every conflict those involved tend to feel that their honor is at stake, and that to give in, even as little as an inch, would diminish their self-respect and dignity. Even to take the first step toward ending a conflict would be regarded as a sign of weakness which, in turn, would greatly damage one's honor. Hence, it is almost impossible for an Arab to come to an agreement in direct confrontation with an opponent. Given the Arab tradition of invective and proclivity to boasting and verbal exaggeration, any face-to-face encounter between two adversaries is likely to aggravate the dispute rather than constitute a step toward its settlement.

The function of the mediator, therefore, is first of all to separate the fighting sides, to make it physically impossible for them to continue the conflict, to force them to stop fighting, and at the same time to enable them to do so without incurring the shame of exhibiting weakness or admitting defeat. After the actual fighting has stopped, the presence of the mediator imposes restraints on both sides, if not over the actual demands or positions, at least in regard to their verbal expression. The entrance of the mediator into a conflict has the same restraining effect also in cases in which the two sides are not involved in actual hand-to-hand fighting but maintain a status of inactive belligerency. This restraint results from the respect in which the mediator is held by both parties to the conflict. The greater the prestige of the mediator and the deeper the respect he commands, the better the chances that his efforts at mediating a dispute will be successful.

For this reason, the role of mediator is in many parts of the Arab world traditionally assigned to members of special descent groups, who as such have a high ascribed status. Among the Shabana of Southern Iraq, for instance, the peacemaking function belongs to the *sāda* class, whose members enjoy a status of nobility based on their generally accepted claim to descent from the Prophet Muḥammad through his daughter Fāṭima. The *sāda* are associated with each tribal segment of the Shabana, but remain free of active fighting and do not become involved in blood feuds. Instead, they take an active part in peacemaking.[1]

A similar function is fulfilled in North Africa by the *mrābṭīn* or marabouts, who are holy or saintly men, with a reputation of good deeds or miracle working. Among the Kabyles of Algeria, who, although Berbers, are heirs to much that characterizes the Arab ethos, the marabouts interfere as soon as a conflict becomes intensified to the point where human life is threatened: they stop the fighting, and then embark on the lengthy process of mediation. This enables the two sides to discontinue the fight without dishonor and shame. This is, as they call it, a "door" to an honorable way out of the dispute. Often in their mediatory efforts the marabouts will try to find fault with the party from whom pardon is being sought, so that a balance can be established and the supplicating party avoid complete humiliation.[2]

It goes without saying that the mediator must be a person whose impartiality is beyond question, and this means that he must not be more closely related to one side in the dispute than to the other. He also must enjoy such a high status that neither of the two disputants can in any way exert pressure on him. Preferably, he should also be a wealthy man, so as to preclude any suspicion of being accessible to bribery. In sum, the ideal mediator is a man who is in a position, because of his personality, status, respect, wealth, influence, and so on to create in the litigants the desire to conform with his wishes.

The mediator often tries to increase whatever personal influence he wields over the disputants by invoking the presumed desires of other individuals whom the litigants are bound to respect. Thus, in trying to persuade a man to give up or, at least, modify a position he has taken, the mediator will frequently say: "Do it for the sake of your father," or brothers, other kinsmen, neighbors, friends, and the like.[3] In most cases, such persuasion, which is applied to both parties in the dispute, brings results, although only after many patient repetitions.

What is the appeal of this argument? Or rather, what is the meaning of the concept of doing something "for the sake" of an individual or of an abstraction such as "the peace of the village"? One underlying assumption undoubtedly is that each individual is obligated by the ties of kinship to act in a manner that his kinsmen find gratifying. The second assumption is that the kinsmen, especially the older ones, are interested in the settlement of any conflict involving their kin group because every conflict represents a potential danger to the honor of the family. A third assumption is that by modifying his position, the disputant can manifest generosity which, in turn, redounds to the honor of his kin group. All these assumptions, of course, remain unspoken. But because they are known to exist and are unquestioningly accepted by everybody as valid and unassailable, the formula, "Do it for the sake of X," has great ethical force and puts considerable psychological pressure on the parties in dispute.

Techniques found effective in one context tend to be applied in others. Thus, the argument, "Do it for the sake of X," is used not only in disputes, but also in bargaining over a piece of merchandise. It is perhaps because of this feature that a mediator or intermediary is often considered indispensable in making sure that one is not cheated in the market place. The procedure of bargaining is evidently regarded as analogous to dispute settling: there is, of course, a dispute over the price, hence the role of the intermediary. Since in the traditional small society both the buyer and the seller are as a rule well known to each other, each of them knows also the male members of the other's family.[4] In these circumstances, the adjuration on the part of the buyer that the seller reduce the price "for the sake of your father" makes sense, because it places the entire transaction in the same category to which the process of dispute-solving belongs. In return, the seller may entreat the buyer to add to the price he offered, "for the sake of your father," or even "my father." If the distance between the price asked by the seller and the one offered by the buyer is still great, one of the two may say, "I shall give so-and-so much for it" (or "I shall give it to you for so-and-so much") "for the sake of your father," or even simply "for your sake." This game has many variants, but a common feature of them all is that it not only leads to successful conclusion of a bargain, but also cements the personal relationship between the two men.

A characteristic expression of kinship cohesion surfaces in connection with disputes. As Ayoub put it on the basis of his observations in a Lebanese Druze village, "The question of rightness of one claim over the other is not a paramount issue so far as one's obligation to support is concerned. Thus, if members of different *ahls* [lineages] quarrel, each can expect support (or neutrality at the very least) from others in his own kin group. . . . "[5] This observation can be generalized: the obligation to support one's kinsman in a quarrel with an outsider exists all over the Arab world, irrespective of the question of right or wrong.

The same mentality expresses itself in the action of the mediators. They, too, "are neither expressly interested in determining the guilt or innocence of any party in the dispute nor the rightness or wrongness of one claim over the other. They mediate. They do not arbitrate. They do not judge."[6] Thus, even if a case has been brought before the court—in all Arab countries there are government-appointed and police-backed courts of justice—and the court hands down its verdict, this does not eliminate the need for mediation. On the contrary. A court verdict does not lead to a reconciliation between the two parties; in order to restore peace in the community and to maintain the solidarity of the group, mediation must continue until reconciliation is achieved. Of course, once a court judgment has been issued, reconciliation is much more difficult to achieve. It is not surprising, therefore, that there is considerable resistance to the use of courts.[7] "A third person is always found ready to interfere between two quarrelling people, or if a mother beats her child, or a person scolds his neighbor."[8] Each of these incidents is considered a conflict situation which calls for outside mediation. As to disputes between husband and wife, the Koran itself (4:35) prescribes that these should be settled through the mediation of two "arbiters," or "judges," one from the husband's and the other from the wife's kin, to effect reconciliation.

Since the mediation of disputes is an important feature of village life, a proper setting has to be provided for it. This is the village guest house, which serves other purposes as well, over and above that of temporary lodging for visitors who, because of the traditional segregation between the sexes, cannot be put up for the night in the house of the people they came to see. The guest house serves also as the meeting place of the men, as the council chamber in which the elders sit, and the courtroom in which intra-village disputes are adjudicated.[9]

The adjudication of a village dispute is never a purely legal matter. In fact, such proceedings are in most cases conducted primarily on the basis of moral or ethical considerations. The very authority of the elders who arbitrate in such disputes is based on their recognized ethical stature. The meetings at which settlements are effected are attended, at the village guest house, by all those who manifest an ethical concern in village affairs, which in practice means all but the youngest. And the decision of the elders is accepted by the disputants and their kinsmen, without any legal means of enforcement, simply because the judgment, once pronounced, represents an ethical and moral imperative. It is in this manner that the folk mores serve as a solid basis for social control.[10]

The intermediary has several other tasks in addition to dispute mediating. One needs an intermediary

> in order not to be cheated in the market place, in locating and acquiring a job, in resolving conflict and legal litigation, in winning a court decision, in speeding government action, and in establishing and maintaining political influence, bureaucratic procedures, in finding a bride, and, in fact, for the social scientist to locate and convince respondents to give an interview.[11]

In both village and town, the za'im—the economically, socially, and politically powerful leader of a major extended family—has the important function of mediating between families or even individuals, thereby keeping disputes out of government courts.[12]

A further function of the mediator is that of resolving the conflict which arises when a woman wants to obtain a divorce and her husband objects. According to Muslim law, a man can easily divorce his wife. All he has to do is to pronounce the words, "You are divorced," in the presence of two witnesses. A wife, on the other hand, has no legal way of obtaining a divorce: she can only run away from her husband's home and take refuge with her paternal family. In addition, among certain Arab tribes she can have recourse to a prodecure in which she asks a mediator to represent her and argue her case with the husband. Among the Awlād 'Alī of the Western Desert of Egypt, a semi-nomadic group of tribes, a woman can "throw herself" upon a respected man in the community and thereby oblige him to give her refuge and start negotiating with her husband with a view to obtaining a divorce from him. The success of the mediator in obtaining the divorce depends primarily on his prestige in the community and his consequent influence on the husband. Therefore, a prudent woman will select a tribal, and not village, chieftain or a generally respected holy man. Incidentally, if the mediator is unable to persuade the woman's kin to return the bride price to the husband and the latter insists on receiving it back, the mediator himself may have to pay the amount in question. Thus the honor that goes with the mediation carries with it a considerable financial risk.[13]

Enough has been said of the traditional role of the mediator and of mediation in Arab folk society to make us expect that this institution is carried over into political life. And, indeed, such methods of resolving conflict are constantly applied on a larger scale to deal with political differences between Arab countries, or between two feuding sides within one state. At this level, too, the mediator has to be an outsider who carries prestige and wields influence, and who can appeal to the feuding parties to end their dispute for the sake of the overriding interest in Arab unity. Outside mediation is such an integral part of Arab political consciousness that once a conflict erupts, it is certain that before long either one of the parties to it will ask an outsider to mediate, or an uninvolved Arab leader from another country will offer his own services or suggest that somebody else should mediate in order to restore Arab brotherhood and unity. Examples in the conflict-torn Arab world of the 1960's abound. We shall confine ourselves to two: the role of mediation in the Yemeni conflict between the Royalists and the Republicans, and in the Jordanian conflict between the commandos and the government.

In September, 1964, when the Second Arab Summit Conference met in Alexandria, the civil war in Yemen between the Royalists and the Republicans was about two years old. One item on the agenda of the conference, which was attended by Field Marshal 'Abdullāh al-Sallāl, President of the Yemeni Arab Republic, was "the financial and moral support that should be given to the Republic of Yemen." On September 5, 'Abdul Khāliq Hassūna, Secretary-General of the Arab League, presented a long report in which he touched upon the problem of Yemen and urged the conference to solve it in order to enable the Arab states to repel the pressing threat of imperialism and Zionism in the Arab world. However, the conference devoted almost all its meetings to discussions of the Israel issue, and adjourned without reaching a decision on the problem of Yemen. Immediately after the conference, Amīr Fayṣal al-Saʿūd, deputy of the King of Saudi Arabia, paid a private visit to President Nasser of the United Arab Republic and arranged for meetings, which actually took place in a few days, in order to come to an agreement over the Yemeni question. Upon the conclusion of these meetings, a communiqué was issued, on September 14, 1964. It stated that agreement had been reached between Saudi Arabia and the U.A.R. to mediate between the two warring Yemeni parties, in order to provide the necessary atmosphere for the solution of the problem by peaceful means. It also stated that Saudi Arabia and the U.A.R. undertook to cooperate in solving the Yemeni dispute, and were determined to put an end to the present military entanglement. As if for good measure, the communiqué included a third item which had nothing to do with the Yemeni war, to the effect that Saudi Arabia and the U.A.R. were determined to cooperate in every field, and to support one another under all political, material, and moral circumstances. This comminiqué was duly published on September 15 in *Al-Ahrām*, the semi-official Cairo daily.

The remarkable thing about this move was that it undertook to mediate between the two sides , although one of them, the Royalists, was actively backed and supplied with arms by Saudi Arabia, and the other, the Republicans, had the armed support of U.A.R. army units. As might be expected, the agreement was not put into effect because Nasser subsequently insisted that the ousted Imām al-Badr of Yemen and his family should not participate in the future government of Yemen, and that the Republican régime should be maintained, while Fayṣal rejected both demands with equal firmness. That the two parties to the mediation effort would take these opposing positions could have been foreseen at the talks. Nevertheless, the Saudi Arabian and U.A.R. leaders could not resist the temptation to assume the role of mediators, as required by Arab tradition.[14]

On November 2, at a secret conference of Royalists and Republicans, a cease-fire agreement was reached which was to come into effect on November 8. One item in the agreement was that on November 23 a national conference of Royalists and Republicans should take place. The cease-fire held for two days, after which the Egyptians resumed their bombing of Royalist positions. The conference, incidentally, never materialized. But Imām al-Badr expressed his hope that King Fayṣal of Saudi Arabia could arrange it with Nasser.[15] That is, he put his faith in outside mediation.

Saudi Arabia continued to support the Royalists, and the U.A.R. seemed intent on building up its armed strength in the country. Tension between Saudi Arabia and the U.A.R. reached an all-time high in July of 1965. On July 22, President Nasser threatened to use force against Saudi Arabia, to "bomb the bases of aggression" in that country. Then came a sudden diplomatic thaw, indeed a reversal, and on August 22, Nasser arrived at Jedda to confer with King Fayṣal about ways of restoring peace to Yemen. On the twenty-fourth, the two heads of state signed an agreement which provided for a withdrawal of all Egyptian forces from Yemen, the cessation of all military aid from Saudi Arabia, and the formation of a force by both countries to back a joint "peace commission." The text of the agreement emphasized that Fayṣal and Nasser had ascertained the wishes of "all the representatives of the Yemeni people and their national forces," and that the purpose of the two heads of state was to enable "the Yemeni people to exercise their free will so that it could provide an atmosphere of peace." That is, they did not judge or decide, but mediated. They also announced that a plebiscite would be held in Yemen not later than November 23, 1966, while on November 23, 1965 (exactly one year before the planned plebiscite), a "transitional conference" of fifty members representing all the national forces and people of authority in Yemen would take place, after due consultation with various Yemeni groups.[16]

On September 9, 1965, the U.A.R. and Saudi Arabia agreed on a joint peace committee to supervise the implementation of the peace terms between the Royalists and the Republicans. A so-called popular conference of the Republicans was held at Janad on October 20, which ended with a resolution calling for the selection of a nine-man committee to choose Republican delegates to the November 23 conference.

The conference actually took place in November and December, 1965. Twenty-five Republicans and twenty Royalists participated, as well as five representatives of the Union of Yemeni Popular Forces, called the "Third Force." However, in the four weeks during which the conference was in session, only three formal meetings were held. Six days after its opening, it was reported deadlocked. On December 24, it was indefinitely postponed, and each side accused the other of leaving the meeting and thereby forcing an adjournment. Faced with this internal impasse, 'Abdul-Rahmān al-Iryānī, leader of the Republican delegation, appealed to the outside mediators once more. He wrote to King Fayṣal and President Nasser imploring them to help: "You alone are in a position to solve the problem. . . ."[17]

But the Yemeni war continued, and so did the active participation in it of Egyptian forces whose attacks included the occasional use of gas bombs dropped from Ilyushin bombers on Yemeni villages.[18]

On January 11, 1966, the Union of Yemeni Popular Forces appealed to Nasser and Fayṣal to help convene a comprehensive Yemeni people's conference. On March 8, the joint U.A.R.-Saudi Arabian peace commission recommended holding a second Haradh conference. The Emir of Kuwait proposed Kuwaiti mediation between the U.A.R. and Saudi Arabia over Yemen on April 4; and on May 16, the brother of King Fayṣal said that Saudi Arabia was agreeable to Kuwaiti mediation. But on May 20, the U.A.R. rejected a Kuwaiti proposal for a joint trip to Saudi Arabia to confer with King Fayṣal. Undismayed, Kuwait announced on June 2 that it would continue its mediation efforts between the U.A.R. and Saudi Arabia, and in the next week the Kuwaiti Foreign Minister visited both countries. He returned to Jedda on the twentieth to continue mediation efforts. On July 30, he announced that U.A.R. and Saudi representatives would soon meet in Kuwait to discuss new proposals for a solution of the Yemeni problem. A draft of a solution based on the Kuwaiti proposals was agreed upon on August 19, and the representatives of the two countries returned to their respective capitals to obtain their governments' acceptance of the tentative agreement. Thereafter, the Kuwaiti draft was never heard of again.[19]

One might think that the experiences sketched above would make the Yemenis distrust further mediation efforts by Arab states. But this was not the case. All that did happen was that hitherto uninvolved Arab states were asked, or offered, to undertake the role of mediators. In the fall of 1966, it was announced that Algeria had agreed to intercede with the U.A.R. to stop the deterioration of the relationship with the Yemeni Republicans, and that Syria, Iraq, and Kuwait also agreed to work for the same purpose.[20]

Finally, the defeat of Egypt by Israel in the Six Day War of June, 1967, gave the impetus to the U.A.R. to withdraw its forces from Yemen. At the Khartoum Summit Conference, which convened on August 29, 1967, Egypt agreed to evacuate Yemen, and Saudi Arabia undertook to halt its own support of the Royalists *after* the Egyptians completed their withdrawal. Two days later a three-nation committee, consisting of representatives of Sudan, Iraq, and Morocco, was established to work out the problems of winding down the war, and to supervise the withdrawal of the Egyptian troops. On September 14, Aden radio announced that U.A.R. troops had begun to withdraw from Yemen, but on October 4 the three-nation committee left for Cairo after complaining that serious obstacles had been put in its way.[21]

President Sallāl's government was overthrown on November 5 of that year, and a new government, headed by a three-man Presidential Council, took over. On December 7, the withdrawal of the Egyptian forces from Yemen was completed, and the Saudis stopped their financial support of the Royalists. However, these steps put an end neither to the war nor to the mediation efforts. In December, 1967, the Royalists laid siege to San'a[22] and the fighting around the capital continued well into January. On January 12, the three-nation mediating committee appealed for an immediate cease-fire. On the eighteenth, the committee ended a week's meetings in Beirut with the decision to refer the Yemeni conflict back to Saudi Arabia and the U.A.R. On June 22, 1968, Yemeni Prime Minister 'Amrī called on Arab leaders to make efforts to improve the relations between Yemen and Saudi Arabia.[23]

Thereafter, the Republicans gradually gained the upper hand, and in May, 1970, it was announced that a final settlement had been reached between them and the Royalists, as a result of which thirty Royalist leaders returned to San'a.

An even more characteristic example of the persistent Arab reliance on mediation is supplied by the protracted sequence of efforts made by several Arab states and leaders to settle the fighting between the Jordanian army and the Palestinian commandos. The acute phase of the struggle between the commandos, who used Jordan as their main base, and King Hussein, as supreme commander of the Jordanian army, lasted well over a year. During this period an identical pattern was repeated with minor variations over and over again: (1) Clashes between the two sides prompted Arab leaders outside Jordan to engage in mediation. (2) As a result of mediation, an agreement was reached between the Jordanian army and the commandos to stop fighting. (3) Conditions were agreed upon under which the commandos could remain in certain delineated parts of Jordan. (4) The agreement was violated, according to each side by the opposite party. (5) Renewed fighting broke out which, in turn, led back to point (1), etc. Many times the whole series of events, from (1) through (5), took place within as short a time as two to three days. Despite the repeated failure of mediation to bring about a settlement, both sides again and again were ready to meet with mediators and agree to settlements proposed by them. Such willingness to go through the procedures of mediation again and again can only be understood as a conditioned reflex based on the reliance on mediation for countless generations.[24]

At the time of writing (1972), it seems that the power of the commandos in Jordan has been effectively crushed. In the fifteen months during which the acute phase of the struggle lasted, there were fifteen outside mediation attempts to restore peace—or about one per month. Leaders from practically every Arab country mediated at one time or another in the conflict, and the increasing number of preceding occasions on which agreements reached as a result of mediation were promptly disregarded never seemed to deter any Arab statesman from trying his hand at this age-old method of conflict resolution.

The attempts at mediation in Yemen and Jordan can serve as a model for the role that this old Arab institution, originally developed within a small, kinship-oriented society, has come to play in modern times in large-scale contests between major Arab powers, in armed conflicts, and in political and diplomatic collisions between Arab states. In addition, the conviction that the only acceptable method of resolving conflict is mediation by a third party, who serves literally as a go-between, commuting back and forth between the two sides until he gets them to accept his solution, influences and, in fact, determines the behavior of Arab leaders also in relation to non-Arab adversaries. The persistent Arab refusal to meet in direct talks with Israel can be considered as a case in point. It appears that in this instance, too, Arab behavior reflects the old tradition of considering the mediator a *conditio sine qua non* for resolving the conflict without loss of face, while the direct peace negotiations, insisted upon by Israel, remain for them a psychological impossibility to accept.

2. "CONFERENTIASIS"

In the United States, when the government or any large public body finds itself confronted with a major problem, the usual method of trying to cope with it is to appoint a committee to study the issue and to make recommendations as to how its solution can be tackled. In the Arab world, the response to a major problem is to convene a conference. If one surveys Arab political behavior in the last two decades or so, one cannot escape the impression that the Arab political leadership suffers from what can best be described as "conferentiasis."

It does not seem to be too far-fetched to see in this predilection for meeting in conference an outgrowth or heritage of two traditional Arab social institutions. One is conflict resolution through mediation, and the other deliberation in council. As to mediation, let us add that, while the efforts of the mediator usually begin in the form of separate meetings with the two litigants, they culminate in one or more joint sessions attended by both parties, as well as by their kinsmen and other supporters. Such a session, presided over by the mediator, is actually a conference which has as its sole purpose the settlement of the conflict pitting the sides against each other. This oft-repeated experience is one of the sources of the Arab readiness to convene a conference for the settlement of any issue, the working out of any plan of action, the passing of any kind of resolution. In the traditional context, the role of the mediator was played out in repeated, small-scale conferences; therefore, the lack of success in resolving a conflict at any one particular conference merely meant that an additional conference had to be convened. Correspondingly, disagreement at a large-scale Arab conference is not taken by the participants as a fiasco, but merely as an inevitable stage in the long and arduous process of reaching an agreement; that is to say, it is considered as nothing more than an indication that the efforts must continue at a subsequent conference. Hence, the frequently observed ritual of concluding Arab conferences, at which little or nothing was agreed, with the announcement that it was resolved to convene another conference, possibly at another place, and probably with a somewhat different cast of participants.[25]

The traditional deliberations in council add the second psychological element to the Arab inclination to meetings in conference. The council of elders, or of adult male members of the community, is an informally constituted consultative body which meets at irregular intervals, but usually more frequently in the nomadic camp than in the agricultural village. Among the Bedouins, the council meets in the tent of the tribal chief; among the villagers, in the guest house. The Bedouin tribal council is the original prototype of the informal deliberative gathering, in which the weight of each man's opinion depends on his age, the size of his family, his reputation, wisdom, eloquence, and personality. The tribal council never votes; it only deliberates and discusses. The shaykh of the tribe is not a chairman of a meeting but rather a host, in whose tent the members of the council are guests, and the rules of polite hospitality are observed. Once the shaykh feels that a definite majority of the council inclines to a certain view (in which, of course, they may well be influenced by the shaykh's own opinion), he will summarize the prevailing views, and at this point, without any formal vote, all know what decision has been reached.

One of the important functions of the tribal council is to elect a new chief at the death of the shaykh. The chieftainship in most Bedouin tribes is the hereditary prerogative of one of the leading families of the tribe, but it is up to the council to decide exactly who among the possibly numerous sons or even nephews of the deceased shaykh should become the new leader. Here, too, no voting takes place; rather, a consensus is gradually allowed to crystallize during the last few years of the aging shaykh's life. In most cases, at the time the old shaykh dies, the decision has long been taken as to his successor.

Before the European control of Arab countries, the village council functioned in a similar way. The one major difference was that many villages consisted not of a single social group (such as the wandering and camping nomadic tribe), but of two or more separate lineages, often called *ḥamā'il* (sing. *ḥamūla).* In some villages, each *ḥamūla* had its own separate council, guest house, and chieftain; and not infrequently there would be considerable tension and feuding among the *ḥamā'il.* In others, the chiefs of all the lineages would form a joint council and recognize the head of the most important lineage as village headman. Thus, even in traditional circumstances, the village council was a more formal body than its tribal counterpart. This formality was enhanced when the Ottoman government, or the local Arab governments, gained sufficient control over the villages to be able to introduce taxation. The council and the headman were made responsible for collecting the taxes in the village, and this in itself resulted in giving formal decision-making powers to the village council. The process of formalization was carried further when the European powers gained control in Arab lands. Voting procedures were introduced, changing the relationship between the people and the leaders, who now became formally elected, and occasionally salaried, officials. The traditional social leadership of the village thus became transformed into a political body. Only one thing did not change: the old love for meetings, council sessions, deliberations, and oratory used as effectively for influencing the listeners as for arguing against other speakers. This, it seems to me, is the traditional background against which one must view Arab political "conferentiasis."

Ever since the creation of the Arab League in 1945 (which, incidentally, came about not through the initiative of the Arab countries but of the British government), inter-Arab conferences have been a permanent feature of Arab political life. Indeed, the conferences and consultations constitute an endless chain.[26]

Each conference is usually preceded by an announcement detailing the important issues on which it will make decisions. In the conference itself, disagreements usually emerge to prevent the participants from actually reaching agreement on the issues discussed. In these circumstances, the decision to convene another conference becomes both a face-saver, maintaining the appearance of unity, and a substitute for the lack of other concrete decisions.

Arab conferences, also, are showcases for several features in the Arab character discussed elsewhere in this book. The Arab disregard of time often finds its expression in the opening a day or so late, in the inability to begin and end sessions at appointed hours, and in the closing several days or hours behind schedule. Arab disunity is expressed in the frequent boycotting of conferences by one or more Arab countries, by walk-outs of delegates or delegations, and by open display of animosities. Arab rhetoricism is manifested in fiery and flowery oratory often quite disproportionate to the concrete issues being discussed. And the Arab proclivity for substituting words for actions shows itself on those rare occasions when a conference does end with agreed-upon resolutions: these, as a rule, sound most impressive but are rarely carried out.

The above generalizations can easily be illustrated by examples. In 1966, the Research Center of the Palestine Liberation Organization in Beirut published a study by Leila S. Kadi of the Arab summit conferences that had taken place in 1936–50 and 1964–66, and which had dealt primarily with the Palestine problem.[27] The gravamen of the book is an indictment of the Arab governments for their failure to act effectively in the Palestine problem and to support the Palestine Liberation Organization. The author is especially critical of the Arab governments and the summitry of the Arab leaders in the 1964–66 period. A typical summit conference, she says, would create a follow-up committee to decide on an issue. This committee

would reach a deadlock; it would refer the issue to the Foreign Ministers to decide on it; a deadlock would be reached here also; and the issue would be referred to the Prime Ministers; these, in turn, because of their inability to reach a decision, would refer the question to the Summit Conference. By the time the issue is finally discussed at the Summit, it would be too late, and the Conference eventually comes out with a unanimous general decision which—more often than not—would not be implemented by the member states.[28]

As a second example, let us give a somewhat more detailed account of the long series of meetings and conferences that were initiated following the fire which damaged the Aqṣā Mosque in Jerusalem on August 21, 1969. Two days later, President Nasser of the U.A.R. said that it had become a sacred duty for all Arab armed forces to war against Israel as a result of the Aqṣā fire. On August 25 and 26, the Arab League's Council of Foreign Ministers met in Cairo. The purpose of the meeting was to consult on the fire in the Aqṣā Mosque in Jerusalem, "to strive for unity of views and action," and, as it was stated subsequently, to "seek effective common action against Israel."[29] Upon adjourning, the Council of Foreign Ministers announced that the Arab League's Joint Defense Council would meet early in November to rally all Arab forces against Israel as a consequence of the fire. After the results of the consultations of the Defense Council became known, a meeting of the Arab kings and presidents, urged by King Hussein, would be considered. At the same time, a plan for a meeting of the heads of all the Muslim states was proposed by King Fayṣal of Saudi Arabia and endorsed by President Nasser of the United Arab Republic and by the foreign ministers of the Arab League states. Saudi Arabia and Morocco were appointed to organize such a meeting, which, it was felt, would strengthen Muslim unity by focusing on an issue on which all Muslim countries were in agreement.

On the same day, *The New York Times* correspondent Dana Adam Schmidt reported from Amman that leaders of the Arab countries most immediately concerned with Israel would meet in Cairo within a few days, to deal with military questions and to prepare a meeting of all Arab heads of state. This, in turn, would pave the way for a meeting of all Muslim heads of state, to be held in Saudi Arabia.

On August 30, King Hussein flew to Cairo for talks with President Nasser preparatory to discussions among the heads of state of Jordan, the United Arab Republic, Syria, and Iraq. Before his visit to Cairo, King Hussein conferred with King Fayṣal at Jedda and discussed with him the plan to convene a meeting of the four states mentioned. Depending on agreement between Hussein and Nasser, the presidents of Syria and Iraq would arrive in Cairo for this meeting on September 1.[30]

Two weeks later, on September 15, 1969, *The New York Times* reported from Cairo that the status of the meeting of the Islamic heads of state scheduled for September 19 in Rabat, Morocco, remained in doubt. On the night of September 13, Egyptian sources had announced a postponement of the meeting; but on September 14, the Moroccan Foreign Minister issued a denial of the Egyptian report and stated that the conference would be held on September 22, in Rabat. However, *The New York Times* reporter in Cairo added that President Nasser seemed unlikely to attend the meeting even if it was held in Rabat as scheduled, and favored a meeting in New York instead, during the session of the U.N. General Assembly, to be attended not by Arab heads of state but by Arab foreign ministers. Since other leftist Arab states were likely to follow Nasser's lead it appeared that, even if the meeting were to take place in Rabat, it would be attended only by Arab monarchs. After considerable difficulties (Pakistan refused to participate), the Islamic Summit Conference did take place in Rabat; and after four days of deliberations, it ended with a declaration to the effect that it gave its full support to the Palestine people for restitution of their usurped rights and their struggle for national liberation.[31]

On November 8–10, a three-day meeting of the Arab League's Joint Defense Council took place in Cairo. Here the participants except Tunisia pledged to give full support to the Palestinian commandos, and it was decided to convene an Arab summit conference in Rabat from December 20 to 22 for the purpose of working out an agreement on a joint all-Arab military confrontation against Israel.

On December 18, two days in advance of the scheduled opening of the conference, King Fayṣal of Saudi Arabia and President Nasser of Egypt met in Cairo to discuss the agenda. The conference was expected to take the form of a war council, but was also described by Moroccan statesmen as a "summit of realism." On the same day, King Hussein of Jordan arrived in Rabat to begin informal talks with King Ḥasan II of Morocco. The next day, several other Arab leaders and envoys arrived in Rabat. On December 20, the day on which the conference was to open, the last representatives of the participating fourteen Arab states and of the Palestinian commandos arrived in Rabat. However, shortly before the conference was scheduled to open at the Hilton Hotel, it was announced that several of the assembled leaders felt too tired after their long flight into Rabat, and that therefore it had been decided to postpone the opening of the conference for a day. The real reason for the postponement seems to have been the desire of President Nasser to conduct last-minute consultations in an effort to reach a reasonable consensus on many complex and controversial issues before the formal opening of the conference. Also, there was a disagreement as to which country's representative should chair the conference. The new time for the opening was set at 10 A.M., December 21, when all that actually took place was the ceremonial opening.

The next day (December 22), the Arab world leaders met in what *The New York Times* described as "secret sessions" to discuss their war plans. On the twenty-third, two oil-producing Arab countries, Kuwait and Saudi Arabia, refused to increase financial support for the strengthening of Arab armies; whereupon President Nasser, Yasir 'Arafāt, and 'Abdul Khāliq Hassūna (Secretary-General of the Arab League) walked out of the conference.

The ceremonial closing session was scheduled to take place on December 24, at 5:30 P.M. This session was boycotted by the Syrian, South Yemeni, and Iraqi delegations, "in anger over the attitudes of their fellow Arabs toward mobilization of the 'Battle of Liberation' against Israel," as *The Times* put it. Leaders of the other Arab states rushed to the villas occupied by the delegations of these three countries to persuade them to attend the closing ceremony. It took some two and a half to three hours to achieve this. In the meantime, the delegates of the other countries waited around in the lobby of the Hilton Hotel. When finally the closing session did take place, it was kept to a brief ten-minute formality. Immediately afterwards, King Ḥasan held a news conference, in which he asserted that the boycott of the closing session by Syria, South Yemen, and Iraq had been the result of nothing more than "doctrinal divergences" among the Arabs, without indicating divergences of purpose.

While it was generally recognized that the Rabat conference ended in a fiasco and a display of disunity among the Arab states, several of them could not be deterred from following their usual procedure of fighting fire with fire and decided, while still in Rabat, to convene yet another conference in Cairo, in January. The countries whose delegations decided on this step were the United Arab Republic, Syria, Jordan, and Iraq.[32]

Mediation and meeting in conference are two examples which illustrate the specific manner in which Arabs synthesize the old and the new. The traditional patterns of conflict resolution and of reaching agreement in council, which for centuries proved adequate for maintaining or restoring the social equilibrium, have been applied by them to new situations that have arisen as a result of the absorption by the modern Arab states of certain elements of Western culture. The conflict between the Royalists and the

Republicans in Yemen, or between the commandos and the army in Jordan, show all the hallmarks of Western-type struggles between two competing factions in a polity. In both countries, the conflict was based on two different understandings of national interests; in both, it was a clash between two nationalisms, and as such quite unlike the local differences which traditionally pitched Saʿd against Ḥaram in Egypt, Qays against Yaman in Palestine and Lebanon, the Ḍanā Bishr and Ḍanā Muslim moieties of the ʿAneze tribes in the North Arabian Desert, or the Beranes and Botr tribes in North Africa. In these traditional struggles the two sides fought primarily for supremacy in the old manner and the fights (unless they got out of hand) were of a semi-ceremonial, almost ritual character, in which rules of chivalry were by and large observed, and bloodshed was kept to a minimum. This is something very different from the type of struggle engaged in by the antagonists in Yemen and in Jordan, who were using not only Western-manufactured weapons (including machine guns, planes, and gas bombs) but also Western methods of warfare aimed at killing off as many of the enemy as possible (including old men, women, children, and other non-combatants). Perhaps in no other area has Arab Westernization borne such deadly fruit.

Whether the Arabs have learned to fight well, by Western standards, that is, with the modern weapons of overkill the West has given them and taught them to use, is not a question that need be raised here. What is relevant is the fact that in these latest inter-Arab fights, in which Western methods of warfare have been adopted together with the Western aims of exterminating the enemy, the old traditional methods of conflict mediation have nevertheless been resorted to, again and again and again. However ineffective these mediation efforts proved to be, they did interrupt the fighting from time to time, they served to remind both sides that the enemy actually was a brother, and thus helped to prevent an escalation of the struggle to war on the well-known Western model.

Practical utility apart, the regularly repeated recourse to mediation introduced a traditional Arab note into these recent inter-Arab wars. The mediatory efforts indicated to all who wanted to see that despite the adoption of Western weaponry, military methods, and war aims, both the leaders and the people have kept alive old Arab traditions, including the very important one which upholds the value of mediated peace against victory in combat.

The persistence of "conferentiasis" among the Arabs, that is to say, the readiness to sit down in council in the hope of being able to iron out differences, must be viewed in a similar light. There is not only something comic and pathetic, but also something noble and touching, in the incessantly repeated attempts of the Arab states to reach an understanding at the conference table. Being Arabs, the leaders cannot help trying their utmost, in most cases by means of fiercely argumentative and grossly exaggerated rhetoric, to uphold their own particular viewpoint; but, being Arabs, they are equally constrained to come together again and again in the hope that, despite what seem to be irreconcilable differences, agreement will ultimately be reached, as it always has been in the tribal council tent and the village guest house.

XV

THE QUESTION OF ARAB STAGNATION

1. THE MESSAGE OF HISTORY

UNTIL THE POST-WORLD WAR I YEARS, MOST ARABS HAD little knowledge of their own historical antecedents, apart from vague popular traditions which were part of Arab folklore and which bore little or no relationship to concrete historical fact.[1] The disregard of the time element was a characteristic feature in these folk traditions, so that people well acquainted with the legendary exploits of a Harun al-Rashid or a Saladdin had no idea when those heroes lived, or how many generations had intervened between them and the present.

It has long been a customary feature of Arab psychology to vent one's anger on the bearer of bad tidings. Numerous historically documented incidents involve a caliph or a vizier who had the head of an innocent messenger cut off simply because his message told of a battle lost or of some other painful event. The messengers who brought the unpalatable intelligence of Arab stagnation since the end of the Middle Ages were nineteenth-century Western historians who had specialized in Arab and Middle Eastern studies. Fortunately for them, they were not physically present when their painful news of Arab decay and torpor reached educated Arabs. But the reaction was exactly as one would have expected: the historians, who had devoted their lifetimes to studying Arab history, were reproached with anti-Arabism. Any critical analysis of Arab history was construed as an attempt to undermine the Arab nation.[2] Several decades had to pass before the message itself, irrespective of its originators and the blow it dealt to self-esteem, made its impact, and a more mature Arab intelligentsia first accepted the historical truth of a protacted epoch of Arab stagnation and then understood the historical lesson contained in it.

A review of the standard history of the Arabs shows the scope of the problem of Arab stagnation. Professor Philip K. Hitti's *History of the Arabs From the Earliest Times to the Present,* written by an Arab, an outstanding historian with unquestionable sympathy for the subject of his lifelong study, and an impeccable scholar, devotes only one-fifteenth of the text space in his long book to a discussion of the post-1517 period.[3] This summary treatment of such a long recent period can have only one reason: for the last 450 years, or at least from 1517 to the days following World War II when most of the Arab states attained independence, there were just not enough important historical events in the Arab world to justify a more detailed treatment.

One is led to the same conclusion by studying the special supplement to the October, 1956, issue of the *Atlantic Monthly* entitled *Perspective of the Arab World*. This is a fine collection of studies from the pens of distinguished Arabists (among them Albert Hourani, Sir Hamilton A. R. Gibb, Ṭāhā Ḥusain, Jamal Muhammad Ahmed, and Ishaq Husseini), edited by William R. Polk, himself a noted student of the Arab Middle East. The supplement concludes with a chronology of fifty-four entries. Of them, twenty-seven cover the 758-year period from 500 to 1258, and twenty-six the period from 1789 to 1956. One single entry ("16th Century–1918: Arabs form part of the Ottoman Turkish Empire, established in the fourteenth century") bridges the 540-year gap between 1258 and 1798. When presented with such a view of Arab history, one is reminded of Oswald Spengler's dictum about the history-less "fellah peoples" with their merely "zoological ups and downs," which did not yield any noteworthy event that could be entered into the chronology. Hitti himself makes the statement that until the conquest of Egypt by Napoleon (1798–1801),

> the people of the Arab world were generally leading a self-contained, traditional, conventional life, achieving no progress and unmindful of the progress of the world outside. Change did not interest them. This abrupt contact with

the West gave them the first knock that helped to awaken them from their medieval slumber. It kindled the intellectual spark that was to set a corner of the Moslem world on fire.[4]

2. CRITICAL VIEWS

Another Arab student of the Arabs, Edward Atiyah, is more outspoken in characterizing the intellectual state of the Arabs before the penetration of Western influences. Until 1798, he says, when Napoleon set foot on Egyptian soil, "the Arabs were still living in the Middle Ages. Socially and intellectually their life had become ossified. They had gradually lost the ability to think their way into fresh fields of endeavour and discovery. . . ."[5] "The mind of Islam seemed to stand still," as Hitti has written elsewhere; the Arab intellect had for centuries been bound "with fetters which it is only now beginning to shake off."[6] These judgments one encounters again and again from the Arab historians. Even an Arab political propagandist speaks of the "spiritual stagnation" of the Arabs, and describes what happened to them during the last four hundred years in almost masochistic detail: Fayez A. Sayegh comments that

> the spiritual stagnation that prevailed over the Arab scene and paralyzed the Arab spirit since the end of the classical Arab Age, and reached its lowest under Ottoman rule which, let us add, lasted for 400 years, was first shaken by the stirrings which occurred in the nineteenth century and which have come to be known as the Arab Awakening.

For centuries, the Arabs "drifted on the periphery of history, and lived and moved in the twilight of being and non-being," and only now, "for the first time since the rise of Islam" have they engaged in a "search for being, for history, for dignity." This awakening expresses itself, among other things, in a search for "new patterns of organization to supplant the moribund, quasi-feudal system and the speedily-disintegrating family and village-structures." The "immediate traditions" of Arab life are, according to Sayegh, "the legacy of centuries of foreign rule or misrule." Of the new, Western democratic principles and institutions, "the Arab is at present adopting merely the forms and shells." Although the Arab "seeks to revive and promote such elements of his age-old traditions as are harmonious with the democratic pattern of life," he still "looks upon these as a foreign importation—if not imposition— . . . in which he looks as clumsy as he would in an ill-fitting, albeit fashionable, garb."

As to the traditional religions of the Arabs (Islam, and, for a small minority, Christianity), these, as Sayegh sees them,

> have shrunk into hollowed catch words, and religious fellowships have degenerated into fossilized groupings, generating blind fanaticism but not edifying communion, stimulating self-seeking attachment but not self-giving loyalties, and serving particular political purposes, disruptive of national unity, instead of promoting inward, loving, joyful, creative spiritual experience.[7]

In 1953—the same year in which Sayegh's pamphlet appeared—Nejla Izzeddin published her book entitled *The Arab World: Past, Present and Future,* which discusses the same subject.

After the golden age of the seventh to thirteenth centuries, she writes, "There followed a long period of stagnation during which the Arabs not only marked time but even lost touch with the creative and liberal values in their own tradition. . . ." Among the factors that brought about this stagnation, the author mentions the Mongol invasion in the middle of the thirteenth century; the Black Death, which swept twice over the Muslim countries in the fourteenth century; the second wave of Mongol hordes at the end of the fourteenth century; and then she continues:

> Yet even more devastating than the visitation which came from without was the drying up of the creative and adventurous spirit within Arab society itself. The keen intellectual curiosity which characterized the preceding period, the passionate and untiring search for knowledge, and the joy of adventure were smothered under a hard crust of dogma and fundamentalism. Free thought was banished, traditionalism reigned in its place.[8]

One of the manifestations of Arab traditionalism is preoccupation with the past. As Fāris and Husayn put it,

> In some respects Arab absorption in their bygone days tends to be a chronic disease. It stems naturally from the general misery of the majority of the people and the wretched social and political conditions since the fall of the Abbasid empire and the Arab states in Spain and North Africa. They live in a splendid past as an escape from the miserable present.[9]

Proceeding to a description of the common mentality characterizing the Arabs, the authors state that

> Until the closing years of the eighteenth century, the Arab world was in a state of near stagnation, ingrown, content with its prevailing conditions, resigned to its fate, and blissfully ignorant of the events unfolding around it. Then the West descended upon the Arab world as a conqueror, bringing its

culture, civilization, and science, its missionaries, moral values, and concepts, its mercantile goods and commodities, and political, economic, and military domination.[10]

Fāris and Husayn recognize that "the cultural famine which ravages Arab life is indeed not novel, nor is it the handiwork of colonial rule, feudal rapacity and local oppression alone" but "its roots go far back into the history of the Arab people." They point to the low position in which Arab society keeps its women as an important contributing factor to this sorry state of affairs. "No wonder," they exclaim, "that the Arab world remains backward, tradition-fettered, and limping behind the procession of human achievement, when woman's status is so low."[11]

Some Arab authors go farther and, taking the fact of Arab decline and stagnation for granted, use it as an explanation of the ability of the Western nations to subjugate the Arabs. Thus, the Muslim Algerian writer Malek Bennabi (b. 1905) argues in his *Vocation de l'Islam* that the Arabs were conquered by the French, in large part, because Arab culture had become uncreative and unable to defend itself.[12]

A younger colleague of Bennabi from neighboring Tunisia, Maḥjūb b. Mīlād (b. 1916), develops the idea of Arab stagnation in greater detail. After referring to the past greatness of the Arabs and enumerating their "immortals," he rejects, as far as Tunisia is concerned, the heritage of Arab decay:

> If . . . the East means that which we have inherited from the centuries of decay, namely the stupidity of blind belief in authority, narrow horizons, shortsightedness, cowardice in confronting reality, neglect of the laws of reality, flight from assuming the responsibilities and the integrity of the intellectual life, then the "new Tunisia" is not of the East nor the East of it!ial[13]

The writings of numerous Arab historians, social analysts, and other literati testify to the complete acceptance of the idea of Arab stagnation. The concept has been internalized and digested by them; they refer to it as to an unquestionable historical fact, and often present it in a stereotyped form. As Ishaq Husseini, a Jerusalem-born professor of Arabic literature at the American University of Beirut, Lebanon, phrased it, "It is against the backdrop of a long and wearisome 'Dark Age' that modern Islam must be viewed."[14] Such a matter-of-fact statement from the pen of a Muslim Arab author, even though it is couched in gentle terms, would have been unimaginable as recently as fifty years ago.

3. WHERE DO WE GO FROM HERE?

Once the historical fact of a centuries-old Arab stagnation had become accepted, its ineluctable implications were faced and efforts were begun to counteract its consequences. The paths to be embarked upon are envisaged diversely by different authors, but most of them agree that traditional Islam in its old form as a total way of life requires modification, reinterpretation, reform. Some writers have advocated the separation of science from religion and the energetic pursuit of scientific advance, on the one hand; and the free interpretation of Islam, with the judicious consideration of Western civilization and its aims, on the other. Others advocate a separation of religion and state, a position endorsed by "the majority of cultured Muslims,"[15] and of course, a most typical example of the acceptance by Muslim Arabs of a modern Western idea. As one writer summarizes it,

> The central problem facing Arab Muslims, and indeed all Muslims today is how to find a new way of life—Islamic in character—which will be halfway between the East and the West and which will provide the internal stability necessary to enable Muslims to face their problems independently. The Arab World can borrow technology from the West but it must find the answers to its deeper problems within itself.[16]

One of the most outspoken critics of the condition of the Arabs as well as one of the most fervent advocates of reform, is 'Abdallāh 'Alī al-Qasīmī. In his book *These Are the Chains,* he starts out with the observation that "Ignorance based on religious doctrine has tied our people with knot upon knot," and then proceeds to analyze the causes of the present-day backwardness of the Arabs and of Muslims in general. As the main cause he isolates "the low state of Islam in every field of human endeavor," which, he says, "carries over into the depressed situation of the individual Muslim as compared to the individual Christian in whichever country the two groups are living side by side." He admits that Muslim Arab "cultural immobility" cannot be overcome, except to the extent to which foreign (that is, Western) influence and training are accepted. He notes that the most isolated Arab country, meaning Yemen, is also the most backward, while conversely the most advanced is the one enjoying most European contacts. Arab humanity *(insāniyya)* belongs to the "abject, frustrated, ignorant, weak" type, and not to the other type of humanity, which is "progress-minded, successful, knowledgeable, strong," and which is found in the West. Al-Qasīmī castigates the Arabs and Muslims for their thousand-year-old conviction that man was created, not for future greatness, but to be inescapably weak in body and mind, and that therefore "stagnation is pleasing to God." Contrary to these age-old Muslim tenets, he says, history shows that man is capable of progress. Both West and East have this capability; but the East neglected its hidden human potential and continues to slumber, while the West "realized its material and intellectual possibilities." Only by reversing its traditional attitude, which sees in the past a process of continuous decay from the glorious days of the Prophet Muḥammad to the pitiful present, and by understanding that man's path has been an unceasing and ever-accelerating advance, can the Arabs and Muslims shake off their lethargy and move forward to increasing political power.[17]

Another Arab author who felt he had to come to grips with the problem of Arab backwardness is Omar A. Farrukh. As the title of his book, *The Arab Genius in Science and Philosophy,* indicates, Farrukh's intention is to extoll the Arab genius, and this lends additional importance to what he has to say about Arab "backwardness." He discusses the great contribution Arabs made to theology, mathematics, the natural sciences, and to two kinds of philosophy, "mental" and "social."[18] But, and this is of crucial significance for our present considerations, none of the outstanding Arab scientists and philosophers he discusses lived later than the fourteenth century. Reading Farrukh's book one therefore gets the impression that from *circa* 1400 on, the Arab genius which is the subject of his study ceased to exist.

More than that, in the Epilogue of the book, which bears the suggestive title "An Outstanding Past, But . . .," Farrukh is drawn into a discussion of Arab backwardness. This begins by emphasizing that "the greatest mark of Arab genius" lay in the fact that "the Arabs alone of the nations remained themselves in every respect, no matter where they went" and contrasts them with the original Aryans who became Greeks in Greece, Latins in Italy, Frenchmen in Gaul, Englishmen in Britain. Then Farrukh faces the issue of Arab backwardness in the modern world. He states that while in "some respects the Arabs are better today than fifty or a hundred years ago," the fact is that "compared with other peoples we have made no advance, we have gained no vital ground; rather we are going backward." And the cause of this backwardness, he finds, lies in the continued Arab preoccupation with "grammar and rhetoric, jurisprudence and mysticism," while the Europeans have advanced to "air raids, flying bombs, and the medicinal use of penicillin. This is inexcusable and unforgiveable." In other words, he attributes Arab backwardness to the Arabs' concentration on their traditional linguistic and theological studies, as contrasted with the technological advances of Europe. Moreover, he attributes "our real backwardness" to the existence of institutions in the Arab countries

> which carry the name of seats of learning, but whose original purpose was to keep sound and profitable learning away from the Arabs, and to offer us only theoretical and elaborate subjects such as could not profit us even if they occupied the whole people . . . at the same time we were cut off from the more important and profitable sciences and arts on which civilization and society turn—and such were studied in Europe by those attending even elementary schools.

The very standards by which the Arabs "continue to measure life . . . were put in our hands to keep us amused and isolated from the true value of contemporary life." The remedy Farrukh recommends for this deplorable condition is twofold: The Arabs "must follow the path followed by our ancestors in order to reach the point which they reached. The ladder they climbed in order to establish their place in the niche of genius is the same one that we must climb." And they must learn Western technology.[19]

4. STAGNATION AND NATIONALISM

The theme of stagnation in the period between the early medieval greatness and the modern Arab awakening is almost a cornerstone in Hazem Zaki Nuseibeh's treatment of the ideas of Arab nationalism. There was a long period, "many centuries of stagnation," he says, following the Turkish conquest of the Arab lands, during which an "apathy and abject dependence" characterized the Arabs. "A static society developed in which inertia, tradition, and imitation became the predominant characteristics," and "the stagnation and the loss of initiative permeated every aspect of life, both material and spiritual." It is not easy to ascertain the causes of the "fundamental spiritual atrophy" that was "at the root of all subsequent retrogressions." But two causes can be singled out as "the first links in the chain of events" which led to "the decline and petrification of the Arab world." They were the Arabs' loss of power and "the decline of religion into outward, formalistic forms." As a result, the social order became permeated by "apathy, enervating quietism and indifference." All this lasted until the "impact of the West" brought about the modern revival of the Arabic-speaking world.[20]

The idea touched on by Nuseibeh in the last phrase quoted is developed by Munif Razzāz, a former secretary-general of the Ba'th ("Renaissance") Party in Syria. Razzāz conveys the impression that, had it not been for the impact of the West, the Arabs would still stagnate. Arab nationalism, Razzāz says, "was born as a response to a challenge, the challenge of Western colonialism." First it had a negative character, but subsequently it acquired a positive one. It undertook the task to "transform the backward character of its own society and to create a new and progressive Arab nation. . . ." From the tenth century on, Islamic society had degenerated, "became stagnant, tranquil, self-satisfied . . . the spirit of innovation was stifled. . . ." This state of affairs "could have lasted forever if no new stimulus had disturbed the prevailing equilibrium. But a stimulus was provided by Western colonialism." The "sudden discovery of what 'Europe' and Western civilization really meant" shook "the slumbering, complacent Muslim Arab world which had lost its driving force." These circumstances forced the Arabs to engage in a painful self-analysis. Since they could not believe "that the values of the 'infidels' were better than the values of the 'faithful,' " they invented and accepted the explanation that "the Muslims had for a long time distorted their own values in their own society, and that the prevailing values within the Arab world were really different from what Islam had taught centuries before." This, in turn, required "a reassessment of their own heritage, to rediscover the old values, to purify Islam. . . ." Thus, the Muslim Arab religious revival movements were born. They failed, because "the European avalanche could only be confronted by its own ideas and values." This recognition brought about a new understanding of what European civilization meant: "in addition to advanced arms and advancing armies," it also represented "notions of freedom, justice, industry, education, modern administration and a new idea of nationalism where the bonds of common language and culture replaced the older bond of faith." In the very struggle of the Arabs for independence, "the main ideal of the various Arab national movements was borrowed from the West itself." They struggled "to achieve independence in order to be able to establish governments and societies on the same lines as the West." After World War II, Arab nationalism discovered and recognized "the problem of social development . . . as part and parcel of the movement itself." Now Arab society "was ready for ideas which were socialist and Marxist in nature, especially if they were associated with ideas of nationalism." The Arab masses turned against their own ruling classes, whom they recognized as "reactionary, corrupt, inefficient, afraid of the emancipation of the masses, and connected directly with Western governments and capital." The successive defeats of the Arabs by Israel strengthened "the Arabs' lack of faith in their own regimes" and augmented their revolutionary fervor. However, the military groups in the Arab countries "justified their existence by the imminent military menace of Zionism" and, in the process, distorted the Arab nationalist movement. True Arab nationalism, as represented by the Ba'th Party,

> is the driving force behind the Arabs in their struggle to create a unified progressive nation that can hold its own among the nations of the world. It was born as the response to the challenge of Western colonialism, but it has outgrown this simple reflex action and become a genuine movement on its own merits.[21]

To sum up, Razzāz argues that, but for the impact of the West, the Arabs would have continued in a state of medieval degeneracy, stagnation, and self-satisfied complacency; the contact with the West, however, provided the driving force for a new social and national awakening.

One more Arab author must be mentioned, albeit briefly. He is Hassan Ibrahim Hassan, former Professor of Islamic History at the University of Cairo and Rector of the University of Assiout, who in the conclusion to his massive religious, political, social, and economic study of Islam touches upon the issue of Muslim stagnation. Like the other Arab authors discussing the subject, Dr. Hassan takes the fact of stagnation for granted, and therefore does not bother to show that this indeed is the case. Instead, he says a few words in explanation of it: "The lagging behind of Islamic nations in general cannot be attributed to the Faith itself, but to international political elements, such as Western Colonisation and the incessant efforts of its missionaries."[22]

5. FIVE STAGES

In summing up the common elements in Arab views concerning this stagnation, one can discern at least five distinct stages. The first and earliest stage was one of naïve unawareness. Before contact with the West, the Arabs, by and large, were blissfully unaware of their cultural decline that had begun in the fifteenth century. Having had no available histories written in Arabic after the end of the Middle Ages, and being of an ahistorical bent of mind, Arab pride focused instead on the great Arab golden age, while the subsequent centuries of stagnation remained largely unknown or at least unconsidered. Following the "opening up" of the Arab lands by the West after Napoleon's conquest of Egypt, and the subsequent emergence of Western scholarly interest in Arab history, this stage gradually gave way to a second in which two interrelated themes were dominant. One was the unavoidably growing awareness of Western technological superiority; the other, the Western-introduced information about Arab history, including Arab stagnation since the end of the Middle Ages. If the former was calculated to shake the centuries-old Arab complacent belief in the superiority of the "House of Islam" as against the inferior "House of War" inhabited by infidels, the latter evoked strong resentment.

A third stage followed after the new insight into Arab stagnation had been internalized and digested. After long stagnation, it was now felt that the hour of awakening had come, the time for a vigorous effort toward advancement, progress, improvement, revival, modernization, all of which were conceived in simple terms of Westernization. At this stage, the blame for Arab stagnation was frequently attributed to the enervating and debilitating effects of four centuries of Turkish domination, which was seen as a period of relentless subjugation and exploitation. Close on the heels of this trend followed a fourth stage, which signified a disillusionment and a reversal. The West was now no longer seen as a prototype to be followed unquestioningly. Western domination over the Arab lands was recognized as but an updated version of Turkish imperialistic exploitation. If the Arab countries were still stagnating and lagging behind in cultural, social, economic, and technological development, they themselves were not to blame for this but the West, which purposely engaged in sinister schemes to prevent the Arab world from catching up with it. This stage has been described as expressive of a deep and fierce hate of, and a mood of revulsion from, the West.[23]

The latest, at this time of writing, is the fifth stage, in which a modification of the fourth can be discerned. No Western power has had colonial dominance over any Arab country since 1963 when Algeria obtained independence. By 1971, even the smallest principalities on the rim of the Arabian Peninsula had shaken off whatever foreign yoke they had been carrying. Rhetoric against Western imperialism, it is true, still continues, but it must sound more and more hollow even to Arab ears. One last issue remains which can be blamed for the lack of progress in the Arab world, that is, for the continued relative stagnation. Internal stagnation or, as modern Arab leaders would rather put it, lack of sufficiently rapid progress on many internal fronts, is being blamed on Israel. As long as Israel exists, the Arabs must, they maintain, bend every effort to liberate that last small piece of land which they consider as being rightfully theirs. Until this purpose is achieved, all other issues must take second place. On the other hand, the Arabs' defeat by Israel (especially in the Six Day War of June, 1967) has become the most powerful stimulant for reform the modern Arab world has experienced.

6. THE ENEMY AS EXEMPLAR

The confrontation with Israel and their defeat by her three times within twenty years (1948, 1956, and 1967) forced the Arabs to take a new, franker, harder, and more searching look at the problem of their stagnation. The painful question, why was a small nation like Israel able to crush the numerically larger and better equipped armies of several Arab countries, not once but three times in a row, demanded an answer.[24] And the search for that answer produced a rich outpouring of books, pamphlets, and articles, which began soon after the 1948 war and is still in progress. Most of these works discuss the weaknesses of the Arabs, their backwardness and its causes, and go into a detailed analysis of the fields in which Arab backwardness is discerned: the Arabs' inability to unite, even when faced with a formidable enemy; their ineffectiveness in trying to solve their social problems; their cultural stagnation; and more of the like. There is general agreement that many areas of Arab national life have reached a critical stage and that much in it has to be radically changed. However, there are differences in approach and emphasis, depending on the ideological orientation of the critics. In an incisive analysis of the Arab writings on the causes and lessons of the 1967 defeat, Y. Harkabi found that they fall into five categories:

The Reformist trend, which emphasizes that the defeat was caused by weaknesses, basic human and social factors, and conditions that characterize the Arab systems of government and the relationship among the Arab countries. Therefore, fundamental changes are required: the social and political order must be reshaped, the educational system must be reformed, and a new Arab created. Arab life and consciousness as a whole must be modernized, the technology must be developed, and the regimes liberalized.[25]

The Revolutionary trend recognizes the same weaknesses but attributes them to the Arab régimes and sees the solution in a general revolution and a radical break with the traditional values. There is, however, no need to wait until all the changes are accomplished, but rather an immediate "popular revolutionary war" must be launched against Israel and this war will develop into a general revolution.[26]

The Islamic trend is represented by those who are sensitive to the moral shortcomings that have spread in the Arab countries, attributing it to a weakening of the adherence to Islam. Arab society, they feel, has degenerated because it turned away from Islam. The remedy for the Arabs' malaise lies in Islam, which alone can give them the strength to continue the struggle with Israel and guarantee their ultimate victory.[27]

The Establishmentarian trend, especially in Egypt, while recognizing the internal Arab weaknesses, minimizes their role in the defeat, which it attributes to accidental circumstances such as errors which can be corrected. Alternately, this approach makes the incompetence of the leadership of the army responsible for the defeat, and sees the remedy in rebuilding the army. The people, it holds, must put their confidence in the political leadership. The solution lies not, as demanded by the previously mentioned trends, in a change of régimes, but, on the contrary, in their strengthening.

Al-Fath (El-Fatah) and the Palestine Liberation Organization take the position that the existence of Israel is the cause of all Arab failings. No attempt to improve internal conditions in Arab countries can be successful as long as Israel exists. Therefore all efforts must be bent on fighting Israel. Only after her liquidation can the Arabs devote themselves to reforming their own house.[28]

A very few examples will have to suffice to show the trends and the extent of the self-criticism that characterizes many of the Arab writings about the defeat by Israel, its causes, and the historical lessons contained in it. One of the first and most important of these appeared as early as August, 1948, almost immediately after the Arab-Israeli war of that year. Its title is *The Meaning of the Disaster,* and its author is Dr. Constantine K. Zurayk (Zurayq), a Syrian Christian Arab and a well-known scholar and educator. The booklet is the more significant since many of the observations contained in it were subsequently repeated again and again in numerous books, pamphlets, and articles published in various parts of the Arab world.

One of the most influential of contemporary Arab intellectuals, Dr. Zurayk emphasizes that the protracted war to "uproot Zionism" will not lead to the victory of the Arabs "as long as they remain in their present condition," and that "the road to this victory lies in a fundamental change in the situation of the Arabs, and in a complete transformation of their modes of thought, action, and life." The reason for the victory of the Zionists was that "the roots of Zionism are grounded in modern Western life while we for the most part are still distant from this life and hostile to it. They live in the present and for the future, while we continue to dream the dreams of the past and to stupefy ourselves with its fading glory." In order to achieve their aim, the Arabs must unite, become progressive, and "establish a sound Arab being." Then Dr. Zurayk goes on to criticize the Arabs for not being permeated by the meaning of the fatherland and for not being united in their aims, while the Zionists are suffused by the dream of building a fatherland for themselves "down to the very marrow of their bones," are united in this will, are grounded in modern Western life, and are ready for rapid advance and progress. Only if the Arabs acquire these characteristics, including the replacement of their "primitive, static mentality" by a "progressive, dynamic" one, will they be able to defeat the Zionists. The Arabs must strive for union among all Arab states, and for economic, social, and intellectual development, and must become progressive, because it was as a result of their progressiveness that the Zionists defeated the Arabs.

As the elements of progressiveness, Zurayk lists (1) technology, (2) separation of religion and state, (3) the transformation of the Arab mind to become "systematized and organized by training in the positive and empirical sciences . . . and keeping as far away as possible from benumbing fancy and insubstantial romanticism," and (4) "the acquisition of the highest mental and spiritual values." He justifies his advocacy of radical progress by arguing that "under the Zionist blows our existing position ended in a terrible material and moral bankruptcy. In this struggle our traditions were of absolutely no avail." The enemy, thanks to having acquired modern civilization, "surpassed us in intensity of belief, in unity of loyalty, and in ability to hold on to people, land, and country just as he surpassed us in weapons of war and in material techniques." This being the case, argues Zurayk, the Arab, too, has "nothing to fear from this national progressiveness."[29]

The argument that, in order to defeat Israel, the Arabs must acquire those characteristics in which the Jews surpass the Arabs recurred with added emphasis nineteen years later, in a second book by Zurayk on the same subject, published in August, 1967, a few weeks after the June war of that year, and entitled *Mā 'ana al-Nakba Mujaddadā (The Meaning of the Disaster Again)*. Here he again attributes the defeat of the Arabs to their cultural and educational shortcomings, compares the Arabs and the Jews, and upholds the latter as the example the former must follow.

> The fact which one must recognize and admit is a civilizational fact; our Arab society and the Israeli society with which we are faced, belong to two different civilizations, or to two different phases of civilization. This is the basic cause of our weakness despite our large numbers, and of the strength of the Israelis despite their small numbers. When we shall reach their level, the problem will be solved by itself. . . .

Dr. Zurayk explains that in talking about "civilization," he is not referring to moral and spiritual values but only to "the modern civilization which excels in its scientific achievements in both theory and practice, and in rationality which develops rapidly and even in spurts. . . ." Somewhat later he returns to the role of science in modern life:

> . . . science is the root also of political ability. We must support other nations or oppose them on the basis of scientific judgment alone, and not on the basis of feelings and emotions; we must shape our inner organization and foreign relations in the light of science. . . .
> Science expresses itself not only in its visible results. . . . Beyond all external phenomena there is a need for a trained and systematic mentality. Such a mentality is not satisfied with imagination and even rises up against it. It believes in reality and experience, and advances towards knowledge on the difficult road which demands patience and exertions; it is equipped with the long breath, with readiness to sacrifice and to forego puny benefits for planning, organization and systematization which it upholds. Science, in its basis, is a way of thinking and a way of life. The main question therefore is: how can we transform Arab society fundamentally and expeditiously from an emotional society which lives in fantasies and is nourished by myths, to a practical, effective, rational, and scientific society? How can we carry out in it the revolution which will obtain for us security, ability, and honor in the modern world? . . .[30]

Several pages later, Dr. Zurayk attempts to answer the question he has posed. The first step in achieving an Arab scientific and productive society and its basic precondition is the belief in the "call for science and productivity," he says, and the zealous endeavor of the political leadership and the intellectual and practical leaders to spread this call among all sectors of Arab society "and to implant it into their brains and souls, until it becomes a part of their feelings and thoughts and a source of their will." The state must make this goal its one basic concern; Dr. Zurayk describes the changes that will have to be introduced, for this purpose, into the governmental machinery itself. Production and development must be stepped up, and the improvisation, the sporadic but short-lived efforts, must be replaced by careful planning, which requires the acquisition of a "planning mentality." The Arab world must involve itself in a war against its own backwardness, and establish a science-based society, for which purpose Arabs must learn to face the truth and must engage in scientific research. The people, too, have important tasks to fulfill: they must take an active part in the affairs of the nation and understand that the struggle and the war are not just the affairs of the government or of certain circles or parties, but of the people as a whole. For this, the people must have political and ideological freedom. Ultimately, the struggle requires that the people develop four characteristics: rationality; love of work and ability to work; discipline and orderliness; and being satisfied with little.[31]

Four months after the appearance of Dr. Zurayk's second booklet, a somewhat longer book on the same subject was published by Dr. Ṣalāḥ al-Dīn al-Munajjid, entitled *The Pillars of the Disaster: A Scientific Inquiry Into the Reasons of the Defeat of June 5*. Dr. Munajjid is a Syrian Arab who studied law at the Sorbonne, was head of the periodicals institute of the Arab League in Cairo, has lived since 1961 in Lebanon, and written several books. Chapter 4 of his book, "Our Scientific Backwardness," opens by quoting a passage from an article by Muḥammad Ḥasanayn Haykal in the October 20, 1967, issue of the Egyptian daily, *Al-Ahrām*. The quotation closes with the statement: "We are facing a skilled and modern enemy, and there is no other solution for the Arab side in the general confrontation but to become likewise skilled and modern." Then Dr. Munajjid embarks on a lacerating analysis of the Arab shortcomings with a ruthless candor which is the more painful since he throughout contraposits Israeli excellence to Arab backwardness. In many respects, his disquisition reads like an elaboration of Dr. Zurayk's thesis except that as against Zurayk's progressivism, Munajjid is emphatically anti-socialistic:

> There can be no doubt that there exists a great difference in the scientific and professional level between Israel and the Arab countries, not only in the military level or the level of the armies, but in all areas of life. For those Jews who came to Palestine are not from among the Oriental Jews who had lived

with us, become Arabized, and upon whom the influences of the climate, the environment and the customs impressed themselves, as well as the common mentality, but from among the European Jews who grew up in a European environment, and acquired knowledge, culture, specialization, acumen, and efficiency, in addition to the hysteria of the Zionist religious faith, which drove them to migrating to and remaining in Palestine.

And this specialization which the Jews had acquired is a comprehensive specialization in all branches of knowledge, and especially in the experimental sciences: mathematics, biology, and the like.

They mastered these sciences, excel in them, and make inventions in their fields. We can count hundreds of Jewish scientists in the natural sciences, e.g. in chemistry, and the atom, while we still lag behind scientifically and technically. We have not mastered the experimental sciences, do not excel in them, and cannot name in them even five scientists of our own.

Also the religious belief—which drives them hysterically towards progress, study, power and superiority—is lacking among us, and especially so since some of our thinkers and educated people want to remove religion and blot it out from our lives.

These Jews have methodical minds which pass judgment with planning and schedules, and calculate the numbers, time and measure of everything; while we have confused minds, which incline to improvisation, are subject to emotions, and are impelled toward recklessness and extremism.

Planning among them [the Jews] extends into all areas: politics and management, economics, social life, industry, education, water supply, agriculture, and communications. This planning aims at improvement, completion and expansion.

While we, there is no planning with us, and if there is any, it is defective, or it aims at destruction and devastation. This is the situation in the revolutionary socialist countries. This is a negative, a lethal, planning.

The Jews adhere to reality, study it in an objective, scientific manner, and act to adapt themselves to reality or to adapt reality to themselves. But we cling to fantasy, delusions delight us, and we passionately love to talk; but soon, how painfully and bitterly reality hits us in the face!

The Jews maintain research centers, they value the scholars, and encourage those centers and those scholars to pure research, because they know that research alone is the single means to a knowledge of reality, to its improvement, and to reaching the desired goals.

But we have no scientific centers and no research institutes, and those which do exist are lifeless and do not function, or there are no expert scientists working in them. Our scientists, from whom we hope for benefits, are spurned and lost.

The Jews, their rich people and their financial institutions in the world donate millions for researches in Israel; but our rich people and our financial institutions, our leaders, our rulers and heads do not contribute a single *gursh* [penny], but ask: Why donate to science?

The Jews derive benefits from all the scientific abilities that can be found among them or which belong to them, whatever their kind or country or orientation. But as for us, we oppress the talented people and drive them away, and every nation benefits from our talents, while we are deprived of them because of the party system which was imposed by the revolutionary socialist regimes. It has become thoroughly clear to all professors and educated people that the educational standard has declined in the primary, secondary and higher schools in Egypt and in Syria. This was commented upon also by the French Orientalist, Professor Jacques Berque, who said: You are afflicted by a frightening cultural misfortune, and coined for this the term "deculturisation."

And lastly, Israel, because of its efforts in science, is advancing with great steps towards self-sufficiency and has begun to export its products—even those of the military kind—to Africa and Asia; while we, because of the socialistic regimes, are moving backward, have not ceased to be dependent on the West, and have not ceased to implore [it] even for light arms.

All these things render Israel scientifically superior to us. Our age is an age of science. He who masters science is in a position to rule and in a position to impose his will.

It is not possible that we should triumph in ignorance.

It is not possible that we should advance in backwardness.

It is not possible that we should prevail with delusions, nor with speeches, songs and talk.[32]

About a year later, the number of writings on the 1967 disaster had grown to such an extent that an Arab lawyer and political leader felt impelled to classify them into several categories and analyze them, prior to offering his own explanations. The author who did this, Dr. 'Abd al-Raḥmān al-Bazzāz, former Prime Minister of Iraq, found that there were ten schools of thought among the Arabs concerning the causes of their defeat:

1. The Arabs were defeated because they did not clean up their internal front, and did not base themselves on scientific socialism. 2. Because they did not give their total reliance to the socialist countries. 3. "Because we still are caught in a medieval mentality." 4. Because our propagandists were unable to raise the morale of our armies. 5. Because we were not truly suffused by a nationalistic consciousness in confronting the enemy. 6. Because our propaganda was unable to rally world opinion to our side. 7. Because we remained separate disunited countries. 8. Because we did not respond to the call of avant-gardist parties. 9. Because our strength was exhausted by inter-Arab conflicts. 10. Because the existing Arab régimes and politicians were not sufficiently responsible.

While not each of these "schools of thought" attributes the defeat to Arab stagnation and backwardness, this explanation figures in several of them, either explicitly (nos. 1 and 3) or implicitly (nos. 4, 5, 7, 8, and 9). All ten seek the reasons for the defeat in the faults of the Arabs in general or blame it on the régimes and the politicians. None of them even as much as touches upon the question of the training and mentality of the Arab soldiers.

After discussing each of these ten explanations in a brief paragraph, and noting that each is countered by an opposite view, Dr. Bazzāz proceeds to present his own view of the major Arab weaknesses that came to light as a result of the defeat:

> I. One Arab country alone can never be strong enough to defeat Israel; hence the Arabs must unite (=7 above). II. Despite the formal agreements among the Arab countries, they often take opposing and even conflicting actions (=9 above). III. The Arabs must establish a united information and propaganda apparatus (=4, 6 above). IV. "There is a lack of planning and preparatory study in our actions; most of our acts are characterized by emotionalism, immediate reaction and lack of a thorough calculation of ultimate consequences." V. As states we act, in general, and in most cases, exactly like the individuals of whom our society is composed. We exaggerate in both love and hate. Our hatred is so exaggerated that we burn all bridges to friendship or to peace. VI. We are inclined to place on others the responsibility for our mistakes. This is a psychic blemish in us, which develops among us from infancy (=10). VII. We must recognize that Israel in itself represents a threat to us, and not only as a basis for the imperialist powers. VIII. We must effect a mobilization of our forces in a manner similar to that of Israel. We must make sure that our army commands "will be equal in their value to the commands of our enemies who are clever, educated, and aware of the meaning of modern wars. . . . The main problem is the raising of the level of the Arab individual . . . so that we shall at least approximate the level of the enemy. . . ."[33]

These quotations suffice to show that there is indeed a strong desire among thoughtful Arabs to introduce far-reaching changes into the traditional texture of their society, and to reshape the Arab man in a new mold. They also show that the enemy, Israel, is being considered by many highly articulate spokesmen as the exemplar which the Arabs must emulate, primarily in order to be able to defeat Israel, but also in order to become progressive, to advance themselves, and to occupy a place of honor in the modern world. This tendency to uphold Israel as an exemplar has become so widespread in Egypt that it has come in for public criticism. On July 14, 1972, the semi-official Cairo daily *Al-Ahrām* carried an article by its editor Muḥammad Ḥasanayn Haykal in which this influential adviser of Egyptian presidents went on record against the large number of Arabs who either had already or were about to visit Israel in the summer of 1972.

Israel wants to deprive the Arabs of their chief weapon, which is their nonacceptance of Israel. . . .

. . .there are now 150,000 Arab citizens who cross over the Jordan bridges every month going to or returning from Israel.

Hundred fifty thousand Arab citizens every month in Israel!

Are we able to comprehend the full meaning—if we ponder this figure, and we must ponder it a long time—the political meaning of the open bridges by which the present state—or crime—of no-peace and no-war is helped?

The meaning of this policy is precisely that it is a method of disarming the Arab rejection of Israel, and it is more powerful than the planes and the tanks and the guns which Israel uses . . . and it is the most dangerous weapon she has. Yet it has become like an ordinary thing . . . like the rhythm of everyday life.

Is this not a disaster?[34]

Haykal's unspoken premise that what the Arab visitors see in Israel must prove irresistibly attractive to them was spelled out in detail in another article, published in *Al-Ahrām* within a few days of Haykal's by a Palestinian writer, Maḥmūd Darwīsh. Darwīsh vents his wrath against the many Arabs who avidly read Arabic translations of books by Israeli authors, making them Arabic best-sellers, and listen to Israeli radio broadcasts. As a result, the attitude of the Arabs has changed from one of contempt for Israel to an exaggerated appreciation bordering on admiration. The Arab public has come to regard Israel's society as a true and healthy form of life where there is much greater freedom. Darwīsh warns that, while the Arabs must know the enemy, this should not mean that they must conduct his propaganda for him.

It seems to be clear that the apprehension that since the Middle Ages the Arab world had been left behind by the West in many areas of civilization —an apprehension which first struck the Arabs when they were easily defeated by Napoleon—was brought into sharp focus, and in a much more painful way, by their defeat by Israel. In the 150 years between these two defeats there was no major war between the Arabs and Western states. Minor skirmishes, such as the Mahdi's capture of Khartoum in 1885 and his subsequent defeat in 1898, were of local significance only and made no impression on the Arab world. Nor was the independence of the three Northwest African French-ruled territories of Morocco, Tunisia, and Algeria achieved in an actual large-scale confrontation between the armed might of a Western country and that of an Arab country.

The result of the Napoleonic conquest of Egypt was the beginning of the Westernization of the Arab world, whose slowly ripening fruit was the achievement of independence by all Arab countries in the mid-twentieth century. What the results of the Arabs' defeat by Israel will be, only history can tell. But one thing is clear already: it has produced an unprecedented fermentation in the Arab world, a search for a change in Arab society, an effort to create a new Arab man, and an immensely intensified desire to shake off the last vestiges of Arab stagnation and takean honored place in the comity of nations of the modern world.

XVI

THE PSYCHOLOGY OF
WESTERNIZATION[1]

1. THE JINNI OF THE WEST

THERE IS A STORY IN THE *ARABIAN NIGHTS* ABOUT A POOR fisherman who one day caught in his net nothing but a cucumber-shaped copper flagon. Disappointed, he was about to throw the flagon back into the sea, when he thought he might as well find out first whether there was anything valuable in it. The mouth of the vessel was closed with a cap, on which was engraved the magic Seal of Solomon. He carefully removed the cap, and, lo, out of the flagon came something like a burst of smoke which assumed the shape of a huge 'ifrīt, a gigantic and powerful jinni. It hovered over the frightened fisherman like a menacing cloud. "Prepare to die!" thundered the demon. "I was locked into this bottle by King Solomon, and thrown into the sea. First I took an oath to make him who would liberate me the richest and happiest man on earth. But as the centuries passed, I became more and more desperate and enraged, until I vowed to kill my liberator. Therefore, you must die!"

"O, mighty 'ifrīt," answered the quick-witted fisherman, "if it is fated that I die, I shall die. But tell me, how is it possible that a huge creature like you should be kept imprisoned in such a tiny flagon? I cannot believe that you were actually inside it."

"I shall show you, O foolish man," said the 'ifrīt. He gradually contracted himself until he became like a little puff of smoke, and disappeared in the flagon.

Quickly the fisherman replaced the cap and said to the 'ifrīt: "Good-bye, my friend. Now back you go into the sea, and you can wait another thousand years before some other fisherman finds you."

"No, wait!" came the barely audible voice of the demon from inside the flagon. "I swear by Allah that if you let me out I shall not harm you, but shall fulfill all your wishes and remain your slave as long as you live."

The fisherman agreed, let him out, and the jinni faithfully fulfilled his oath.[2]

I am reminded of this story as I observe the encounter between the Arab world and the West. The Arabs, too, have found in the sea a magic flagon, out of which, once they could not resist the temptation of opening it, came pouring an overwhelming array of Western cultural accomplishments. Soon they felt that unless they could control this flood of intrusive Western offerings, their own traditional culture would suffocate. They tried to coax this jinni of the West back into its flagon, force him to do their bidding, fulfill their wishes, enable them to select what they desired and reject what they disliked—but the name of Allah and the magic Seal of Solomon did not seem to work any longer. The Arab fisherman and the jinni of the West became locked in a gigantic struggle taking place simultaneously on both a physical and a spiritual level, a struggle which is the more dangerous for the fisherman since he can never be sure in his mind whether he really wants to accept or to reject a particular gift, and whether the jinni offers it to him with a benevolent smile or a sardonic grin.

There is an Algerian song, written around 1900 in colloquial Arabic, in which Western civilization is personified as a ghoul—a particularly obnoxious subvariety of demon. In one version which was current in the early years of this century in Mitidja, the plain south of the city of Algiers, the ghoul of the West is depicted as huge of size, prodigious in strength, and exceedingly ugly. He is the master of all sorts of magical tricks, but is also unscrupulous, bestial, greedy for wealth, and, in contrast to the fisherman's 'ifrīt, an unbeliever, who violates the moral precepts of Islam. Nevertheless, according to the song, in the end the ghoul is subdued, and either converted or killed.[3] The difference between the Algerian singer's approach to the jinni (or 'ifrīt or ghoul) of the West and my own is that they foresee its defeat by the traditional forces of the Arab world, while to me, looking at the great encounter some seventy years later, such an outcome seems highly doubtful.

2. EGYPT—A CASE HISTORY

The first confrontation between the Arab world and the jinni of the West took place in 1798, when Napoleon arrived in Egypt and conquered it without encountering serious resistance. Up to that time the Arabs, including both the educated and the illiterate masses, lived in the naïve belief that their way of life, centered upon Islam, was the best that mankind had achieved. Although by 1798 most Arab countries had been held in subjection by the Ottoman Turks for almost three centuries (since 1516–17, to be exact), by a peculiar twist of logic the Arabs identified with the Turks even while hating them. It was the sword of Islam wielded by the Turks which prevented the infidels from breaking out from their "House of War," and it was as the heir of the Prophet Muḥammad that the caliph in Constantinople held sway over all the rooms that comprised the "House of Islam."

This complacency was traumatically shattered by the appearance of Napoleon in Egypt. As a result, the Arabs "awoke to a disagreeable reality in which their countries, their resources, their civilizations, their very souls were menaced by a Europe which was rich and powerful beyond belief, and which, in its limitless self-confidence, aggressiveness, and acquisitiveness, seemed to be bringing the whole world within its grasp."[4]

At first the reaction was reserved, skeptical, or resentful. The story is told that while Napoleon was still in Cairo, the French, to impress the natives, launched a *"montgolfier,"* a large balloon filled with hot air which at the time was the last word in French civilizational achievement. The reaction of the Egyptians was very different from what the French had expected. It was expressed by an Arab chronicler in these terms: "The French fabricated a monster which rose up into the sky with the intention of reaching and insulting God. But it rose only to a feeble height, then fell back, ridiculously impotent." Later, the same sentiment was expressed—with such a fine irony that it needed unusual sensitivity to feel it—in the courteous phrase with which a Muslim, confronted by the industrial application of science, complimented a European: "All that you still want for is to suppress death" (meaning, of course, that death and eternal life, the domain of God, are the only things that really count).[5]

Soon, however, more and more Egyptians changed their tune. Once the initial shock wore off, the first reaction was admiration accompanied by a readily understandable desire to learn from the West. With all their pride and egocentricity, the Arabs were and are a pragmatic people, willing to learn from anybody as long as they feel the learning will benefit them. France defeated us, they argued after the Napoleonic conquest, because the French evidently know things we don't; let us therefore learn from France. Within an astonishingly short time after the withdrawal of the French occupation forces from Egypt, in fact within seven years thereafter, the ruler of Egypt, Muḥammad ʿAlī Pasha, sent a group of students to study in Europe; true, not to France as yet, but to Italy. By 1818, there were twenty-three Egyptian students in Europe; and in 1826, as the first of several large groups, forty-four students were sent to Paris.[6]

Nor was this all Muḥammad ʿAlī did in order to equal the West. He made valiant, albeit unsuccessful, stabs at industrializing Egypt by importing textile plants and building sugar factories. He appointed the foreign consuls in Alexandria to a Board of Sanitation for the purpose of combatting the plagues that ravaged Egypt year after year. The success of this effort could soon be seen in the rapid increase of the Egyptian population. He imported numerous instructors from France to staff his newly established military schools, and founded a Polytechnic Institute and a Medical College, the latter headed by a French director. He set up a press which printed translations of European technical works, as well as newspapers in both Arabic and French. He transformed Alexandria into a modern city resembling Marseilles or Naples. Muḥammad ʿAlī himself was so imbued with the wish to emulate the West that, toward the end of his life, he once commented that he had found Egypt "utterly barbarous" and that he tried to improve it.[7] While he was engaged in these projects, the rich upper classes in Egypt began to learn French and to imitate the manners and customs of the Europeans who had become attracted to Egypt by the extraordinary business opportunities it offered. To them were added the representatives of European governments, and before long a privileged class of foreigners developed in Alexandria and Cairo, to which the rich native Egyptians who could afford it assimilated with gusto. Nobody doubted the superiority of everything the Europeans stood for. If there were some who did, and gave expression to their feelings, they were silenced by ridicule.

The lower classes (at the time there was no middle class to speak of) stood uncomprehendingly in the face of this development. For them, the "Frank," as they referred to European Christians without distinguishing among nationalities, remained what he had been for centuries: an unbeliever, a godless, immodest, immoral, and evil dog of a person, worthy only of contempt, or perhaps commiseration because of his benighted ways. That this miserable foreigner should be the companion and friend of their own Khedive and pashas, and that, moreover, the Egyptian Muslim notables themselves should be eager to associate with him, adopt his clothes, speak his language, eat in his house, and prefer his ways to those of their own Muslim fathers —this was simply impossible to understand.

The attitude of the Europeans was one of blithe superiority to the upper-class Egyptians, with whom, however, they shared the traditional contempt for the fellahin and the ignorant, non-Westernized masses in the cities. Despite a certain resentment evoked among the upper-class Egyptians by the emergence of a European class on top of them, the lure of Western technology and gadgetry, backed as it was by the prestige of the conquerors, proved irresistible. By the second half of the nineteenth century in Egypt, Syria, and Iraq (in that order) "Western clothing, Western furniture, Western sports, and Western languages developed a snob appeal that cast reflections on everything Arab or 'native.' "[8]

The Europeanization of Egypt continued, with some interruptions, under Muḥammad 'Alī's successors. Under the French-educated Isma'īl Pasha (ruled 1863–79), the Suez Canal was completed. The festivities celebrating the opening of the canal in 1869 were attended by six thousand guests, including a glittering gathering of European crowned heads which would have been unusual even in Paris. Incidentally, the building of the canal cost £11,500,000, while Isma'īl spent another million on the opening ceremonies. Before long, however, the European-Egyptian honeymoon was over. By 1876, Isma'īl had accumulated a state debt of almost £100 million sterling, and the European powers insisted on more and more control in order to safeguard their investments. In vain did Isma'īl assert, as he was fond of doing, that "Egypt was a part of Europe"; in vain did upper-class Egyptians send their sons to study in Europe and seek out in Cairo and Alexandria the company of resident or visiting Europeans. The European halter began to cut into the cheeks of the Egyptian camel.

The situation led to the emergence of political parties, in itself a European institution. Among them was Colonel 'Urābī Pasha's army group of "pure Egyptians," which embraced nationalistic ideas—another borrowing from Europe. Nationalist excesses in Alexandria served as a pretext for England to occupy Egypt in July, 1882, and to re-establish European control over the country. Egypt now became virtually a British colony, ruled autocratically by Sir Evelyn Baring (later Lord Cromer) from 1883 to 1907. The improved conditions in the country were manifested in the rapid increase of the population—from 6.8 million in 1883 to 12.3 million in 1914. (By 1972, Egypt's population reached 35 million.)

Egyptian developments in the nineteenth century can serve as a model of all nineteenth-century Arab-European relations: everywhere the first frightening appearance of the European was followed by an enthusiastic reception of his gifts, which made Arabs eager to acquire the magic Europe had to offer. At this early stage, Europe appeared almost like a fertility demon. It brought an increased yield in every field: in population, in health, in government revenue, in traffic, in commerce, in wealth. But soon it appeared that there was a bill to pay for all this: the jinni that came across the White Middle Sea (as the Arabs call the Mediterranean) gave much but demanded in exchange subservience, termed by him "control." It was at this point that the Arab spirit asserted itself: it appropriated a trait that the West did not at all intend to offer to the Arabs, the idea of nationalism, which soon proved both contagious and effective. One of its major consequences was that, before long, the European control came to be felt intolerable by increasing segments of the Arab populations. The struggle for national independence that thereupon ensued, beginning at different times in different places and pursued with diverse intensities and methods, is part of the recent political history of the Arab world and need not concern us here. However, its success might be indicated by three dates and three numbers. Until the end of World War I, no single Arab country was fully independent; thereafter, and until the end of World War II, there were two: Saudi Arabia and Yemen. Then the pace of achieving independence accelerated, and by 1971 all Arab states, numbering no less than eighteen, had become sovereign political entities.

But it was precisely in the process of achieving their political independence that the jinni-nature of Western culture revealed itself to the Arabs. Indeed, there was something uncanny about the way in which the West managed to increase its cultural influence as its political hold weakened. For it is a fact that in most parts of the Arab world, decrease in political dependence on the West came to be accompanied by an increase in Western cultural influences. Consequently, more and more thoughtful Arabs came to feel that what the Arab countries had achieved in winning their political independence from the European powers had to be paid for by their increasing cultural subservience to the West. This changeover from political to cultural dependence, and, more particularly, the increasing awareness of, and chafing against, European culture, engulfed the Arabs in a new set of psychological problems.

Struggle for political independence tends to unite a subject people. This general observation proved true again and again in many of the Arab countries. Political independence was a great and overriding issue, which overshadowed internal differences and important cultural divergencies. However, once independence was achieved, and the adversary represented by the colonial power removed from the scene, internal cultural differences gained in importance and became painfully divisive.[9] In such a situation, national leaderships tend to look for a new external issue which can fan the fire of national aspirations. The Palestine problem, with the goal of eliminating Israel, has been used as such an all-Arab cause ever since 1948. Should it be solved, in whatever way, it can be foreseen that the presence of foreign oil companies in Arab lands will become a problem that more and more will be felt to be intolerable. On the positive side, there is always the psychologically irresistible appeal that the idea of Arab unity, either in the form of Pan-Arabism or in a more modest formulation of a federation between two or more Arab states, has for the Arab mind.

3. THE ISSUE OF TECHNOLOGICAL DOMINATION

The modern-day encounter between the Arabs and the West has many emotional strands which are not always easy to disentangle. In historical perspective, the Arabs see the West as a young disciple who has overtaken and left behind his erstwhile master, medieval Arab civilization. Now it is the turn of Arabs to sit at the feet of their former pupil, a role which is beset by emotional difficulties. In theory, the problem does not appear to be too great. It was relatively easy to advise the Arabs that the acquisition of Western science is the road to liberation from Western domination. This is precisely what Jamāl al-Dīn al-Afghānī did as early as 1882. One of the great figures of modern Islam, Afghānī recognized and stated emphatically that the British and French conquests in the Middle East, from Tunisia to Afghanistan, were made possible by science and that, therefore, the Arabs must acquire science if they want to liberate themselves from Western domination. "In reality," he said, "this usurpation, aggression and conquest has not come from the French or the English. Rather it is science that everywhere manifests its greatness and power."[10]

Carrying Afghānī's idea farther, Norman Daniel, an Arab expert of the British Council who has spent sixteen years in Arab countries, observes that "in the second half of the twentieth century the effects of Western technological development are being felt much more widely than they were in the imperial age" in the nineteenth century, and that "this is one reason why there is more bitter resentment" of the West in the Arab world today than there was in the past. After enumerating a long list of "alien artifacts" with which the young Arab growing up today finds himself surrounded, Daniel concludes that "it is apparent to every Arab that the world into which he is born is dominated by Western technology."[11]

This, in turn, creates a demand in the Arab countries for industrial development, in which they see the only road leading to liberation from their industrial domination by the West. When Western economic experts advise them to "concentrate on developing their natural agricultural resources, and leave industrial development to countries better endowed for the purpose," they resent this economically sound advice. More than that, they see in it "a trick to rob the underdeveloped countries of the sources of power."[12] This attitude has its parallel in a quite similar position taken by Arab authors in a different but related field—the accusation they leveled against the West to the effect that the West has purposely withheld technological education from the Arabs and thereby prevented them from liberating themselves.[13] While such allegations express eloquently the Arab feeling that the Arabs have so far been unable to catch up with Western technology, they shift the blame for this state of affairs from themselves to the West.

There can be no doubt as to the eagerness with which those Arabs who could afford it took to the use of Western appliances, utensils, gadgets, which were intrinsically attractive and useful, as well as prestigious. In the course of the struggle for political independence, Arabs quickly learned that the only way to fight the West was with its own weapons. Hence, Western technology gained one more significant value: it became the instrument for liberating the Arab countries from Western rule. Once independence was achieved, the continuing flow of Western-made artifacts into the Arab countries—newly liberated and therefore doubly sensitive to every manifestation of residual Western domination—was perceived as more and more intolerable. What is the use of political independence, it was asked with increasing frequency, if technologically, and therefore economically, we remain dependent on the West, in fact enslaved by it? The answer was to seek technological and economic advancement. But here serious obstacles soon emerged.

For one thing, except for its oil—which in itself is, of course, an enormous asset—the Arab world as a whole is relatively poor in mineral deposits. It lacks the requisite raw materials for significant industrial development.[14] Middle-sized, privately owned firms using modern technology—which played such an important role in the West and more recently in Japan— have failed to emerge in most Arab countries, and have been discouraged by nationalization in Egypt, Iraq, and Syria.[15] A more serious obstacle toward economic independence is represented by a particular set of features in the traditional Arab ethos which has already been discussed.[16] The unwillingness of the Arabs to "dirty their hands," to engage in manual labor, is a trait not easily overcome. To it is added the specific Arab form of the general Mediterranean inclination of "taking it easy," which is expressed in the Spanish *"mañana,"* the Italian *"dolce far niente,"* and the Arabic *"buqra"* ("tomorrow"). Among the Arabs, this tendency to leave things undone unless there is a compelling immediate reason is both more pronounced and more general than among the peoples of the north shore of the Mediterranean. The combination of these traits creates a mental climate which is not favorable for industrialization. Among other things, industrialization requires conscientious attention to maintenance, from small, incidental repairs to major overhauls; the traits referred to militate against regular maintenance and cause many problems in trying to operate industrial plants and machines efficiently.

It is not suggested here that the traits which make industrialization difficult are specific to the Arab mind. Quite the contrary. The national character of the Western peoples, those imbued with what Max Weber termed "the Protestant ethic," is the only one within which personality traits conducive to industrialization seem to be thoroughly at home. Even within the modern West, a southerly clime, as exemplified by the Mediterranean, appears to be unfavorable to industrialization: witness the difference between industrialized northern Italy and northern Spain, and the poor, rural south in both countries. Outside the West, industrialization has readily struck roots only in a very few exceptional cases. It is interesting to observe that where it has done so, for example in Japan, modern Western technology was not felt to be something alien, threatening the local, traditional culture, even though the latter lacked an original technological component. It would seem that a main reason for the difference between the outstanding success of Japanese industrialization and the relatively indifferent results of industrialization in the Arab countries must be sought in the difference between the Japanese and Arab national character.

In his analysis of the Arab attitude to technology, the Swiss Arabist Hans E. Tütsch observed that the Arabs are conscious of the fact that the technology which dominates their way of life to an almost unlimited degree is the technology of alien nations. In the entire Arab world there is practically no mechanical production which is not dependent on the great production centers of the Western world. This technological retardation, Tütsch finds, is related to the static world view of Islam to which the Western thirst for knowledge and theories of cognition are alien. The Arab world, and the Middle East as a whole, holds that it already has the answers to all the questions of a simple life. This is why in the Arab countries there are no "men who ponder the mysteries of their visible and invisible surroundings," no "do it yourself" fans, "no laboratories, and no philosophical schools which are not hedged in by the barriers of dogma."[17]

In considering the Arabs' attitude to technology, clear distinction must be made between their use of technological products and their willingness or ability to engage in technological production. It has often been observed that the Arabs are willing and even eager to accept whatever the West offers them in the way of machinery and gadgetry. The problem arises in connection with the production aspects of technology. The foundations on which technology rests remain unexplored, and the *making* of machines and gadgets, as distinct from their *use,* remains alien. Georges Ketman—a French writer who was born in Cairo in 1927 of Syrian, Afghan, and German origin—has commented that the Arabs' most serious failure in the modern world is their "inability to master the language of technology."[18] While this approach is clearly simplistic, the Arabs undoubtedly belong among the many peoples of the world whose national character does not constitute a spontaneously fertile soil for industrialization. This does not mean that Arab countries cannot or will not industrialize. The fact is that prodigious efforts are being made in that direction in several Arab countries. But the process will doubtless be a slow and arduous one. It will require a major re-educational effort, during which the whole configuration of the Arab national character will have to undergo modification.

Nor does the Arabs' disinclination to technological production mean that they have no technical aptitudes. Ingenious technological devices were invented and used by the Arabs in the past, among them the giant water wheels which lifted up water from rivers; the wind towers which directed refreshing breezes from the roof into the rooms below; and underground water channels. The Arabs have excelled in shipbuilding; the weaving of textiles; the knotting of carpets; steelmaking; brass work; and many more technological areas. But the heyday of these technical skills has long past; most of the crafts have either declined or totally disappeared, and the ancient installations have fallen into disuse. As a result, one of the main difficulties in introducing modern technology into the Arab world is that such an attempt must, among other things, cope with the problem of imparting technological skills to people who for several generations have had little or no opportunity to utilize whatever aptitude they may possess in this field. A related problem is that technological skills can be acquired only by people who have an interest in them or an inclination to developing them, and the traditional Arab disdain for manual labor constantly militates against such a course.

4. FOCUS, VALUES, AND CHANGE

A discussion of the psychology of Westernization in the Arab world must present the differences between the culture of the West and the culture of the Arabs. This is a difficult thing to undertake, because to represent "the West" and "the Arab world" as if each of them were a homogeneous entity requires a high level of abstraction and generalization. In reality, of course, both "worlds" can be construed as homogeneous only when viewed from a considerable distance. These were the main considerations that prompted me some years ago to suggest the use of the term "culture continent" for both the Middle East, of which the Arab world is the central part, and the Western world; and to insist that each of these two "culture continents" is made up of several, mutually delimitable "culture areas."[19]

Keeping these reservations in mind, one can nevertheless make an attempt (superficial though it must be) to point out what appear to be the basic differences between the two cultures and the "national character" formed by them. These differences can best be presented by concentrating on the cultural foci, that is, the dominant concerns which exist in every culture, and which comprise the areas of activity and belief in which the greatest awareness of form exists, the most discussion of values is heard and the richest variety in structure can be discerned, and which are most highly prized by the carriers of the culture. Among the focal concerns of the West one can mention, by way of illustration, technology, scientific inquiry, the belief in and preoccupation with progress—which also means that innovation and change are considered benefits in themselves—nationalism, democracy, basic individual freedoms, and the like. None of these concerns were focal in the Arab world; in fact, they barely existed, until they were introduced by Westernization. As against them, the Arab world has had a complement of dominant concerns of its own which lacked counterparts in the modern West, such as religion, traditionalism, familism, sexual modesty, and the like. These focal concerns are so pronounced that they can be used with advantage to characterize an entire culture, to draw its profile, as it were.[20]

One might expect that a society would exhibit great resistance to change in the focal areas of its culture; there is a sentimental attachment to them, and therefore they command loyal adherence, which would militate against the introduction of innovations. On the other hand, innovations to cultural features lying outside these focal areas might encounter no resistance.[21] But in a culture in which traditionalism is pronounced, change and innovation in every area of culture are inhibited. Moreover, in such a culture, the greater the antiquity of a feature, the greater its traditional value, and, hence, the greater the resistance to changing it.

If, however, a culture is innovation-oriented, as Western culture is, one can expect an inverse correlation: the closer a feature is to the cultural focus, the greater the interest and willingness to introduce innovations into it, because innovations are *a priori* considered improvements and as such desirable. In such a culture the focal concerns, because of the great interest they attract, are subject to a constant search for possible improvements. This explains why in a change-oriented culture, such as the American, it is precisely in the dominant concerns (for example, technology) that one finds the greatest and fastest rate of change; while in those areas of the culture which are not focal, such as the established religion, the change is less pronounced—not because of resistance to change as such, but because of lack of interest in them. The characteristic attitude toward these areas is, "Let good enough alone"; while in the focal concerns nothing is ever felt to be good enough, and incessant experimentation goes on to develop superior alternatives.

In modern Western culture, the new is considered better than the old, and thus change in itself is considered a good; in tradition-bound Arab cultures, the old is regarded as better than the new, and thus the retention of the existing order is considered a good. When the early-nineteenth-century Western students of the Near East embarked on their investigations of what they liked to call at the time "Bible Lands," one of the first features that struck them was precisely this traditionalism which permeated Arab life. In fact, their impression of the tradition-bound nature of the Arab world was so strong that they coined the phrase "the immovable East." It appeared to them as if the life of the people in the Near East, their manners and customs, their ways of thinking and feeling, had remained unchanged ever since antiquity. This approach resulted in numerous studies whose purport was to show the similarities between biblical life and life observed in the contemporary (i.e., nineteenth-century) Arab scene, especially in the villages, in Palestine and the neighboring countries.[22] The burden of the message of these studies was that these amazing similarities showed to what extent life in the Bible Lands had remained unchanged ever since the days of Abraham, David, and Jesus; in other words, that the East was indeed "immovable."

This naïve view is now a thing of the past. A more critical approach has taught us that the Near East was not "immovable" at all; changes have occurred in both its social and cultural life. But these changes were minor, or slow, compared to the rapid changes that have occurred in the Western world in the last two hundred years. Revealed religion is undoubtedly a strong factor in developing Arab traditionalism: if a society believes that its religion was revealed by God at a certain time in the past to its greatest religious leader, it cannot help developing a mentality which considers adherence to religious tradition as a supreme value, and, by extension, must come to regard all tradition in the same light. Inevitably, it is believed that the age in which the revelation took place was the greatest and noblest period in its history, followed by gradual decay as the distance between the new generations and the original revelation increased. Every innovation is a sin because it increases this distance. If change is sought, it is only in the direction of return to the original, pure, perfect state of religion. This belief, which in itself is a potent factor militating against everything new, was strikingly characterized by Nabih Amin Fāris: "Piety and virtue lie in obedience and conformity *(ittibāʿ),* while nothing is more repugnant than change and innovation *(ibtidāʿ).*"[23] And there are other factors as well which make traditionalism a dominant attitude in Arab culture. Familism, with the dominance of the paterfamilias and elders and their veneration, carries with it a preference for the staid ways of the older generation and their unquestioning adoption and continuation by the younger. The meagerness of the material resources also militates against emergence of an innovative spirit: it creates the feeling that one must be satisfied with one's ability to eke out a living by traditionally approved and proven methods, rather than risk starvation by experimenting with new ones.

Needless to say, any feature introduced from the West is an innovation, and therefore, sight unseen, encounters a tendency on the part of the tradition-bound Arabs to oppose it. A Western feature must indeed be possessed of most readily apparent advantages to be accepted with little or no opposition. Also, it must lie well outside the focal concerns of traditional Arab culture. Technological features which do not seem to threaten any of the traditionally embedded values are the most readily accepted. The traditional lack of concern with technology means that there is no traditional opposition to technological novelties such as a radio, a kerosene lamp, heater, or stove, a steel plow, an iron thresher, a motor-driven water pump, and the like. Where traditionalism does play an important role in preventing or hampering the introduction of Western innovations is in those areas of life which are linked with the basic values. Among these figure such features as familism, personal relations, sexual modesty and, to a lesser extent, the traditional arts and crafts, especially the verbal arts. All these are held in high esteem not merely because they represent old traditions in Arab life, but also because they are hallowed by religion.

Arab culture and Middle Eastern culture in general are part of Eastern culture, yet of all Eastern cultures they are closest to the West both historically and geographically. Several Arab thinkers have in recent decades emphasized the affinity of the Arab world with the West rather than with the great Asiatic cultures that lie to the east of Arabia. Yet there can be no doubt that the two cultures, that of the West and that of the Arab world, are characterized by widely divergent positions. Arab, and generally Middle Eastern Muslim, culture is closely related to the East, to the cultures of South, Southeast, and East Asia.[24]

The contrasting orientations of the East and West are summarized in a striking paragraph by Franco Nogueira:

> The distance between the two worlds—West and East—was in fact considerable. The premises of life were different and, frequently, opposing. Existence was oriented to mutually exclusive or non-coinciding values. The social and moral stages of the one and the other were so disparate that a meeting was

not viable. To a rural and agricultural society, Europe was unexpectedly opening the doors of urbanism and industrialization. To the patterns of an ancient feudalism, of a patriarchal matrix, in which the individual and the state were subordinated to the family, the West counterpoised the primacy of the human person and of the state organism. To a pluriform religiosity, partaking simultaneously of Confucian, Hindu, Buddhist and Islamic traditions, the West responded with a philosophy of Hellenic origin and a religion with Hebraic and Christian roots. The millenary concerns of a developed culture dedicated entirely to literary forms of ethical and social content and impregnated with philosophical subjectivism were disregarded by the Western obsession with scientific invention, seeking control of physical factors and progress in the area of the natural sciences. For the cult of ancestors the West substituted a practical social humanitarianism. On the notion of personal obedience, which revered the wisest or the oldest, the European superimposed a concept of organic discipline sanctioned by general law. In contrast with the system of accepting reality for extra-rational motives, the European defended and practiced the principle of rationalistic, selective and detailed criticism. Apparently disdaining culture as an end in itself, the West proclaimed its utilitarian sense in the struggle for life. The physical dynamism of European man collided with the contemplative inertia of Asiatic man. The intuitive imagination of the latter clashed with the objective intelligence of the former. And in this way there continued to develop between the two that moral abyss whose repercussions are still in progress.[25]

The intrusion of Western culture challenges not only Arab traditionalism but also other dominant Arab concerns.

5. FIVE DOMINANT CONCERNS

Next to traditionalism, and closely connected with it, is familism. Elsewhere I defined familism as "the centrality of the family in social organization, its primacy in the loyalty scale, and its supremacy over individual life."[26] The traditional Arab family (as well as the Muslim family in the non-Arab parts of the Middle East) is characterized by six features, each one of which supports and strengthens the dominance of familism in Arab life: it is extended, patriarchal, patrilineal, patrilocal, endogamous, and occasionally polygynous. A family with such traits cannot but reign central and supreme in both social and individual life.

Familism has been so deeply embedded in the Arab mind that larger social aggregates have traditionally been conceived as mere extensions of families. The lineage (called *"ḥamūla"* in the villages in several Arab countries) is but an enlarged super-family, whose original progenitor lived six to eight generations ago. Similarly, an entire tribe, even if numbering thousands, is considered the offspring of one single, mythical or eponymous ancestor. By a maximal extension of this kinship principle, all the Arabs in all countries of the Arab world are considered or believed to be the descendants of either of the two primal fathers. It is but the application of this traditional familism when Arabs speak of the brotherhood of all the Arabs and, in theory, represent all inter-Arab conflicts as mere "family quarrels."

The extension of the principle of familism in another direction results in the participation of the individual in all larger social groupings, not on an individual basis but through his family. Theoretically, and this is reflected in common parlance, the guilds and other occupational groups are also viewed as if they were large families or tribes. Political parties, wherever they have developed, are similarly the outgrowths of families and of the family-based relationship between the *za'īm* (strong man) and his clients.

It is not at all difficult to understand that those who have a vested interest in maintaining familism—which includes all those individuals who occupy the middle and upper rungs in the family hierarchies, that is, practically everybody except the youngest men and boys—are strongly opposed to any change that would disrupt the family or even weaken it. Now the fact of the matter is that all elements of Westernization tend to do precisely this. If you send a girl to school she will be less likely to accept unquestioningly her parents' choice for a husband. If a boy goes to school, he is likely to entertain ideas of his own as to what work he wants to engage in and where he wishes to live. Even apparently innocuous technological features can gradually and insidiously set in motion a chain reaction which ultimately touches upon the sacrosanct values of familism and other dominant concerns. While it cannot be said that processes such as these are always consciously examined, both traditionalism and familism create a state of mind which is generally, and in principle, suspicious of foreign-born innovations.

Another value challenged by the West, that of personal relationship, is closely associated with familism. An individual who grows up in a small society in which familism is a dominant theme and the family the actual framework of life is used to relating to everyone on a highly personal basis. All the people he meets in the course of a normal day's routine are known to him personally, and are in many cases related to him in some degree. To encounter someone not known to him from before is quite an unusual event; if it occurs, both sides will spend considerable time discussing their ancestry and relatives in the hope of finding somewhere a connecting link; only thereafter will they approach the subject that brought the stranger in the first place to the village or tribe. In the traditional Arab town, contacts were not confined to personal acquaintances to the same extent; but even there, especially in the old towns with their tightly sectionalized residential structure,[27] personal relationship was the one within which the individual had been habituated to move with ease.[28]

A complementary feature of this type of social organization is that there is an intense social interaction between the individual and the other members of his group. As Sania Hamady put it, "Every member interferes in his life to steer or mislead him. He may not make decisions without consulting his near relatives and the senior members of his group." He "lives in a compact organization in which everyone knows everyone else's business. His every utterance or deed goes through the censorship exercised by his group. He is constantly subjected to the value judgments that are passed on all his words and actions."[29]

It seems to me that it is in this emphatically personal and intense character of all or most social contact in traditional society that we must see one of the sources of the Arab inclination toward a "personalization of problems" that has been commented upon by several students of the Arabs. Hans Tütsch, the Swiss Arabist, remarked that

> the personalization of problems goes so far in the Arab countries that even material, technical difficulties accompanying the adoption of elements of Western civilization are considered as resulting from human malevolence and felt to be a *humiliation*. The Arabs, who have accepted Western law and European institutions, whose clothing, food, means of transportation, yes, life as a whole, are more and more determined by Western technology and science, of course experience always new "humiliations" which in other places would be considered normal difficulties of growth, and eliminated. Where the Arab encounters an obstacle he imagines that an enemy is hidden. Proud peoples with a weak "ego structure" tend to interpret difficulties on their life path as personal humiliations and get entangled in *endless lawsuits* or throw themselves into the arms of *extremist political movements*.
> *A defeat in elections,* a risk that every politician must face in a democracy, appears to be such a humiliation that an Arab can thereby be induced without further ceremony to take up arms against the victor and the legal government, or to ally himself with those who promise him success the next time. . . .[30]

While this may be somewhat exaggerated, there is unquestionably an element of truth in the observation that the Arab "feels enemies, humiliations, triumphs where the Occidental makes allowances for material, objective, and, in any event, impersonal difficulties."[31] There can be no doubt that, with their customary acuity and sensitivity to personal issues, the Arabs gradually became fully aware of the actual changes that ensue in the character of social contact once Westernization begins to penetrate their ranks. The replacement of personal by impersonal contact, coming as it does closely on the heels of the breakdown or weakening of the patriarchal extended family, thus becomes an added factor to relating negatively to the West.

Nor is the Western insight that problems and events affecting individuals are brought about, partly at least, by objective circumstances calculated to make the Arab feel better about his defeats or more elated about his successes. On the contrary. As long as he could attribute these occurrences to personal factors, he was moving in a terrain thoroughly familiar. The intrusion of impersonal, objective factors into his world makes the Arab feel impotent in overcoming defeat, and diminishes his gratification from a success which now appears as not having been the result of his ability to overcome personal antagonists.

The corruption of the sexual mores of the young, and especially of the girls, is one of the most frequently and most bitterly voiced complaints against Westernization. As we have seen, this is a particularly sensitive area within the general morality of the Arab world, all of which is solidly anchored in religion. Any change introduced from the West into the sexual conduct is, therefore, over and above its intrinsic impermissibility, an affront to that pivotal aspect of Muslim life which is religion. Not to mention that other, older and deeper meaning which the sexual morality of the woman has for the Arab man. It is easy to see that any Western-influenced innovation in Arab sexual mores would force a revaluation of the entire Arab ethics of virtue.

Yet another important concern has been challenged by the West: that of folk arts, folk crafts, and folklore. However, the passing of these creative expressions of the Arab folk spirit is regretted today by relatively few Arabs, because the number of those who know them and value them has rapidly diminished in the course of the last few decades. The various manifestations of traditional Arab folk culture—such as folk stories, folk poetry, proverbs, sayings, riddles, folk songs, folk music—and the various visual forms of folk art—such as embroidery, the embellishment of all kinds of objects with decorative patterns, basketry, pottery, jewelry, and so on—were media in which a superb esthetic sense used to express itself, and they enriched the life of the people everywhere, rich and poor alike. Today, much of this is irretrievably lost. The traditional objects and utensils which used to be decorated with beautiful old patterns have been largely replaced—even in

285

in remote villages and Bedouin encampments—by mass-produced equivalents, factory-made either in the West or, after the Western pattern, in a big industrialized Arab city. Nobody seems to bemoan the fact that this process has brought about, or will bring about in the near future, the complete disappearance of centuries-old arts and crafts. The radio is replacing the music that used to be made on all possible occasions, and the spread of literacy militates against the retention in memory of the treasures of oral literature.

While most other aspects of Westernization encounter varying degrees of resistance, this disappearance of the esthetically satisfying and/or useful arts seems to be taken by the Arab world in its stride. The reason for this indifference appears to lie in the generally shared conviction that Western-manufactured goods are superior to the products of local Arab handicraft, and that the adoption and widest possible use of the former represents an advancement, a modernization of Arab life. The issue of esthetic impoverishment of Arab life incurred in the course of this development is shrugged off (if acknowledged at all) as an unimportant side effect.

Of all the dominant concerns of Arab culture, Islam is the most solidly entrenched in the Arab psyche and faces the smallest risk, in fact, no risk at all, of being supplanted by the dominant religion of the West. The danger that Westernization represents for Islam is a different one. The penetration of Western culture into Arab lands introduces a feature that young Arabs are increasingly inclined to adopt: the typical Western attitude to religion. None of them would dream of converting to any of the numerous Christian denominations represented in their midst, but they learn to relate to Islam the way Westerners relate to their religions. This means, first of all, that they learn to consider Islam not as a total way of life, but as a religion which in a certain area of life imposes specific duties upon them and prescribes the relationship they must have to God. As tradition-bound Muslims see it, Westernization introduces a dichotomy into Arab life, which had been one organic whole, Muslim in its totality; now it has become partly Muslim and partly secular. While this dichotomy is in itself a sin, because it removes part of human life from divine guidance, still worse is the development which inevitably follows and which leads to a progressive expansion of the secular area of life at the expense of the religious. At the end of this road, as Muslim traditionalists see it, is a duplication of what has happened to the West: a complete subordination of all human endeavor to materialistic goals, with a corresponding total abandonment of religion and the morality it teaches.[32]

Closely related to this idea is the oft-encountered conviction that the Arabs, because of their Muslim religion, are "spiritual," while the irreligious West is materialistic and immoral. This belief in the "spirituality" of the Arab world has often been criticized, and even held up to ridicule, by Arab thinkers. Several young Arab writers decades ago "resolved to adopt and preach" the idea, as Khālid Muḥammad Khālid put it, "that the Orient's *raison d'être* is to be a source of spiritualities; that it must remain so and not otherwise; and that the importation of Western materialistic principles is a mistake unworthy of the Orient's past and magnanimous tradition." Which doctrine is summarily and sarcastically dispatched by Khālid by asking, What about Western technological achievements?[33]

The fear that the Muslim world may be heading in the direction of a pernicious Western materialism is also voiced by Fazlur Rahman, a Western-educated modern Muslim theologian and director of the Islamic Research Institute of the Government of Pakistan in Karachi. Many Muslims argue or feel, says Dr. Rahman, that

> the Muslims are fundamentally and inalienably spiritual whereas the West is purely materialistic, and that all that the East has to do in order to develop is to borrow the technological (material) skills of the West and, together with the spirituality that it possesses already, all will be well.

This argument had the consequences in the East of "creating a false sense of placidity and superiority in conservative circles" while it has also been responsible for "the development, in the so-called Westernized classes, of a naked and frightening form of materialism which recognizes hardly any moral demands whatsoever. . . ." Against this development, as well as against the materialism of communism, Islam's "old spirituality is ineffective: it is by and large the secularized intellectual who talks of the 'New Society' and whenever he thinks it convenient also unhesitatingly exploits the name of Islam."[34] These observations hold good for the Arab world as they do for Pakistan, and they epitomize the position of orthodox, and even moderately conservative, Muslim Arab thinkers on the impact of the West in the religious area.

6. WESTERN STANDARDS AND MASS BENEFITS

As against the Muslim misgivings over the West and Westernization, those who look through Western eyes at its results get the impression of a great, beneficial, many-faceted series of changes, which have brought about great improvements in the lives of the average Arab. No Arab author, as far as I am aware, has ever given unstinting praise to what Westernization has meant for the Arab world. However, some analysts have gone so far as to list, side by side with the evils that the West has introduced into their world, the benefits that the Arabs have reaped from their contact with the West. Let us mention among these Muḥammad Kurd 'Alī, who in his early book *Islam and Arabic Civilization* (published in Arabic in 1934) lists the positive features adopted by "the East," that is, by the Arabs, from the West. These, according to him, are: The meaning of fatherland and patriotism, including such Western forms of public institutions as parliaments, certain law courts, and the like; the press, journalism, and translations from Western literature, including fiction and scientific works; certain sciences, such as economics, medicine, and so on; and an improved educational system.

In addition, Kurd 'Alī gives full recognition to the superiority of Western technology, especially in the fields of agriculture and industrial production, medicine, transportation, military science, administration, and so forth. He recommends the adoption of these features, and emphasizes that there is nothing wrong in accepting them from the West, since "on the day of their rise the Westerners took from the Arabs all they could use, and now they are giving back some of that which they learned from our forebears to which they have added in accordance with the progress of the times."[35]

There can be no doubt that the impact of the West has not only brought about profound changes in many aspects of life in the Arab countries, but also forced the Arabs to take an entirely new look at the world, at life, and, in particular, at the relationships between men. There are quite a number of basic axioms which the West developed in the course of the last two or three centuries and which, once the Arab world became acquainted with them, appeared also to it as self-evident and beyond any question. The most important of these can be subsumed under the heading of mass benefits, and one can state generally that the Arab world has unquestioningly accepted all the individual features which in the West are understood by this term, such as general education, literacy, nutritional standards, health and hygienic services, social security, and democratic processes. Those few small Arab countries in which the sudden growth of oil revenues provided the government with sufficient income have been transformed into welfare states—in itself a Western concept, of course, which involves the ultimate in realizing the ideal of mass benefits in all areas of human life. A hundred years ago, the same income would have been hoarded in the rulers' treasuries and the populace left living in exactly the same way as it had lived before. Today, there is no question about giving the people more and more of those things which are the required mass benefits according to Western thought. In those Arab countries in which the gross national product does not permit such luxuries—and 99 per cent of all the Arabs live in such countries—the ideal of mass benefits has been adopted and is being upheld by the governments, whether their political orientation is socialistic or conservative, and efforts are being made to raise the standard of living of the people.

Most Arab governments, moreover, have adopted the habit of measuring the progress of their countries by the Western yardstick of such mass benefits, and not by any traditional local gauge of achievement. For instance, they present the statistics of the increasing percentages of children attending primary schools (a recently introduced Western innovation) and not the percentages of children attending *kuttābs,* or Koran schools, which have been the mainstay of traditional Arab education for centuries. Apart from a few extreme orthodox traditionalists, nobody questions the desirability of developing secular primary education at the expense of the *kuttāb.* Nor does anybody question the need to teach all children and, if possible, illiterate adults how to read and write, although the idea of general compulsory elementary education was a specific and unique modern Western development, and the Arabs in particular could argue against introducing it into their countries by pointing to their own golden age in which a few educated individuals reached unsurpassed heights in the midst of an almost totally illiterate population. Despite this great precedent in their own history, all the Arab leadership and most of the people have unquestioningly and uncritically adopted the Western view about the value of literacy, which has become in their eyes a *summum bonum,* irrespective of its actual practical value for, let us say, camel-breeding nomadic tribes. Obviously, I am not advocating the discontinuation of the Arab effort at spreading literacy, but merely wish to point out that whereas in the past the knowledge of reading and writing was a specialized skill in the Arab world, much like being a swordsmith or a brassworker, under the impact of the West the view that reading and writing is a must for everybody has been adopted and is being put into practice, without, to the best of my knowledge, ever questioning the theoretical assumption underlying this particular feature of Western civilization.

This example, to which others could be added from different areas of life, illustrates the attitude that characterizes the Arab judgment of Westernization. The slightest remaining survivals of Western domination are fiercely resented. The economic dependence of the Arab countries on the West is felt to be an indignity and often drastic measures are taken to eliminate it. Western cultural superiority in such areas as technology is grudgingly admitted and the Arab world's superiority in the spiritual realm compensatorily stressed. But the major basic assumptions of Western culture have been accepted, and any questioning of their validity for the Arab world would be rejected with indignation. Thus, while opposing the West, and often hating it, the Arab world sees itself and evaluates itself through Western spectacles. It compares all its areas of achievement with those of the West, and wherever it falls short of the West it feels itself wanting. This is the predicament of the Arab world in the last third of the twentieth century.

7. THE SINISTER WEST

What is of crucial significance for an understanding of the Arabs' reaction to the West is not so much the very fact that the Western impact has changed, or is in the process of changing, their entire lives, but rather their almost obsessive preoccupation with Westernization, its phenomena and problems, its analysis and evaluation, the emphatic reiteration of what is good and what is bad in it, and prescriptive suggestions as to what of it should be accepted and what rejected. The specific positions on these issues are so many that they defy classification. They could, perhaps, be arranged on a scale, starting with the views of those who reject everything the West has to offer, and ending with those who advocate that everything should be accepted. But irrespective of the position they take on this question, almost all Arab thinkers agree that the West is responsible for Arab stagnation in modern times.[36] A few of them, it is true, seem to have difficulties in making up their minds, and end up both blaming the West for Arab stagnation and absolving it from responsibility for this. The Algerian Malik Bennabi criticizes those who blame the West for the Arab *malaise,* but also asserts that Europe has displayed arrogance in bringing its science to the lands of the Arab world which are backward only because Europe "has thrown them back."[37] Similarly, Anwar al-Jindī, a popular modern Egyptian writer, quotes with evident pleasure many statements by Western Orientalists extolling the greatness of Islam and its unique ability to satisfy the human soul in every age, but at the same time goes to considerable lengths to prove that Western Arabists were guilty of a sinister plot to undermine and destroy Islam.[38]

Fāris and Husayn exhibit this same ambivalent view of the role of the West in relation to the Arabs. They criticize the theory which blames Western colonialism for the Arab ills, calling it mere self-deception, and hold that the key which will open the doors to Arab progress is internal intellectual development. On the other hand, they too succumb to the tendency of blaming others for the deplorable conditions they find in the Arab world. The "others" in this case are Britain and France. These two colonial powers have destroyed "the geographic unity of the Arab world" and "endeavored to destroy its social, economic, and spiritual unity and tried their best to delay its progress. They moved very slowly in the field of education." As far as the British were concerned, their "obstruction of native industry took many forms." They "invigorated Iraqi feudalism and strengthened its foundations." Furthermore, "by bestowing upon the tribal population special privileges not enjoyed by the urban, and by preserving tribal customs and practices incompatible with the norms of civilized societies and with the spirit of good citizenship, the processes of urbanization and progress were impeded." The British did this because their main concern was "to keep the country divided, the tribal sheiks in constant strife, and the people ignorant. . . ." The net result of this policy was that "the majority of the population of Iraq have remained tribal and primitive, enslaved by their sheiks and chieftains, illiterate, ridden by disease, malnutrition, and even hunger, and exist with a generally depressed standard of living.[39] And the authors go on to analyze similarly the French policies in those Arab countries which were under French control.

Quite often when an Arab author gives any measure of credit to the West, he exposes himself to attacks by others unwilling to concede that the West has done anything good for the Arabs. Thus, an anonymous critic in his attack on Mikhā'īl Nu'ayma reiterates with added emphasis that "Western colonialism is the single cause of ignorance, poverty, and sickness; Western colonialism alone is responsible for the diseases rampant in Arab lands, and the bloody tragedy called Palestine."[40]

In order to lend verisimilitude to the accusation that the West is responsible for the stagnation and backwardness of the Arab world, Arab authors and leaders frequently resort to the device of depicting in glowing colors the state of affairs in Arab lands before the European intrusion. For example, it is part of the doctrine of orthodox Moroccan nationalism that before the French occupation, conditions in the country were excellent. "The educational system, even for girls, had been flourishing. The sultan had been on the point of carrying out the boldest reforms of modernism when the foreigners pinned his arms. . . ." Even the lot of the religious minorities under the pre-French régime had been "enviable, as is usual under a truly Islamic system of government."[41]

In the 1950's, just enough foreign domination was left in some parts of the Arab world to supply a basis for the argument, voiced by numerous Arab authors, that the lack of "complete independence" was the factor responsible for the backwardness of the Arab intellectual endeavor:

> Only when no trace whatsoever of foreign influence remains on Arab soil can there be any real progress in matching the economic pace set by other nations. And only with the success of this endeavor will the Arabs be qualified to occupy an appropriate international position. This position once attained, the Arabs will be able to demonstrate the full measure of their capability and to contribute to the progress of mankind as they have done in days gone by.[42]

While none of the Arab authors writing about the interrelationship between the Arabs and the West denies that the Western impact has profoundly affected Arab life, they express a variety of often conflicting views as to the concrete aims the West wished to achieve in bringing its offerings to the Arab world. There is, however, a common denominator to all these opinions: it is taken for granted that the West had, and still has, selfish and sinister aims in its dealings with the Arabs.

As early as 1930, the view was expressed that the West had inundated the Arab world with the products of its own intellectual output in the fields of philosophy, literature, and so forth, in order to swamp the Arab spirit and thereby weaken the Arab peoples. An article published in the Cairo newspaper *Al-Fath* says:

> . . . the intruders may colonize the hearts of men and women—that is the ultimate loss, the final collapse. The real danger approaches us from the *spiritual war* that Europe is *methodically* conducting against the spirit of Orientals in general and Muslims in particular, with the aid of its philosophical books, its novels, its theaters and films, and its language. The aim of this *concerted action* is of a psychological nature—to cut off the Oriental peoples from their past. What a conquering Europe fears more than anything else is this consciousness of the past which is beginning to awaken in the hearts of the Indians, the Chinese, and especially the Arabs. . . .[43]

Another view accuses the West of doing precisely the opposite: purposely withholding the intellectual aspects of its culture while offering only its technology, its materialism, and other "false gods" to the Arab world. In this way the West hoped to weaken the Arabs by turning them away from their own traditional spiritual values without enabling them to substitute Western values in their stead. Thus, the European colonial powers brought about a cultural decline in the Arab world. This view is embraced by Charles Malik, a Lebanese Christian Arab philosopher of considerable renown, who stated in 1952 that "One can show that if there is lack of unity, lack of responsibility, lack of sincerity, lack of understanding and lack of love in the Near East [which for Malik is primarily the Arab world], the Near East caught on these things largely from the West." And in discussing the issue of lack of understanding he remarks, "The West did not offer the highest goods of its positive tradition, but the false gods of modern Western civilization: nationalism, materialism, Communism."[44]

Within a year, a very similar idea was expressed by Fayez A. Sayegh, who emphasized that the West is to blame for not having presented its true values—he enumerates Plato, Aquinas, Shakespeare, Goethe, and Dostoyevsky—which "represent the authentic character of the West . . . more boldly and persuasively. . . ." Since the West failed to do so, the Arabs on their part also failed to make a distinction between the secular, predatory, imperialist, and economically exploitative West on the one hand, and the "authentic West," on the other, and consequently rejected the chance the West offered for their salvation and edification, thereby courting "spiritual stagnation."[45]

A third view holds that the West has withheld from the Arabs its technological know-how in order to keep them weak and prevent them from developing economically. One of those who think along these lines is Omar A. Farrukh, who insists that "We must also be prepared to make use of the scientific and technical knowledge which the West has gained so that we may be able to compete in this narrow world both in the material and in the spiritual struggle." As we have seen earlier, Farrukh also accuses Arab seats of learning of purposely keeping sound and profitable sciences away from the Arabs while enticing them instead to study useless theoretical and elaborate subjects.[46] While Farrukh refrains from specifying that the West is to blame for this state of affairs in Arab institutions of learning, his meaning becomes clear when one reads the same complaint in the writings of another Arab author who is less reticent. In an essay entitled "The Future of Culture in Arab Society," Dr. Muḥammad Kamel Ayyad, a teacher of philosophy at the Higher Teachers College of Damascus and the author of several studies on Arab political and cultural problems, first blames the Arabs for not having appropriated more than they did from the storehouses of Western culture—the only work by Schopenhauer translated into Arabic is his polemic against women. He even reproaches the Arabs for having fallen far behind the West in the study of their own cultural heritage. But then—and here he comes to the argument that clarifies Farrukh's thesis—he goes on directly to accuse the Western Orientalists of "promoting imperialist designs." Because of these sinister imperialist designs, Dr. Ayyad maintains, many of those Western Orientalists were employed "in the Foreign Ministries of Western governments, assiduously editing and publishing the works of Muslim and Hindu mystics and fostering the opinion that there was no hope of saving world civilization from decline and disaster except in a return to the 'spirituality' of the East." But one must not be misled by such pronouncements. These Western Orientalists were all part of an imperialist plot. They fostered interest in the "spiritual" culture of the Orient for one reason only: they were intent on keeping the Orient, and especially the Arab world, in a state of spiritual torpor in which all its energies were concentrated on things spiritual and other-worldly, so that they should have neither the interest nor the energy to learn from the West the only thing that really mattered—technology. It is precisely in the vital areas of technology, science, industry, propaganda, and organization that the imperialist West tried to prevent the Arab world from achievement. It deliberately discouraged the Arabs "from adopting modern culture and thereby liberating themselves from Western domination." Its purpose was to reserve modern civilization to the Western nations and to make other peoples cling to their ancient culture, their "spiritual" heritage. This is why the West was only ready to support Arab institutions that studied the Arab cultural heritage, such as rhetoric, Arabic grammar, Islamic mysticism, and the like, but did not help the Arabs organize laboratories, acquire technical equipment, or establish chairs for comparative literature, modern criticism, and the art of the novel.

In apparent contradiction, Dr. Ayyad then goes on to describe how Western civilization in the past fifty years flooded the Arab world with industrial products as well as its own laws and ideologies. As a result of this, the Arabs have adopted from the West new industrial techniques, inventions, architecture, town planning. Even the family and the status of women have changed under the impact of the West. The West introduced urbanization, created a new working class, caused feudalism to collapse, raised the standard of living, and aroused the masses to clamor for their rights. It is in this direction, he says that the Arab states must push for further development, because what they need in order to survive in this age of competition and strife is to acquire modern technology, industries, economic planning, and sciences.[47]

Dr. Ayyad's argument that the West has purposely encouraged the Arabs to concentrate on their spiritual heritage in order to keep them in a state of intellectual torpor is a new—fourth—variant in the series of accusations leveled by Arab thinkers against the sinister West.

The fifth is that the West maliciously falsified and distorted Arab history in order to diminish the Arabs' pride in their past which alone can inspire them to a great national effort. This idea is expressed by 'Abd al-Raḥmān al-Bazzāz. This Iraqi author and political leader emphasizes that three things must be realized before Arab nationalism and Islam can be fully reconciled: (1) The Arabs must free themselves "from the intellectual power of the West and its imported concepts, and . . . must think independently and with originality about [their] problems, affairs, and history." (2) They "must work earnestly and sincerely to present anew our nation's past and to write our history in correct scientific manner, in order to *eradicate these distorted* pictures and to put a stop to these iniquitous judgments, to tear out those black pages which the pens of prejudiced intriguers have drawn." And (3) "We must look to Islam, which we cherish so much and which we believe to be the reflection of the Arab soul and its spiritual source which does not exhaust itself. . . ."[48]

As we see, two of these three preconditions to a reconciliation between Islam and Arab nationalism involve taking a stand against the West and against what the West has taught the Arabs. Yet Bazzāz seems unaware of the contradiction between his call for a rejection of Western "imported concepts" and his demand that the Arabs write their own history "in correct scientific manner": the very idea of writing history in a scientific manner is a Western one, as are the critical methods of historiography without which no rewriting of Arab history is possible.

8. THE HATRED OF THE WEST

Western students of the Arab world have repeatedly remarked on the violent hate that Arabs feel for the West. Wilfred Cantwell Smith wrote in the mid-1950's: "Most Westerners have simply no inkling of how deep and fierce is the hate, especially of the West, that has gripped the modernizing Arab."[49] A few years later, Bernard Lewis made an almost identical observation in speaking of "the mood and wish that united many if not most Arabs" in 1955: it was, he found, that of "revulsion from the West, and the wish to spite and humiliate it," to which "dramatic and satisfying expression" was given by "Nāṣir's [President Nasser] Russian arms deal in Sept. 1955." "In the twilight world of popular myths and images, the West is the source of all evil—and the West is a single whole. . . ." All this, Lewis concludes, has not only created "real problems, through the economic, social and political dislocations to which it gave rise," but has engendered a "cultural inferiority complex."[50]

Lewis's explanations do not touch upon one fundamental question that will inevitably arise in the minds of those who study the relationship between the West and the rest of the world: Why is it that of all the nations who find themselves in a similar situation *vis-à-vis* the West, this hatred of the West and this "cultural inferiority complex" in relation to it arose in a most pronounced form precisely among the Arabs? The Japanese are certainly at least as much indebted to Western culture and technology as are the Arabs; moreover, in World War II the West let them feel its armed superiority in a horrible manner. Thereafter, their country was occupied and ruled by America for a number of years. And yet there is no evidence in Japan of anything even approaching the Arab hatred of the West and the Arab cultural inferiority complex. Or, take the several Black African states that had been French colonies in the recent past and whose cultural tenor, after they gained independence, remained thoroughly French. No comparable hatred of the West, no similar cultural inferiority complex, characterizes them in their relations with the West in general or France in particular. Consider the case of India. The peoples of this huge subcontinent were under British rule for two centuries. Their relationship to Britain during that period was similar to the relationship of the Arab states to Britain or to France from the end of World War I—and in the case of the North African states and Egypt, from an earlier period—until their independence. Nevertheless, in India and in Muslim Pakistan one finds little of the hatred of Britain or of the West that characterizes the Arab states. India resented the partition of the subcontinent and the establishment of a separate Pakistani state just as much as the Arabs of Syria or Iraq or Egypt resented the partition of Palestine and the establishment of Israel in part of it. Yet this political disagreement with Britain and the West did not lead to a hatred, nor did it create a cultural inferiority complex.

Here we have, then, a number of ex-colonial nations, all of whom had largely similar experiences with the Western powers and all of whom are today in a similar situation with reference to the intrusive, dominant, and often overwhelming Western culture. If of them all only the Arabs display that hatred of the West and that cultural inferiority complex which has been noted by both Arab and foreign observers, the cause evidently does not lie in the colonial and post-colonial experiences of the Arabs, but in a different set of factors.

These other factors must be sought in two areas: One is the pre-colonial past or, more precisely, the way in which the pre-colonial past lives in the consciousness of ex-colonial peoples. The other is their specific modal personality. The two are, of course, connected. The past is viewed through the spectacles of the modal personality. Thus, where bravery, aggressiveness, and fighting ability are important features and values in the modal personality, the view of the past will emphasize these features in the national history. On the other hand, the consciousness of the past is an important factor in the formation of the modal personality. If the past is known or believed to have been a time of glorious victories, this will leave its mark on the modal personality by inclining it toward an imitation of the ancestral ways which will reinforce such personality traits as aggressiveness and bravery.

In applying these considerations to the relationship of the various ex-colonial peoples to the West, we find that of all of them only the Arabs had in the past contributed directly and most significantly to the cultural development of the West. The educated Arabs, whose number increases year by year, know that only a few centuries ago their people were superior to the West in all fields of cultural endeavor of which the West today is so proud. In their understandable ethnocentrism, many of them exaggerate the role Arab culture played in preparing the ground for the great European upsurge beginning with the Renaissance. As Wilfred Cantwell Smith put it, "The Arabs feel more intimately the early glory of the past Muslim-Arab greatness than do any other Muslim group; and feel more tautly the nostalgia. The Arab sense of bygone splendour is superb." And elsewhere he comments, "Arab Islam . . . is uninterested in and virtually unaware of Islamic greatness after the Arab downfall. For it, in 1258 (the fall of Baghdad), or for Egypt in 1517 (the Turkish conquest), Islamic history virtually came to an end."[51] The West, therefore, is a cultural upstart, and to have to learn from it is for the Arabs a position verging on dishonor.

The second factor is also partly a matter of historical knowledge and consciousness. Although some Arab intellectuals smart under what they consider Western distortions of Arab history,[52] and Arabs in general have attained a knowledge of their own past mainly as a result of Western efforts,[53] the fact is that of all the ex-colonial nations, only the Arabs can look back at long historical contacts with the West. Only they had met the West repeatedly in battle, defeated it, and subjected it to their rule. This happened in Spain as early as the eighth century, while as late as the eighteenth, after the leadership in the "House of Islam" had passed to Turkey, South-Central Europe as far north as Hungary was still under Muslim domination. In the Arab historical view, it should be remarked, when it comes to confrontation with the West, Turkey is considered an extension of the Arab world and the Turkish defeats of Christian Europe are looked upon as victories of Islam—of which the Arabs were and remained the founders, the spreaders and the core, even while Turkey became its mailed fist. In the view of some modern Arab authors, these past victories of the Arabs were inspired by their Islamic faith. Muḥammad Quṭb says that if the Arabs can regain their disciplined faith, they will, as did the early Muslims, defeat the great empires of the world.[54] Defeat and domination by an adversary who formerly had been weaker than the Muslim armed might are thus more painful to the Arabs than for nations who throughout their historical contacts with the West have always experienced it as superior in military power.

The Arabs' emotional dependence on their past is paralleled by the rejection of the West and what it stands for. It is because of this rejection that the Arab's

> self-assertion assumes the exclusive character that it does; and, obversely, the more the Arab furthers his rather pathological inclination to seek in himself —that is to say, in his past—the sole basis for his present awakening and future self-determination, the more hopelessly imprisoned within the narrow cell of himself he becomes, and the more hostile to any form of creative interaction with the Western spirit he grows to be.[55]

298

The third factor is that of religion. Indeed, religion is such an important feature in the Arabs' anti-Western stance that it should perhaps have been mentioned in the first place. However, the same religion, Islam, is shared by other countries which do not manifest anything even remotely resembling the Arab anti-Western animus. From this difference one can conclude that Islam alone, that is, without the consciousness of past cultural and military superiority to the West touched upon above, is not a sufficient motivation for the emergence of a strong hatred of the West among ex-colonial nations. Only when the conviction of being possessed of the only true religion (which is shared by all Muslims) is coupled with the knowledge of past cultural and military superiority (which only the Arabs can have) does this combination result in a mutual reinforcement of the anti-Western feeling as found among the Arabs. Only among the Arabs could a belief emerge that their religion, Islam, helped them in the glorious centuries of their past to achieve a cultural and military superiority over the West. Therefore, only the Arabs have to face the bitter reality that in recent centuries they have lost both these superiorities. Given the Arabs' belief in divine predestination, this reversal of pre-eminences cannot but be considered by them a preordained event which, in turn, casts doubt on their value in their own eyes. Since for the traditional Muslim it is inconceivable to reproach or even question God, the blame for the Arab reversal is put on the Arabs themselves, primarily in terms of moral, that is, religious shortcomings. Or, in an illogical but emotionally much more satisfactory manner, the West itself is held culpable for all that befell the Arabs.

What is particularly resented is the rich array of external manifestations of Western superiority in all the material, economic, technological, and organizational fields. These attainments, which are constantly exhibited or, as the Arabs see it, flaunted by the West, endow it with superior power. This is especially annoying to the Arab mind because it has been conditioned to regard all such shows as secondary to the true values of morality and religion, in which, they sincerely believe, the West is emphatically wanting and thus very much inferior to the Muslim Arabs. When they nevertheless find that they are unable to resist imitating the West in all the things the West considers important, and that in doing so they involuntarily adopt the scale of values which they think is upheld by the West, their resentment easily escalates into hatred.

There are a number of other now familiar features in the Arab modal personality which predispose Arabs to an anti-Western stance, and which do not exist, or are present to a much smaller degree, in the modal personalities of other ex-colonial nations. Among these is the proclivity to exaggeration, which not only inclines the Arabs to overemphasize and reiterate what they feel toward the West, but actually intensifies those feelings. Another is the sense of marginality which never allows an Arab to detach himself from his traditional culture and environment as completely as a British-educated Indian could, and, conversely, makes it equally impossible for him to ignore Western culture as totally as does a Japanese Zen *roshi*. The Arab's marginality always causes him discomfort, which at times can grow very acute, and for which either consciously or unconsciously he blames the West. Closely connected with his marginality is the Arab's ambivalence toward both his own traditional culture and the modern culture of the West, which makes his hatred of the latter the stronger the more he is attracted to it. His extremely keen sense of honor is yet another factor creating in him a suspicion, of which he cannot rid himself, that by imitating the West he might be debasing himself; and since he cannot stop imitating the West, he hates it for luring him into a dishonorable posture. To all this must be added the Arab's proclivity to blaming others for his own shortcomings and failures. Since the West is the most readily available scapegoat, it must take most of the blame, with which goes inevitably most of the hate.

So far we have spoken of the psychological bases of the Arabs' hatred of the West. The cultural inferiority complex which the Arabs experience in relation to the West can be explained by referring to the opposite pole in the ambivalence that characterizes the attitude to the West. If their hatred of the West is a manifestation of the negative pole of this ambivalence, the Arabs' inferiority complex is the outcome of its positive pole. While they would rarely admit to "loving" Western culture, it exerts upon them an irresistible attraction, because it comprises so much they want to have as soon as they learn that it exists. It is the very presence of the West, with all the enticements its civilization contains, with all the new values it introduces, and with all the genuine improvements in everyday life it makes possible, that produces in the Arab world a cultural inferiority complex. As Wilfred Cantwell Smith phrases it, "It is by Western standards that the Arabs are weak, by imported criteria that their self-esteem is undermined. A defeat by superior power not only curtails one's freedom; it also demonstrates or reminds one of one's impotence."[56]

Arab authors, as a rule, are reluctant to speak about the Arab hatred of the West. What they prefer to do, instead, is to list and analyze the factors that create in the Arabs an oppositon to Western influences. The explanations of Arab writers as to why the Arabs are inimical to the West were gathered and summarized by J. Desparmet as early as in 1932. According to him, the ultimate basis of all objections to the West is the religious "fervor" or "jealousy" which fires the Muslim Arab and from which he derives or deduces all kinds of other objections.[57]

9. ARABS AND TURKS

Finally, in discussing the psychological motivations of Arab hatred of the West, the question must be asked, Why did the Arabs single out the West as the object of their hate rather than Turkey? After all, the Arab lands were exposed to Western incursion and domination for about a hundred years only; whereas the Turks ruled the Arab world for four centuries. Moreover, the Turkish yoke weighed much more heavily on the necks of the Arabs than did that of the European colonial powers. Economically, the Turks bled the Arab lands white. They considered the Arabs subject peoples whose only roles in life were to pay heavy taxes to the Turks and to serve in the Turkish-officered armies of the Ottoman Empire. In exchange for these services the Turks treated the Arabs with contempt, administered harsh justice, and were always ready to mete out cruel punishment. And yet, in retrospect, the memory of the four-centuries-long cruel Turkish rule evokes in the Arabs much less resentment and hate than the memory of the one-hundred-year-long European domination which, in comparison, was humane and enlightened.

One reason for this undoubtedly lies in the religious identity between Turks and Arabs. The Turkish sultan was not only the temporal head of the Ottoman Empire, but also the caliph, the religious head of all Sunnī Islam. Whether or not the Arabs liked to see the caliphate held by a Turkish sovereign, he still was in their eyes the caliph, the legitimate successor of the Prophet Muḥammad, to whom obedience was due.[58] Whatever injustices and cruelties were committed against the Arabs by the officers of the Turkish government and army, the Sultan-Caliph as the symbol of Islam could not and was not held culpable. This also meant that the hate felt by the Arabs against individual Turkish potentates, such as the notorious Aḥmad Pasha, surnamed al-Jazzār, "the butcher," the despotic ruler of Syria and Lebanon for many years, was, as a rule, not generalized and extended to all the Turks. While the name of al-Jazzār, who died in 1804, still lives "as a synonym of terror and cruelty,"[59] the hatred of the Turks in general, even if it was intense during their misrule over the Arab lands, has long become a thing of the past.

As against this, the European powers were Christian. And Christians were for the Arabs an undifferentiated human conglomerate, the infidel enemy. For the untutored mind which was always the great majority in the "House of Islam," all Christendom was one: moreover, every group of Christians was considered to be a typical representative of all "Franks," that is, Christians. The very circumstance that the people who from the nineteenth century on managed to establish themselves as the new masters of the Arabs were Christians made it almost inevitable that the Arabs should generalize their animosity and make all Christendom, or the entire West, the object of their resentment and hatred. Every individual act of aggression, every particular injustice, real or imagined, was considered as expressive of what the Christian West as a whole stood for and became an added irritant exacerbating and embittering the Arabs' attitude to the West.

Another point is the different historical experiences the Arabs had with Turkey on the one hand and with the West on the other. It is a psychological law that people nurture a greater hatred toward those who have been their inferiors in the past and then succeed in outdistancing them, than toward those who proved their superiority from the very first moment of their encounter. As far as the Arabs are concerned, the Turks belong to the latter, the West to the former category. Ever since the Ottoman Turks established their rule in Anatolia (after 1300), the Arab-Turkish encounters always spelled defeat for the Arabs and victory for the Turks. After a short period of indecisive rivalry between the Turkish and the Egyptian sultan in the late fifteenth and early sixteenth centuries, expressed in repeated conflicts on the borders between Asia Minor and Syria, the Turks conquered Syria in 1516 and Egypt the following year. Thereafter, for more than three centuries, until the rise of the European colonial powers, the Turks were in Arab eyes the invincible champions of Islam, who, it is true, bore down heavily with their feet on Arab necks, but who also brought down on Christian necks the victorious sword of Muḥammad. Such an overlord an Arab may resent, and attempt to rebel against, but he certainly cannot hate him as intensively as he can the infidel Christian.

The outcome of the early encounters between Christians and Arabs was, as a rule, Christian defeat. This engendered a feeling of superiority in the Arabs, with a complementary feeling of disdain for the Christians. When the Arabs conquered lands ruled by Christians, and allowed the Christian remnants to live in the midst of the Muslims as *dhimmīs,* or protected, second-class citizens, this disdain grew into contempt. For centuries no Christian power was a match for the Muslim Arabs. The limits of the Arab expansion were set less by Christian armies than by natural obstacles. When the tide turned and the Arabs were gradually pushed back by Christian Europe, and especially when, from 1798 on, Christian Europe began to make inroads into Arab lands, the haughty disdain the Arabs had nurtured toward *Rūm* (Christendom) became transformed into impotent rage, and ultimately into fierce hate.

Here, then, was a classical example of group hatred intensified by the historical reversal of a power relationship. What cannot be forgiven the rival outgroup is not so much the fact that it has gained the upper hand, as the circumstance that it managed to do so after it had for long been forced to play the role of the underdog. No comparable reversal of historical roles has occurred on a worldwide scale between any other two cultures.

10. FACING THE FUTURE

Never in their thirteen-centuries-old history, since they broke out of their isolation in the Arabian Peninsula, have the Arabs faced a challenge comparable in magnitude to the one represented by their encounter with the modern West. For the first time they have been put on the defensive, not militarily—that has happened in the past—but culturally. No sooner had the West established contact with the Arab world than it began to study Arab history, Arab religion (i.e., Islam), Arabic literature, and other manifestations of Arab culture. Before long, Western Arabists (or Orientalists, as they used to be called) knew more about these subjects than the best Arab scholars themselves, so that if the latter wanted to devote themselves to a serious scientific inquiry into their own history, religion, or literature, they had, in the first place, to read the books and studies written by their Western colleagues. Scholarship is supposed to know no nationalities, but Arab pride could not help being hurt by this state of affairs. To recognize the superiority of Western technology and to adopt it did not touch Arab sensibilities; after all, the West specialized in technical development, let us therefore use its inventions, gadgets, machines. But to have to learn from the West the full story of Arab literature and Muslim religion and the full course of Arab history—subjects which for centuries were studied in such venerable Arab institutions as al-Azhar and other famous mosque-schools—this was difficult to take. No wonder that some modern Arab scholars, their nationalistic suspicions aroused, accused Western Arabists of having worked for the foreign ministries of their respective governments and having purposely falsified or distorted Arab history.

Nevertheless, serious Arab scholars turned to Western studies of Arab history, religion, and literature and learned from them. One of the least palatable things they had to recognize was that with the end of the Middle Ages the Arabs had sunk into a torpor, that they stagnated and remained in a state of cultural somnolence until awakened by the West. There can be no doubt that the Arab historians, writers, and social critics learned the idea of Arab stagnation well. Indeed, so well that they became much more critical of Arab shortcomings than outside Arabists have ever been. In the past, too, Arabs were known to have a penchant for criticizing Arabs—but the often poisonous criticisms were always directed against other Arabs, not against the critic's own group. Now, under the impact of the Western presentation of Arab stagnation, Arab criticism of Arabs underwent two developments. First it became general, that is, directed not against a particular competitive Arab group, but against the Arab people as a whole. Secondly, it turned inward and included the critic's own group, often even going so far as to single out the ingroup for the sharpest barbs. This self-criticism is, next to nationalism, the most important intellectual development that has taken place in the Arab world under the influence of the West.

Of course, the point of Arab self-criticism was (and is) directed not so much to past failings as to present shortcomings. Much more irksome than the decline that had begun six or seven centuries ago, and for which there were several external causes ready to blame, was the recognition that today, after more than a century and a half of contact with the West, the Arabs were still lagging behind the West culturally, economically, and in many other areas whose importance they unquestioningly accepted from the West. Why, it was asked with increasing frequency and impatience, are we still largely uneducated, economically weak, technologically underdeveloped, with most of our people exposed to diseases and to poverty? The answer, given the specific political and power relationship between the Arabs and the West, and the particular proclivities of the Arab mind, is as ingenious as it is contrived: The West, because of selfishly sinister motivations, has kept the Arabs down, prevented them from acquiring the vital skills it possesses, and withheld from them either its technical know-how, or its intellectual accomplishments, or both.

Whatever the particular Arab explanation for the continuing Arab cultural lag relative to the West, and whether favorably or unfavorably inclined toward the West, the Arab mind must and does recognize that the West possesses a culture which is at least partially superior to the one the Arabs have received from their forebears and cherished for centuries. Whatever the Arabs' opinion about the West's attitudes and intentions toward them, whether they consider the West a benevolent jinni or a horrible ghoul, the things the West has to offer and the Arabs can acquire from it are irresistible. Yet not a few thoughtful Arabs are sore afraid that the Arab soul will be the price they will have to pay for the gifts of the West. They shudder at the prospect that the end result of all the turmoil of modernization that is seizing one Arab country after another will be a chain of Arab states that will differ from Western countries only in retaining Arabic as their language and a greatly weakened and secularized Islam as their religion. While we of the West may not quite grasp the aversion and apprehension evoked by this prospect in the mind of conservative Muslim Arabs, many of them feel that it would be much too high a price to pay for the elimination (or alleviation) of social shortcomings and the introduction of Western amenities.

Yet the die is cast. The gifts of the jinni of the West are gradually finding their way into the most remote corners of the Arab world. Resistance to them is short-lived and waning. First imperceptibly, then more and more palpably, they change the traditional Arab order of life. What is more important, they change the Arab mind. "Old" used to be synonymous with "good," and "new" or "innovation" the equivalent of "bad" or even "sinful." This evaluation epitomized a way of life, a state of mind. Where as much as a radio, a motor-driven pump, a vaccine against an illness is introduced, the most tradition-bound mind is forced to make an adjustment away from the old equations. The "new" must be recognized as "good," as better than the "old." And the process of Westernization has begun.

The problem that the Arab mind faces as it struggles with the issues of Westernization is not whether it should welcome it or resist it. That problem was from the very first moment on (say, from the day Napoleon set foot on Egyptian soil) a theoretical one, whose practical outcome had long been decided at the time the Arab mind first became aware of it. The historical concatenation of circumstances brought it about that, as in all other parts of the world into which the West penetrated, Westernization would proceed apace, indeed, must proceed, and that resistance to it was useless, in fact, impossible. To slow it down, to retard it, that was possible; but to prevent it from spreading was not.

The issue still open to the Arab mind is a different one; it consists of a number of interrelated questions. Should the Arab countries encourage and facilitate the adoption of a capitalist, a socialist, or a Communist variety of the Western economic systems? Similarly with regard to political organization: should they endeavor to fashion their emerging polity after a democratic, a rightist-dictatorial, or a leftist-Communist one-party pattern? What are those specific elements in the traditional Arab culture whose retention is worth fighting for? Respectively, in what way can and should economic, political, and cultural features brought in from the West be modified so as to give them an Arab character? In brief, while recognizing that the Westernization of the Arab world is inevitable, a good many options still remain, and upon the choice among them will depend the future political, economic, social, and cultural physiognomy of the Arab world, and the future shape of the Arab mind.

CONCLUSION

THE PICTURE OF THE ARAB MIND AS IT EMERGES FROM THE foregoing discussion is a complex one. Different processes of enculturation, which begin at birth but for which preparations are made even before birth by the fervent hope of the mother, father, and entire family that the expected child will be a boy, mold a boy and a girl into two substantially disparate personalities. The consciousness of male superiority and female inferiority is impressed into the mind of both male and female infant, and is reinforced with the passage of the years until, by the time adulthood is reached, it becomes a deeply internalized feature of consciousness. The stereotype of men and women, as it lives in the mind of both sexes, is a basic component of Arab life which exerts considerable influence on the social order in general and on personal relations in particular.

Infancy is also the time in which other component features of the Arab modal personality are formed. Important among them are the tendency to rely on the past, on established precedent and time-honored custom; the disinclination to make efforts with a view to changing existing situations; the unwillingness to persevere for the purpose of deferred achievement; and the proclivity to resort to oral threats as an expression of displeasure without following them up by action.

The acquisition of his language adds a special dimension to the Arab personality. Arabic, used with great virtuosity even by the uneducated, illiterate majority, becomes much more than a mere medium of oral communication: it develops into an artistic instrument whose utilization can provide great emotional satisfaction to the speaker and can make an equally great emotional impact on the listener. It is in this specific, emotionally colored quality language has for the Arab, in the sensate satisfaction he derives from the sound, rhythm, and cadence of Arabic, that one must seek the psychological bases of his inclination to rhetoricism, exaggeration, over-assertion, and repetition, and of his tendency to substitute words for actions. On the other hand, the absence of exact tempora in the Arabic language appears to be correlated with the disregard of the time element and with the lack of time sense that is an oft-observed characteristic of the Arab personality.

The Western-inspired spread of literacy introduced the first break in the psychological integrality of the Arab mind and the Arabic tongue. As elementary education, and with it the knowledge of literary Arabic, spread, more and more Arabs came to recognize that the language they spoke was but a vulgarized version of the pure and fine literary Arabic, a smattering of which they acquired but full mastery of which most of them could never attain. This bilingualism was topped by a second one, that of Arabic and a European language, which was introduced into the society and the school system by whatever European colonial power gained control over the country. Typically, the result of this Arabic-Western bilingualism was to force those Arabs who acquired a working knowledge of the European language to admit to themselves that Arabic (whether the colloquial or the literary variety) was an inferior medium, a language inadequate for the expression of many thoughts and things which had become important for them as a result of their French or English education.

Arabic-French or Arabic-English bilingualism is one of the most readily apparent manifestations of that marginality which engulfed the educated élite in most Arab countries about the turn of the century. Other expressions of marginality can be found in practically all aspects of life: in housing, furnishing, clothing, food, social forms, behavior patterns, workings of the mind, and even emotions. As a result, many members of the educated élite in Arab countries developed an ambivalent attitude to both cultures: the traditional Arab culture from which they wished to break away but which continued to have a hold on them, and the modern Western culture to which they wished to assimilate but which they were unable to internalize completely. This ambivalence, in turn, can lead—as recognized by Arab students of the Arab personality—to *izdiwāj*, or a split personality, which itself is, of course, a Western psychological concept. As far as social structure is concerned, the acquisition of a Western language and culture resulted in a cultural dichotomy in most Arab countries between the Westernized or Westernizing élite and the tradition-bound masses. The consequent disruption of the cultural continuum between the lower and upper reaches of Arab society created a sense of alienation or estrangement between the two, and an anomalous situation in which two culturally largely alien sectors lived side by side in the same country and even in the same city.

The dichotomy between the Westernized élite and the traditional masses finds one of its most trenchant expressions in the political field. With a very few exceptions (notably in the Arabian Peninsula), the political leaders of the Arab world are all Westernized men, all know either English or French (occasionally better than Arabic), and all are inclined to measure the cultural, social, and economic level of their countries by Western standards rather than by their own time-honored traditions which they tend to consider outmoded. Whether they are hereditary monarchs or presidents; whether their political orientation is pro-Western, neutral, or emphatically anti-Western; whether they rule autocratically, dictatorially, or democratically; whether they are heads of state or occupy positions in their government one or more rungs beneath the summit—almost all the Arab political leaders are deeply influenced by the West. And, being Westernized, they cannot help looking with Western (or near-Western) eyes at the interests of their non-Westernized, traditional Muslim Arab countrymen who constitute the majority of the population in every Arab state. Their task, therefore, as they see it, is twofold: to bring Western-inspired innovations to their peoples, and to re-educate them so that they should see in those innovations improvements and be willing to accept them.

Turning our attention to the traditional components of the Arab personality, we find that they fall into two main categories: a pre-Islamic Bedouin substratum, which continues to live on in the folk culture of the traditional majority; and the Islamic component, superimposed on the first one and often merging with it imperceptibly. The Bedouin element in the Arab personality consists of such features as the sense of kinship, loyalty, bravery, manliness, aversion to physical work, and a great emphasis on honor, "face," and self-respect. It also finds its expression in such institutions as

309

raiding, blood revenge, and hospitality, the last including the syndrome of protection for those in need of it, and generosity. A special, and very important, complex within the Bedouin tradition is the sexual honor of the women, which is interpreted in most cases very stringently, and on which depends the honor of the woman's entire paternal family.

The Islamic component of the Arab personality is seen in the specific way in which Islam permeates the totality of life, that is, in its normative function; in its psychological effect in providing a sustaining force; in its particular belief system; in its religiocentrism; and in the teleology or purposive orientation it gives to life. It also inculcates a belief in predestination, commonly referred to as fatalism, which creates a specific mental predisposition and is a source of both great weakness and great strength. As long as things go tolerably well, Muslim fatalism has a retarding effect: it makes people averse to any effort directed toward seeking betterment. When misfortune strikes, it is an inestimable asset: it imparts to people the ability to bear with equanimity the hardest blows of fate, since everything that happens to man is the will of God. In both bad and good fortune it can lead to improvidence and to lightheaded squandering because "Allah is the provider."

A conspectus of the pre-Islamic and Islamic components in the Arab personality leads to the recognition that Arab ethics embrace both folk elements, largely pre-Islamic in origin, and Koranic-Islamic features. That particular compartment of ethics which has been called "ethics of virtue" is found, upon closer inspection, to be composed of largely pre-Islamic elements, and to be centered on the imperative of preserving one's "face," and on its correlate, that of avoiding shame. An analysis of the focal moral norms discloses that while these fall into such categories as courage, hospitality, generosity, and honor, ultimately they all revolve around the one central issue of self-respect. Moreover, since in the Arab view a man's self-respect depends primarily on the respect others have for him, the entire Arab ethical system is basically other-determined or outward-oriented. What is important for this type of ethical outlook is not feelings, intentions, and other internal values of morality, but the outwardly manifested behavior patterns which alone serve as the basis for the judgment others pass on the character of an individual. Thus shame, and not guilt, is the main factor in determining conduct.

While Arab conduct is of the conforming type, requiring the individual to behave in a manner approved by his social environment, Arab culture provides a vent through which suppressed emotions can, at least occasionally, break into the open. This culturally approved outlet is the flare-up of temper, flashes of anger, aggression, and violence, which are condoned by society and readily forgiven. This type of behavior tends to veer from one extreme to the other, being polarized between the two contrasting syndromes of self-control and wild outbursts of aggressivity. While these seizures last, Arab temperament goes on a rampage and hostility can easily become irrational. Once they pass, sincere contrition follows, accompanied by bafflement and a total lack of comprehension of what one has done and how one could have done it.

It would appear that there is some connection between this disjointed type of behavior and the relative lack of correlation among the three functional planes of human existence: thoughts, words, and actions. Arab thought processes are relatively more atuonomous, that is, more independent of reality, than the thought processes typical of Western man. Nor is Arab verbal formulation influenced by reality to the degree to which it is in the West. Arab thought tends more to move on an ideal level, divorced from the Procrustean bed of reality. Arab speech likewise tends to express ideal thoughts, and to represent that which is desired or hoped for as if it were an actual fact in evidence, rather that cleave to the limitations of the real. There is thus among the Arabs a relatively greater discrepancy between thought and speech on the one hand and action on the other. In action, one is hemmed in by reality; thoughts and words, however, manage to retain a relative independence from reality.

Additional insight into the working of the Arab mind can be gained from a consideration of the Arab arts, music, and literature. In the visual field, the Arabs have focused on decorative arts, which can be interpreted as an inclination to adhere to ideal constructs and a concomitant neglect or disregard of, even disdain for, visible reality as expressed in natural forms. In music, the same tendency exists but does not strike us so strongly because music is in Western culture too the one art form which is least correlated with reality. Musical notes and sequences are the invention of the human mind in both cultures. Where Arab music differs from Western is in its tonal raw material and its structure. Both Arab decorative art and Arab music are characterized by a seemingly unending repetition of the same small-sized element, with or without minor variations. The same feature has been discerned in Arab architecture as well as in Arab literature. However, all this—the entire physiognomy of Arab artistic, musical, and literary

311

expression—is rapidly changing and moving toward Western forms.

The tension between unity and conflict which characterizes social relations within Arab countries as well as inter-Arab political relations can be taken to constitute yet another example of the variance between the ideal and the real in the Arab mind. Arab unity has been for a long time the ideal to which popular sentiment has been attracted and the political leadership has paid lip service. But reality often makes a mockery of this ideal and pits one Arab group against the other and one Arab nation or country against the next. True, conflicts do not always take the form of bloody wars, but can be merely small-scale and relatively innocuous free-for-alls with no other weapons but sticks and stones, or altogether devoid of physical violence expressing themselves only in verbal abuse and invective. But all the varied levels of fighting bear unmistakable witness to the conflict proneness of the Arabs and to the fact that fellow Arabs, rather than outsiders, are the Arabs' "favorite" enemies. In recent decades, more and more Arab voices have been raised in criticism against this proclivity to internal conflict and have called for the realization of the old and hitherto elusive ideal of Arab unity.

A society as strife-torn as that of the Arabs could not but develop machinery for resolving conflicts and restoring peace between warring and fighting parties of whatever description. The traditional institution of mediation was the concrete form taken by this peacemaking effort. The same institution is relied upon by the Arabs in the large-scale conflicts which have raged among them in the last decade. The untiring repetitive recourse to mediation time and again in the same continuing conflict is a remarkable testimony to the Arabs' unshaken reliance on this tradition-honored method of conflict resolution, even within the unaccustomed context of modern Western-type warfare. Another example of the application of traditional methods to problems of the modern Arab world is what I termed "conferentiasis." The prototype of the numerous and frequently reconvening inter-Arab conferences is the *majlis,* the council in the guest tent of the Bedouin shaykh. Many features characterizing modern Arab conferences can be elucidated by reference to the tribal council and by a comparison with its highly informal procedures.

A very specific component was added to the Arab mind when Western scholarship presented Arab literati with the historical drama of medieval Arab greatness followed by centuries of stagnation. Arab critics soon outdistanced their Western colleagues in chastising the Arabs for their backwardness, cultural decline, indeed, fossilization. The thrust of these melancholy representations was always positive: they intended and actually managed to awaken the Arab mind from its medieval slumber, implanted in it the desire to recapture ancient glories and take its place alongside the West in the cultural vanguard of humanity. Nationalism was thought by many to be the panacea for all Arab ills, and Arab nationalism contributed greatly to the liberation of the Arab homeland from the Atlantic to the Persian Gulf.

At the same time Arab nationalism became tainted by a strong anti-Western streak. While it had to be recognized that the West was the prime mover in bringing about the Arab awakening, in introducing sanitation, general education and other mass benefits into the Arab world, the West assumed for the Arab mind the character of a sinister jinni, a hateful enemy and a convenient whipping-boy who could be blamed for all the problems that beset the Arabs. The encounter with the West produced a disturbing inferiority complex in the Arab mind which in itself made it more difficult to shake off the shackles of stagnation. The next challenge the Arab mind must meet is to cease measuring Arab achievements with Western yard-sticks and to work for a regeneration of the Arab world by building on its own, by no means negligible, capabilities.

THE ARAB WORLD: AREA AND MID-YEAR POPULATION ESTIMATES

Country	Area (sq. kms.)	1950	1960	1970	Natural Increase	Density per sq. km. (1970)
NORTH AFRICA						
Morocco (const. monarchy)	445,050	8,950,000	11,640,000	15,530,000	33.0	35
Algeria (republic)	2,381,741	8,750,000	10,800,000	14,012,000	32.2	6
Tunisia (republic)	164,150			5,140,000	30.3	31
Libya (republic)	1,759,540	1,030,000	1,350,000	1,938,000	37.0	1
Arab Republic of Egypt	1,001,449	20,460,000	25,920,000	33,330,000	27.6	33
Sudan (republic)	2,505,813	9,070,000	11,850,000	15,700,000	30.5	6
THE FERTILE CRESCENT						
Syria (republic)	185,180	3,500,000	4,560,000	6,100,000	32.2	33
Lebanon (republic)	10,400	1,620,000	2,110,000	2,790,000	23.2	268
Jordan (const. monarchy)	97,740		1,640,000	2,320,000	33.1	24
Iraq (republic)	434,924	5,200,000	6,890,000	9,440,000	33.8	22
THE ARABIAN PENINSULA						
Saudi Arabia (kingdom)	2,149,690	4,890,000	5,980,000	7,740,000	27.3	4
Yemen (republic)	195,000	3,620,000	4,430,000	5,730,000	27.3	29
People's Democratic Republic of Yemen	287,683	810,000	990,000	1,280,000	27.3	4
Oman (sultanate)	140,797	390,000	490,000	657,000	30.0*	3
United Arab Emirates	83,600	80,000	90,000	180,000		
Qatar (sheikdom)	22,014	20,000	50,000	79,000	30.0*	4
Bahrain (sheikdom)	598		160,000	215,000		360
Kuwait (emirate)	16,000	150,000	280,000	710,700	35.9	44
TOTAL	11,881,369	68,540,000	89,260,000	122,891,700		10

*Includes immigration
Sources: *United Nations Demographic Yearbook 1970* and *United Nations Statistical Yearbook 1971.* The majority of the data contained in the table are United Nations estimates.

APPENDIX II

The Judgment of Historians: Spengler and Toynbee

OSWALD SPENGLER AND ARNOLD TOYNBEE, BY FAR THE MOST outstanding representatives of the morphological approach to history, based their characterization of Arab culture on a perusal of a large amount of historical material and historical studies which were available to them at the time they wrote their respective surveys of man's major cultural flowerings. Their presentation of the life history of Arab culture is closely interwoven with their judgment of the Arab mind. A brief review of what these two great Western historians have to say about the Arabs is, therefore, of interest in connection with the topic of this volume.

1. SPENGLER

In a long chapter of his *Decline of the West,* entitled "Problems of Arab Culture,"[1] Oswald Spengler discusses the historic cultures of the Near East from the earliest times to the present. The beginnings of these cultures, he maintains, go back to ancient Babylonian civilization,[2] and they comprise ancient Persian, Jewish, Christian-Byzantine, and Muslim formations, all of which are subjected to his analytic scalpel. Yet the very fact that he titles his chapter "Problems of Arab Culture" indicates that of all the particular cultures he considers as belonging to this group, he regards Arab culture as the most characteristic and, perhaps, also as the most central and significant. This becomes apparent also from the terminology Spengler coins and consistently uses to characterize this group of cultures.

A Spenglerian term that recurs frequently is the expression. "fellah culture." The subchapter immediately preceding that dealing with the problems of Arab culture is entitled "Primal Peoples, Culture Peoples, Fellah Peoples." [3] To the first category belong peoples prior to the emergence of their culture. To the second, peoples who are the carriers of historic cultures. Spengler takes considerable pride in what he calls his "decisive discovery" of the true interrelationship between cultures and peoples. Since in the same paragraph in which he makes this statement he also gives his generalized evaluation of Arab culture, it is worth quoting *in extenso:*

> It must be stated with utmost clarity: the great cultures are something entirely original, something that rises up from the deepest grounds of the psyche *(Seelentum)*. However, peoples under the spell of a culture are, in their inner form and in their entire appearance, not the authors but the *products* of this culture. . . . "The Arabs" have not created the Arab culture. On the

contrary. The magian culture, which began in the time of Christ, produced as its last great nation-creation the Arab people which, like the Jewish and Persian peoples, represents a religious community, that of Islam. World history is the history of the great cultures.[4]

In Spengler's cultural morphology, every cultural flowering must be followed by decline and cultural death. As he puts it: "I term that which follows a culture 'fellah peoples,' after their most famous example, the Egyptians since Roman times."[5] And he explains:

What primal peoples and fellah peoples experience is that oft mentioned zoological up and down, a planless happening, in which, without aim and without measured duration, many things occur but in a meaningful sense nevertheless nothing happens.[6]

The religions of such fellah peoples necessarily become

fellah religions, in which the contrast between cosmopolitan and provincial piety has again vanished as has that between primitive and high culture . . . The religion has become completely historyless; where once decades signified an epoch, now even centuries have no more meaning, and the ups and downs of superficial changes only prove that the inner form (Gestalt) is set with finality.[7]

Spengler repeatedly and consistently characterizes Arab culture as "magian." Nowhere does he define explicitly what he means by this term, but he enumerates in various passages the traits of the "magian soul":

. . . the magian soul of the Arab culture appears, awakening in the time of Augustus in the lands between the Tigris and the Nile, the Black Sea and Southern Arabia, with its algebra, astrology and alchemy, its mosaics and arabesques, its caliphates and mosques, the sacraments and holy books of the Persian, Jewish, Christian "late antique," and Manichaean religions.[8]

The magian world view is characterized by a feeling of limitedness, of being confined, in fact, of living in a cavelike world.[9] This cave-feeling is expressed, says Spengler, in the religious architecture of all the faiths that developed within the realm of magian-Arab culture: in that of the basilicas of the Christians, Hellenistic Jews, and Baal cults, in the Mithraeums, the Mazdaic fire temples, and the mosques. All these are expressions of the same psyche (Seelentum): "the cave-feeling."[10] The most essential expression of this cave-feeling is the dome. It is in the "central dome structure" that "the magian world-feeling finds its purest expression."[11]

This cavelike perception of space is paralleled, says Spengler, by a similarly cavernous awareness of time.

The first thing that the man of this culture, from poorest slave and porter to prophet and Caliph, feels over him as Kismet [fate] is not the limitless flight of times which never allows the lost moment to recur, but a beginning and an end of "these days" which are immutably fixed and ordained and between which human existence takes its place foreordained ever since the beginning. Not only World-space, but World-time, too, is cave like, and from this follows an inner, truly magian certainty: everything has "a time", from the Savior's advent whose hour was stated in ancient texts, to the smallest everyday activities, in which the Faustian [i.e., Western] haste becomes senseless and unintelligible. . . .[12]

This results in a historical view of the given time as it is still natural for the Muslim people today. The world view of the people falls naturally into three major parts: the beginning, the development, and the destruction of the world. For the Muslim, with his deeply ethical outlook, the essential parts of the development of the world are the salvation story and the ethical way of life. . . .[13]

Magian human existence is led by the feeling of *this* time and the viewing of *this* space to quite a specific type of piety which also can be termed cave like: a *will-less* submission which knows nothing at all of the spiritual ego, and which finds in the spiritual We, that has entered the quickened body, a mere reflection of the divine light. The Arabic word for this is "Islam," submission . . . Islam is precisely the *impossibility of an I as a free power vis-à-vis the divine*. . . . In the entire cosmic cave there is only *one cause* which is the *immediate* ground of all visible effects: the deity, which itself has no longer any reasons for its acts.[14]

It is out of this feeling that the "purely magian idea of grace" is derived.[15]

One of the most intriguing theses in Spengler's morphology of world history is his observation that the spread of the Arab-magian culture preceded the Arab armed conquests. After the time of Augustus, says Spengler, this Arab-magian culture began to be diffused over an increasingly large part of the ancient world and, in the course of the subsequent centuries, all of North Africa, as well as Spain and part of France in the West, and Southwest Asia plus India and Turkestan in the East, became spiritually the domain of magian culture. This cultural conquest prepared the ground for the armed conquest of that entire huge world area in the seventh century:

> This alone explains the enormous vehemence with which Arab culture, liberated at last artistically as well by Islam, hurled itself upon all the lands which had inwardly belonged to it for centuries. It was the mark of a psyche which senses that it has no time to lose, which is affrighted noticing the first signs of age before it has had youth. This liberation of magian mankind is unparalleled. Syria is conquered, one should say, *delivered,* in 634; Damascus falls in 635; Ctesiphon in 637. In 641 Egypt and India are reached, in 647 Carthage, in 676 Samarkand, in 710 Spain; in 732 the Arabs stand before Paris.[16]

As to psychology, in the sense of the doctrine concerning the soul, Spengler observes that "the magian soul-image is characterized by a strict *dualism of two mysterious substances: spirit and soul.*"[17] This inner, psychological, microcosmic dualism is paralleled by an outer, supernatural macrocosmic dualism: "God and Devil, Persian Ormuzd and Ahriman, Jewish Yahweh and Beelzebub, Islamic Allah and Iblis, the absolute good and the absolute evil. . . ."[18] Accordingly, "magian man sees history as the great cosmic drama of creation and destruction, the struggle between soul and spirit, good and evil, God and Devil, a strictly delimited happening with one single *peripeteia* as its high point: the appearance of the Redeemer."[19]

Subsequently, Spengler points out that the same basic dualism exists, for magian man, in other realms as well:

Truth is for the magian way of thinking *a substance,* and lie or error another one. It is the same essential dualism as in the strife between light and darkness, life and death, good and evil. As substance truth is identical once with God, once with the spirit of God, once with the word. . . . A magian revelation is a mystical process in which God's eternal and un-created word —or *the deity as word*—enters into a man in order to obtain through him the "revealed," sensate form of sounds and especially of letters. *Koran means "reading."* Muhammed glimpsed in a vision written scrolls preserved in heaven which he—although he had never learned how to read—was able to decipher "in the name of the Lord" (Sura 96; cf. 80:11 and 85:21). This is the form of revelation which in this culture is the rule, and in others not even the exception.[20]

In another passage, Spengler has more to say about the mystery that magian man felt enveloped him:

The world of magian man is filled with a fairy-tale atmosphere. Devils and evil spirits threaten man, angels and fairies protect him. There are amulets and talismans, mysterious lands, cities, buildings and beings, secret letters, the Seal of Solomon and the philosophers' stone. And over all this is poured a glittering cave-like light which is always threatened with being swallowed up by a ghostly darkness. . . .[21]

Even in the Arab-magian psychology, that is, the doctrine about the non-material components of man, says Spengler, one can discern the echoes of the magian world view:

. . . souls are in depth discrete entities; the *Pneuma* [spirit] is one and always the same. Man possesses a soul, but he *merely takes part* in the spirit of the light and the good. The divine descends into him and in this manner binds all the individuals there below with the One in the above. This primal feeling which dominates the entire faith and opinion of all magian men, is something quite unique; it separates not only their world-view, but also every kind of magian religiosity, from every other in the kernel of its existence. This culture was, as has been shown, quite specifically, the culture of the middle. . . . All religions of the magian culture, from the creations of Isaiah and Zarathustra to Islam, constitute a complete inner unity of world-feeling. . . .[22]

The proclivity for mystery underlies, according to Spengler, Arab art, architecture, and scientific effort as well.

The arabesque and the cave-like vault of the mosque were part of Arab culture; out of this world-feeling developed alchemy with its concepts of mysteriously effective substances such as the "philosophers' mercury," which is neither a material nor a property, but something that magically underlies the colored substance of metals and can effect the transformation of one into the other.[23]

When the magian soul does not express itself in magic and mystery, it at least indulges in "indeterminacy." One of the characteristics of algebra, invented by Arab culture, is the "indeterminacy of the unnamed Arabic numerals."[24]

This magian culture, says Spengler, "is geographically and historically the most central in the group of high cultures, the only one which has had contact spatially and temporally with almost all other cultures."[25]

However, while the spirit of magian culture is homogeneous, it expresses itself in many different languages: "There was here a closed group of magian national literatures of a homogeneous spirit but in *several* languages . . . for a nation of the magian style has no mother tongue. . . ."[26]

A magian nation, sustained by such a culture and world view, differs essentially from other nation types:

> A magian-style nation is the community of the believers, the union *(Verband)* of all those who know the right road to salvation and who are inwardly bound together through the *ijmā'* [consensus] of this faith. One belongs to an antique nation through the possession of citizenship; to a magian nation —through a sacral act: to the Jewish through circumcision, to the Mandaean or Christian through a quite specific type of baptism. What the citizen of a foreign city was for an antique people, the unbeliever is for a magian one. With him there can be no contact and no intermarriage . . . the magian nation is practically identical with the concept of the Church [i.e., the religious community]. The antique nation is inwardly bound to city, the Western to a landscape, the Arab knows nether fatherland nor mother tongue. An expression of the latter's world-feeling is but the script of which each "nation" develops one of its own immediately after its emergence. But precisely because of this the *magian* national feeling, in the fullest sense of the word, is so inwardly and solid. . . .[27]

Elsewhere, too, Spengler emphasizes that the criterion of nationhood in the magian culture is religion, and that members of a given magian religio-national group insist on holding themselves separate from members of other such groups:

> In the magian [i.e., Islamic-Arab] legal world there exists no *connubium* between members of different faiths . . . how could, in a Syrian village, a Monophysite Christian man marry a Nestorian Christian woman? They may have been the descendants of the same tribe *(Geschlecht)* but they belonged to two juridically different "nations."
>
> This Arab concept of the nation is a new and totally decisive fact. In the Apollonian [i.e., Western] culture, the boundary between homeland and foreign parts lay between two cities; in the magian—between any two religious communities.[28]

The latest formation of a magian religio-national community was the Muslim-Arab nation. This new nation, says Spengler,

> with its passionate soul so full of character, was created through the *consensus* of the new faith. This nation is, like the Christian, Jewish and Persian, not homogeneous racially, nor is it connected to a homeland; therefore, it did not "emigrate," but achieved its enormous expansion through the absorption into its union of the greater part of the early magian nations. All these nations passed at the end of the first millennium into the form of fellah peoples. It is as fellah peoples that the Christian peoples of the Balkan Peninsula have ever since lived under Turkish rule, as did the Parsees in India and the Jews in Western Europe.[29]

The concept of the "fellah peoples" was made by Spengler into a key concept of his historical morphology: "Fellah peoples . . . are rigid objects of a movement coming from the outside, which exercises itself upon them without meaning and in accidental thrusts."[30]

According to Spengler, after a civilization reaches the overripe stage at which it develops big cosmopolitan cities, it inevitably enters a period of "appalling depopulation." This era lasts for several hundreds of years.

> The entire pyramid of culture-bearing man vanishes. It is being reduced from the tip downward: first the cosmopolitan cities, then the provincial towns, and finally the countryside. . . . Finally, only the primitive blood remains, which, however, has been robbed of its strong and promising elements. Thus the *type of the fellah* emerges.[31]

Having come from the outside, from the field of general historiography, to the study of the five-thousand-year-old history of the Near East, Spengler felt rather pleased with what he called his "discovery" of "Arab culture." He introduces his brief capsule of Arab cultural history with the words: "This Arab culture is a discovery." Then he goes on:

> Its unity had been suspected by the late Arabs, but it escaped the Western historians so completely that one cannot find even a good designation for it. On the basis of the dominant language one could term the pre-culture and the early period Aramaic, the late period, Arabic. . . . The Arab spirit, however, mostly under a late-antique mask, cast its spell over the emerging culture of the West, and Arab civilization, which in the folk psyche of Southern Spain, Provence and Sicily is superimposed that of antiquity . . . became the model after which the Gothic spirit was educated. . . .[32]

2. TOYNBEE

Toynbee's affinity with Spengler has been noted in a general way by a number of his critics,[33] and even by a student of Spengler's precursors.[34] Several years ago, the present author made an attempt to show in some detail Toynbee's dependence on Spengler, in particular in the concept of "fossil" peoples which re-echoes, down to specific terms and turns of phrases, Spengler's portraiture of "fellah peoples."[35]

Spengler's Arab or magian culture re-emerges in Toynbee's "Syriac Society" or "Syriac Civilization." This began with King Solomon (tenth century B.C.), but did not develop its universal religion until the emergence of Islam in the seventh century A.D. The constituent ethnic elements of the two are practically identical. This civilization, says Toynbee, "has three great feats to its credit. It invented the Alphabet; it discovered the Atlantic; and it arrived at a particular conception of God which is common to Judaism, Zoroastrianism, Christianity and Islam." The alphabet was invented, probably, by the Phoenicians, who also discovered the Atlantic. Monotheism was invented by the Israelites.[36] The role of Islam was, as Toynbee sees it, that it endowed the Syriac Society, at last, with an indigenous universal church and thereby enabled it, after centuries of suspended animation, to give up the ghost in the assurance that it would not now pass away without leaving offspring; for the Islamic Church became the chrysalis out of which the new Arabic and Iranic civilizations were in due course to emerge.[37] It was through Islam that both the Iranic and the Arabic civilizations were affiliated to the Syriac civilization.[38]

Toynbee devotes considerable attention to the causes and circumstances of what he terms the breakdown of the two Muslim civilizations. In the thirteenth century, he explains, Southwest Asia received a blow from the Mongols under whose impact it "is still prostrate" today, "even after the passage of 700 years." This thirteenth-century Mongol devastation was followed by the fifteenth-century West European diversion of the World's sea-routes away from the Levant and the Red Sea." These two developments between them explain "the decline and eclipse of South-West Asia and Egypt in the sixteenth, seventeenth, and eighteenth centuries." Then, as if oblivious that a few lines earlier he had pronounced the area "still prostrate," Toynbee adds: "This makes the recovery of this region in the nineteenth century and thereafter all the more remarkable and impressive."[39]

Elsewhere, Toynbee pinpoints the date of the breakdown of the two Muslim civilizations more closely:

> . . . a scrutiny of the histories of the Iranic and Arabic Muslim civilizations revealed strong evidence of these two societies having broken down in the second decade of the sixteenth century of the Christian Era . . . when . . . Ottoman Sunni Iranic Muslim Power [conquered] the sister Arabic Muslim Society.[40]

The question of why and how Arabic Muslim society suffered its breakdown is dealt with by Toynbee in some detail in others parts of his *magnum opus* as well. On balance, he finds that of the two baneful historical events, the Mongol invasion in the thirteenth, and the Ottoman conquest of the Arab lands in the sixteenth century, it was the latter which gave Arab society the *coup de grâce:*

> . . . there is nothing in the record to suggest that, within this span of some 250 years [from the last quarter of the thirteenth to the first quarter of the sixteenth century], the Arabic peoples had prepared the way for the Ottoman aggressor by doing themselves any fatal injury with their own hands. It is true that this Arabic Society had not shown any marked signs of promise before the time when it was submerged by the Ottoman flood; for the loneliness of Ibn Khaldun's star is as striking as its brilliance. Yet the apparently aimless turbulence of Ifrīqīyah under the Hafsids, as well as the apparently lifeless torpidity of Egypt under the Mamluks, may have masked the vigorous and purposeful progress of a healthily growing society from infancy through childhood towards adolescence; and we have no valid warrant, in the Arabic history of that age, for pronouncing dogmatically that the Arabic Society would never in any event have burst into flower if the Ottoman conquest had not blighted it.
>
> Thus in Arabic history we might seem to have one case in which the breakdown of a civilization can be traced to the destructive effect of an alien society's impact. . . .[41]

However, the breakdown suffered by the Arab lands as a result of the Ottoman conquest is not seen by Toynbee as a total disintegration of the body social. On the contrary. In Egypt, for instance, underneath the "exotic military crust" of the Janissaries, the indigenous Arabic Society of Egypt still continued to lead its separate and self-sufficient life, in which the peasantry and the 'ulamā and the urban guilds of merchants and artisans each played their interdependent parts, and all recognized one another's respective functions in the corporate life of their common body social.[42]

Turning to Arab society in the present time, Toynbee wonders whether it is "simply displaying the effects of a temporary shock on the morrow of a harrowing experience which, after all, has not proved fatal?"[43]

In any case, in contrast to Spengler, Toynbee does not consider the Arab society as an example of a "fellah people," or, in Toynbee's own terminology, a "fossil." According to Toynbee, the fossils of the otherwise extinct Syriac civilization include the Monophysite Christians of Armenia, Mesopotamia, Egypt, and Abyssinia, and the Nestorian Christians of Kurdistan and Malabar, as well as the Jews and the Parsees. Islamic civilization is counted by him among the four "living societies" that exist in the present world in addition to Western society, the other three being the Orthodox Christian, the Hindu, and the Far Eastern.[44]

As can be readily seen from this summary of Toynbee's views of Arab society and culture, his approach is characterized by a certain ambivalence. On the one hand, he frequently refers to the "breakdown" of Arab civilization and traces the historical events and circumstances that dealt the Arab world a blow under whose impact it is still prostrate today. On the other, he speaks of the "remarkable and impressive recovery" of the area from the nineteenth century on. He even goes so far as to reinterpret boldly the "apparently lifeless torpidity" of the most populous Arab country, Egypt, in the Mamluk era as being a mere mask under which Egyptian society actually experienced a "vigorous and purposeful progress" and a healthy growth.

When it comes to an evaluation of the Muslim Arab outlook on life, Toynbee is again of two minds. On the one hand, he goes along with D. B. MacDonald in his judgment of the scope of the tradition-bound outlook on the world and on life which still characterizes a major part of Muslim Arab world. He finds that there is a "catholic indifference" to anything that is not directly of moment for his life in This World or the next which is enjoined upon every pious Muslim by the precepts of orthodox Islamic theology. Moreover,

> this is not simply theological; it is in the very texture of the Muslim mind. We can say: 'This is an interesting book'; in Arabic you cannot express that idea . . . . Even curiosity, in the highest and finest sense, we cannot render [in Arabic]. . . . The free, self-determining, self-developing soul may not walk its own path, however innocently, but must fit itself to the scheme and pattern of schools.[45]

Elsewhere, however, in seeming contrast, Toynbee remarks that "the thinking faculty played a more responsible part in Islam than in Christianity."[46]

Self-contradictory evaluations of a similar kind are given by Toynbee of the Arab attitude to other races. He quotes the observation of the noted Arab historian al-Balādhurī to the effect that the Arabs use the term "ḥamrā" (ruddy) as a deprecatory epithet for their northerly subjects, and refers to the oft-encountered Arab pronouncement about "the comely swarthiness of their own Arab breed."[47] Elsewhere, however, he remarks that there is no color prejudice among the Arabs, and that they mingle relatively freely with Negroes in Africa.[48]

The sum total of all this is that the student of Toynbee's *Study of History* remains quite unenlightened as to what, on balance, is Toynbee's impression, evaluation, and judgment of the cultural position of Arab society today in global perspective.

APPENDIX III

The Arab World and Spanish America: A Comparison

REFERENCE WAS MADE IN THE MAIN TEXT TO THE PREVALENT ARAB view which considers all Arabs as constituting one single nation despite the present fragmentation of the Arab world into eighteen independent states. In Chapter XIII we discussed the significance of this pervasive idea of Arab unity in some detail, but it seems appropriate here to consider for a moment the uniqueness of such a conviction of theoretical unity for so large a number of sovereign political entities. This uniqueness can best be pointed up by comparing the Arab world with the only other similar group of nations, that of the Spanish American states. The similarities between the two are numerous; and the differences between them on the issue of unity are striking.

Spanish, with some dialectal variation, is spoken in seventeen countries in America; Arabic, with greater dialectal differences, in eighteen countries in the Middle East. Catholicism, the dominant religion in Spanish America, is the religion also of Portuguese-speaking Brazil, the largest country on the South American continent; of several smaller island republics; and of Spain, the European mother country whose colonial offshoots developed into the Spanish American states. Islam, the dominant religion in the Arab world, is also the religion of the two large non-Arab countries in the Middle East itself, Turkey and Iran, and of several countries outside the Middle East with populations much larger than those of the biggest Arab states.

The independence of the Spanish American countries, which preceded that of the Arab states by about a century, was won by a series of fierce revolutionary wars. By 1825, the last Spanish forces were expelled from the mainland. In the course of this liberation movement, the four former Spanish vice-royalties broke up into the present seventeen republics. This process of fragmentation continued until 1839. Simón Bolívar's dream of a league of free, constitutional republics became translated into the reality of numerous mutually hostile dictatorships.

In the Arab world, Turkey played roughly the role that Spain had in Spanish America. Both Turkey and Spain experienced their great colonial expansion around 1500. Both treated their conquered territories as colonies. The concept of a dominant mother country seeking to confer benefits on the peoples of her colonies was as alien to Turkey as it was to Spain. But there were differences in the power relationship between the two sets of countries. Spain sent her conquering armies overseas, imposed her language, her religion, and her culture on the Indians of Spanish America, and sent a considerable number of settlers who remained in the newly conquered lands, intermarried or interbred with the natives, and established themselves over them as an aristocratic upper class. Turkey, too, sent her armies to conquer the Arab lands, but she did not impose her language on the native Arab populations. As far as religion was concerned, the Turkish state religion, Islam, was itself an importation of an earlier age from the same Arab lands which the Seljuks first conquered in the eleventh and the Ottomans in the sixteenth centuries. Thus, Turkish Muslims ruled over Arab Muslims and there was no religious barrier between them. Nor did Turkish settlers in considerable numbers move into the Arab lands. Only the highest officials of the vilayets and sanjaks—into which the Arab lands were divided under Turkish rule—were Turks, as were most officers of the army. The lower officialdom and the common soldiers were Arabs. Lack of settlers meant a minimum of intermarriage, and the absence of any attempt to introduce Turkish culture. For four centuries, the Arab lands of the Fertile Crescent were governed by handfuls of Turks, concentrated for the most part in the major cities. So Turkish-Arab relations in no way paralleled the economic, social, and cultural web that was woven between subject natives and dominant newcomers in Spanish America in the three centuries of Spanish colonial rule.

There was also a considerable difference as to the demographic effect of the conquest in America and in the Arab lands. While the Turkish rule over the Arabs was invariably harsh and often cruel, the Turks did not cause anything even faintly reminiscent of the demographic devastation that followed the Spanish conquest of America. It has been estimated that wars, slavery, and above all epidemic diseases, introduced by the Spaniards, resulted in an elimination of no less than 95 per cent of the native population by 1650, that is, within 150 years of the arrival of the first *conquistadores.*[1] Nothing like this was done or caused to happen by the Turks, under whose rule the Arab populations remained numerically as stationary as they had been before. What did happen was that the oppressive and exploitative Turkish rule sapped the vitality, energy, and initiative of the Arabs to such an extent that the entire period of Turkish domination was for the Arabs a historyless time, an era of stagnation (cf. Chapter XV). In this connection it is interesting to note that while fighting among hostile Arab factions occurred quite frequently in this period, for example, among the rival Qays and Yaman moieties,[2] there was no significant armed struggle against the Turkish overlord. This represents a sharp contrast to Spanish American developments, in which numerous native leaders arose and revolution followed revolution until independence was won. Middle Eastern history knows no Arab Bolívar, no San Martín, no Iturbide, no Guerrero; in fact, no revolutionary uprising against the Turks.

Even at the most opportune time, when Turkey was involved in a life-and-death struggle with the Western Allies in World War I, the only Arab revolt, a small-scale and rather insignificant one at that, was organized by a British officer, T. E. Lawrence, and the few Arabs who participated in it came from those groups who had never been touched more than peripherally by Turkish rule. Only after World War II did a thoroughly Frenchified Maghribite Arab leadership raise the standard of revolt against French colonial rule and, after a relatively brief, although hard and bloody, struggle gain independence for Tunisia, Morocco, and Algeria. The Arab countries of the Fertile Crescent, however, had been handed independence a few years earlier by the French and British mandatories as the fruit not of armed struggle but of negotiation.

One more difference, and this a psychologically most significant one, can be pointed out between the Spanish- and the Arabic-speaking groups of countries. In Spanish America, there is a general but rather amorphous consciousness in the educated classes of the Spanish origin of their history, their culture, and their religion, and a correspondingly general and diffuse consciousness of the relatedness of one Spanish American country to the others. But neither the leaders of the Spanish American countries nor the intellectuals in them nor the people at large ever express a belief in the national unity of the several American nations, let alone a national unity between them and Spain, although the latter is fondly referred to as "*la madre patria.*" In fact, any talk about a political union of one's own country and one or more other Spanish American states would be considered as verging on treason.

In the Arab world, on the other hand, the leaders of each country frequently declare that their country is part of "the Arab nation."[3] This tenet is embodied in the constitutions of several Arab countries. The theoretical assumption of the national unity of all the Arab countries, however, does not seem to be conducive to the development of actual harmony and cooperation among them. On the contrary: in practically every part of the Arab world there is tension between the rival concepts of *qawmiyya* (all-Arab nationalism) and *waṭaniyya* (the particularistic nationalism of each Arab country.)[4]

As against this contrast, a similarity in the political development of the two groups of countries can be noted. The early revolutionary leaders in Spanish American planned a democratic form of government for their newly liberated countries. Instead, what happened very soon was that autocratic dictators, so-called *caudillos,* seized power, and it took several decades until here and there, sporadically, democratic forms managed to establish themselves.

Quite a similar process could be observed in the Arab countries, although the prime agents in its first phase were not the Arab political leaders themselves, but the foreign—British and French—Mandatory governments. The Mandatory powers that ruled over the newly established Arab countries of Syria, Lebanon, Transjordan, and Iraq, as well as the colonial powers in the Arab countries of North Africa, had the intention of gradually training the countries under their dominance to become democracies upon attaining independence. Yet soon after these countries gained independence, whether as a result of armed revolt or negotiations, the democratic forms of government were discarded and dictatorships introduced in their stead. In many cases, both in Spanish America and in the Arab world, the governance fell into the hands of military régimes. As far as the Arab countries are concerned, these régimes in essence (though not in form) do not differ much from the indigenous forms of tyrannical autocracy that had been typical of government in the region for millennia.[5]

In view of the similarities and differences noted above, it is interesting to see the views expressed by an Arab leader about the social and economic conditions in South America and the lessons the Arab countries can learn from them. After touring Latin America in 1960, Ben Youssef Ben Khedda, who soon thereafter was to become President of the Provisional Government of the Republic of Algeria, published an article in the French edition of *El-Moudjahid* (January 5, 1961) entitled "Impressions d'une tournée en Amerique Latine." In it he attributes the social and economic backwardness he discerned in Latin America to the fact that the early revolutionary leaders had failed to obtain complete economic and political independence for their nations, an omission whose aftereffects can still be felt even after a century. Neo-colonialism, he states, had been allowed to continue in the form of economic exploitation, a possibility Algeria must avoid by pressing for a complete revolution resembling that of Castro's Cuba. Ben Khedda was impressed by the statement of General Cardenas of Mexico: "Try to grasp for complete independence or it will take you another century to realize real independence as with us in Latin America."[6] When Ben Khedda wrote his article, Algeria was still embroiled in her struggle for independence from France. He therefore saw the position of the Latin American countries from the point of view of that struggle. Having focused his attention on the issue of total independence, he overlooked certain details such as the fact that the Latin American struggle for independence was directed against Spain and Portugal, and that the complaint of neo-colonialism in the Latin America of the 1950's (and 1960's) was directed against another power, the United States, whose political and economic influence in the Latin American countries began many years after they had won total independence from their European mother countries.

The true lesson that the Arab countries can and should learn from studying the situation in which the Latin American states find themselves at present is a different one. Once a nation has gained independence from the country which exercised colonial rule over it, it must jealously guard its hard-won independence and not allow the chance of momentary advantage to lure it into an alliance with another, more powerful and technologically and industrially much more advanced, nation, because such an alliance is only too likely to turn before long into neo-colonial subjugation.

NOTES

I THE ARABS AND THE WORLD

1. Gamal Abdul Nasser, *Egypt's Liberation: The Philosophy of the Revolution,* Washington, D.C.: Public Affairs Press, 1955, pp. 85–86, 88 ff., 109–111.

2. See the criticism of Nasser's analysis of the position of Egypt by Giorgio Levi Della Vida, *Aneddoti e svaghi arabi e non arabi,* Milan and Naples: R. Ricciardi, 1959, pp. 146–147. It is interesting to note that Sāṭi' al-Ḥuṣrī, the outstanding exponent and popularizer of Arab nationalist doctrine, in a discussion with Fatḥī Riḍwān stated that on the basis of language and culture Egypt was a part of the Arab world with which her relations were a hundred times closer than with the rest of Africa. Egypt's ties with the North African countries, he said, were those of history, language, and culture, the same bonds which unite her with Arabia, Syria, and Iraq. Cf. his *Al-'Urūba Awwalan (Arabism First),* 2nd ed., Beirut: Dār al-'Ilm li'l-Malāyīn, 1955, pp. 90–94, 96–99; as summarized by L. M. Kenny, "Sāṭi' al-Ḥuṣrī's Views on Arab Nationalism," *The Middle East Journal,* vol. 17, no. 3 (Summer, 1963), p. 245.

3. On Islam in general, cf. Hamilton A. R. Gibb, *Mohammedanism,* New York: Mentor Books, 1955; A. S. Tritton, *Islam: Belief and Practices,* London: Hutchinson University Library, 1951.

4. Raphael Patai, *Golden River to Golden Road: Society, Culture and Change in the Middle East,* 3rd ed., Philadelphia: University of Pennsylvania Press, 1969, pp. 13ff. It should be pointed out that to speak of "the culture" of the Middle East involves considerable generalization.

5. On the Arabs, cf. Philip K. Hitti, *History of the Arabs,* 8th ed., London: Macmillan, 1964; Bernard Lewis, *The Arabs in History,* London:Hutchinson,

1950; Abdullah M. Lutfiyya and Charles W. Churchill (eds.), *Readings in Arab Middle Eastern Societies and Cultures,* The Hague: Mouton, 1970; and consult also the *Encyclopaedia of Islam,* new ed., Leiden: Brill, 1960– .

6. The interested reader will find fine summaries of these historical and cultural processes in the *Encyclopaedia of Islam,* s.v. *al-'Arab* and *'Arabiyya.*

7. These views are cited by Nabih Amin Fāris and Mohammed Tawfik Husayn, *The Crescent in Crisis: An Interpretive Study of the Modern Arab World,* Lawrence, Kan.: University of Kansas Press, 1955, pp. 177–178.

8. Jabra I. Jabra, "Arab Language and Culture," in Michael Adams (ed.), *The Middle East: A Handbook,* New York: Praeger, 1971, p. 174. Sāṭi' al-Ḥuṣrī defined as an Arab anyone whose native language is Arabic, *op. cit.,* p. 11; Kenny, op cit., p. 234.

9. Clifford Geertz, *Islam Observed,* New Haven, Conn.: Yale University Press, 1968, p. 65.

10. Cf. e.g., Fāris and Husayn, *op. cit,* p. 24: "Arab history is a living reality in the minds of Arab masses because it and Islam are to them one and the same thing."

11. This has been pointed out by Gustave E. von Grunebaum in his *Islam: Essays in the Nature and Growth of a Cultural Tradition,* New York: Barnes and Noble, 1961, p. 203; cf. also p. 202.

II THE GROUP ASPECTS OF THE MIND

1. It might be mentioned here that there are numerous books in whose title the word "mind" appears in combination with the name of a large human group. A few of these can be listed here: Hans Kohn, *The Mind of Germany,* New York: Scribner's, 1960, as well as two other books by the same author, one on the mind of modern Russia and the other on the mind of France. Lily Abegg, *The Mind of East Asia,* London: Thames and Hudson, 1952. Gerald Abrahams, *The Jewish Mind,* Boston: Beacon, 1962. W. E. Abraham, *The Mind of Africa,* Chicago: Chicago University Press, 1963. Franz Boas, *The Mind of Primitive Man,* New York, 1911 (rev. ed., New York: Macmillan, 1938), and Claude Lévi-Strauss, *The Savage Mind* (in the original French, *La pensée sauvage*), Chicago: Chicago University Press, 1966. Most recently, a small book in Arabic appeared under the title *The Arab Mind Between the Wars: 1918–1939,* by 'Alī Ḥajj Bakrī, Beirut, 1972.

2. The descriptive study of the human body has for several centuries been the domain of a special science, that of anatomy. Almost as old is the study of the functioning of the human body, the science of human physiology. In the last hundred years or so, the study of physical differences between human races has been put on a scientific basis in physical anthropology. All these disciplines involve varying degrees of abstract terminology and thinking.

3. Ralph Linton, "Foreword," in Abram Kardiner, *et al., The Psychological Frontiers of Society,* New York: Columbia University Press, 1945, pp. vii–viii. Cf.

also Ralph Linton, *The Cultural Background of Personality,* New York: Apple-ton-Century-Crofts, 1945, pp. 129, 131, etc.

4. Clyde Kluckhohn and Henry A. Murray (eds.), *Personality and Culture,* 2nd ed., New York: Alfred A. Knopf, 1967, p. 595.

5. It should be added here that more recently those anthropologists who are still interested in the "culture and personality" approach (on this see below) no longer emphasize the early enculturative experiences of the individual to the exclusion of later environmental influences. They pay, instead, more attention to precisely those factors in the sociocultural setting to which the individual is exposed as long as he lives. Cf. E. Adamson Hoebel, "Anthropological Perspectives on National Character," *The Annals of the American Academy of Political and Social Science,* vol. 370 (March, 1967), p. 6. "Present interest is in research-ing the processes by which individuals acquire the patterned norms that charac-terize their cultures *throughout* the felicities *and* vicissitudes of life." That is to say, the interrelationship between culture and personality is now seen as an ongoing process in which the individual is influenced by culture, and in turn influences it, throughout his lifetime.

Whether or not we go along with this interpretation of culture and personal-ity, it cannot be doubted that each individual's personality traits contain one complement molded by culture. Some students of national character define the scope of its study narrowly, others widely. One of the narrowest approaches is that of Geoffrey Gorer, who considers "motives" as the only legitimate subject matter of this study. He defines the very "concept of national character or basic character structure" as "an attempt to isolate and describe the motives shared by the members of a society who manifest the same shared habits or culture." However, later in the same essay, perhaps feeling that the term "motive" as commonly used is too limited for his purposes, Gorer rephrases his own defini-tion and says: "The concept of national character refers to the structuring and combination of traits or motives." Cf. Geoffrey Gorer, "The Concept of Na-tional Character," in Kluckhohn and Murray (eds.), *op. cit.,* pp. 249, 257.

It is in this latter, or in an even broader, sense that most students of national character see the subject matter of their scholarly quest. They find that not only motives shared by the members of a society go into the national character, but also goals, behavioral traits, beliefs, and values. By no stretch of meaning could, for instance, the traits of rhetoricism, prevarication, hospitality, or submissive-ness be subsumed under "motives." Yet there can be not the slightest doubt that these traits, and many others like them, are integral parts of the national character of the Arabs.

6. Cf. Alex Inkeles, "Some Sociological Observations on Culture and Personality Studies," in Kluckhohn and Murray (eds.), *op. cit.,* p. 580.

7. Cf. Don Martindale, "The Sociology of National Character," *The Annals of the American Academy,* vol. 370 (March, 1967), p. 35.

8. Ibn Khaldūn, *The Muqaddimah: An Introduction to History,* translated from

330

the Arabic by Franz Rosenthal, New York: Bollingen Series, Pantheon Books, 1958, vol. I, pp. 299, 302–303. Cf. also pp. 303–304.

9. *Op. cit.,* vol. I, p. 305.

10. Maqrīzī, *Description topographique et historique de l'Égypte.* Mémoires publiés par les membres de la mission archéologique française au Caire, vol. 17, Paris: Leroux, 1900, pp. 121, 126, 133, 135–138.

11. Michel Feghali, *Proverbes et dictons syro-libanais,* Paris: Institut de l'Ethnologie, 1938, pp. 78–88.

12. Cf. von Grunebaum, *op cit.,* p. 209.

13. Ṭāhā Ḥusain, *Mustaqbal al-Thaqāfa fī Miṣr (The Future of Culture in Egypt),* Cairo: Maṭba‘at al-Ma‘ārif wa-Maktabatuha, 1938, 1944. Available also in an English translation by Sidney Glazer, Washington, D.C.: American Council of Learned Societies, 1954.

14. *Ibid.,* pp. 6–11, 30–39, 62–64, as summarized, respectively excerpted, by von Grunebaum, *op cit.,* pp. 209–215.

15. Henri Habib Ayrout, S.J., *The Egyptian Peasant,* Boston: Beacon Press, 1963, pp. 136–37, 147–48; Carlo Landberg, *Proverbs et dictons de la province de Syrie, section de Sayda,* Leiden: Brill, 1883, p. 170.

16. Maqrīzī, *op. cit.,* p. 139. A modern attempt at analyzing the Arab mentality in general is that of Isma‘īl Mazhar, in his book *Whathbat al-Sharq (The Attack of the East),* Cairo, 1929.

17. Patai, *op. cit.,* pp. 13ff.

III ARAB CHILD-REARING PRACTICES

1. As Kluckhohn and Murray have stated, "In the greater number of cases . . . the similarities of character within a group are traceable less to constitutional factors than to formative influences of the environment to which all members of the group have been subjected. Of these group-membership determinants, culture is with little doubt the most significant. . . . Those who have been trained in childhood along traditional lines, and even those who have as adults adopted some new design for living, will be apt to behave predictably in many contexts because of a prevailing tendency to conform to group standards." The same observation can be applied not only to action patterns but also to the motivational systems of individuals. Thus, "the values imbedded in a culture have special weight among the group membership determinants." Cf. Kluckhohn and Murray (eds.), *op. cit.,* pp. 53ff. and esp. pp. 58–59.

   Similarly, Abram Kardiner points out that certain aspects of culture (those which he terms "primary institutions") affect the developing personality of the child more than others, and by the time the child grows up he will have developed behavioral dispositions based on these primary institutions. These behavioral dispositions will constitute his character. Cf. Kardiner, *op. cit.,* p. 25.

The actual channels through which such behavioral dispositions are instilled into the child are its parents and other individuals who surround it in its early years. These socializing and enculturating agents mold the personality of the child by requiring him to conform to the patterns which they consider the proper ones. They reward the child when he or she conforms to their patterns, and punish him whenever he acts in a manner considered wrong by them. By the time the child reaches adolescence, the do's and don'ts hammered into him by his elders will have become internalized, so that he will continue to obey them in adult life even without external compulsion; and, what is more important for sociocultural continuity, he will insist on imparting them to his children. This is how the cultural heritage of a human aggregate persists from generation to generation, and this is how national character is transmitted. These considerations make it necessary that we begin our analysis of the Arab mind by examining Arab child-rearing practices.

2. Much of this material has been collected in Patai, *op. cit.*, pp. 412ff.

3. Edwin T. Prothro, *Child Rearing in the Lebanon,* Cambridge, Mass.: Harvard Middle Eastern Monograph Series VIII, 1961; Hilma Granqvist, *Birth and Childhood Among the Arabs,* Helsingfors: Söderstrom, 1947; Hamed Ammar, *Growing Up in an Egyptian Village,* London: Routledge and Kegan Paul, 1954; Horace M. Miner and George de Vos, *Oasis and Casbah: Algerian Culture and Personality in Change,* Ann Arbor, Mich.: University of Michigan, 1960.

4. Patai, *op. cit.*, p. 414.

5. Prothro, *op. cit.*, p. 123.

6. On early personality development, cf. J. W. M. Whiting and I. L. Child, *Child Training and Personality: A Cross-Cultural Study,* New Haven, Conn.: Yale University Press, 1953.

7. Patai, *op. cit.*, pp. 439–440.

8. *Ibid.*, pp. 412ff.

9. Sir Geoffrey Furlonge, *Palestine Is My Country: The Story of Musa Alami,* New York: Praeger, 1969, pp. 4–5. The book consists basically of transcribed tape recordings of the reminiscences of Musa Alami, who was born in Jerusalem in 1897.

10. Sania Hamady, *Temperament and Character of the Arabs,* New York: Twayne Publishers, 1960, p. 172; William A. Darity, "Some Socio-cultural Factors in the Administration of Technical Assistance and Training in Health," *Human Organization,* vol. 24, no. 1 (Spring, 1965), p. 80.

11. Cf. Prothro, *op. cit.*, p. 66.

12. See Patai, *op. cit.*, pp. 97ff.

13. *Op. cit.*, pp. 441–442, and sources there, to which should be added Miner and de Vos, *op. cit.*, p. 58. Dr. E. T. Prothro, in a private note (dated May 26, 1971), informed me that, according to one of his informants, this practice stopped in Lebanon after the child began talking and walking.

14. Ammar, *op. cit.*, p. 121.

15. *Op. cit.*, p. 120.

16. Patai, *op. cit.,* pp. 444ff., 477, and sources there.
17. *Op. cit.,* pp. 413–414, and sources there.
18. D. C. McClelland, J. W. Atkinson, R. A. Clark, and E. L. Lowell, *The Achievement Motive,* New York: Appleton-Century-Crofts, 1953; cf. also Whiting and Child, *op. cit.,* pp. 61ff.
19. See Prothro, *op. cit.,* p. 25.
20. Raphael Patai, "General Character of the Society," in R. Patai (ed.), *The Republic of Lebanon,* New Haven, Conn.: Human Relations Area Files, 1956, p. 22. This statement is quoted by Prothro, *op. cit.,* p. 18, in a somewhat altered form.
21. Prothro, *op. cit.,* pp. 50–51.
22. *Op. cit.,* p. 146, quoting A. J. Meyer, J. Chami, and Y. A. Sayigh.
23. *Ibid.,* pp. 149ff.
24. *Ibid.,* pp. 151–152.
25. Patai, *op. cit.,* pp. 100–102.
26. *Ibid.,* pp. 98–99, 105–106.
27. Prothro, *op. cit.,* pp. 152.
28. *Ibid.,* p. 146.

IV UNDER THE SPELL OF LANGUAGE

1. Jabra, "Arab Language and Culture," in Adams (ed.), *The Middle East: A Handbook,* p. 175.
2. See Patai, *Golden River,* pp. 179ff.
3. Al-Tha' ālibī, *Fiqh al-Lugha,* Cairo, 1284, 3; cited by 'A. 'A. al-Dūrī, *Al-Judhūr al-ta'rikhiyya li'l-Qawmiyya al-'Arabiyya (The Historical Roots of Arab Nationalism),* Beirut, 1960, p. 46; as quoted by Bernard Lewis, *The Middle East and the West,* Bloomington, Ind.: Indiana University Press, 1965, p. 86.
4. Alvaro, "Indiculus Luminosus," in *España sagrada* XI: 274, as quoted by Philip K. Hitti, *History of the Arabs,* 7th ed., New York: Macmillan, 1960, pp. 515–516.
5. Jabra, *op. cit.,* pp. 177–178.
6. Charles A. Ferguson, "Myths About Arabic," in Joshua A. Fishman (ed.), *Readings in the Sociology of Language,* The Hague: Mouton, 1968, p. 377; cf. pp. 375–376.
7. *Op. cit.,* pp. 375–379. Cf. also Laura Nader's strictures on Ferguson's report on dialect rating, *op. cit.,* pp. 278ff.
8. Haim Blanc, "Style Variations in Spoken Arabic," in Charles A. Ferguson (ed.), *Contributions to Arabic Linguistics,* Cambridge, Mass.: Harvard Middle Eastern Monographs Series III, 1964, pp. 87–88. How far modern literary Arabic still is from being an adequate medium for scholarly writing can be illustrated by a few examples taken, incidentally, not from the technical world where the lack of Arabic scientific terminology may be expected, but from the social sciences. Dr. Ḥāmid 'Ammār in his book *Fī Binā' al-Bashar (On the*

Building of Man), published in Sirs al-Layān, U.A.R., 1964, found it necessary to give in footnotes the English equivalents of several Arabic terms he uses in his text. For example, when he uses the word "*tajrīb,*" he explains in a footnote (my translation from the Arabic): "*Tajrīb* is the translation of the English expression 'experimentation' " (p. 117). In a similar manner he explains the Arabic expressions he uses for "*a priori,*" "naïve realism," "reproductive and creative," "character building," "regression," etc.

9. This figure is reached by subtracting the number of non-Arabs from the totals contained in the table on page 314.

A word is in place here about the survival, within the Muslim Arab core area, of a few relatively small communities that had successfully resisted either Islamization or Arabization or both. Those who resisted Islamization while adopting Arabic as their mother tongue were, as a rule, adherents of the pre-Islamic monotheistic religions, Judaism and Christianity. It was part of the teaching of Muḥammad that these monotheistic "peoples of the book" should not be forced to convert to Islam (as was done with pagans), but allowed to follow their own religions as long as they accepted Muslim overlordship. They thus became *dhimmīs,* protected people, subject to head-tax, restrictions, and humiliations, but enabled to find their niche in the ethnic patch-quilt of Arab lands. While retaining their religions, most of these Jewish and Christian communities assimilated linguistically to the Muslim Arab conquerors of their countries, together with the other population elements.

Those communities which adopted Islam while retaining their own languages fall into the same category as the general populations of the large countries lying in the non-Arab Muslim belt that surrounds the Muslim Arab core area. In at least one typical case, that of the Kurds, such a community occupies a marginal position between inner, Muslim Arab countries (Iraq and Syria), and outer, Muslim but non-Arab countries (Turkey and Iran). In fact, in the case of the Kurds, it is merely a political accident that the area inhabited by one part of the community was incorporated (by the victorious Allies after World War II) into Iraq, while another comparable segment of the Kurdish community was left within truncated Turkey, and a third in Iran.

10. Edward Atiyah, *The Arabs,* Baltimore, Md.: Penguin Books, 1955, p. 96.

11. Philip K. Hitti, *The Arabs: A Short History,* Princeton, N.J.: Princeton University Press, 1943, p. 21.

12. See Albert Hourani, "Arabic Culture: Its Background and Today's Crisis," *Perspective of the Arab World,* an *Atlantic Monthly* supplement (October, 1956), pp. 125, 127. We shall return to the issue of the Arabs' black and white vision in Chapter X.

13. Cairo, 1945, p. 120, as quoted by Moshe Zeltzer, *Aspects of Near Eastern Society,* New York: Bookman Associates, 1962, p. 255.

14. Furlonge, *op. cit.,* p. 152.

15. Dana Adam Schmidt, *Yemen: The Unknown War,* New York: Holt, Rinehart and Winston, 1968, p. 208.

16. Interview with Mr. 'Abdu'l-'Azīz Zu'bī, in Jerusalem, on July 19, 1971. Mr. Zu'bī's comments reminded me of what Nasser wrote almost twenty years earlier: "It sometimes appears to me that we content ourselves overmuch by wishful thinking. In flights of fancy we fulfill our desires and enjoy in imagination things which we never bestir ourselves to realize." Cf. Nasser, *op. cit.*, p. 64. Cf. also Malcolm Kerr, *The Arab Cold War 1958–1967*, 2nd ed., London: Oxford University Press, 1967, p. 112, who remarks that the actions following the Syrian-Egyptian agreement of April, 1963, were "the product of an absurd situation in which symbols seemed to count for everything and reality for nothing."

17. M. M. Bravmann, *The Arabic Elative*, Leiden: Brill, 1968, pp. 5, 6.

18. *Op. cit.* pp. 1, 38, 42.

19. Hussein of Jordan, *My "War" with Israel*, as told to and with additional material by Vick Vance and Pierre Lauer, New York: William Morrow, 1969, pp. 82–83.

20. Arabic news broadcast of the Egyptian Broadcasting Service from Cairo in the first quarter of 1957. My translation from the Arabic text printed in Richard S. Harrel, "A Linguistic Analysis of Egyptian Radio Arabic," in Ferguson (ed.), *Contributions to Arabic Linguistics*, p. 57.

21. The page numbers refer to Arnold Hottinger, *The Arabs*, Berkeley and Los Angeles: University of California Press, 1963, which, on pp. 312–313, contains the English translation of excerpts from Ḥusayn's article.

22. Mostefa Lacheraf, "The Future of Algerian Culture," in *Temps Modernes* of November 30, 1963, pp. 20–22, as translated into English and quoted by David C. Gordon, *The Passing of French Algeria*, London: Oxford University Press, 1966, p. 192.

23. E. Shouby, "The Influence of the Arabic Language on the Psychology of the Arabs," *The Middle East Journal*, vol. 5, 1951, pp. 298–299.

24. *Op. cit.*, pp. 300–301.

25. *Op. cit.*, p. 300.

26. E. T. Prothro, "Arab-American Differences in the Judgment of Written Messages," *Journal of Social Psychology*, vol. 42, 1955, as reprinted in Lutfiyya and Churchill, *op. cit.*, pp. 706, 710, 711–712.

27. Interview with Dr. Sami Farah Geraisy in Nazareth on July 27, 1971.

28. Prothro, *Child Rearing in the Lebanon*, p. 109; cf. also pp. 107, 149.

29. *Time* magazine, May 3, 1971, p. 24.

30. Ṣādiq Jalāl al-'Aẓm, *Al-Naqd al-Dhātī Ba'd al-Hazīma* (*Self-Criticism After the Defeat*), Beirut, Lebanon: Dār al-Ṭalī'a, 1968; as summarized by Sylvia G. Haim, "The 'Lesson of Japan' Put to a New Use," in Sylvia G. Haim (ed.), *Arab Nationalism and a Wider World*, Middle East Area Studies Series V, New York: American Academic Association for Peace in the Middle East, 1971, p. 6.

31. Hussein of Jordan, *op. cit.*, pp. 21, 46. The sequence of inter-Arab negotiations is critically presented in Kerr, *The Arab Cold War 1958–1967*.

32. Hussein of Jordan, *op. cit.*, p. 51, 52.
33. Majid Khadduri, *Republican Iraq: A Study in Iraqi Politics Since the Revolution of 1958.* London: Oxford University Press, 1969, pp. 166, 170, 172, 279.
34. Hottinger, *op. cit.*, p. 314.
35. Address to the Palestine Club in Alexandria on December 13, 1953; printed in Gamāl 'Abdu 'l– Nāṣir, *Khuṭab wa-Taṣrīḥāt 1953–1959 (Addresses and Declarations)*, Cairo: National Publishing House, in the series *Ikhtarna Laka (We Selected for You)*, vol. I, p. 153, as quoted by Y. Harkabi, *'Emdat ha-'Aravim b'Sikhsukh Yisraēl-'Arav (The Arabs' Position in the Israel-Arab Conflict)*, Tel Aviv: Dvir, 1968, p. 374. A similar observation was made by Elie Salem in his article "Form and Substance: A Critical Examination of the Arabic Language," *Middle East Forum*, Beirut (July, 1958), p. 18.
36. *Al-Ahrām*, January 17, 1964; as quoted by Harkabi, *op. cit.*, p. 375.
37. Leonard Berkowitz, *Aggression: A Social Psychological Analysis*, New York: McGraw-Hill, 1962, pp. 196–197. However, cf. Berkowitz's own reservations about the catharsis hypothesis, *ibid.*, pp. 197ff., as well as those of G. W. Allport, *The Nature of Prejudice*, New York: Doubleday, 1958, p. 56, and R. E. L. Faris, "Interaction Levels and Intergroup Relations," in Muzaffer Sherif (ed.), *Intergroup Relations and Leadership*, New York: Wiley, 1962, p. 27.
38. Shouby, *op. cit.*, p. 295.
39. Malek Bennabi, *Vocation de L'Islam*, Paris, 1954, as quoted by David C. Gordon, *North Africa's French Legacy*, Cambridge, Mass.: Harvard Middle Eastern Monographs Series IX, 1964, p. 56.
40. Judith R. Williams, *The Youth of Haouch El Harimi, A Lebanese Village*, Cambridge, Mass.: Harvard Middle Eastern Monograph Series XX, 1968, pp. 118, 125.
41. Cf. Franklin Fearing, "An Examination of the Conceptions of Benjamin Whorf in the Light of Theories of Perception and Cognition," in Harry Hoijer (ed.), *Language in Culture*, American Anthropological Association Memoir Series, no. 79 (December, 1954), p. 47.
42. As Carl Brockelmann put it: "The study of the usage of the Semitic tempora is rightly considered one of the most difficult chapters of Semitic syntax, because it [i.e., the meaning of the tense forms] oscillates strongly in the individual Semitic languages themselves, and because it is difficult to represent them [the Semitic tempora] by the categories of the modern Indo-Germanic languages." Brockelmann goes on to say that the Arab grammarians themselves term the two tenses *māḍī* (i.e., past) and *muḍāri'* (i.e., "similar to the noun in taking case endings"). Cf. Carl Brockelmann, *Grundriss der vergleichenden Grammatik der semitischen Sprachen*, Berlin: Reuther und Reichard, 1913, vol. II, p. 144. My translation.
43. Hans Bauer, *Die Tempora im Semitischen*, Leipzig: J. C. Hinrich, 1910, pp. 25, 42; my translation. Cf. also Kjell Aartun, *Zur Frage Altarabischer Tempora*, Oslo: Universitetsforlaget, 1963.
44. This enumeration of the various meanings the Arabic perfect and imperfect

verb form can take largely follows A. Socin, *Arabische Grammatik,* 10th ed. by Carl Brockelmann, Berlin: Reuther und Reichard, 1929, pp. 94–100.

45. Cf. De Lacy O'Leary, *Colloquial Arabic,* London: Routledge and Kegan Paul, 1963, pp. 109–160; and Hilma Granqvist, *Marriage Conditions in a Palestinian Village,* Helsingfors: Societas Scientiarum Fennica, 1932, pp. 48–49. Cf. also Haim Blanc, *Communal Dialects in Baghdad,* Cambridge, Mass.: Harvard Middle Eastern Monographs Series X, 1964, pp. 117–118.

46. Edward Sapir, "The Status of Linguistics as a Science," *Language* (Charlotteville, Va.: Linguistic Society of America), vol. 5 (1929), p. 209.

47. Harry Hoijer, "The Sapir-Whorf Hypothesis," in Hoijer (ed.), *Language in Culture,* p. 93.

48. Benjamin L. Whorf, *Collected Papers on Metalinguistics,* Washington, D.C.: Department of State, Foreign Service Institute, 1952, p. 11, as quoted by Hoijer, *op. cit.,* p. 93.

49. Whorf, *op. cit.,* p. 5.

50. *Op. cit.,* pp. 33, 44, 21.

51. Fearing, *op. cit.,* p. 49

52. The difference between Western and Arab time perception was noted and commented upon by Oswald Spengler, who, however, did not relate it to differences in language, but to the two different world views, the Faustian of Western culture and the Magian of Arab culture. See Appendix II.

53. Cf. Sir Hamilton Gibb, *Arabic Literature,* Oxford: Clarendon Press, 1963, p. 80.

54. Franz Rosenthal, *A History of Muslim Historiography,* 2nd ed., Leiden: Brill, 1968, p. 14. On the character of Arab historiography in general, cf. *ibid.,* pp. 66ff., and G. M. Wickens, "Islamic Historical Writing," *Encyclopedia Americana,* 1971, vol. 14, p. 239.

55. Rosenthal, *op. cit.,* p. 15.

56. *Ibid.,* p. 251.

57. *Ibid.,* p. 250.

V THE BEDOUIN SUBSTRATUM OF THE ARAB PERSONALITY

1. Max Weber in his analyses of national traits often traced them back to the behavioral model supplied by strategic social strata. Thus, e.g., he argued that the Junkers, who were an important and influential sector in German society, had a strong impact on the German national character as a whole. Cf. Max Weber, *From Max Weber: Essays in Sociology,* translated by Hans Gerth and C. Wright Mills, New York: Oxford University Press, 1958, pp. 386–395. It is in this Weberian sense that the Bedouins impressed their stamp on Arab society.

2. Jacques Berque, *The Arabs: Their History and Future,* New York: Praeger, 1964, p. 174.

3. Cf. Lewis, *The Middle East and the West,* p. 48.
4. Jabra, *op. cit.,* p. 175.
5. Berque, *op. cit.,* p. 164.
6. In a lecture he delivered in 1951 on "The Personality of the Iraqi Individual," and subsequently in two books, entitled *Wu'āz al-Salāṭīn (Exhorters of Rulers),* Baghdad, 1954, and *Uṣṭūrat al-Adab al-Rafi' (The Myth of the Noble Literature),* Baghdad, 1957. The latter study is termed "sensational" by Berque, *op. cit.,* pp. 269, n.3, and 270–272.
7. Cf. Khadduri, *Republican 'Iraq,* p. 73. Dr. Khadduri identifies the Zubayd as "a tribe traditionally associated with the tribes of Qaḥṭān, presumed to have migrated from the north of the Hijaz," and the Bani Tamīm as a Shī'ite tribe "reputed to have belonged to the tribes of 'Adnān of southern Arabia." Either Dr. Khadduri, or the family tradition he records, seems to be inaccurate. Qaḥṭān is the famous ancestral name of the *southern* division of the Arab tribes. Their original home was Southwestern Arabia. It is from there, and not from the north of Hijaz, that some Qaḥṭān tribes migrated to the Iraqi region west of the Euphrates. As to 'Adnān, he was the eponymous ancestor of the *northern* Arabian tribes. Incidentally, the Zubayd are to this day represented in Syria, where they form one of the two subdivisions of the 'Arab el-Jebel of the Hawran region, as well as in Iraq where they comprise three groups. The Bani Tamīm are found in Southern Iraq, and the Sunnī Muslims in the city of Basra consider themselves as their descendants. Cf. Patai, *Golden River,* pp. 183ff., 210, 216–217, 260, 451.
8. Berque, *op. cit.,* p. 165. Cf. also Robert A. Fernea, *Shaykh and Effendi: Changing Patterns of Authority Among the El Shabana of Southern Iraq,* Cambridge, Mass.: Harvard University Press, 1970, p. 77. The inhabitants of the town of Daghara and its environs, who have been settled agriculturalists for several generations, "proudly claim descent from the great Bedouin tribes of the Arabian Peninsula and the Syrian Desert."
9. Berque, *op. cit.,* p. 29.
10. On the early Arab concept of *muruwwa* in the sense of *virtus,* that is, manly virtues, and the ethical duties comprised in it, cf. M. M. Bravmann, *The Spiritual Background of Early Islam: Studies in Ancient Arab Concepts,* Leiden: Brill, 1972, pp. 1–7.
11. Cf. Patai, *Golden River,* pp. 425–428.
12. Abū Tammām (d. 849), *Ash'ār al-Ḥamāsa (Verses on Bravery),* ed. Freytag, Bonn, 1828, p. 171.
13. Hitti, *History of the Arabs,* pp. 24–25.
14. Patai, *Golden River,* pp. 253–254.
15. Hamady, *op. cit.,* pp. 48–49. Cf. also below, Chapter X.
16. George Antonius, *The Arab Awakening,* Philadelphia: J. B. Lippincott, 1939, p. 89; Fāris and Husayn, *op. cit.,* p. 30.
17. Leila S. Kadi, *Arab Summit Conferences and the Palestine Problem (1936–1950), (1964–1966),* Palestine Books No. 4, Beirut, Lebanon: Research Centre, Palestine Liberation Organization, 1966, p. 189.

VI BEDOUIN VALUES

1. The Arabic term for protection, *"Jiwār,"* derived from the verb *jāra,* to lose one's way, means extending protection to a *jār,* i.e., a stranger or neighbor who comes and asks for asylum. The Arabic root is cognate to the Hebrew *gēr,* which means a stranger who sojourns among the people and must therefore be protected. Cf. Exodus 22:20: "And a stranger shalt thou not wrong, neither shalt thou oppress him . . ." Exodus 23:9: "And a stranger shalt thou not oppress, for ye know the heart of a stranger, seeing ye were strangers in the land of Egypt." Leviticus 19:23: "The stranger that sojourneth with you shall be unto you as the homeborn among you, and thou shalt love him as thyself." Deuteronomy 10:18–19: "He [God] loveth the stranger, in giving him food and rayment. Love ye therefore the stranger . . ." Deuteronomy 24:17: "Thou shalt not pervert the justice due to the stranger . . ."

2. Hitti, *History of the Arabs,* pp. 25–26.

3. See Ahmed Abou-Zeid, "Honour and Shame Among the Bedouins of Egypt," in J. G. Peristiany (ed.), *Honour and Shame: The Values of Mediterranean Society,* Chicago, Ill.: The Chicago University Press, 1966, p. 255.

4. Bertram Thomas, *Arabia Felix,* New York: Charles Scribner's Sons, 1932, pp. 211–212.

5. Richard T. Antoun, "Conservatism and Change in the Village Community: A Jordanian Case Study," in *Human Organization,* vol. 24, no. 1 (Spring, 1965), p. 7.

6. Antoun, *op. cit.,* p. 8.

7. Hamady, *op. cit.,* pp. 77, 81.

8. Cf. *ibid.,* pp. 77–83; Musil, *op. cit.,* pp. 455–470.

9. The above is based on my personal experiences and observations among the Arabs of Jerusalem. As to the last point, cf. also Tore Nordenstam, *Sudanese Ethics,* Uppsala: Scandinavian Institute of African Studies, 1968, p. 88.

10. Nordenstam, *op. cit.,* 77–78, 81.

11. Musil, *op. cit.,* p. 256; Ammar, *Growing Up in an Egyptian Village,* pp. 137ff.; Patai, *Golden River,* pp. 412–417.

12. Hamady, *op. cit.,* p. 59.

13. *Ibid.,* p. 60.

14. See, e.g., Peristiany (ed.), *Honour and Shame: The Values of Mediterranean Society,* and in it especially Pierre Bourdieu, "The Sentiment of Honour in the Kabyle Society," pp. 191–241; and Ahmed Abou-Zeid, "Honour and Shame Among the Bedouins of Egypt," pp. 243–259; also Hamady, *op. cit.,* pp. 34–39, 50–54.

15. As quoted by David C. Gordon, *Women of Algeria: An Essay on Change,* Cambridge, Mass: Harvard Middle Eastern Monograph Series XIX, 1968, p. 33.

16. See, e.g., Ahmed Abou-Zeid, *op. cit.,* p. 251.

17. Safia K. Mohsen, "The Legal Status of Women Among the Awlad Ali," *Anthropological Quarterly,* vol. 40, 1967, p. 160.

18. *Encyclopaedia of Islam,* new ed., 1960, s.v. *'Aṣabiyya.*
19. Al-Mubarrad, *al-Kāmil,* ed. W. Wright (Leipzig, 1864), p. 229, I, 3, as quoted by Hitti, *History of the Arabs,* pp. 27–28.
20. Hitti, *ibid.* Cf. also the analysis of *'aṣabiyya* by Muhammad Rashid Rida (1865–1935), the well-known Syrian-Egyptian author and editor, in the Cairo monthly *Al-Manār,* XXXIII (1933), pp. 191–192, as translated in Sylvia G. Haim, *Arab Nationalism: An Anthology,* Berkeley and Los Angeles: University of California Press, 1962, pp. 75–77.
21. Antoun, *op. cit.,* p. 9; cf. also Victor F. Ayoub, "Conflict Resolution and Social Reorganization in a Lebanese Village," *Human Organization,* vol. 24, no. 1 (Spring, 1965), p. 12.
22. See Herbert H. Williams and Judith R. Williams, "The Extended Family as a Vehicle of Culture Change," *Human Organization,* vol. 24, no. 1 (Spring, 1965), p. 63, quoting *The Lebanese Balance of Payments for 1961,* prepared by Khalil Salem, Beirut: Economic Research Institute, American University of Beirut, 1964 (in Arabic).
23. See, e.g., Ali Othman and Robert Redfield, "An Arab's View of Point IV," University of Chicago Round Table, no. 749, August 5, 1952; Patai, *Golden River,* pp. 96, 384, 395, 436, 523.
24. Nordenstam, *op. cit.,* p. 101.
25. Cf. John Bagot Glubb, "Glubb Pasha Analyzes the Arab Mind," *The New York Times Magazine,* November 18, 1956, p. 38.

VII   THE BEDOUIN ETHOS AND MODERN ARAB SOCIETY

1. Cf. Nordenstam, *op. cit.* p. 74. Cf. Bourdieu's analysis of what he terms "ethos of honor" in Kabyle society, Pierre Bourdieu, *op. cit.,* in Peristiany (ed.), *Honour and Shame,* pp. 228ff.
2. Aḥmad ibn Ḥanbal, *Musnad,* Cairo, 6 vols, vol. III, p. 425; as quoted by Reuben Levy, *The Social Structure of Islam,* Cambridge: University Press, 1957, p. 193. Subsequently (p. 194), Levy remarks that Muḥammad "appears to have adopted the tribal terminology for good and evil," which, of course, is another example of the Islamization of pre-Islamic Arab moral ideas.
3. Nordenstam, *op. cit.,* pp. 75, 123.
4. Cf. e.g. Alois Musil, *The Manners and Customs of the Rwala Bedouins,* New York: American Geographical Society, 1928, pp. 451, 455ff., 471–472, 483.
5. Yochanan Peres, "Modernization and Nationalism in the Identity of the Israeli Arab," *The Middle East Journal* vol. 24, no. 4 (Autumn, 1970), p. 488.
6. With some exceptional and marginal cases which are discussed in Chapter VIII, "The Realm of Sex."
7. Cf. Ignaz Goldziher, *Muhammedanische Studien,* Halle, 1889, vol. I, p. 13; *Encyclopaedia of Islam,* new ed., s.vv. *ḥamāsa, djiwār.* On the nomadic values shared by the settled populations in the Fertile Crescent, cf. Fernea, *op. cit.,* p. 77. On the nomadic origins of the values in the wider Mediterranean area,

cf. Germaine Tillion, *Le Harem et les cousins,* Paris: Editions du Seuil, 1966.

8. Cf. Nordenstam, *op. cit.,* p. 107.

9. Bourdieu, *op. cit.,* in Peristiany (ed.), *Honour and Shame,* pp. 209–210.

10. *Op. cit.,* p. 212.

11. Ahmed Abou-Zeid, *op. cit.,* in Peristiany (ed.), *Honour and Shame,* p. 259.

12. Nordenstam, *op. cit.,* p. 106.

13. *Ibid.,* pp. 109, 111–114.

14. Hussein of Jordan, *op. cit.,* pp. 60–61.

15. *Ibid.,* pp. 65–66.

16. *Ibid.,* p. 66.

17. *Ibid.,* p. 71.

18. *Ibid.,* pp. 82–83.

19. *Ibid.,* pp. 82–83.

20. *Ibid.,* p. 88.

21. *Ibid.,* pp. 92–93.

22. Michel Feghali, *Proverbes et dictons syro-libanais,* Paris: Institut d'Ethnologie, 1938, pp. 80, 81; as quoted by Hamady, *Temperament and Character of the Arabs,* p. 63.

23. Landberg, *Proverbes et dictons du peuple Arabe,* p. 45.

24. Cf. Hamady, *op. cit.,* p. 63.

25. Carleton S. Coon, *Caravan: The Story of the Middle East,* revised ed., New York: Holt, Rinehart and Winston, 1965, p. 170.

26. Cf. David P. Ausubel, "Relationships Between Shame and Guilt in the Socializing Process," *Psychological Review,* vol. 62, no. 5 (September, 1955), pp. 379, 382, 389.

27. Hamady, *op. cit.,* p. 35; cf. pp. 34–39.

28. Prothro, *Child Rearing in the Lebanon,* p. 94; Ammar, *Growing Up in an Egyptian Village,* pp. 109f., 126, 128, 135, 137, 185f., 191f.

29. Cf. 'Ammār, *Fī Binā ul-Bashar (On the Building of Man).*

30. *Ibid.,* p. 79. The Arabic phrase *"al-namaṭ al-ijtimā'ī li-shakhṣiyyat al-Masrī"* (literally, "the social mode of the Egyptian's personality") seems to be Dr. 'Ammār's rendering of what in English would be "the Egyptian modal personality."

31. *Ibid.,* pp. 79–91. My translation and summary.

32. Ṣādiq Jalāl al-'Aẓm, *Al-Naqd al-Dhātī Ba'd al-Hazīma (Self-Criticism After the Defeat).* The section summarized above is found on pp. 69–90. The entire book has been excerpted in Harkabi (ed.), *Leqaḥ ha-'Aravim mi-T'vusatam (Arab Lessons From Their Defeat),* Tel Aviv: 'Am 'Ovēd, 1969, pp. 71–114. The above summary is based on these excerpts.

33. William A. Darity, "Some Sociocultural Factors in the Administration of Technical Assistance and Training in Health," *Human Organization,* vol. 24, no. 1 (Spring, 1965), p. 81.

34. See Harold Q. Langenderfer, "The Egyptian Executive: A Study in Conflict," *Human Organization,* vol. 24, no. 1 (Spring, 1965), p. 94.

35. Kevin G. Fenelon, "Technology," in Adams (ed.), *The Middle East: A Handbook,* p. 453.
36. Williams, *op. cit.,* p. 124.
37. Patai, *Golden River,* pp. 81, 268–270, 276.
38. *Ibid.,* pp. 268–271, and literature in the footnotes, to which should now be added Lothar Stein, *Die Šammar-Ǧerba: Beduinen im Übergang vom Nomadismus zur Sesshaftigkeit,* Berlin: Akademie Verlag, 1967. Cf. also the earlier study of Henri Charles, S.J., *La Sédentarisation entre Euphrate et Balik,* Beirut, Lebanon, 1942.
39. Patai, *Golden River,* p. 311.
40. In some Arab countries, such as Egypt, the workers do not have the right to strike; cf. Langenderfer, *op. cit.,* p. 91.

VIII   THE REALM OF SEX

1. Cf. Ahmed Abou-Zeid, "Honour and Shame Among the Bedouins of Egypt," in Peristiany (ed.), *op. cit.,* p. 256. On *'ird,* cf. also Musa Kazem Daghestani, *Etude sociologique sur la famille Musulmane contemporaine en Syrie,* Paris: Leroux, 1932, p. 58. The irreparability of a woman's *'ird* in the view of Arab villagers and their general view of female sexuality are discussed in some detail by Richard T. Antoun, "On the Modesty of Women in Arab Muslim Villages: A Study in the Accommodation of Traditions," *American Anthropologist,* vol. 70, no. 4 (August, 1968), pp. 671–697.
2. Nordenstam, *op. cit.,* p. 94.
3. Pierre Bourdieu, "The Sentiment of Honor in Kabyle Society," in Peristiany (ed.), *op. cit.,* p. 220.
4. Fulanain (pseud.), *The Marsh Arab: Haji Rikkan,* Philadelphia: Lippincott, 1928, pp. 243ff.
5. Nordenstam, *op. cit.,* p. 97.
6. *Op. cit.,* p. 96.
7. Sources in Patai, *Golden River,* pp. 445–446.
8. *Ibid.,* pp. 447–455, and sources there in the footnotes.
9. *Ibid.,* pp. 457–459.
10. Edgar Barton Worthington, *Middle East Science,* London: His Majesty's Stationery Office, 1946, p. 157.
11. Deuteronomy 11:17. On this whole subject of R. Patai, *Sex and Family in the Bible and the Middle East,* New York: Doubleday, 1959, pp. 80ff.
12. Miner and de Vos, *op. cit.,* pp. 82–83.
13. Gordon, *Women of Algeria,* pp. 64–65.
14. Mouloud Feraoun, *Journal 1955–1962,* Paris, 1962, as quoted by Gordon, *Women of Algeria,* p. 52.
15. Miner and de Vos, *op. cit.,* p. 80; cf. also Antoun, *op. cit.,* pp. 678–679.
16. Nordenstam, *op. cit.,* p. 96.
17. The quotes are from Mme Fadéla M'Rabet, *La Femme Algérienne,* Paris, 1964, as quoted by Gordon, *Women of Algeria,* pp. 70–72.

18. Sayed Kotb, *Social Justice in Islam*, translated by John B. Hardie, Washington, D.C.: American Council of Learned Societies, 1953, pp. 49ff.

19. A *fatwa* (religious decree) issued on July 11, 1952, by the Commission of Fatwas of al-Azhar, as quoted and summarized by Gordon, *Women of Algeria*, pp. 33–34.

20. See, e.g., Freya Stark, *A Winter in Arabia*, London: John Murray, 1940, p. 200, on the survival of pre-Islamic words in the women's language in Hureidha in Southern Arabia. On women's religion in Arab lands, cf. Patai, *Golden River*, pp. 463ff.

21. Sigmund Freud, *Beyond the Pleasure Principle*, London: Hogarth Press, 1922, p. 69.

22. Berkowitz, *Aggression: A Social Psychological Analysis*, pp. 17, 267ff.

23. Carl Gustav Jung, *Two Essays on Analytical Psychology*, New York: Meridian Books, 1956, p. 277.

24. *Op. cit.*, p. 136.

25. Florence Goodenough, *Anger in Young Children*, London: Oxford University Press, and Minneapolis, Minn.: University of Minneapolis Press, 1931, p. 138, as summarized by Lydia Jackson, *Aggression and Its Interpretation*, London: Methuen, 1954, pp. 20–21.

26. Jackson, *op. cit.*, p. 27.

27. J. Dollard, L. W. Doob, N. E. Miller, O. H. Mowrer and R. R. Sears, *Frustration and Aggression*, New Haven, Conn.: Yale University Press, 1939, and London: Routledge and Kegan Paul, 1944, p. 1. Also Berkowitz, *op. cit.*, p. 26.

28. Levon H. Melikian and Edwin Terry Prothro, "Sexual Behavior of University Students in the Arab Near East," *Journal of Abnormal and Social Psychology*, 1954, vol. 49, pp. 63–64; Prothro, *Child Rearing in the Lebanon*, p. 120.

29. Raphael Patai, *Man and Temple in Ancient Jewish Myth and Ritual*, Edinburgh: Thomas Nelson, 1947 (2nd ed., New York: Ktav Publ., 1967), p. 156; cf. also p. 146.

30. Edward Atiyah, *An Arab Tells His Story*, London: John Murray, 1946, p. 68.

31. Melikian and Prothro, *op. cit.*, pp. 62–64.

32. Cf., e.g., Eldon Rutter, *The Holy Cities of Arabia*, London: 1928, p. 80: "A husband never walks with his wife, even though the destination be the same."

33. The custom was observed and recorded by Gertrude Joly, "The Woman of the Lebanon," *Journal of the Royal Central Asian Society*, vol. 38 (1951), pp. 179ff. The interpretation is mine.

34. Musil, *Manners and Customs of the Rwala Bedouins*, p. 240.

35. Edward William Lane, *The Manners and Customs of the Modern Egyptians*, London: Everyman's Library Edition, n.d., pp. 184–185, 435–437.

36. About the Tuareg culture area, see Patai, *Golden River*, pp. 66, and map opp. p. 61.

37. Yāqūt, *Geographical Dictionary*, ed. Ferdinand Wüstenfeld, 6 vols., Leipzig, 1866–73, vol. IV, pp. 481–482.

38. Ibn Baṭṭūṭa, *Riḥla*, ed. C. Defrémery and B. R. Sanguinetti, 4 vols., Paris, 1853–59, vol. II, pp. 227f.

39. The Wahhābīs forced the Merekede to renounce this custom, whereupon for two years scarcely a drop of rain fell. This was regarded by the Merekede as a punishment for having abandoned the laudable rite of hospitality practiced for centuries by their forefathers, and they applied to 'Abdu 'l-'Azīz, the Wahhābī chieftain, for permission to honor their guests as before, which he granted. After describing this, Burckhardt remarks that he first heard of the extraordinary custom of the Merekede tribe during his travels among the Syrian Bedouins, but could give no credence to the story. But, he continues, "I can no longer entertain a doubt on the subject, having received both at Mekka and Tayf, from various persons who had actually witnessed the fact, most unequivocal evidence in confirmation of the statement." About another South Arabian tribe, the Bani Yām, Burckhardt reports that when a man undertakes a trip, he takes his wife to the house of a friend who replaces the husband during his absence. Cf. J. L. Burckhardt, *Travels in Arabia*, London: Henry Colburn, 1829, pp. 448, 453, and *Notes on the Bedouins and Wahábys*, London, 1831, vol. 1, pp. 179–180. Cf. also William Robertson Smith, *Kinship and Marriage in Early Arabia*, Cambridge, 1885, pp. 139f.

40. Count Carlo Landberg, *Arabica*, Leiden, 1897, vol. IV, pp. 25–27, 33; vol. V, p. 168; *Études*, Leiden, 1905, vol. II, pp. 203, 907–916, 944, 972.

41. Cf. also Julian Morgenstern, *Zeitschrift für die Alttestamentliche Wissenschaft*, vol. 49 (1931), p. 48; Joseph Henninger, "Die Familie bei den heutigen Beduinen," *Internationales Archiv für Ethnologie*, 42, 1948, p. 46.

42. S. I. Curtiss, *Ursemitische Religion*, Leipzig, 1903, p. 49; George Wyman Bury (Abdullah Mansur), *The Land of Uz*, London: Macmillan, 1911, p. 135; H. St.-John B. Philby, *Arabian Highlands*, Ithaca, N.Y.: Cornell University Press, 1952, p. 28, 241; Père Mariede Saint Elie Anastase, "La femme du désert autrefois et aujourd'hui," *Anthropos*, vol. 3 (1908), p. 188.

43. Philby, *op. cit.*, pp. 28, 142, 146, 168, 275, 447, 451, 644; also *Sheba's Daughters*, London: Methuen, 1939, p. 46.

44. Melikian and Prothro, *op. cit.*, pp. 60, 63.

45. *Op. cit.*, p. 60.

46. Alan Dundes, Jerry W. Lead, and Bora Özkök, "The Strategy of Turkish Boys' Verbal Dueling Rhymes," *Journal of American Folklore*, vol. 83, no. 329 (July–September, 1970), pp. 325–349.

47. Levy, *The Social Structure of Islam*, p. 234.

48. Walter Cline, *Notes on the People of Siwah and El Garah in the Libyan Desert*, Menasha, Wisc.: General Series in Anthropology, 1936, p. 43. Byron Khun De Prorok, *In Quest of Lost Worlds*, London: F. Muller, 1935; Robin Maugham, *Journey to Siwa*, London: Chapman and Hall, 1950; and others supply colorful details about Siwan homosexuality which, however, need to be checked out by an anthropologically trained observer.

49. Cline, *op. cit.*, p. 43.

50. Melikian and Prothro, *op. cit.*, p. 60.

51. Lane, *op. cit.*, p. 303.

52. *Arabian Nights,* translated by Richard Burton, vol. VII, p. 161, n. 10; cf. Levy, *op. cit.,* pp. 233–234.
53. Lane, *op. cit.,* p. 303.
54. Winifred S. Blackman, *The Fellahin of Upper Egypt,* London: Harrap, 1927, p. 43.
55. Ayrout, S. J., *The Egyptian Peasant,* pp. 146–147.
56. Sources quoted by Levy, *op. cit.,* p. 234.
57. See also H. St.-John B. Philby, *Arabian Jubilee,* New York: John Day, 1953, p. 110; cf. also pp. 111–112, 132, 245.
58. Cf., e.g., Philby, *Arabian Highlands,* p. 80.
59. Richard H. Sanger, *The Arabian Peninsula,* Ithaca, N.Y.: Cornell University Press, 1954, p. 15.
60. This subject is treated in some detail in Patai, *Golden River,* pp. 470–478. Sources there, pp. 530–531.
61. Lane, cf. also p. 305.
62. See Berque, *op. cit.,* p. 271. As to opposition to Westernization, see Patai, *Golden River,* pp. 386ff., chapter 14, "Resistance to Westernization," and below, Chapter XVI.
63. Berque, *op. cit.,* p. 271.

IX THE ISLAMIC COMPONENT OF THE ARAB PERSONALITY

1. Arnold J. Toynbee, *A Study of History,* abr. ed., Oxford, 1947, p. 487.
2. Rebecca West, *Black Lamb and Grey Falcon,* New York: The Viking Press, 1943, p. 298.
3. Patai, *Golden River,* p. 327; cf. *ibid.,* pp. 322–344, the chapter on "Religion in Middle Eastern, Far Eastern, and Western Culture."
4. Abu 'l-Ḥasan ‘Alī al-Ḥasanī al-Nadwī, *Mā dhā khasara 'l-ʿalam bi-'nhiṭāt al-Muslimīn? (What Has the World Lost Through the Decline of the Muslims?) 2nd ed., Cairo, 1951, pp. 185–202;* as summarized by G. E. von Grunebaum, *Modern Islam,* 1964, pp. 252–253.
5. However, the reader might find instructive the penetrating critical analysis of Nadwī in von Grunebaum, *ibid.,* pp. 244–257.
6. Cf. Wilfred Cantwell Smith, *The Meaning and End of Religion,* New York: Macmillan, 1962, pp. 110ff., which contains an excellent analysis of what Islam means to the Muslim world.
7. Cf. *Encyclopedia of Religion and Ethics,* s.v. Fate, vol. V, pp. 794ff.; and Levy, *op. cit.,* pp. 225–226.
8. Cf. e.g., Genesis 16:12, 25:23; Judges 13:5; Jeremiah 1:5; Matthew 1:21; Luke 1:14–17; and Romans 9:11–12.
9. Cf. *Encyclopedia of Religion and Ethics,* s.v. Predestination, vol. X, pp. 231ff.
10. Levy, *op. cit.,* pp. 205–207.
11. The Koran contains several references to books or records kept in heaven in which all the deeds of men are recorded, cf. 83:7–9, 18–20; 84:7–12; 34:3.

12. Hilma Granqvist, *Birth and Childhood Among the Arabs,* Helsingfors: Söderstrom & Co., 1947, p. 177; cf. pp. 62, 227, n. 22.
13. Lane, *op. cit.,* pp. 69, 291.
14. *Ibid.,* pp. 477–478. We note in the last sentence the echo of the old Koranic idea that man can do good only if God so ordains. This prayer is similar to the one recited by Jews in their New Year and Day of Atonement rituals. However, among the Jews since the *Haskala* (Enlightenment), only a diminishing percentage still attaches any literal meaning to these prayers.
15. Afîf I. Tannous, "Group Behavior in the Village Community of Lebanon," *American Journal of Sociology,* vol. 48 (1942), pp. 233, 236–237.
16. Hamady, *op. cit.,* p. 72.
17. Cf. R. Patai, "Musha'a Tenure and Cooperation in Palestine," *American Anthropologist,* vol. 51, no. 3 (July–September, 1949), pp. 436–445.
18. *Ibid.,* p. 441.
19. Cf. al-Maqrīzī, *Description topographique et historique de l'Egypte,* p. 138.
20. Hamady, *op. cit.,* p. 81, quoting Tritton, *Islam: Belief and Practices,* p. 128, who, however, only says: "History and literature are full of fantastic tales of open-handed giving and there must be some truth behind them."
21. Feghali, *Proverbes et dictons syro-libanais,* pp. 605, 606; Walter Cline, "Proverbs and Lullabies from Southern Arabia," *American Journal of Semitic Languages and Literature,* vol. 57 (1940), p. 291.
22. G. E. von Grunebaum, *Medieval Islam: A Study in Cultural Orientation,* 2nd ed., Chicago: University of Chicago Press, 1953, pp. 127–128.
23. Cf. Patai, *Golden River,* pp. 35–36.
24. Hamady, *op. cit.,* pp. 187–188.
25. Granqvist, *Birth and Childhood Among the Arabs,* pp. 177–181; cf. also Lane, *op. cit.,* p. 291.

X EXTREMES AND EMOTIONS

1. T. E. Lawrence, *Seven Pillars of Wisdom,* London: Jonathan Cape, 1940, p. 36. Cf. also Berque, *op cit.,* p. 265.
2. Cf. Léon Gauthier, *Introduction a l'étude de la philosophie Musulmane,* Paris: Leroux, 1923, pp. 34–36; my translation. Already Maqrīzī sought to establish a correlation between climate and character, cf. Maqrīzī, *op. cit.,* pp. 121, 133.
3. Gauthier, *op. cit.,* pp. 37–64. Emphasis in the original.
4. Blackman, *The Fellahin of Upper Egypt,* pp. 23–24.
5. *Ibid.,* p. 129.
6. *Ibid.,* p. 38.
7. Ayrout, *op. cit.,* pp. 141–145.
8. Hamady, *op. cit.,* pp. 54–55.
9. Hazem Zaki Nuseibeh, *The Ideas of Arab Nationalism,* Ithaca, N.Y.: Cornell University Press, 1956, p. 152. Cf. also Berque, *op. cit.,* p. 283, quoting Henri

Corbin, *L'imagination créatrice dans le soufisme d'Ibn Arabi,* Paris: Flammarion, 1958.

10. Hamady, *op. cit.,* pp. 43–54. Cf. also Furlonge, *Palestine Is My Country,* p. 21.

11. Mohammed Neguib, *Egypt's Destiny,* London: Victor Gollancz, 1955, p. 139.

12. Khadduri, *Republican Iraq,* p. 52.

13. Fayez A. Sayegh, *Understanding the Arab Mind* (pamphlet), published by the Organization of Arab Students in the United States, New York (June, 1953), pp. 13, 14.

14. Lewis, *The Middle East and the West,* p. 95.

15. Smith, *op. cit.,* pp. 158–159.

16. Harkabi, *'Emdat ha-'Aravim b'Sikhsukh Yisraēl-'Arav (The Arabs' Position in the Israel-Arab Conflict),* pp. 376–378, 380.

17. Morroe Berger, *The Arab World Today,* New York: Doubleday Anchor Books, 1954, pp. 160–161. There is no contradiction between Berger's observation about the Arabs' predilection for adopting plans, and mine on the Arab aversion to long-range planning. He speaks of the modern, Westernized Arabs, who are still the minority, and I of the tradition-bound majority. Berger himself adds, p. 161: "One can sense here the influence of religious fatalism too; it is all very well for mortals to make plans, but they ought not to challenge fate by trying to realize them." On the slow and rather hesitant adoption of economic planning in a few Arab countries in recent years (since 1951), see Albert J. Mcyer, *Middle Eastern Capitalism,* Cambridge, Mass.: Harvard University Press, 1959, pp. 96–103.

18. In contrast to them, cf. Fernea, *op. cit.,* p. 78: "The 'real world' of superordinate and subordinate human relations and the 'ideal world' of equality before God seem nowhere to have achieved better mutual accommodation than in the predominantly Islamic states of the world."

XI   ART, MUSIC, AND LITERATURE

1. These exceptions are discussed by Jacques Berque, *op. cit.,* pp. 213ff. On Arab art in general, cf. Ernst Kühnel, *The Minor Arts of Islam,* Ithaca, N.Y.: Cornell University Press, 1971.

2. E. g.: "Angels do not enter the house which contains a dog or an image"; "On Resurrection Day God will consider the image-makers as the men most deserving punishment"; "Those who make pictures will be punished on Resurrection Day; it will be said to them: Give life to what you have created." Cf. Ernst Kühnel, "Islam," *Encyclopedia of World Art,* New York: McGraw-Hill, vol. VIII (1963), p. 332.

3. On the Arab shadow theater, cf. Jacob Landau, "Shadow-Plays in the Near East," *Edoth, A Quarterly for Folklore and Ethnology* (Jerusalem), vol. III, nos. 1–2 (October, 1947–January, 1948), pp. 33–72 (in Hebrew), and pp. xxiii–lxiv (in English).

4. Cf. Kühnel, *The Minor Arts of Islam,* p. 333.
5. Berque, *op. cit.,* p. 219.
6. A "cent" in musicology is a one-hundredth part of a Western semitone; i.e., a quarter-tone has 50 cents, a semitone 100, a full tone 200, and an octave 1200. This method of measuring the tone pitches of different non-Western musical traditions was first suggested by Sir A. J. Ellis, "On the Scales of Various Nations," *Journal of the Society of Fine Arts,* London, 1885.
7. Henry George Farmer, "Mūsīkī," in *Encyclopaedia of Islam.*
8. Henry George Farmer, *Oriental Studies: Mainly Musical,* London: Hinrichsen, 1953, pp. 54–55.
9. Edith Gerson-Kiwi, "The Transcription of Oriental Music," *Edoth,* vol. III, nos. 1–2 (October, 1947–January, 1948), p. xviii.
10. Cf. Henry George Farmer, "Arabian Music," in *Grove's Dictionary of Music and Musicians,* 5th ed., New York: St. Martin's Press, 1955, vol. I, pp. 185–186; and Eric Werner, "The Eight Modes of Music," *Hebrew Union College Annual,* vol. 21 (1948), pp. 211–255.
11. Farmer, *Oriental Studies,* pp. 55–56.
12. Hamilton A. R. Gibb, *Arabic Literature: An Introduction,* 2nd ed., Oxford: Clarendon Press, 1963, p. 3.
13. *Ibid.,* p. 15.
14. Musil, *The Manners and Customs of the Rwala Bedouins,* pp. 78ff.
15. *Ibid.,* pp. 283–284.
16. Salem, "Form and Substance: A Critical Examination of the Arabic Language," p. 17.
17. Dr. Fū'ad Zakarīyā, "Mustaqbal al-Mūsīqā fī Miṣr" *(The Future of Music in Egypt),* *Al-Majalla* (June, 1957), p. 102; as quoted by Berque, *op. cit.,* pp. 219–220.
18. Dr. Ḥusayn Fawzī, *Al-Mūsīqā al-Simfūniyya (Symphonic Music),* p. 17; as quoted by Berque, *op. cit.,* p. 223.
19. Berque, *ibid.*
20. *Ibid.,* pp. 228–230.

XII BILINGUALISM, MARGINALITY, AND AMBIVALENCE

1. See Frank Ralph Golino, "Language and Cultural Identity in North Africa" (mimeographed) paper presented to the Conference on North Africa in Transit, Columbia University, March 22–23, 1971, p. 3.
2. *Op. cit.,* pp. 8, 10, 11, quoting A. Demeersman, "Contribution a l'étude de la relation entre la langue Arabe et la personnalité de la Tunisie," *IBLA: Revue de l'Institut des Belles Lettres Arabes à Tunis,* No. 92, 1960.
3. *Op. cit.,* pp. 11–12, quoting Tunisian Prime Minister Hedi Nouira, as reported in *Al-Amal,* December 20, 1970.
4. *Op. cit.,* p. 12, quoting *Agence France Presse,* December 30, 1970, and *Le Monde,* January 3–4, 1971.

5. *Op. cit.*, p. 18.
6. *Op. cit.*, pp. 19–21.
7. John Simmons, "Factors Associated with School Achievement: Rural Boys in Tunisia" (mimeographed) paper presented to the Conference on North Africa in Transit, Columbia University, March 22–23, 1971, p. 6.
8. *Op. cit.*, pp. 10, 12, 13, 18, 26, 33, 44.
9. *Op. cit.*, pp. 13, 14, 26, 27, 29, 34.
10. *Op. cit.*, p. 14.
11. In most Arab countries, only a minority of the six- to thirteen-year age group is attending schools. Cf. Patai, *Golden River*, p. 491.
12. Blanc, *op. cit.*, pp. 85, 151–152.
13. *Ibid.*
14. The concept of marginality was first introduced by Robert Ezra Park (1864–1944), and subsequently made the subject of a full-length study by Everett V. Stonequist, *The Marginal Man: A Study in Personality and Culture Conflict*, New York: Charles Scribner's Sons, 1937.
15. See, e.g., Roger Le Tourneau, "North Africa: Rigorism and Bewilderment," in G. E. von Grunebaum (ed.), *Unity and Variety in Muslim Civilization*, Chicago: University of Chicago Press, 1955, pp. 231–54; Benjamin Rivlin, "Cultural Conflicts in French North Africa," *The Annals of the American Academy of Political and Social Science*, vol. 306 (July, 1956), pp. 4–9 (discussing the problems of marginal man in North Africa in general); Hisham Sharabi, "The Crisis of the Intelligentsia in the Middle East," *The Muslim World*, vol. 47, 1957, pp. 187–193; Pierre Bourdieu, *Sociologie de l'Algérie*, Paris: Que Sais-Je? Presses Universitaires de France, 1958, pp. 90–126; etc. I found especially instructive and insightful the discussions of Arab marginality in North Africa by David C. Gordon, *North Africa's French Legacy, 1954–1962*, pp. 54–64; and in Morocco by John P. Halstead, *Rebirth of a Nation: The Origins and Rise of Moroccan Nationalism 1912–1944*, Cambridge, Mass.: Harvard Middle Eastern Monographs Series XVIII, 1967, pp. 135–141.
16. Allal al-Fassi in interviews with John P. Halstead on June 22 and 23, 1959; see Halstead, *op. cit.*, p. 139.
17. Mohammad Lyazidi in an interview with Halstead on June 23, 1959; see Halstead, *op. cit.*
18. Georges Naccache, in *Al-Afkar* (July, 1961), pp. 14–16, as quoted by Gordon, *North Africa's French Legacy*, p. 112.
19. The expression is that of Jean Amrouche, in *Afrique-Action*, January 23, 1961, p. 3, as quoted by Gordon, *North Africa's French Legacy*, p. 52.
20. Hussein of Jordan, *My "War" with Israel*, p. 47. This kind of joking has almost become institutionalized in Turkey, where it has developed into a contest of rhyming insults spiced with obscenities. See Alan Dundes, Jerry W. Leach, and Bora Özkök, "The Strategy of Turkish Boys' Verbal Dueling Rhymes," *Journal of American Folklore*, vol. 83, no. 329, (July–September, 1970), pp. 325–349.
21. John Bagot Glubb, "Glubb Pasha Analyzes the Arab Mind," p. 38.

22. Cf. Charles F. Gallagher, "Language and Identity," in Leon Carl Brown (ed.), *State and Society in Independent North Africa,* Washington, D.C.: The Middle East Institute, 1966, p. 93.

23. Albert H. Hourani, *Syria and Lebanon,* London: Oxford University Press, 1946, pp. 70–72 (dealing with the problems of marginal man in Syria and Lebanon, which countries had been under French mandatory rule since the end of World War I).

24. Gordon, *North Africa's French Legacy,* p. 8.

25. *Ibid.,* pp. 44–46.

26. Frederick H. Harrison and Ibrahim Abdelkader Ibrahim, "Some Labor Problems of Industrialization in Egypt," *The Annals of the American Academy of Political and Social Science,* vol. 305 (May, 1956), p. 118.

27. *Op. cit.,* pp. 116, 118.

28. Gordon, *North Africa's French Legacy,* p. 118; cf. also pp. 20, 76.

29. David C. Gordon, *The Passing of French Algeria,* London: Oxford University Press, 1966, pp. 200, 201.

30. Louis J. Cantori, "Local Leadership Characteristics of the Istiqlal Party of Morocco" (mimeographed) paper presented to the Conference on North Africa in Transit, Columbia University, March 22–23, 1971, p. 4.

31. Sigmund Freud, *Totem und Tabu,* Leipzig-Vienna-Zürich: Internationaler Psychoanalytischer Verlag, 1925, p. 40.

32. Cf. Ḥalīm Barakāt, *'Awdat al-Ṭā'ir ilā 'l-Baḥr (Return of the Flying Dutchman [or Sailor] to the Sea),* Beirut: Dār al-Nahār, 1969; as analyzed by Trevor J. LeGassick, "Some Recent War-Related Arabic Fiction," *The Middle East Journal,* vol. 25, no. 4 (Autumn, 1971), p. 495. Other treatments of Arab ambivalence can be found in J.-P. Charnay (ed.), *L'ambivalence dans la culture arabe,* Paris: Anthropos, 1967; and, most recently, in C.A.O. van Nieuwenhuijze, *Sociology of the Middle East,* Leiden: Brill, 1971, pp. 37, 187, 278, 656–657.

33. It is a well-known fact that the infrequent press conferences granted by the King of Morocco are invariably held in French. Cf., e.g., Charles F. Gallagher, "Language and Identity," in Brown (ed.), *State and Society in Independent North Africa,* p. 75.

34. This subject, the disruption of the cultural continuum in the Arab countries as a result of Westernization, is dealt with in greater detail in Patai, *Golden River,* pp. 372ff. The traditional cultural continuum between rural and urban society in Morocco has been recently referred to by Clifford Geertz, *Islam Observed,* pp. 5–6. He also remarks, p. 64, on the "difference in cultural identity" that emerged as a result of European influence.

35. Patai, *Golden River,* pp. 373–374.

36. 'Abdullāh 'Alī al-Qaṣīmī, *Hādhī Hiya 'l-Aghlāl (These Are the Chains),* Cairo, 1946, p. 309, as translated and quoted by von Grunebaum, *Islam: Essays in the Nature and Growth of a Cultural Tradition,* pp. 218, 220, 221.

37. 'Alī Ḥasan al-Wardī, *Shakhṣiyyat al-Fard al-'Irāqī (The Personality of the Iraqi*

Individual), Baghdad, 1951. A German translation of this lecture was published by G. Krotkoff under the title "Die Persönlichkeit des Irakers. Ein Beitrag zur Sozialpsychologie," in *Bustan,* no. 1 (1961), pp. 7–11.

38. Fāris and Husayn, *op. cit.,* p. 178.
39. *Ibid.;* cf. Berque, *op. cit.,* pp. 270–271.
40. Hisham Sharabi, "Political and Intellectual Attitudes of the Young Arab Generation," in Tibor Kerekes (ed.), *The Arab Middle East and Muslim Africa,* New York: Praeger, 1961, pp. 20, 60–61.
41. The Arabs' ambivalent attitude toward their own historical past will be discussed in Chapter XVI. See also Charles D. Cremeans, *The Arabs and the World: Nasser's Arab Nationalist Policy,* New York-London: Published for the Council on Foreign Relations by Praeger, 1963, p. 132.
42. Barakāt, *'Awdat al-ṭā'ir ilā 'l-Baḥr (Return of the Flying Dutchman [or Sailor] to the Sea),* p. 55, as quoted by LeGassick, *op. cit.,* p. 495.

XIII   UNITY AND CONFLICT

1. Von Grunebaum, *Modern Islam,* pp. 277–278.
2. Muḥammad Abu-Zahra, *Al-Waḥda al-Islāmiyya (Islamic Unity),* Cairo: al-Maktab al-Fannī, 1958; as summarized in Fahim I. Qubain's valuable bibliography, *Inside the Arab Mind,* Arlington, W.V.: Middle East Research Associates, 1960, p. 25.
3. Fatḥī Yakun, *Risālat al-Qawmiyya al-'Arabiyya (The Mission of Arab Nationalism),* n. p., n.d. (probably Beirut, *ca.* 1959), as summarized by Qubain, *op. cit.*
4. Lewis, *The Middle East and the West,* p. 88.
5. As quoted in William R. Polk, "Generations, Classes and Politics," in Kerekes (ed.), *The Arab Middle East and Muslim Africa,* p. 118; and in von Grunebaum, *Modern Islam,* p. 226. Subsequently, the Third Congress of Arab Writers formulated a similar definition and programmatic description of *qawmiyya;* cf. von Grunebaum, *Modern Islam,* pp. 235–236.
6. Cf. 'Abdullāh al-'Alāyilī, *Dustūr al-'Arab al-Qawmī (The National Constitution of the Arabs),* 1st ed., Beirut, 1941, pp. 88–95; as translated by Sylvia G. Haim, *Arab Nationalism: An Anthology,* pp. 120–127.
7. Nabīh Amīn Fāris, *Al-'Arab Al-Ahyā (The Living Arabs),* Beirut, 1947, pp. 102 ff.; translated by von Grunebaum, *Modern Islam,* pp. 195–196.
8. Fāris and Husayn, *op. cit.,* pp. 21–30. The quotations are from pp. 28–30.
9. The above is a summary made by G. E. von Grunebaum, of an article by 'Abdarraḥmān Azzām, published in *al-'Arab,* Jerusalem, August 27, 1932. See von Grunebaum, *Modern Islam,* pp. 284–285.
10. Von Grunebaum, *Modern Islam,* p. 285.
11. *Encyclopaedia of Islam,* new ed., s.v. *Ayyām al-'Arab.*
12. Pierre Bourdieu, "The Sentiment of Honour in Kabyle Society," in Peristiany (ed.), *Honour and Shame,* pp. 201–202, 235, n. 7. On the role of the mediators, see the next chapter.

13. Nuseibeh, *op. cit.*, p. 15.

14. See, e. g., Fulanain (pseud.), *op. cit.*, p. 112.

15. Ruth Benedict, *Patterns of Culture*, London: Routledge, 1935, pp. 141ff.

16. Cf. *Kitāb al-Aghānī*, vol VIII, p. 109; *Encyclopaedia of Islam*, old ed., s.v. *Mufākhara;* supplement, 1938, p. 151.

17. 'Abdul Raḥmān al-Bazzāz, *Hādha Qawmiyyatunā (This Is Our Nationalism)*, Cairo: Dār al-Qalām, 1964, chapter 3.

18. Nāṣir al-Dīn al-Nashāshībī, *Al-Waḥda wa-Qaḍiyyat Falasṭīn (The Unity and the Problem of Palestine)*, Kutub Qawmiyya *(Nationalist Books)* no. 109, May 15, 1961, pp. 28–29; and *Tadhkirat 'Awda (Return Ticket)*, Beirut: Al-Maktab al-Tajjārī, July, 1962, pp. 117–118; as quoted by Harkabi, *'Emdat ha-'Aravim b-Sikhsukh Yisraēl-'Arav (The Arabs' Position in the Israel-Arab Conflict)*, pp. 324–325.

19. See Ignaz Goldziher, *Abhandlungen zur Arabischen Philologie*, vol. I, Leiden, 1896, "Über die Vorgeschichte der Higā-Poesie," pp. 1–105.

20. *Encyclopaedia of Islam*, new ed., s.v. *Hidjā'.*

21. A survival of the *hijā* on the popular-juvenile level can be seen in the Turkish boys' custom of engaging in oral duels in which the insults and obscenities hurled at each other must rhyme. Cf. Dundes, Lead, and Özkök, "The Strategy of Turkish Boys' Verbal Dueling Rhymes," pp. 325–349.

22. See Patai, *Golden River*, p. 181.

23. *Op. cit.* p. 183; cf. also *Encyclopaedia of Islam*, new ed., vol. I, pp. 544ff.

24. Reinhart P.A. Dozy, *Spanish Islam*, London: Chatto and Windus, 1913, p. 66, and Arabic sources there.

25. Hitti, *History of the Arabs*, p. 281. On the whole phenomenon of dual organization in the Middle East, cf. also Patai, *Golden River*, pp. 177–250.

26. See C. F. Volney, *Travels Through Syria and Egypt in the Years 1783, 1784, and 1785*. London, 1788, vol. II, p. 203; cf. Hamilton A. R. Gibb and Harold Bowen, *Islamic Society and the West*, vol. I, part I. London: Oxford University Press, 1950, p. 268.

27. E.g. in Ramallah, cf. Miriam Zarour, "Ramallah: My Home Town," *The Middle East Journal*, vol. 7, no. 4 (Autumn, 1953), pp. 431–432; and in Syria, cf. Carsten Niebuhr, *Reisebeschreibung nach Arabien und andern umliegenden Ländern*, Copenhagen, 1778, vol. II, p. 447.

28. See Patai, *Golden River*, pp. 226–228; and Gibb and Bowen, *op. cit.*, for the fights between the Sa'd and the Ḥarām moieties in Egypt. It might be added that the Awlād 'Alī Bedouins of the Western Desert of Egypt are to this day divided into two moieties, one called Awlād 'Alī al-Aḥmar ("The Red Awlād 'Alī"), and the other Awlād 'Alī al-Abyad ("The White Awlād 'Alī"). Cf. Ahmed Abou-Zeid, "Honour and Shame among the Bedouins of Egypt," in Peristiany (ed.), *Honour and Shame*, p. 248.

29. Dozy, *op. cit.*, p. 126.

30. Patai, *Golden River*, p. 187 and sources there.

31. Ameen Fāris Rihani, *Mulūk al-'Arab (Kings of the Arabs)*, 3rd ed., Beirut,

1953, vol. I, p. 117; as quoted by Fāris and Husayn, *op. cit.*, p. 179.

32. Blackman, *op. cit.*, pp. 129–131.

33. Ammar, *Growing Up in an Egyptian Village*, pp. vii, 44, 45, 47, 61.

34. Joseph Chelhod, "Les Structures dualistes de la société Bédouine," *L'Homme*, Paris, 1969, vol. 9, no. 2, pp. 108–109.

35. Patai, *Golden River*, pp. 218, 240.

36. Jacques Berque, "The Social History of an Egyptian Village in the Twentieth Century," in Louise E. Sweet (ed.), *Peoples and Cultures of the Middle East*, vol. II, New York: The Natural History Press, 1970, pp. 194, 215, 217.

37. Patai, *Golden River*, p. 219.

38. *Ibid.*, pp. 180ff.

39. The above sketch of Lebanese conflict patterns is based on the excellent and detailed analysis by Samih K. Farsoun, "Family Structure and Society in Modern Lebanon," in Sweet (ed.), *op. cit.*, vol. II, pp. 257–307. In his footnotes, Dr. Farsoun quotes much of the literature on the subject.

40. Khadduri, *Independent Iraq*, p. 36.

41. See Prothro and Melikian, "Social Distance and Social Change in the Near East," pp. 3–11.

42. Nasser, *Egypt's Liberation*, pp. 35–36.

43. Hussein of Jordan, *My "War" with Israel*, pp. 26, 28, 29, 34, 36.

44. Khadduri, *op. cit.*, pp. 24, 223. On pp. 277–278 Khadduri refers to the internal conflicts among the Kurds of Iraq.

45. Fāris and Husayn, *op. cit.*, pp. 59, 86, 93, 113, 124, 134, 150, 153, 157–167, 170–172.

46. Kadi, *op. cit.*

47. *Ibid.*, pp. 191–193.

48. Cf. Berger, *op. cit.*, p. 160.

49. Cf. Hamed Ammar, *Growing Up in an Egyptian Village*, pp. 54, 107-08, 110, Cf. also Hilma Granqvist, *Marriage Conditions* II: 172, n.3, and *Child Problems Among the Arabs*, Helsingfors: Söderstrom, 1950, p. 81; Afif I. Tannous, "Extension Work among the Arab Fellahin," in Edmund de S. Brunner *et al.* (eds.), *Farmers of the World*, New York: Columbia University Press, 1947, pp. 78–100.

XIV   CONFLICT RESOLUTION AND "CONFERENTIASIS"

1. Fernea, *Shaykh and Effendi*, p. 96. In neighboring Iran the mediator plays a similarly important role, cf. Reinhold Löffler, "The Representative Mediator and the New Peasant," *American Anthropologist*, vol. 73, no. 5 (October, 1971), pp. 1077–1091.

2. Bourdieu, "The Sentiment of Honour in Kabyle Society," in Peristiany (ed.), *Honour and Shame*, pp. 196, 201, 235, 237.

3. Cf. Antoun, *op. cit.*, p. 10.

4. This is the case even in a big city like Tripoli in Lebanon with its 180,000

inhabitants; cf. John Gulick, "Old Values and New Institutions in a Lebanese Arab City," *Human Organization,* vol. 24, no. 1 (Spring, 1965), p. 52. On Arab bargaining techniques, including the attempt to establish social or familal contact between buyer and seller by locating common friends or relatives, cf. Fuad F. Khuri, "The Etiquette of Bargaining in the Middle East," *American Anthropologist,* vol. 70, no. 4 (August, 1968), pp. 698–706.

5. Victor F. Ayoub, "Conflict Resolution and Social Reorganization in a Lebanese Village, *Human Organization,* vol. 24, no. 1 (Spring, 1965), p. 13.

6. *Ibid.*

7. *Ibid.*

8. Hamady, *op. cit.,* pp. 48–49.

9. Antoun, *op. cit.,* p. 8.

10. On this subject, cf. Antoun, *ibid.*

11. Farsoun, *op. cit.,* p. 270; cf. also pp. 281–285, and Meyer, *Middle Eastern Capitalism,* pp. 36–37, on the esteem in which the mediator or middleman is held in the Arab East.

12. Farsoun, *op. cit.,* p. 282.

13. Safia K. Mohsen, "The Legal Status of Women among the Awlad Ali," *Anthropological Quarterly,* vol. 40, 1967, pp. 162–165. On the role of mediation in connection with marriage and in the life of a Jordanian village in general, cf. Richard T. Antoun, *Arab Village: A Social Structural Study of a Transjordanian Peasant Community,* Bloomington, Ind.: Indiana University Press, 1972, pp. 66–68, 80–81, 85, 95, 100–103, 110, 117–123, 137–139.

14. Kadi, *op. cit.,* pp. 127, 129, 146–148.

15. Cf. Schmidt, *Yemen: The Unknown War,* pp. 205, 208–209, 213.

16. *Ibid.,* pp. 236–237, 305–306.

17. *Ibid.,* pp. 241–244.

18. *Ibid.,* pp. 257–273.

19. *The Middle East Journal,* vol. 20, no. 4 (Autumn, 1966), p. 516; vol. 21, no. 1 (Winter 1967), pp. 84–85.

20. *Ibid.,* vol. 21, no. 1 (Winter, 1967), p. 85; vol. 21, no. 2 (Spring, 1967), p. 253.

21. *Ibid.,* vol. 21, no. 4 (Autumn, 1967), p. 524; vol. 22, no. 1 (Winter, 1968), p. 72.

22. Schmidt, *op. cit.,* pp. 294ff.

23. *The Middle East Journal,* vol. 22, no. 2 (Spring, 1968), p. 191; vol. 22, no. 4 (Autumn, 1968), p. 494.

24. *Ibid.,* vol. 24, no. 4 (Autumn, 1970), p. 506; vol. 25, no 1 (Winter, 1971), pp. 69, 71, 72; vol. 25, no. 2 (Spring, 1971), pp. 236, 237; vol. 25, no. 3, (Summer, 1971), p. 378; vol. 25, no. 4 (Autumn, 1971), pp. 511–512.

25. A case in point illustrating this feature of Arab conferences and consultations (i.e., to conclude them with the announcement that an agreement has been reached to reconvene for the purpose of working out an agreement) has been noted by Malcolm Kerr in his *The Arab Cold War 1958–1967,* pp. 98, 102 (cf. also pp. 97ff.): "The agreement reached in April 1963 between the Ba'th and

Nasser was no more than a statement of good intentions for the future. . . ."
". . . all that had been exchanged was a commitment to come to terms in the future."

26. There are, of course, many inter-Arab conferences on other topics of interest, such as economics, technical problems, education, etc. A detailed picture about the frequency of inter-Arab conferences can be obtained by perusing the volumes of the *Record of the Arab World (Documents, Events, Political Opinions)* published in Beirut, Lebanon, by The Research and Publishing House, and edited by Jebran Chamieh. E.g., in March, 1971, alone no less than fourteen such conferences took place and are recorded in the March, 1971, issue of the *Record.*

27. Kadi, *op. cit.*

28. *Ibid.,* p. 188.

29. *The New York Times,* August 26, 1969.

30. *Ibid.* Aug. 31, 1969.

31. *The Middle East Journal,* vol. 24, no. 1 (Winter, 1970), p. 54.

32. The above account is based on reports of *The New York Times,* November 11–12 and December 18–26, 1969, 18–26, 1969, and on the Chronology of *The Middle East Journal,* vol. 24, no. 1 (Winter, 1970), p. 54; vol. 24, no. 2 (Spring, 1970), p. 185.

XV THE QUESTION OF ARAB STAGNATION

1. It is interesting to note that the Arabs' ignorance of their own past, including their former greatness, was observed as early as the fourteenth century by Ibn Khaldūn, who says: "Most Arabs do not even know that they possessed royal authority in the past, or that no nation had ever exercised such (sweeping) royal authority as had their race." See Franz Rosenthal's translation of Ibn Khaldūn's *The Muqaddimah: An Introduction to History,* vol. I, p. 308.

2. This was the case even as late as the early 1950's, when the Arabic original of Omar ('Umar) A. Farrukh's book, *The Arab Genius in Science and Philosophy,* 2nd ed., Beirut, Lebanon, 1952, was published. Its English translation (by John B. Hardie) was published in Washington, D.C.: American Council of Learned Societies, 1954; see pp. vii–viii.

3. Cf. Hitti, *History of the Arabs,* 8th ed., 1964. The two-volume, 1800-page *Cambridge History of Islam* (Cambridge: University Press, 1970) makes even shorter shrift of the history of Arab lands in the Ottoman period. The sixteenth and seventeenth centuries are touched upon only occasionally and tangentially within the context of the history of the Ottoman Empire, while the eighteenth and nineteenth centuries are dealt with in a sketchy historical summary of eighteen pages which tells little more than what the Turks, the French, and the British did in those countries.

4. Hitti, *History of the Arabs,* p. 745.

5. Atiyah, *The Arabs,* p. 73.

6. Hitti, *The Arabs: A Short History*, pp. 128–129. On pp. 212–213 Hitti attributes Arab stagnation to the oppressive rule and excessive taxation by the Ottoman Turks.

7. Sayegh, *Understanding the Arab Mind*. The quotations are found on pp. 27–29 of this pamphlet.

8. Nejla Izzeddin, *The Arab World: Past, Present, and Future*, Chicago, Ill.: Regnery, 1953, pp. 57–58.

9. Fāris and Husayn, *op. cit.*, p. 25. In the footnote to this passage p. 178, the authors refer to Ma'rūf al-Rusāfī, *Nahnu wa'l-Māḍī (We and the Past)*, Cairo, 1931, pp. 34–36, where this Arab tendency is described and strongly criticized. Sayegh also comments on the great "Arab preoccupation with the past . . . the glories of the past often suggest themselves as a comfortable compensation for the humiliations of today. . . .", *op. cit.*, p. 35. Many years before these authors, the French Arabist P. Lapie recognized that the Arab soul *(âme)* was oriented in its entirety toward the past; cf. P. Lapie, *Les civilisations tunisiennes*, as quoted by Gauthier, *op. cit.*, p. 19.

10. Fāris and Husayn, *op. cit.*, p. 46.

11. *Op. cit.*, pp. 168, 172.

12. Bennabi, *Vocation de l'Islam;* as quoted by Gordon, *North Africa's French Legacy*, p. 111.

13. Mahjūb b. Mīlād, *Tūnis Bayn al-Sharq wal-Gharb (Tunisia Between East and West)*, Tunis, 1956, pp. 22ff., as translated by von Grunebaum, *Modern Islam*, p. 208.

14. Ishaq Husseini, "Islam Past and Present," in *Perspective of the Arab World, an Atlantic supplement* (October, 1956), p. 171.

15. *Op. cit.*, p. 172, referring to Aḥmad Amīn, 'Alī 'Abdel-Rāzik, and Khālid Muḥammad Khālid.

16. *Op. cit.*, p. 171.

17. Al-Qaṣīmī, *Hādhi Hiya 'l-Aghlāl (These Are the Chains)*, Cairo, 1946, pp. 12–70; as summarized by von Grunebaum, *Islam: Essays in the Nature and Growth of a Cultural Tradition*, pp. 216–219.

18. The extravagant claims made by Farrukh for the medieval Arab intellectual and spiritual greatness are analyzed by von Grunebaum in *Modern Islam*, pp. 221–222.

19. Farrukh, *op. cit.*, pp. 155–158.

20. Nuseibeh, *The Ideas of Arab Nationalism*, pp. 35–40.

21. Munif Razzaz, "Arab Nationalism," in Adams (ed.), *The Middle East: A Handbook*, pp. 353–355, 358–362. Cf. also Munif Razzaz, *The Evolution of the Meaning of Nationalism*, New York: Doubleday, 1963.

22. Hassan Ibrahim Hassan, *Islam: A Religious, Political, Social and Economic Study*, distributed by Khayat's, Beirut; printed at The Times Printing and Publishing (P. Sh. G.), Baghdad, Iraq, 1967 (publication subsidized by the University of Baghdad), p. 532.

23. Cf. Smith, *Islam in Modern History*, p. 159, n. 203; Lewis, *The Middle East and the West*, p. 133.

24. Cf. A. L. Tibawi, "Towards Understanding and Overcoming the Catastrophe," *Middle East Forum,* vol. 44, no. 3 (1968), pp. 35–42.
25. This view is represented, among others, by Constantine K. Zurayk (Zurayq), in his book *Ma'nā al-Nakba Mujaddadā (The Meaning of the Disaster Again),* Beirut, 1967, which is discussed below.
26. This view is embraced, e.g., by Dr. Ṣādiq Jalāl al-'Aẓm in his book *Al-Naqd al-Dhātī Ba'd al-Hazīma (Self-Criticism After the Defeat);* and by Ḥusayn Mirwa, in his article *"Tarīqūna Ilā Taghayyur al-Insān al-'Arabī" (Our Road to Changing the Arab Man),* in *Al-Adāb,* vol. 15, no. 7–8 (July–August, 1967), pp. 34–37. Also Nājī 'Alūsh represents the radical-revolutionary position, in *Jadal al-Hazīma wa'l-Naṣr (Discussion of the Defeat and the Victory), Dirāsāt 'Arabiyya,* vol. 3, no. 11 (September, 1967), pp. 5–16.
27. This trend is represented, among others, by Dr. Ṣalāḥ al-Dīn al-Munajjid in his book *The Pillars of the Disaster;* see below.
28. Y. Harkabi (ed.), *Leqaḥ ha-'Aravim mi-T'vusatam (The Arabs' Lessons From Their Defeat),* Tel Aviv: 'Am 'Ovēd, 1969, pp. 12–13. This valuable volume contains Hebrew translations of writings or excerpts from writings by twelve Arab authors, including those mentioned in the preceding three footnotes.
29. Cf. Constantine K. Zurayk, *The Meaning of the Disaster,* translated from the Arabic by R. Bayly Winder, Beirut: Khayat's, 1956, pp. 34–41.
30. Constantine K. Zurayk, *Ma'nā al-Nakba Mujaddadā (The Meaning of the Disaster Again),* Beirut, Dār al-'Ilm lil-Malāyīn, August, 1967; as translated in Harkabi, *op. cit.,* pp. 185–187.
31. *Op. cit.,* pp. 194–201.
32. Cf. Dr. Ṣalāḥ al-Dīn al-Munajjid, *A'midat al-Nakba: Baḥth 'Ilmī fī Asbāb Hazīmat 5 Khazīrān (The Pillars of the Disaster: A Scientific Inquiry Into the Reasons of the Defeat of June 5th),* Dār al-Kitāb al-Jadīd; first printing, Dec. 1967; second printing Shebat 1968, 199 pp. The quoted part is on pp. 127–143. My translation from the Arabic.
33. 'Abd al-Raḥmān al-Bazzāz, *"Kayfa Yarbaḥ al-'Arab al-Ḥarb" (How Will the Arabs Win the War?)* in *Ḥawl al-Nakba al-Ḥādira (About the Present Disaster),* Al-Dār al-Sa'ūdiyya li'l-Nashr, March, 1968, Summarized on the basis of the full translation into Hebrew in Harkabi, *op. cit.,* pp. 258–281.
34. My translation from the Arabic.

XVI THE PSYCHOLOGY OF WESTERNIZATION

1. Cf. Patai, *Golden River,* the chapters on "The Dynamics of Westernization" and "Resistance to Westernization," pp. 364–406.
2. My paraphrase of "The Story of the Fisherman with the 'Ifrīt," *Alf Layla wa-Layla,* Cairo: Sa'īd 'Alī al-Khuṣūṣī, n.d., vol. I, pp. 15–18; English translation by Richard F. Burton, *The Book of the Thousand Nights and a Night,* privately printed by the Burton Club, n.p., n.d., vol. I, pp. 38–45, 60ff.
3. J. Desparmet, "Les Chansons de Geste de 1830 à 1914 dans la Mitidja," *Revue*

Africaine, vol. 83 (1939), pp. 192–226, esp. pp. 212–213, 225–226; as quoted by von Grunebaum, *Modern Islam,* p. 203.

4. Lewis, *The Middle East and the West,* p. 45.

5. Cf. E.-F. Gautier, *Moeurs et coutumes des musulmanes,* Paris: Payot, 1949, pp. 18–19.

6. Lewis, *The Middle East and the West,* p. 39.

7. Sydney N. Fisher, *The Middle East: A History,* 2nd ed., New York: Alfred A. Knopf, 1969, pp. 284–285.

8. Cremeans, *The Arabs and the World,* p. 53.

9. Cf. the theoretical discussion of cultural crisis by David Bidney, *Theoretical Anthropology,* New York: Columbia University Press, 1953, pp. 436–437; and "Culture Theory and the Problem of Cultural Crisis," in Lyman Bryson, *et. al.* (eds.), *Approaches to Group Understanding (Sixth Symposium, Conference on Science, Philosophy and Religion),* New York, 1947, pp. 553–573.

10. As quoted by Norman Daniel, "Westernization in the Arab World," in Adams (ed.), *The Middle East: A Handbook,* p. 517.

11. Daniel, *op. cit.,* p. 517.

12. *Ibid.,* p. 518.

13. See below.

14. Samir A. Makdisi, "Natural Resources, Economic Structure and Growth," in Adams (ed.), *The Middle East: A Handbook,* p. 401.

15. Robert E. Mabro, "Industrialization," in Adams (ed.), *The Middle East: A Handbook,* p. 446.

16. See Chapter V, "The Bedouin Substratum of the Arab Personality."

17. Hans E. Tütsch, "Arab Unity and Arab Dissensions," in Walter Z. Laqueur (ed.), *The Middle East in Transition,* New York: Praeger, 1958, pp. 14–15.

18. Georges Ketman, "The Egyptian Intelligentsia," in Laqueur (ed.), *op. cit.,* p. 483.

19. Cf. Patai, *Golden River,* pp. 13–72. Cf. also on this issue, von Grunebaum, *Modern Islam,* p. 175.

20. This definition of cultural focus largely follows that of Melville J. Herskovits, "The Processes of Cultural Change" in Ralph Linton (ed.), *The Science of Man in the World Crisis,* New York: Columbia University Press, 1945, pp. 164–165; and Herskovits, *Man and His Works,* New York: Alfred A. Knopf, 1948, pp. 542, 544. One must keep in mind that to speak of the focal or dominant concerns of a culture is merely a convenient shorthand for saying that most individuals who make up a society are more concerned with those particular aspects of their culture than with others. Or, to put it in even more precise terms, the dominant (or focal) concerns in a culture are those cultural features which constitute the prime preoccupation of the modal personality in that culture. Another important feature in the interrelationship between cultural focus and modal personality is that the latter not only puts high value on the focal aspects of his culture, but considers them ethnocentrically as superior to corresponding features in other cultures.

21. In propounding the above as a working hypothesis, I part company with Herskovits, who held that it is precisely the focal aspects of the culture in which cultural change is most likely to occur. See Herskovits, *Man and His Works,* p. 544, and pp. 550–551, where he uses my observations on culture contact between Jews and Arabs in Mandatory Palestine as an example for his thesis.

22. Cf. Patai, *Sex and Family in the Bible and the Middle East,* p. 15.

23. Nabih Amin Faris, "The Islamic Community and Communism," in Laqueur (ed.), *op. cit.,* p. 353.

24. In speaking of the cultures of the East, and in particular of the great religious systems of Islam, Hinduism, Buddhism, Taoism, Confucianism, and Shintoism, F. S. C. Northrop emphasized in his influential *The Meeting of East and West* (New York: Macmillan, 1947, p. 313) that "to specify the philosophical and religious differences entering into the constitution of the cultures of the East is at the same time to possess inescapable interconnections and identities. It is the unity provided by these essential relations and identities which merges the cultures of the Oriental countries into one traditional culture of the Far East." It is to a juxtaposition of this Eastern culture and its similarly abstracted Western counterpart and to the search for reconciliation between these two cultural entities that Northrop's book as a whole is devoted.

25. Cf. Franco Nogueira, *A Luta Pelo Oriente,* Lisbon: Junta de investigações do ultramar. Estudios ciências politicas e sociais 4, 1957, pp. 15–16. Translation by Daphne Patai.

26. Patai, *Golden River,* p. 350.

27. *Ibid.,* p. 313.

28. Cf. on this subject the comment of Coon, *Caravan: The Story of the Middle East,* p. 7.

29. Hamady, *Temperament and Character of the Arabs,* p. 32.

30. Cf. Hans E. Tütsch, *Vorderasien im Aufruhr,* Zurich: Neue Zürcher Zeitung, 1959, pp. 141–142. My translation from the German. Italics in the original.

31. Von Grunebaum, *Modern Islam,* p. 176.

32. In an earlier context we have seen that this is how Nadwī sees what took place in the West; cf. Chapter IX, fn. 4.

33. Khalid Muhammad Khalid, *From Here We Start,* Washington, D.C.: American Council of Learned Societies, 1953, p. 43. The Arabic original of this book was published in Cairo in 1950.

34. Fazlur Rahman, *Islam,* Garden City, N.Y.: Doubleday Anchor Books, 1968, p. 313.

35. Muḥammad Kurd 'Alī, *Al-Islām wa-'lHaḍāra al-'Arabiyya (Islam and Arab Civilization),* Cairo, 1934, vol. I, pp. 351–363; as quoted and summarized by von Grunebaum, *Islam: Essays in the Nature and Growth of a Cultural Tradition,* pp. 206–207.

36. Among the few Arab authors who at least partly exonerate the West from the responsibility for Arab stagnation, one can mention 'Abd al-Raḥmān al-Bazzāz, Maḥjūb Ben Mīlād, Mikhā'il Nu'ayma (Nāima), and Musa Alami,

"The Lesson of Palestine," *Middle East Journal* (October, 1949), pp. 373–405. However, the tendency to blame the West is sufficiently widespread to have attracted the attention of both Arab and Western scholars. Among the latter, let us quote two of the most prominent ones. Wilfred Cantwell Smith, *Islam in Modern History,* p. 100, refers to "the usually vague but persistent Arab tendency to identify the ills of its own society with its imported (Western) institutions." In April, 1954, Smith says, he saw this tendency "come into sharp focus" in the street demonstrations against elections, parliamentarianism, and the whole formal democratic process, together with reaction and corruption. And Bernard Lewis, *The Middle East and the West,* p. 96 says: "An Israeli scholar has defined the difference between the religious and nationalist approaches to events in this way: as believers in a religion 'our forefathers gave praise to God for their successes, and laid the blame for their failures on their sins and shortcomings. . . .' As members of a nation, 'we thank ourselves for our successes, and lay the blame for our failures on others.' " See also Charles D. Cremeans, *The Arabs and the World,* p. 130. The Arabs' tendency to blame others for their own failures has emerged most recently as a disturbing element in the Arab-Soviet relations. According to a dispatch dated Beirut, Lebanon, January 29, 1972, and published in the January 30 issue of *The New York Times,* "Eastern European sources here said that blaming others for their failures had been a main reason for Arab weakness." The news item also refers to the demonstrations that took place in a number of Arab capitals after the 1967 war, during which the demonstrators "chanted slogans blaming the Russians for not coming to the Arabs' assistance during the war."

37. Bennabi, *op. cit.,* pp. 16–17, as quoted by von Grunebaum, *Modern Islam* p. 204. Italics supplied.
38. Anwar al-Jindī (al-Jundī), *Al-Fikr al-'Arabī al-Mu'āṣir fī Ma'rakat al-Taghrīb wa'l-Tab'iyya al-Thaqāfiyya (Contemporary Arab Thought in the Struggle of Westernization and Cultural Imitation),* Cairo, Maṭba'at al-Risāla, c. 1961, pp. 447–458.
39. Fāris and Husayn, *op. cit.,* pp. 93–95.
40. As quoted by von Grunebaum, *Modern Islam,* p. 235.
41. Robert Montagne, *Révolution au Maroc,* Paris, 1953, pp. 312–313; as summarized by von Grunebaum, *Modern Islam,* pp. 220–221.
42. Anonymous Arabic brochure published by the Société Arabe in Cairo; translated under the title "Que veulent les Arabes?" in *Orient,* vol. V (1958), pp. 171–180; and summarized by von Grunebaum, *Modern Islam,* p. 229.
43. As quoted by von Grunebaum, *Modern Islam,* p. 218, following J. Desparmet, "Le réaction linguistique en Algérie," *Bulletin de la Société de Geographie d'Alger et de l'Afrique du Nord,* vol. 32 (1931), p. 13, n. 43.
44. Charles Malik, "The Near East: The Search for Truth," *Foreign Affairs,* vol. 30 (January, 1952), reprinted in Haim (ed.), *Arab Nationalism: An Anthology,* pp. 189–228. The above quote is from pp. 22–23. Cf. also the cogent remarks of Tütsch, "Arab Unity and Arab Dissensions," in Laqueur (ed.), *op. cit.,* pp. 15–16.

45. Sayegh, *op. cit.*, pp. 38–39, 46.

46. Farrukh, *op. cit.*, pp. 155–158.

47. Muhammad Kamel Ayyad, "The Future of Culture in Arab Society," in Laqueur (ed.), *op. cit.*, pp. 462–477.

48. Cf. 'Abd al-Raḥmān al-Bazzāz, *Al-Islām wa'l-Qawmiyya al-'Arabiyya (Islam and Arab Nationalism)*, Baghdad, 1952; as translated by Haim (ed.), *Arab Nationalism: An Anthology*, pp. 187–188. Cf. also the small English collection of Bazzāz's wrtings published by the Embassy of the Republic of Iraq in London (printed by S. Austin), 1965, under the title *Al-Bazzaz on Arab Nationalism*, p. 48.

49. Smith, *Islam in Modern History*, p. 159, n. 203.

50. Lewis, *The Middle East and the West*, pp. 133–136.

51. Smith, *Islam in Modern History*, pp. 94–95.

52. Cf. al-Bazzāz, *op. cit.*, pp. 187–188.

53. Cf. Lewis, *The Middle East and the West*, p. 135.

54. Muḥammad Quṭb, *Shubuhāt ḥawl al-Islām (Doubts About Islam)*, Cairo, 1954; as summarized by Smith, *Islam in Modern History*, p. 159.

55. Sayegh, *op. cit.*, pp. 35–36.

56. Smith, *Islam in Modern History*, p. 99.

57. J. Desparmet, "Les réactions nationalitaires I," *Bulletin de la Société de Géographie d'Alger*, vol. 33 (1932), pp. 178–179. The passage is quoted in French by von Grunebaum, *Modern Islam* p. 189, n. 23.

58. Cf. Sāṭi' al-Ḥuṣrī, *Al-Muḥāḍara al-Iftitāḥiyya (The Opening Lecture)* (an address given at the opening of the Institute of Higher Arab Studies in Cairo in 1954), pp. 13ff., as summarized by L. M. Kenny, "Sāṭi' al-Ḥuṣrī's Views on Arab Nationalism," *The Middle East Journal*, vol. 17, no. 3 (Summer, 1963), p. 246.

59. Hitti, *History of the Arabs*, 7th ed., p. 733.

APPENDIX II

1. Cf. Oswald Spengler, *Untergang des Abendlandes*, München: Oskar Beck, 1922, vol. 2, pp. 225–399; in the English translation by Charles Francis Atkinson, the chapter is entitled "Problems of the Arabian Culture"; see *The Decline of the West*, New York: Alfred A. Knopf, 1926, p. 187. Since the English translation is frequently imprecise, I retranslated from the German all the quotations appearing in this chapter. All emphases are in the original.

2. P. 227; *Decline* 2: 189.

3. The English translation renders: "Primitive, Culture-Peoples, Fellaheen," 2:159. In the German original, "Urvölker, Kulturvölker, Fellahenvölker," pp. 189–224.

4. *Untergang* 2:203; *Decline* 2:170.

5. *Untergang* 2:202; *Decline* 2:169.

6. *Untergang* 2:204; *Decline* 2:170–171.

7. *Untergang* 2:387–388; *Decline* 2:314–315.
8. *Untergang* 1:237–238; *Decline* 1:183.
9. *Untergang* 1:97, 228; 2:283; *Decline* 1:71, 174; 2:233.
10. *Untergang* 1:271; *Decline* 1:209.
11. *Untergang* 1:274; *Decline* 1:211.
12. *Untergang* 2:289–290; *Decline* 2:238.
13. Here Spengler quotes M. Horten, *Die religiöse Gedankenwelt des Volkes im heutigen Islam,* p. xxvi; see *Untergang* 2:291; *Decline* 2:239.
14. *Untergang* 2:292–293; *Decline* 2:239–240.
15. *Ibid.*
16. *Untergang* 1:276–277; *Decline* 1:213.
17. *Untergang* 1:393ff. and 2:283ff; *Decline* 1:305ff. and 2:233ff.
18. *Untergang* 1:402; *Decline* 1:312.
19. *Untergang* 1:468; *Decline* 1:363.
20. *Untergang* 2:299; *Decline* 2:244.
21. *Untergang* 2:288; *Decline* 2:237.
22. *Untergang* 2:285–286; *Decline* 2:234–235.
23. *Untergang* 1:494; *Decline* 1:382.
24. *Untergang* 1:99; *Decline* 1:72 translates: "Arabian indeterminateness of number."
25. *Untergang* 2:228; *Decline* 2:190.
26. *Untergang* 2:229; *Decline* 2:191.
27. *Untergang* 2:208–09; *Decline* 2:174.
28. *Untergang* 2:80; *Decline* 2:69.
29. *Untergang* 2:214; *Decline* 2:178.
30. *Untergang* 2:447; *Decline* 2:362.
31. *Untergang* 2:125; *Decline* 2:105.
32. *Untergang* 2:50; *Decline* 2:42.
33. E.g., Maurice Samuel, *The Professor and the Fossil,* New York: Alfred A. Knopf, 1956, p. 28, quoting Herbert I. Muller, *The Uses of the Past,* 1952; Franz Borkenau, "Toynbee and the Culture Cycle," *Commentary* (March, 1956), pp. 239ff. H. Michell in his study "Herr Spengler and Mr. Toynbee," *Transactions of the Royal Society of Canada,* vol. XLII, ser. III (June, 1949), Sect. 2, pp. 103–113 (reprinted in M. F. Ashley Montagu [ed.], *Toynbee and History,* Boston, Mass.: Porter Sargent Publisher, 1956, pp. 77–78) keeps largely to observations on general similarities in attitudes and the "great central theme" of the two authors, although he notes that "Spengler is an almost indispensable prerequisite to Toynbee. . . ."
34. Hans Joachim Schoeps, *Vorläufer Spenglers,* Leiden: Brill, 1955, p. 98.
35. R. Patai, "Toynbee's Dependence on Spengler," *Judaism,* vol. 6, no. 2 (Spring, 1957), pp. 134ff.
36. Toynbee, *A Study of History,* abridged ed., pp. 92ff.
37. *Op. cit.,* p. 145; cf. p. 19.
38. Toynbee, *A Study of History,* London: Oxford University Press, 1954, vol. VII, p. 393; cf. also pp. 53, 410.

39. *Op. cit.,* vol. XII: *Reconsiderations,* 1961, p. 475.
40. *Op. cit.,* vol. IX (1954), pp. 411–412.
41. *Op. cit.,* vol. IV (1939), pp. 112–113.
42. *Ibid.*
43. *Ibid.,* pp. 113–114.
44. *Op. cit.,* vol. I (1934), p. 35; vol. XII (1961) pp. 292–293.
45. *Op. cit.,* vol. X (1954), p. 8, note 1, quoting D. B. MacDonald, *The Religious Attitude and Life in Islam,* pp. 120–121.
46. *Op. cit.,* vol. VII (1954), pp. 730–732.
47. *Op. cit.,* vol. VIII (1954), p. 567, quoting al-Balādhurī, *Kitāb Futūḥ al-Buldān (The Book of the Conquests of the Countries),* Engl. transl. New York: Columbia University Press, vol. I (1916), p. 441; vol. II (1924), p. 251.
48. *Op. cit.,* vol. I (1916), p. 226.

APPENDIX III

1. Edward Wellin, in the *Encyclopedia Americana,* 1971 ed., s.v. Latin America, vol. 17, p. 6.
2. Patai, *Golden River,* pp. 218ff.
3. After writing the above passage I found that Malcolm Kerr has commented on this difference between the Arabs and the Latin Americans: "Why the idea of unity is so strong among Arabs—so much more than among Latin Americans, for instance, or the English-speaking nations—is a mystery that neither Arab nor western historians have satisfactorily explained." In the next sentence, Kerr calls this idea of unity among the Arabs an "obsession" which is "an important psychological force." Cf. Kerr, *The Arab Cold War 1958–1967,* p. 1.
4. This subject is discussed by Charles F. Gallagher, "Language, Culture, and Ideology: The Arab World," in K. H. Silvert (ed.), *Expectant Peoples: Nationalism and Development,* New York: Random House Vintage Books, 1967, pp. 216ff. Cf. also Chapter XV here.
5. Dr. Abdul Rahman al-Shahbandar, a leading Syrian thinker and statesman, foresaw and advocated this development in 1936: "If an Arab country achieves complete independence, then the best government for it would be an authoritarian but just one," because the Arabs had as yet no experience with parliamentary forms of government. Cf. his book *Al-Qaḍāyā al-Ijtimāʿiyya al-Kubra fī 'l-ʿAlam al-ʿArabī (The Major Social Issues in the Arab World),* Cairo, 1936, p. 93; as quoted in Nuseibeh, *The Ideas of Arab Nationalism,* p. 161.
6. The above summary of Ben Khedda's article is based on Gordon, *North Africa's French Legacy,* pp. 119–120.

INDEX

Arabic names and words beginning with the article *al-* are listed under the letter following the article.

7294